Big Data Surveillance and Security Intelligence

Big Data Surveillance and Security Intelligence
The Canadian Case

Edited by David Lyon and David Murakami Wood

UBCPress · Vancouver · Toronto

30 29 28 27 26 25 24 23 22 21   5 4 3 2 1

Printed in Canada on FSC-certified ancient-forest-free paper (100% post-consumer recycled) that is processed chlorine- and acid-free.

Library and Archives Canada Cataloguing in Publication

Title: Big data surveillance and security intelligence : the Canadian case / edited by David Lyon and David Murakami Wood.
Names: Lyon, David, editor. | Wood, David Murakami, editor.
Description: Includes bibliographical references and index.
Identifiers: Canadiana (print) 20200333143 | Canadiana (ebook) 20200333887 | ISBN 9780774864176 (hardcover) | ISBN 9780774864190 (PDF) | ISBN 9780774864206 (EPUB)
Subjects: LCSH: Electronic surveillance – Canada. | LCSH: Intelligence service – Canada. | LCSH: Cyber intelligence (Computer security) – Canada. | LCSH: National security – Canada. | LCSH: National security – International cooperation. | LCSH: Data protection – Canada.
Classification: LCC JL86.I58 B54 2020 | DDC 327.1271—dc23

Canadä

UBC Press gratefully acknowledges the financial support for our publishing program of the Government of Canada (through the Canada Book Fund) and the British Columbia Arts Council.

Printed and bound in Canada by Friesens
Set in Helvetica Condensed and Minion by Apex CoVantage, LLC
Copy editor: Francis Chow
Proofreader: Judith Earnshaw
Indexer: Delano Aragão Vaz
Cover designer: Alexa Love

UBC Press
The University of British Columbia
2029 West Mall
Vancouver, BC V6T 1Z2
www.ubcpress.ca

Contents

Figures and Tables

Figures

Tables

Preface

THIS BOOK EXAMINES one of the most pressing issues in the organization of society today: the application of new data practices to both global systems and everyday devices – in this case, those that have to do with national security. The editors have been involved in research on surveillance in relation to security for over two decades, but it is difficult to think of innovations as far-reaching and consequential as those involving so-called big data. This is because they rest on novel ways of using data, enabled by massive computing power, and because they touch the lives of everyone. Intelligence gathering in the era of social media and the Internet of Things cannot but implicate and involve all citizens, domestically as well as in other countries, not just those conventionally thought of as suspicious, risky, or threatening.

The book is the product of a large-scale research project involving several Canadian universities as well as partners and collaborators in other countries, with its central node at the Surveillance Studies Centre at Queen's University in Kingston, Ontario. Other lead researchers are from Université Laval, the University of Ottawa, and the University of Victoria, along with St. Andrew's University in Scotland. This project is underwritten by a five-year Partnership Grant from the Social Sciences and Humanities Research Council (SSHRC), in which academic researchers work collaboratively with partners from both public policy and civil society. More specifically, it comprises expert papers shared at a very stimulating and fruitful research workshop held in Ottawa, in which both academics and members of privacy commissions and civil liberties groups contributed papers for discussion.

We are very grateful to the SSHRC both for the funding opportunity and for the doors it opened for our research to be carried out in active cooperation with our Canadian government policy and compliance bodies (the Office of the Privacy Commissioner in Ottawa and the British Columbia Office of the Information and Privacy Commissioner) *and* non-governmental organization partners (the International Civil Liberties Monitoring Group in Ottawa and the BC Civil Liberties Association). These partnerships are evident in the chapters of this book.

Abbreviations

ARPANET	Advanced Research Projects Agency Network
ASD	Australian Signals Directorate
ATIP	Access to Information and Privacy
BCCLA	British Columbia Civil Liberties Association
BCOIPC	British Columbia Office of the Information and Privacy Commissioner
BRUSA	Britain-USA [Agreement]
CANUSA	Canada-USA [Agreement]
CBNRC	Communications Branch of the National Research Council
CNE	computer network exploitation
COMINT	COMmunications INTelligence
COMSEC	Communications Security (part of the CBNRC)
COTC	Canadian Overseas Telecommunications Corporation
CRA	Canada Revenue Agency
CRTC	Canadian Radio-television and Telecommunications Commission
CSE	Communications Security Establishment
CSIS	Canadian Security Intelligence Service
DARPA	Defense Advanced Research Projects Agency
DEW	Defense Early Warning
DGI	Director General Intelligence
DNI	Digital Network Intelligence
DNR	Dial Number Recognition
DPI	deep packet inspection
EFF	Electronic Frontier Foundation
FINTRAC	Financial Transactions and Reports Analysis Centre of Canada
FISC	Foreign Intelligence Surveillance Court
FLQ	Front de libération du Québec
FVEY	Five Eyes
GAC	Global Affairs Canada

GCHQ	Government Communications Headquarters
GCSB	Government Communications Security Bureau (NZ)
HUMINT	HUMan INTelligence
IAC	Intelligence Advisory Committee
ICAMS	International Campaign Against Mass Surveillance
ICLMG	International Civil Liberties Monitoring Group
ICT	information and communications technology
ILC	International Licensed Carriers
ILP	intelligence-led policing
IMINT	IMagery INTelligence
ISIL	Islamic State of Iraq and the Levant
ISP	Internet service provider
LESAs	law enforcement and security agencies
LTAP	Long-Term Accommodation Project
MITACS	Mathematics of Information Technology and Complex Systems consortium
NAE	New Analytic Environment
NAM	New Analytic Model
NDA	*National Defence Act*
NIM	National Intelligence Model
NSA	National Security Agency (US)
NSICOP	National Security and Intelligence Committee of Parliamentarians
NSIRA	National Security and Intelligence Review Agency
OCSEC	Office of the Communications Security Establishment Commissioner
ODAC	Operational Data Analysis Centre
OPC	Office of the Privacy Commissioner
PCLOB	Privacy and Civil Liberties Oversight Board
PIPEDA	*Personal Information Protection and Electronic Documents Act*
SCISA	*Security of Canada Information Sharing Act*
SIGINT	SIGnals INTelligence
SIRC	Security Intelligence Review Committee
SIS	Secret Intelligence Service (MI6)
SLA	specialized lawful access
SMO	Social Movement Organization
SOCMINT	SOCial Media INTelligence
SOIA	*Security of Information Act*

SSO	Special Source Operations
TIA	*Total* (later, *Terrorism*) *Information Awareness*
TIMC	Tutte Institute for Mathematics and Computing
TSP	telecommunications service provider
UKUSA	UK-USA [Agreement]

Big Data Surveillance and Security Intelligence

Introduction

David Lyon and David Murakami Wood

"Everything has changed" in the wake of big data, declared the Canadian Communications Security Establishment (CSE).[1] While some more skeptical analysts may raise an eyebrow at this, it is undoubtedly the case that the modes of analysis of communications described as "big data" have produced huge changes in the pursuit of national security. Far from being an exclusively Canadian phenomenon, this is a global process in which agencies worldwide work together using new methods of data analytics to try to identify risks to national security with a view to preventing or pre-empting the possibility that those risks might become realities. The title of our book, *Big Data Surveillance and Security Intelligence: The Canadian Case,* thus sums up a crucially important trend, one that calls for serious and critical analysis.

While this process is global, one cannot hope to grasp the import and impact of what is happening by attempting to capture the complete global scene. Thus, this book is primarily about what is happening in Canada, to follow how the big data changes came about in one country. Of course, this pulls us right back into the broader picture because the Canadian experience is deeply influenced by others, especially through the so-called Five Eyes partnership of Australia, Canada, New Zealand, the United Kingdom, and the United States. But the case of Canada remains central to what follows. It is not at all identical to the experience of others and contains important markers for ongoing analysis.

First, it is vital that the two terms "security intelligence" and "surveillance" appear together. The former, a growing activity of any nation-state, requires the latter, which has to do with the purposeful collection and examination of personal data. Of course, all manner of information handling may be carried out for national security, but the aim is to discover human activities potentially detrimental to the proper functioning of the nation-state. One way this occurs is through open-source data gathering, changes in which indicate the enormously enlarged scope of personal data gathering and sifting in the twenty-first century. During the Second World War, "open-source intelligence" referred to the monitoring of enemy radio stations for clues about hostile activities. Today it has expanded exponentially to include the monitoring of the Internet and especially social media. This is the primary origin of the tremendous troves of data referred to as "big."

Second, as the following chapters indicate, parallel linked trends are apparent in national security intelligence. One is the expansion of the notion of security to cover a range of fields not previously designated as such. In the field of international relations, "securitization" refers to the designation by governments of their citizens and those of other countries as matters of security. This means that extraordinary means – rendition to other countries for questioning or even torture, for example, as happened to Maher Arar and other Canadians after the terrorist attacks of 11 September 2001 – may be used in the name of security. Not only persons but also certain kinds of events, such as musical or athletic activities, or sites, such as sidewalks with no vehicle barriers, may also be newly considered as security risks. The second trend is the one already alluded to, of gathering data from sources that only recently – in the twenty-first century – have become available.

Each of these trends underscores the importance of discussing the activities of communications security and security intelligence in Canada and around the world. And they also point to the need for a deeper understanding of the ways in which surveillance has become such an essential player in each area, along with others, such as domestic policing, that are also securitized and also increasingly depend on big data.[2] As far as national security is concerned, the big data connections started to become publicly clear with the whistle-blowing activities of American security operatives such as William Binney, Thomas Drake, Mark Klein, and, especially since 2013, Edward Snowden. What they demonstrated was both the widened sweep of surveillance – often called "mass surveillance" – and the profound dependence of the national security agencies of all countries on telecommunications and Internet corporations for the acquisition and then the promiscuous use of personal data.

Third, then, is the notion of a big data age. While it may be premature or misleading to adopt big data as a key descriptor for an historical era, it is nonetheless essential to recognize and assess the impact of big data practices in multiple areas of corporate and governmental life. If one turns to Google's Internet dictionary for a definition of big data, you may find this: "extremely large data sets that may be analyzed computationally to reveal patterns, trends, and associations, especially relating to human behavior and interactions." This is very instructive because it speaks not only to the volume of data but also to the dependence on massive computer power, the production of correlations between disparate factors, and the predominant focus on human activity. What is missing is a sense of the enthusiasm with which big data "solutions" are often sought, and the relative lack of critical reflection on the limits on and ethics of what can be achieved using such methods.

The "big data" buzzword may have a limited shelf life but what it points to is highly significant. At CSE, the relevant phrase is "New Analytic Model" (Chapter 6). The key idea is to take advantage of the availability of rapidly growing quantities of data available through the Internet but especially consequent on the rise of social media. The fact that the platforms also learned to monetize what was previously referred to as "data exhaust" also meant that such data were sought more vigorously. Rather than relying on conventional modes of analysis, we can now mine and analyze such data, using algorithms, to discover previously unnoticed patterns of activity. While big data is often summarized by attributes such as volume (of data), velocity (speed of analysis), and variety (the expanding range of usable datasets), its core is practices. As danah boyd and Kate Crawford note, it is the "capacity for researchers to search, aggregate and cross-reference large data-sets."[3] They also ask some telling questions about such data practices.

It is hardly surprising, however, that security intelligence services would wish to exploit new possibilities for learning from the mass of metadata that actually answers queries a private detective agency might have – such as location, time, and type of transaction and communication, along with identifying details of participants. From about 2009 in Canada, it became clear that legal warrant was sought for such data gathering and analysis. However, as hinted at in the designation of big data as a *buzzword,* hard ontological and epistemological questions are easily glossed over. Such practices are all too often marred by what Jose van Dijck calls "dataism," a secular belief in the "objectivity of quantification and the potential for tracking human behaviour and sociality through online data," along with the presentation of such data as "raw material" to be analyzed and processed into predictive algorithms.[4] The potential for new analytics *and* the potential problems that arise from this are discussed throughout this book.

It is also worth noting, however, that the processes involved are ones that are also visible in everyday life, not only in the arcane world of national security intelligence and surveillance. After all, the data concerned are frequently gleaned from what David Lyon calls "user-generated surveillance," referring to the ways in which contemporary new media encourage the sharing of information and images and the proliferation of online communications and transactions that yield highly consequential metadata.[5] This parallels Bernard Harcourt's account, which explores processes of quotidian self-exposure, where people "follow" others, "sharing" information as they roam the web and as they themselves are "followed" by multiple commercial and governmental organizations that obtain access to the same data.[6] The corporate use of such data has now reached such major proportions that theorists such as Shoshana Zuboff now dub this "surveillance capitalism," a process that has far-reaching and profound political, economic, and social repercussions. This is the crucial context for the present study.[7]

The words that form the title of our book sum up what its authors are at pains to reveal as they debate the big data surveillance involved in today's security measures, seen especially in intelligence gathering and analysis dependent on big data practices. The book does not question the need for forms of national security or policing as such, but it does raise many questions about the ways in which new kinds of data production and analysis challenge conventional and time-honoured practices within such agencies. The book queries the rapid and wholesale departure from earlier traditions of national security activity, along with the ethics and legal instruments that have governed these areas in the past, but it does so with a view to the future of national security, not with a nostalgic view of what went before. After all, during the twentieth century many questions were also raised about national security and policing measures. There is a long history of reasoned and principled assessment of such endeavours, to which this book makes a further contemporary contribution.

Situating Security Intelligence

Security intelligence encompasses a large number of diverse state activities. Broadly speaking, we are talking about espionage, or spying, although much of what takes place under this banner is far from the popular images of Cold War espionage, whether John le Carré's cynical British Secret Intelligence Service (SIS, or MI6) spooks or the antics of *Mad* magazine's "Spy vs. Spy." Such HUMINT (HUMan INTelligence) operations remain important, but with the rise of, first, telecommunications, and then computing, and their now inescapable and ubiquitous combination, HUMINT has increasingly been overtaken by SIGINT (SIGnals INTelligence) and associated specialist domains, including COMINT (COMmunications INTelligence), IMINT (IMagery INTelligence), and SOCMINT (SOCial Media INTelligence).

Much security intelligence activity is conducted in secret, and for long periods of the history of security intelligence this secrecy has been felt to be both necessary and inevitable. There have been occasional voices raised, questioning or criticizing such assumptions and what Clive Ponting, in the context of the British state, called the "culture of secrecy."[8] Therefore, only some of what we know of security intelligence agencies and their history and activities has come via official channels in often belated formal releases of historical information (after thirty, fifty, or seventy years). Some more has come through the Canadian *Access to Information Act* (*ATIA*) or the British and American *Freedom of Information Acts* (*FOIA*). As we have already noted, however, much of the most significant revelations have come through the actions of activists and whistle-blowers in acquiring and publicizing information that would otherwise have remained hidden.[9]

While espionage dates back to the beginnings of government, there are some generally accepted milestones in the history of Anglo-American intelligence, into which the Canadian system fits. A dedicated HUMINT office was first set up under Francis Walsingham during the reign of Elizabeth I in England, but such initiatives remained both sporadic and specific in their targeting (Walsingham's efforts were mainly targeted at the Catholic threat to England's nascent Protestant regime). State intelligence activity gradually increased, especially during the long period of warfare in Europe in the eighteenth century and into the Napoleonic Wars of the early nineteenth century. The eighteenth and nineteenth centuries also saw the emergence of internal political policing with the "new police," whose roles included the breaking up of reform meetings and demonstrations and the "moving on" of the urban poor and homeless. The nineteenth century also saw the first British legislative interest in the targeting of emerging communications systems by state surveillance. Of particular note was the 1844 scandal in which an Italian exile, Joseph Mazzini, who was resident in London, discovered that the British government was secretly opening his mail, prompting parliamentary discussion and demands for accountability and reform.[10]

The story of intelligence in the Anglo-American world cannot be treated separately from settler-colonial control and policing. It was in India, for example, where British colonial officers pioneered the use of fingerprinting and databases of personal biometric information for identification. This was mainly to ensure prompt payment of taxes imposed by the British Raj, but the use of fingerprints to combat resistance and insurgency as well as more conventional crimes followed. Fingerprinting spread from India to Ireland, Britain's nearest colony, and then to the imperial metropole of London and other major cities in the United States and in the Dominion of Canada.

Early security concerns in what would become Canada centred on the conflict between France and the United Kingdom over territory that belonged to neither but was claimed by both, as well as on Indigenous peoples, whose land it was and who continued in many cases to fight against the tide of settler-colonialism. Within British colonial territory, the additional internal threat of the Fenians, Irish republicans seeking to free their country from British rule, became an additional concern, and as the nineteenth century progressed, strongly racialized concerns about immigration from China and India, as well as freed African slaves from the United States and Canada, moved to the fore. However, there was hardly anything resembling a security intelligence apparatus at this time.

Meanwhile, in the United States arguments about the nation's own potential overseas empire beyond the frontier that had its terminus at the Pacific appeared to have been settled almost by circumstance with the results of the Spanish-American War and the US acquisition of the Philippines. The United States instituted an intensive military governance program that conflated both crime and terrorism and saw a "solution" to the problem in counter-insurgency operations.[11] Counter-insurgency thereafter proved a rich vein for new intelligence services that were created in the twentieth century, notably the Army Intelligence Agency (later the Defense Intelligence Agency) and the Central Intelligence Agency (CIA), deployed with debatable success in Europe after the Second World War via the Gladio network, and over a longer period in Latin America, following the Monroe Doctrine, which asserted US hegemony over the American hemisphere. The tactic of essentially manufacturing threats that could be disrupted was also the modus operandi of the Federal Bureau of Investigation (FBI) on the US mainland.

The postwar period in the United States saw the migration and ascent of security intelligence from a fringe activity often run largely by enthusiasts and amateurs to the core of the state during the Cold War, with intelligence agencies – as expert bureaucracies with the greatest access to secret information, burgeoning budgets, and the least accountability to elected bodies – constituting the core of what has been variously called the permanent, secret, or deep state.

With Britain's economy grievously damaged by the war and its imperial power broken, the postwar period also saw the United States confirmed as the new centre of the anglophone world, and military and security intelligence arrangements were among the first to recognize this new reality. Conventional histories still emphasize NATO cooperation. This was (and is) undoubtedly important, but in the security intelligence field there is no doubt that secret and unacknowledged accords have long marked the new reality. The signing of the Britain-USA Agreement (BRUSA) in 1943 set the stage for the UK-USA Agreement (UKUSA) in 1946, which confirmed American dominance over the still extensive British imperial intelligence networks. The United Kingdom was vital not just for its personnel and expertise but also because one major legacy of British imperial power was its centrality in international undersea cable networks. Any SIGINT agency with global aspirations was going to want the ability to tap those cables, and the integration of UKUSA agencies into existing and new cable and domestic telecommunications systems was a priority from this time.

The United States made it a priority to bring in British white settler-colonial dominions (Canada, Australia, and New Zealand). For SIGINT, a Canada-USA Agreement (CANUSA) was signed in 1948, and Australia and New Zealand's intelligence services (originally as a single entity) were brought into the emerging system in 1956. These were the founding "second parties" to what later became known as the Quadripartite Agreement and later, more informally, the Five Eyes (FVEY), with the United States as "first party." The reconstruction of postwar intelligence agencies in the defeated former Axis powers (West Germany, Italy, and Japan in particular) was also achieved with US and Allied oversight (often involving many of the same people who had worked for the former fascist security intelligence agencies), and the new security intelligence agencies became "third parties" in the emerging US-dominated international security intelligence system. Other eventual third parties included members of NATO and countries propped up with US military aid during the Cold War, such as Thailand and Israel.

The postwar period also saw the rapid rise of SIGINT, facilitated by both this international system and the spread of existing technologies like the telephone and new technologies of computing. The historian of intelligence Bernard Porter has argued that SIGINT became increasingly central from the 1950s onward, and that the "the future of intelligence clearly lay with 'Sigint' and the new technology."[12]

Compared with the United States and the United Kingdom, Canadian participation was relatively insignificant during this period. Canadian universities contributed to CIA research projects in psychological manipulation and torture. Canadian SIGINT did not really become important until the emergence of the National Research Bureau in the 1960s and its eventual more public identity as the Communications Security Establishment of Canada (CSEC, latterly CSE).[13] For much of this time, the most important Canadian contribution consisted of hosting multiple tiny Arctic installations that formed part of what was called the DEW (Defense Early Warning) Line, designed to protect the United States, and to a lesser extent Canada and Britain, against Soviet long-range bomber and later ICBM (intercontinental ballistic missile) attack, and its successors.[14]

While Canada struggled in many ways to establish a meaningful international security intelligence role independent of the United States, internally it adopted tactics that were strongly reminiscent of the FBI's domestic version of counter-insurgency. The Royal Canadian Mounted Police (RCMP), by global standards a rather strange hybrid policing and internal security organization more akin to London's Metropolitan Police Service – with its dual local/regional conventional policing and national anti-terrorism/internal security roles – than to any other organizational equivalent, was infamously revealed to have been involved in multiple illicit activities in order to uncover enemies within.[15]

This sparked a national inquiry, the McDonald Commission (Royal Commission of Inquiry into Certain Activities of the RCMP), which led to the removal of the RCMP's internal security intelligence role and the creation of the Canadian Security Intelligence Service (CSIS) in 1984. However, the post-9/11 environment has once again muddied the never entirely clear blue waters that separate CSIS's security intelligence role from the RCMP's policing mandate. As CSIS has grown in power and influence, pressure has grown for it to have more active capabilities to – in the words of the *National Security Act, 2017* (formerly Bill C-59) – "disrupt" terrorist plots and so on. In addition, the RCMP still maintains what can only be described as a political policing role, akin to the Special Branch of London's Metropolitan Police, targeting what it describes as "domestic" or "multi-issue extremists" (who include environmental activists, Indigenous peoples' rights organizations, Quebecois separatists, and more).[16] As a result, CSIS has developed its own extensive databases, in line with the US Department of Homeland Security's "fusion centers," created after 9/11. There are multiple proposals in Canada for similar organizations to share data and cooperate operationally, following a model that was tested for the 2010 Winter Olympics in Vancouver.[17]

By 2010, Canada was four years into the decade-long government of Stephen Harper, who had promised to change Canada "beyond recognition." This seems far-fetched, particularly in retrospect and in the long-term historical view taken here, but there were a number of key changes in the area of security intelligence with which the country is still wrestling. Harper's approach in general was to favour increasing the legal powers of state security intelligence organizations, with a corresponding reduction in human rights, particularly privacy. Arguments over what became known as "lawful access" were not a consistent factor over Harper's ten years in power but became increasingly important, particularly after 2009.

Successive public safety ministers, Peter van Loan and Steven Blaney, and Justice Ministers Rob Nicholson and Peter MacKay, and above all Vic Toews, who held both portfolios at different times, joined Harper in these attempts to enact legislation giving police and security intelligence greater powers. The initial push in 2009 came through two bills: Bill C-46, the *Investigative Powers for the 21st Century Act,* and Bill C-47, the *Technical Assistance for Law Enforcement in the 21st Century Act.* Key features, which were to recur in almost all later bills, centred on allowing warrantless police access to many aspects of Internet communications. Security fears associated with the Vancouver Winter Olympics may have had something to do with it, but terrorism, serious crime, and other threats were cited. Although this pair of bills did not attract enough support, a second attempt came in 2011 with Bill C-30, the *Protecting Children from Internet Predators Act,* whose title demonstrates the kind of rhetoric deployed to justify lawful access provisions. This again failed.

The Harper government did not limit itself to parliamentary avenues. In 2012, the CSIS was effectively given more leeway with the elimination of the CSIS Inspector-General's Office, the body responsible for monitoring CSIS. Instead, it was to be held accountable by the Security Intelligence Review Committee (SIRC), which was made up of part-time federal appointees. The federal Office of the Privacy Commissioner (OPC), although with no direct oversight of the security intelligence services, is important in setting a tone with regard to privacy and related human rights; here too Prime Minister Harper attempted to stack the deck, appointing a career government security lawyer, Daniel Therrien, when the opportunity arose, over more directly qualified candidates who were favoured in the privacy law community. Both SIRC and Therrien gradually discovered their teeth, however, and have bitten back to some extent against both the government that appointed them and its Liberal successor.

In 2013, there was another attempt to introduce lawful access legislation: Bill C-13, the *Protecting Canadians from Online Crime Act,* purportedly to tackle cyber-bullying but containing provisions that were almost identical to the previous unsuccessful attempts. It again struggled, although a revised version was eventually enacted as SC 2014, c 31. Of course, 2013 was a landmark year for security intelligence because of the revelations of US National Security Agency (NSA) contractor Edward Snowden. He was far from the first nor was he the most highly placed NSA whistle-blower, but the huge cache of internal training documents and slides he revealed was carefully curated with the assistance of major newspapers and resonated with the public as no previous revelation had.

Canada initially seemed far from the centre of the action, even though the documents confirmed that CSE was in fact a long-time junior partner of the NSA. It was also revealed, however, that CSE had its own mass surveillance programs. This should have been a national scandal, but for several years afterwards CSE managed to avoid the consequences of the Snowden revelations that other Five Eyes agencies faced. Instead, it moved into a slick new building whose basement would hold massive supercomputing power – essential for the movement to big data analysis.[18] Far from its being reined in, the year after the Snowden revelations saw a more concerted attempt to extend CSE's powers. This time the rationale was "lone wolf" terrorist attacks in Quebec and Ottawa and the rise of ISIS in the Middle East. Bill C-51 used tactics that the Conservative government had previously used to bury difficult legislation: it was included as part of an omnibus bill, making it difficult to deal with the quantity and detail. Bill C-51 provided CSIS with greater foreign and domestic powers and more explicit immunity from accountability in the use of these powers. Documents released in response to access to information requests to the Canadian security services revealed that the state fears that drove Bill C-51 were much more related to environmental and Indigenous opposition to the oil industry in Alberta (reflected in both the grassroots Idle No More and anti-pipeline movement), resulting in RCMP infiltration and surveillance of such groups throughout this period.

Bill C-51 sparked massive opposition, much more so than the previous failed attempts, but was ultimately successful even though the Harper government looked tired and out-of-date compared with the Instagram-friendly new Liberal leader, Justin Trudeau. Trudeau had refused to oppose Bill C-51, claiming instead that his government would review the provisions of the bill in a consultation process. The resulting Bill C-59 (*National Security Act, 2017*) finally received royal assent in June 2019. Such is the importance of this bill and its predecessor that they are considered in multiple chapters of this book.

As for the intelligence relationship between Canada and the United States, the situation is less certain in the age of President Donald Trump. In 2011, Canada and the United States signed a special declaration titled *Beyond the Border: A Shared Vision for Perimeter Security and Economic Competitiveness,* aiming "to enhance our security and accelerate the legitimate flow of people, goods and services." Had this vision progressed, it would have tied Canadian sovereignty further to that of the United States in line with post-9/11 trends. There were hints of expansion of the extraterritorial powers of the US Customs and Border Protection agency in places such as Pearson International Airport in Toronto, but the aggressive anti-migrant and anti–free trade policies of President Trump seem to have at least temporarily derailed such continental security efforts. Further, Trump has struck at the other foundational elements of the postwar settlement (e.g., international law, the United Nations, NATO, and the European Union) but, despite his frequent denunciations of the deep state and the intelligence agencies that he claims are conspiring against his government, not yet the Five Eyes network. There can be no doubt that security intelligence co-operation continues, but it is difficult to assess how much long-standing arrangements may have been (or may yet be) damaged by the authoritarian populist turn in the United States.

It is in this nested series of contexts – from technological transformation and global networks to political machinations in Ottawa – that we present these reflections on Canadian security intelligence and surveillance in the big data age. For the longest time, security intelligence has depended on classic knowledge practices of the modern era, such as deductive reasoning and explanatory logic, augmented since the mid-twentieth century by successive phases of computer and communications development. Such information technologies became significant in new ways with the creation of the Internet – itself originating in military defence – which facilitated both more rapid and global surveillance networks and also, in the twenty-first century, the rise of platforms and social networking. These generated massive amounts of data as the participation of ordinary users grew exponentially, which major corporations learned to harvest for profit. It is these data above all that gave the impetus to big data intelligence gathering and analysis, which is the subject of the rest of this book.

Security, Surveillance, and Big Data: A Road Map

This book is divided into five parts, each tackling a significant aspect of security intelligence and surveillance in a big data age. The chapters are written both by practically minded academics who wish to understand the issues through the prism of actual processes and events, and by others from policy fields who are very aware of the significant debates. Part 1, "Understanding Surveillance, Security, and Big Data," begins on a large canvas. In Chapter 1, Midori Ogasawara paints a picture of how security surveillance is seen from within national security agencies by operatives who courageously questioned their practices. Her interviews with Mark Klein and Edward Snowden show clearly how such agencies collaborate with big data corporations and the kinds of impact this has for everyday surveillance practices. Such collaboration is a global phenomenon, as clearly visible in Canada as in the United Kingdom or the United States and elsewhere – one that raises crucial questions about where responsibility lies for the kinds of pre-emptive surveillance, along with profit making, characteristic of today's situation.

This is followed by Chapter 2, from Christopher Prince, a researcher at the Office of the Privacy Commissioner of Canada, who notes that law and policy have become more complex and contested, that surveillance powers are difficult to grasp, and that when it comes to intelligence gathering the view is positively murky and mysterious. He offers a commentary on how this works out in Canada, concluding appropriately that clarity is called for at every level. He neatly summarizes some ways this could happen, and warns that while surveillance may be necessary, it is not a solution to everything.

Chapter 3 focuses on anti-terrorism features as a key rationale for intensified surveillance within both security agencies and policing services. The question must be asked, however: Do the shifts towards data analytics offer genuine benefits to the process of finding reliable and rights-respecting ways of combatting terrorism? According to a long-time expert in the field, the answers are not at all straightforward. Civil liberties are likely to take a hit, and without the hoped-for benefits. So why pursue this route? There are many reasons, suggests Stéphane Leman-Langlois, but none is compelling.

The question of big data may be pursued in even greater detail if a particular case – here, financial tracking – is examined. In Chapter 4, Anthony Amicelle and David Grondin note the ways in which algorithms form part of the essential infrastructure of security surveillance, especially as it applies to terrorist financing and money laundering. In Canada, the Financial Transactions and Reports Analysis Centre of Canada (FINTRAC) uses algorithm-based alerts to sniff out suspicious activity and govern the movements of suspects. It is not clear, however, whether the limitations of such methods are understood by their practitioners.

Part 2 focuses on "Big Data Surveillance and Signals Intelligence in the Canadian Security Establishment." Chapter 5, by Bill Robinson, carefully tracks the specificities of Canadian SIGINT history through different phases, showing what is distinctive about Canadian approaches as well as what Canada shares with other nations. It is a fascinating and important story, especially as the recently discerned tendencies of governments to turn their attention to internal "security" have antecedents. Today's CSE has grown greatly since the postwar days, however, and no longer passively receives but actively hunts for data. Among other things, this makes it more difficult to tell "targets" and "non-targets" apart.

Chapter 6 explores in more detail one recent, crucial aspect of these changes – the shift within CSE to a "New Analytic Model" starting in 2012. Scott Thompson and David Lyon use material provided by Access to Information and Privacy (ATIP) requests to show that, in the same period that the United Kingdom and United States made similar moves, big data analysis became the order of the day at CSE. Along with growing dependence on tech corporations and their software, there is a much greater reliance on computing expertise and practices – "sandbox play," for instance – and a reduced role for legal and ethical intervention appears to be the perhaps unintended consequence of these developments.

Another angle of the work of CSE – examining the interception of Internet communications – is investigated by Andrew Clement in Chapter 7. The agency itself is secretive and, unlike its US partner, the NSA, no truth-tellers have come forward, as Edward Snowden did, to indicate more precisely what goes on in the Edward Drake Building in Ottawa. Clement's evidence strongly suggests that CSE intercepts Canadians' domestic Internet communications in bulk – as do the NSA in the United States and the Government Communications Headquarters (GCHQ) in the United Kingdom – which is not legally permitted. The "airport Wi-Fi" case from 2014 is just the first of several telling examples explored here. Clement's case is one that should give pause not only to anyone professionally concerned with privacy or those seeking stronger digital rights or data justice but also to CSE and, indeed, every single Canadian citizen.

Part 3 focuses on the "Legal Challenges to Big Data Surveillance in Canada." In Chapter 8, Micheal Vonn sets the tone for the section with her analysis of what can be learned from SIRC reports about the conduct of CSIS, an agency as shrouded in secrecy as CSE. One report suggests that CSIS data acquisition practices are "essentially unmoored from law." Vonn cuts sharply through the language used by CSIS, showing that data collection is not collection, a threshold is not a threshold, and guidelines are not guidelines. Is this data collection proportionate, necessary, and relevant? If not, it may be unconstitutional, and the Bill C-59 "solution" to these problems may not be a solution.

This issue segues neatly into Craig Forcese's Chapter 9, which is devoted to Bill C-59, although readers may conclude that this analysis is slightly more sanguine about the bill than the previous chapter. Nonetheless, it is a trenchant critique from a leading legal scholar. He carefully distinguishes, for example, between surveillance as watching on the one hand and the "potential watching" enabled by new mass data-gathering methods on the other. The chapter clearly understands the challenges of big data surveillance but concludes that despite its limitations, Bill C-59 is a definite improvement on current legal measures.

These difficulties are echoed in a different area of surveillance – policing – that nonetheless raises issues very similar to those that must be explored with national security. In Chapter 10, Carrie Sanders and Janet Chan look at how big data methods are actually used by police (much more is known about their activities than about CSE and CSIS). Their findings are very instructive for grasping the scope of this shift not only within the police but also within security agencies. The connecting word is "security," which each body has a mandate to protect. The agencies' desire to pre-empt and prevent security breaches, such as terrorism, is matched by the police claim to be detecting and disrupting crime – in each case, leaning more heavily on big data. Like some other authors discussing security agencies in this book, Sanders and Chan query police services' knowledge and capacity to fully understand "the capabilities and limitations of big data and predictive policing." Responsible representatives of the security agencies acknowledge this deficit too.

Part 4 then moves beyond formal legal challenges to consider active "Resistance to Big Data Surveillance" by security intelligence agencies on the part of civil society. In Chapter 11, Tim McSorley and Anne Dagenais Guertin survey three revealing cases of resistance to government surveillance in Canada since 2001: Stop Illegal Spying (2013), Stop Online Spying (2011), and the International Campaign Against Mass Surveillance (2004). They argue that each campaign did make a difference because each was clearly targeted, created coalitions of interest, and used diverse tactics to make its claims and mount its cases.

These three case studies are complemented by another – the protests against government surveillance enshrined in Bill C-51 from 2014. In Chapter 12, Jeffrey Monaghan and Valerie Steeves see this as unprecedented grassroots opposition to surveillance in Canada. It succeeded, they argue, due to new forms of "connective action" using social media as well as conventional tactics, and because it not only built on previous protests but also took advantage of external events – notably the Snowden disclosures – to buttress its case. On the other hand, Monaghan and Steeves recognize that future success will depend once again on a variety of circumstances and tactics.

Finally, Part 5, "Policy and Technical Challenges of Big Data Surveillance," considers these challenges with a view to showing how the debates over big data surveillance might be pursued towards appropriate goals. This book began with the issues faced at CSE and this theme recurs with Christopher Parsons and Adam Molnar's Chapter 13, which analyzes its accountability for signals intelligence. They propose new requirements for reporting CSE activities – transparency at the legal, statistical, narrative, and proportionality levels that would help accountability be not only vertical, towards oversight bodies, but also horizontal, for citizens in general, particularly those who have concerns because of their own awareness, through personal experience of how data issues affect them.

In Chapter 14, Andrew Clement, Jillian Harkness, and George Raine return to the unresolved controversies over "metadata," seeing it as the "fraught key to big data mass state surveillance." It is good that this is tackled by individuals with computer science expertise because all too often the black box remains unopened. As they note, in the hands of state actors, "metadata can provide the basis for highly intrusive intervention into people's lives." The authors draw on a study of more than 500 documents released by Snowden that show how metadata may be used to build detailed life profiles of those surveilled. It is clearly not "context, not content," as often claimed. Surveillance researchers, security intelligence agencies, and critics of mass surveillance are each offered vital guidance in light of this.

The book concludes with an afterword by Holly Porteous, who agreed to reflect on both the original research workshop and the chapters of this book from her unique perspective as a former employee at CSE. Limited as it is by what she is able to say in the context of her former employment, the value of this chapter lies in its offering of a rare glimpse into the thinking of CSE personnel, acknowledging the correctness of many conclusions reached in our book while also questioning others in a very constructive fashion and providing a number of fruitful avenues for further research that could fill gaps and develop new insights. We are delighted to have this valuable coda to pull together so neatly the central themes of the book while simultaneously offering a constructively critical view of where informed scholarship should focus its analysis.

Conclusion

We started with CSE's assertion that "everything has changed" in an age of big data. Our brief historical sketch shows that this is far from the first time that this argument has been made, and that the changes that are undoubtedly occurring have deeper roots themselves, as well as potentially profound consequences. It is also worth emphasizing that while a turn to a New Analytic Model would seem to indicate a further shift from what has traditionally been understood as HUMINT to SIGINT, there are two main caveats. First, security intelligence agencies, whether SIGINT or HUMINT, are established bureaucratic organizations subject to the self-perpetuating logic of bureaucracies identified by Max Weber early in the twentieth century.[19] HUMINT agencies persist even as a lot of what they now do and will increasingly do is indistinguishable technically from the ostensible function of SIGINT agencies. Second, and despite the first caveat, a lot of what happens from policing up to national security still has nothing directly to do with big data. Human sources, tipoffs, infiltration, provocation, and much more besides remain central modes of operation for security intelligence and political policing.

Many questions remain as to data's centrality and "bigness." As Carrie Sanders shows, in the world of policing, big data practices are often marginalized compared with these older, more trusted human methods.[20] It appears that this also holds for national security HUMINT work. Perhaps the officers who doubt big data's universal usefulness are right to do so: Stéphane Leman-Langlois is profoundly skeptical about the historical effectiveness of big data analysis techniques, arguing that most of the lessons that have supposedly been learned relate to very specific situations that are not applicable in the national security context.[21] The effective use of data is often narrower and smaller than the hype.

And finally, there are many questions about how the movement towards big data affects how security intelligence agencies can be controlled and held accountable, and their powers and reach in some cases rolled back. The cases offered here present some contradictory lessons. Perhaps it is unlikely that any legal, regulatory, or political oppositional activities on their own are going to prevent the accumulation of ever larger collections of data and the application of ever more "intelligent" analytic techniques, but that does not provide a carte blanche for the collection of all or any data, for all or any data-mining processes, and for all or any applications. Above all, the pernicious technocentric story of endless and unstoppable technical progress must be challenged when it comes to security intelligence agencies, because their activities can profoundly yet often silently and secretly affect human rights, civil liberties, and the conditions for human flourishing in Canada.

Notes

1 CSE refers to this not as big data but as the "New Analytic Model." See Chapter 6.
2 See, e.g., Chapter 10.
3 danah boyd and Kate Crawford, "Critical Questions for Big Data," *Information, Communication and Society* 15, 5 (2012): 662–79.
4 Jose van Dijck, "Datafication, Dataism and Dataveillance," *Surveillance and Society* 12, 2 (2014): 197–208.
5 David Lyon, *The Culture of Surveillance: Watching as a Way of Life* (Cambridge: Polity, 2018).
6 Bernard Harcourt, *Exposed: Desire and Disobedience in the Digital Age* (Cambridge, MA: Harvard University Press, 2015).
7 Shoshana Zuboff, *The Age of Surveillance Capitalism* (New York: Public Affairs, 2018).
8 Clive Ponting, *Secrecy in Britain* (Oxford: Basil Blackwell, 1990), 10.
9 Such revelations have a long history in themselves; see David Murakami Wood and Steve Wright, "Before and After Snowden," *Surveillance and Society* 13, 2 (2015): 132–38.
10 David Vincent, *The Culture of Secrecy in Britain, 1832–1998* (Oxford: Oxford University Press, 1998).
11 Alfred W. McCoy, *Policing America's Empire: The United States, the Philippines, and the Rise of the Surveillance State* (Madison: University of Wisconsin Press, 2009).
12 Bernard Porter, *Plots and Paranoia: A History of Political Espionage in Britain, 1790–1988* (London: Routledge, 1992), ix.
13 See Chapter 5.
14 P. Whitney Lackenbauer and Matthew Farish, "The Cold War on Canadian Soil: Militarizing a Northern Environment," *Environmental History* 12, 4 (2007): 920–50.
15 Reg Whitaker, *Secret Service: Political Policing in Canada: From the Fenians to Fortress America* (Toronto: University of Toronto Press, 2012).
16 Andrew Crosby and Jeffrey Monaghan, *Policing Indigenous Movements: Dissent and the Security State* (Toronto: Fernwood, 2018).
17 For more on CSIS, see Chapter 8.
18 See Chapter 6.
19 Max Weber, *Economy and Society*, ed. Guenther Roth and Claus Wittich (Berkeley: University of California Press, 1978).
20 See Chapter 10.
21 See Chapter 3.

Part 1
Understanding Surveillance, Security, and Big Data

1

Collaborative Surveillance with Big Data Corporations
Interviews with Edward Snowden and Mark Klein

Midori Ogasawara

> *When reporters asked, they [AT&T] would give this strange statement, "we don't comment on matters of national security," which implicates them right there. National security? I thought you were a telephone company!*
> – Mark Klein, from my interview in May 2017

One of the most striking facts about today's security intelligence is an extensive collaboration with technology companies, which traffic, store, and use people's digital footprints, often employing so-called big data practices. It is worth remembering that people who accused tech companies of cooperating with governments for state surveillance were usually seen as paranoid or labelled conspiracy theorists without evidence, until Edward Snowden's revelations in June 2013. Although there were a few whistle-blowers prior to Snowden on tech-intelligence collaborative surveillance, such as former AT&T employee Mark Klein, their claims were neither understood nor accepted by the public to the extent that Snowden's were.[1]

By disclosing top-secret documents of the US National Security Agency (NSA), the former contractor unveiled the systematic way tech giants like Google, Microsoft, Apple, and Facebook have worked with NSA to provide volumes of personal data on their customers. The Snowden documents have also shown in subsequent research by investigative reporters that major telecommunications enterprises, such as AT&T and Verizon, have helped the NSA set up mass surveillance facilities at landing points for transoceanic cables. Through these specifically named Internet and telecommunications companies and their documented involvement, people finally realized that governments could actually seize *their* personal data and communications, and that it mattered to *them*. Surveillance became everyone's issue because most of us were familiar with Google and Apple and used the private services they provided, while having only a murky view of state surveillance.

The names of secret partners were deeply hidden. Their extensive cooperation with security intelligence was the vital key to "Collect It All," the NSA's new imperative, established since the US "War on Terror."[2] In one secret NSA slide,

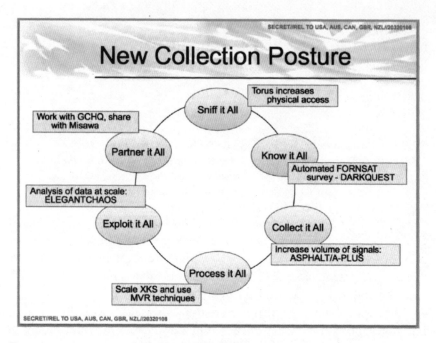

Figure 1.1 A top secret NSA slide for the 2011 conference of the Five Eyes, showing NSA's new organization for "Collect It All." | *Source*: Glenn Greenwald, *No Place to Hide: Edward Snowden, NSA, and the US Surveillance State* (Toronto: Signal, 2014), 97.

the full circle of the "New Collection Posture" is completed with "Partner It All" and enables the starting point of "Sniff It All" (Figure 1.1). But how and why did private companies become good partners of security intelligence for numerous, unwarranted wiretappings? What made the two work together for mass surveillance behind the scenes?

This chapter examines the development of collaborative surveillance between security intelligence and tech companies, and the effect of the collaboration on the political and judicial spheres. Security intelligence and tech companies rapidly developed strategic relationships induced by political economic incentives. The main resources for my analysis are two personal interviews I had with whistle-blowers from both the security intelligence side and the corporate side, Snowden in 2016 and Klein in 2017. It should be noted that the main focus of these interviews was on Japan-US relations, because the activities of the NSA had rarely been contextualized in Japanese politics before. However, Snowden and Klein explained in the interviews the mechanisms of worldwide surveillance networks, of which Japan, Canada, and many other countries are part. Because the worldwide networks are basically American systems, technically supported by American big data companies, and the NSA shares the data collected from those networks with other foreign agencies, it can be said that the NSA systems are also used as a major vehicle for security intelligence in other countries to obtain data. In this sense, Canada's foreign intelligence agency, the Communications Security Establishment (CSE), has been getting more data from the NSA than the Japanese Ministry of Defense has, as the NSA categorizes Canada in its closest group of the Five Eyes network (United States, United Kingdom, Australia, New Zealand, Canada), or the "second parties" in sharing classified data, while placing Japan among the "third parties" with the rest of the US allies. Thus, the basic mechanisms of collaborative surveillance between the NSA and tech companies to be described in this chapter are relevant to Canadian intelligence agencies, to which the NSA and tech companies have been feeding the data. Furthermore, because of the long-standing Five Eyes relationship, the NSA's collaborative techniques with tech companies can imply similar relations and methods that CSE might have developed with Canadian tech companies.

Although worldwide surveillance networks, enabled by state collaboration with private actors, are continuously hidden, the expanded networks have been affecting global political landscapes and redrawing judicial borders of state surveillance. To demonstrate this, I will provide a Japanese example, and my main argument will be the apparent global tendency to legalize the currently illegal state surveillance of citizens. Snowden elaborated on the NSA's strategies to compel the Japanese government to pass certain surveillance legislation while he worked as the NSA's secret contractor in Japan. This legislation, called the *Secrecy Act,* helped the NSA remain covert and practise further illegal surveillance in Japan, and hid the Japanese government's involvement.[3] Similar stories about other US allies are unreported as yet. But the Five Eyes and other European countries have also passed legislation to expand state surveillance over citizens under the political anti-terror discourse of the past two decades, including Canada's Bill C-51 and France's "Big Brother Laws."[4] Together, they create a global wave of legalization of previously illegal surveillance of citizens. This phenomenon strongly resonates with and confirms NSA's policy-making strategies as explained to me first-hand by Snowden.

In what follows, I will first describe a dominant format of the NSA's dragnet surveillance, which emerged in the early stages of the War on Terror and which Klein witnessed in 2004. It was built in part on telecommunications infrastructure in the private sector and presumably proliferated to other locations, as told in Snowden's detailed story of the Special Source Operations (SSO). The partnerships with tech companies are shrouded in secrecy, and if the secrecy is breached, immunity follows *retroactively,* in order not to punish the NSA partners that aided the illegal tapping. Second, what Snowden calls "natural incentives" are present in every chain of collaboration, rather than coercive orders. I will lay out the political economic interests tying the two entities together before analyzing two kinds of collaboration, which the NSA categorizes as "witting" and "unwitting" relationships. In the former, the information and communications technology (ICT) companies know that they are delivering data to the NSA; in the latter, the data are delivered without the consent of the collaborators. The unwitting relationships are often established outside the United States, through a technological "backdoor," with foreign intelligence agencies. The two together keep pushing the boundaries of data collection and secrecy globally. As a significant outcome of the globalized collaboration, I examine the Japanese case of surveillance laws – the *Secrecy Act*, the *Wiretapping Act*, and the *Conspiracy Act* – and discern a judicial trend towards legalizing previously illegal mass surveillance, in relation to the NSA's collaborative strategies.[5] The early format of retroactive immunity is sustained and reinforced in the trend, which allows the extra-judicial activities to replace the rule of law.

Built-in Format of Dragnet Wiretapping

Mark Klein was one of the earliest whistle-blowers regarding the NSA's unwarranted wiretapping programs. He worked for AT&T, one of the oldest and largest telecommunications companies in the United States, as a communication technician who dealt with hardware and troubleshooting on long distance digital circuits.[6] When he was transferred to a branch located in downtown San Francisco in 2004, he came across the NSA's covert operation and collaboration with AT&T.[7]

At the "611 Folsom Street office," as it was known after Klein's whistle-blowing, he discovered a device called a "splitter cabinet" while troubleshooting a long distance circuit. The circuit did not work well when connecting to the splitter cabinet. Klein noticed that the splitter cabinet, when copying something, degraded the signal, and this could cause problems. He called a management technician who knew about the cabinet. The technician came from a secret room downstairs, cleared by the NSA. He helped Klein solve the problem, but Klein became aware of how the splitter worked. It was copying data and sending them down to the NSA's server. The splitter was not helping the data flow but duplicating data for the NSA.

For Klein, the shock lay in the fact that the circuits connected to the splitter cabinet carried local and domestic communications. The US government had occasionally admitted that the NSA eavesdropped on international communications, but denied spying on domestic ones between US citizens. "What I revealed was that they were collecting purely domestic traffic in San Francisco, so that meant they were collecting everyone's data. The story about, 'We're just getting international,' was just a cover story," said Klein.

Why everybody? Klein also found the points at which the NSA accessed the networks: peering links. He explained to me:

> "Peering links" are a typical term for the links that connect one network with others, and that's how you get the Internet. So AT&T's domestic fiber network connects to other companies' networks, like Sprint or what have you, with peering links so that people who are not AT&T, their messages can get to the AT&T network. By tapping into peering links, you get a lot more of everybody's communications, not just AT&T's. The fact that they did this in San Francisco and they were tapping into peering links, people were really upset when I revealed that.

Klein did not want to be part of the illegal unwarranted wiretapping, but could not take immediate action for fear of losing his decent job. Later in 2004, the company offered a financial package for the employees around his age who wanted to retire. He took this opportunity and retired, taking with him engineering documents that proved how the splitter cabinet was connected to NSA equipment. He brought the documents to the Electronic Frontier Foundation (EFF), an advocacy group for privacy and free expression in the electronic age. In 2006, the EFF sued AT&T on behalf of its customers, for violating privacy law by collaborating with the NSA in an illegal program to intercept citizens' communications.[8] Klein supported the EFF lawsuit as a witness and his documents were submitted to the court as evidence in *Hepting v AT&T*.

The Bush administration quickly intervened in this private case, however. The government petitioned the court to dismiss the case on the grounds of state secret privilege. Though the court rejected the petition, the government eventually succeeded in getting the controversial *Foreign Intelligence Surveillance Act [FISA] of 1978 Amendments Act of 2008* enacted by Congress, under which AT&T was awarded so-called retroactive immunity. Law is principally non-retroactive, but it was an exception. The 2008 amendments allow the Attorney General to require the dismissal of lawsuits over a company's participation in the warrantless surveillance program if the government secretly certifies to the court that the surveillance did not occur, was legal, or was authorized by the president, whether legal or illegal.[9] As a result, in 2009, a federal judge dismissed *Hepting* and dozens of other lawsuits over AT&T's collaboration with the NSA in illegal wiretapping.

The EFF also sued the NSA and other government agencies in 2008, and Klein's documents from AT&T were again provided as evidence that AT&T had routed copies of Internet traffic to the NSA's secret room. By then, there was more public exposure from other whistle-blowers regarding NSA mass surveillance. However, the Obama administration also moved to dismiss this case, claiming that litigation over the wiretapping program would require the government to disclose privileged "state secrets" and that the wiretapping program was immune from suit, using the same logic the Bush administration had pursued.[10] Though the case is not completely over, Klein believes that President Obama effectively contained it. "The government has a million ways to kill a lawsuit against the government. So I don't hold out any hope for lawsuits," he commented.

Klein's early revelations of NSA mass surveillance systems, in the first few years after the United States declared the War on Terror in 2001, illuminate two aspects of the collaboration between the NSA and ICT companies. One is that the collaboration appears to have started at the foundation of the existing facilities built by the telecommunication giants. When I visited 611 Folsom Street after my interview with Klein, this reality became more tangible, because the building is located at a busy street corner in downtown San Francisco. The secret room was set up at a location familiar to locals and visitors, but not many pay attention to the black building, which has few windows and looms large, like a huge data box in the city centre. The NSA began a massive wiretap within the telecom's facility in this populated area, and the same systems were disclosed in other AT&T facilities by the *New York Times* and the *Intercept*.[11] The more wiretapping points there were, the more personal data were acquired. This built-in format of dragnet tapping would grow to sites beyond the telecoms' branches, as Snowden later revealed, to a worldwide scale.

The other important aspect of the early collaboration between the NSA and its partners is how devotedly the government protected the private partners that had delivered the data. The government created a very exceptional, retroactive law that turned illegal actions of the telecoms into legal ones. Retroactive immunity nullified the law that banned warrantless wiretapping against citizens, and the presidential order, whether legal or illegal, replaced the law. No responsibility and accountability could be demanded if the rule was retroactively changed after the game had started. Retroactive immunity is fundamentally opposed to the rule of law and democratic oversight by Congress and the people. This type of immunity has become an increasingly common strategy used by governments to expand partnerships for mass surveillance worldwide, as I discuss later. The strategy has drastically changed the boundaries between legal and illegal state surveillance. My interview with Mark Klein highlights the early format that enabled collaborative surveillance, both physically and judicially.

Natural Incentives for Collaboration

Though Klein clearly exposed the collaborative relationships between the NSA and telecommunications companies for mass surveillance systems, the pioneering whistle-blower found it difficult to publicly prove what the NSA had spied on. He did not have NSA security clearance. "I was working down in the nitty-gritty, down at the hardware connecting things up. I didn't have the big view." Edward Snowden walked into the right spot, in Klein's view, to show the big picture. "Snowden had the best evidence possible, actual documents from inside NSA. What more could you ask for?"

Snowden explained to me various methods of NSA mass surveillance, including the Special Source Operations, which he believes plays a central role in today's covert data acquisition.[12] As he told me, "The government calls this bulk collection, and everyone else calls it mass surveillance." The SSO is typically set up at the landing sites of the international transoceanic cables. The telecommunications companies from different countries jointly build and operate these cables, and locate the landing stations on the shore to sort data traffic. According to Snowden, the NSA requires the telecoms to set up a room for the NSA to copy all data going through the landing sites. Based on classified NSA documents that Snowden disclosed in 2013, it has been revealed that the major landing sites were part of their wiretapping programs, such as those code-named FAIRVIEW, STORMBREW, or BLARNEY.[13] The landing sites are called "choke points" by the NSA and this is where tapping devices are embedded in the communication hubs owned by ICT companies. This method has a very similar format to the one that was built into the major communications infrastructure at 611 Folsom Street in 2004, and appears to have evolved to a global scale.

Snowden said: "This is the real central problem because this is the way the majority of spying happens today. It's not done through satellite, although of course that's still done, but not majority. It comes from these ocean cables." He argues that SSO is more intrusive than the NSA's other highly controversial program, the PRISM program. PRISM shocked the world in 2013, revealing how covertly well-known Internet service providers like Microsoft, Yahoo!, Google, Apple, and others have cooperated with the NSA. According to Snowden, however, the government is more likely to pursue knowledge of individual cases than knowledge from all the customers in PRISM, and there is an intermediate step where the government sends requests for certain online accounts to the company, and then the company pulls all the information directly from the servers and gives an exact copy to the government. With SSO, on the other hand, once the NSA has a telecom company set up the splitter cabinet, "then the company doesn't really have to do anything ever again, because NSA has basically a perfect copy of everything that's coming over those lines, all the time," just like duplicating all data going through the domestic communications cables in San Francisco.

Why did the NSA develop this method as today's major source of security intelligence? The spy agency asked itself that in one of the Snowden documents, which also indicates the reasons. "Why SSO?" Because "SSO is 'Big Data.'" It can capture up to "60% of content" and "75% of metadata" in a digital data stream.[14] There is no definition of big data in this document, but it is easy to assume that big data includes not only actual correspondence among people, such as telephone calls, emails, and text messages, but also human behaviour, both online and offline, such as what people searched online and where they went. Big data provides the NSA with a wider scope of information to predict what people would like to do next.

Snowden described the actual process behind the scenes – how the NSA negotiated with its partners to set up choke points at the landing sites. The NSA normally pays the company for a room where it puts all its equipment, including its servers. The NSA attaches special locks to the room and allows only staff with security clearance to enter. It then asks the company to run the cable through the NSA's equipment, to copy all the data it wants. The telecoms do not deal with what the NSA does with that data. "But, there is no real case here where these companies don't know about it," asserted Snowden.

Why do big data corporations cooperate with these illegal wiretapping programs? Snowden points out that these companies take the NSA's requests into their business calculations. To expand the service areas and access new networks, the company needs to obtain permissions and approvals from the government. If the company got into trouble with the NSA by refusing the requests, it might lose an opportunity to increase profits, resulting in a shrinking of its business. "So, they've got a little bit of leverage with the government," says Snowden.

> Not that they are really threatened by the government, but the government goes, "Well, it's in our interests to help them build this new site or do whatever, because they'll give us access too." And so, it's this kind of culture that nobody sees, because this all happens secretly. But it's the nature of how intelligence works ... you don't want to think about villains. What you want to think is what are the natural incentives for all of the people engaged at every level of the process? What, if you were in their position, what would you do? And, suddenly, it becomes obvious why everything works out the way that it does; everybody is just scratching each other's back.

On the government side, where Snowden once belonged, he experienced a similar culture of political economic incentives within the organization, which encouraged avoiding trouble and following the existing tacit rules, for job security and promotion. If any lawmakers attempted to stop the process, they could find themselves in a politically vulnerable situation. If any incidents occurred, they could be blamed or retaliated against by the intelligence agency that can find anyone's weak spot and leak personal data to achieve its goals. It would be a safe choice for lawmakers to let the intelligence agency do what it wants, so they suffer no consequences at all. "It's not a product of evil ... It's a product of incentives in the system. Secrecy corrupts the process of democracy." Because few challenge the secret power of security intelligence, the intelligence agencies transcend democratic power and simultaneously undermine democratic decision making.

Snowden attributes the rapid expansion of collaborative surveillance to political economic incentives active at both ends – the NSA and ICT companies. From a cautious perspective, delivering customers' data to the NSA does not directly profit the ICT companies. Rather, it violates customers' privacy and other rights and organizational compliance, and may damage business by harming public trust. This would be another story if the collaborations were all hidden. Secrecy would nudge the ICT companies to avoid problems with the authorities, and to choose the political economic benefits of conformity. In fact, when the secret was revealed by the whistle-blowers, angry customers began accusing the companies, as the EFF sued AT&T on behalf of its customers. Thus, secrecy is a necessary condition for "natural incentives" to come into effect and for growing the political economic incentives. The NSA and ICT companies can "scratch each other's backs" while people don't know that their data are actually used in the deal.

If all these processes had been transparent from the very beginning, the political economic incentives would have been more likely to turn into business risks because customers would stop using the services or sue the companies. Collaboration based on illegal surveillance inherently requires secrecy, and secrecy lets the incentives work for both ends – the government and the private sector. However, an end to the secrecy initiated by Klein, Snowden, and other whistle-blowers did not end the collaboration. With secrecy removed, the government took formal action to wrench the legal standard towards illegal practices, by passing laws to legalize the unprecedented scale of state surveillance. Instead of secrecy, the government invented and provided retroactive immunity to its partners, to protect their illegal involvement in mass surveillance

Witting and Unwitting Relationships

For the NSA, protecting and expanding its partners has been an important keystone of the War on Terror imperative of Collect It All. The diagram of this imperative consists of six stages in a cycle: Sniff It All, Know It All, Collect It All, Process It All, Exploit It All, and Partner It All (see Figure 1.1).[15] The last stage is particularly relevant, as it guarantees the means of collecting personal data through communication infrastructure as much as possible.

Snowden's analysis is this: "In many cases, the way it works, the biggest ICT companies are the ones that are working the most closely with the government. That's how they got to be big and that's why they don't have any trouble with regulatory problems, and they got all the permits they need." The largest American telecoms, AT&T and Verizon, have been reported as having "extreme willingness to help" the NSA.[16] A smooth relationship with the government helps business grow, so political economic incentives are convincing. The NSA aims to eventually set up an SSO at all landing sites of all international transoceanic cables to gear up for Collect It All.

Snowden told me that these SSO collaborations between the government and businesses are called "witting" relationships in NSA terms: the executives know that they are working with the intelligence agency and that information is closely shared with other intelligence agencies, such as the Five Eyes or the second parties.[17] For example, participants in PRISM, such as Microsoft, Facebook, Google, and Apple, are involved with witting relationships, as are AT&T and Verizon in the SSO.

Much less known are the "unwitting" relationships, where companies are unaware that they are providing data to the NSA. These are unilateral programs in which the NSA sets up tapping devices within ICT equipment and uses them as a "backdoor" to absorb data to its servers.[18] For example, according to Snowden, the NSA encourages foreign governments to set up their own network equipment, whether in Afghanistan or Japan, so the foreign governments order these high-tech appliances from ICT companies, many of which are based in the United States. When the equipment is shipped from or transits the United States, the NSA attaches tapping devices to the product. "So we made them into a kind of Trojan Horse where you install it on your network and it works perfectly for you but it also works for us without you knowing."

Those more deeply hidden unilateral programs directly assist anti-terror tactics of identifying targets by location technologies and attacking them remotely by drones. The point here is that the NSA sneakily develops unwitting relationships in order to push the limits of witting relationships towards Partner It All. In fact, the NSA has established both types of relationships with thirty-three countries called third parties, including Japan, Germany, France, Brazil, and Mexico.[19] These countries are diplomatically US allies, so they often cooperate with NSA surveillance by offering and exchanging data. Simultaneously, however, the NSA surveilles these countries, including German chancellor

Angela Merkel's mobile phone,[20] former Brazilian president Dilma Rousseff's calls,[21] and Japan's thirty-five telephone lines connected to ministries.[22] Thus, witting and unwitting relationships were combined and often against the same targets for various purposes. This shows the inherently unequal, ambiguous relationships with allies as partners.

One NSA document Snowden and I discussed in the Japanese context clearly indicates that the NSA had been collecting data from Japan in the SSO program called FAIRVIEW.[23] The piece of correspondence, dated 23 August 2011, reported:

> On 5 Aug 2011, collection of DNR and DNI traffic at the FAIRVIEW CLIFF-SIDE trans-pacific cable site resumed, after being down for approximately five months. Collection operation at CLIFFSIDE had been down since 11 March 2011, due to the cable damage as result of the earthquake off of the coast of Japan ... FAIRVIEW operations will continue to task collection for all new and restored circuits.[24]

"DNI" refers to Digital Network Intelligence and "DNR" is apparently Dial Number Recognition. According to the investigative news organization Pro-Publica, which reported on this document jointly with the *New York Times,* CLIFFSIDE is a cable station operated by AT&T in Point Arena, California.[25] The submarine cable landing at Point Arena is connected to Japan, where AT&T's counterpart, Japan's NTT Communications, admitted one of the cables was repaired on that date.

Another transoceanic cable, Trans-Pacific Express, is also a part of the SSO program STORMBREW, according to the *New York Times.*[26] The Trans-Pacific Express was jointly constructed by telecommunications companies from China, Taiwan, Korea, Japan, and the United States. In the United States, it is operated by Verizon; in Japan, the landing station is again run by NTT Communications. NTT is the oldest and largest telecom in Japan, which fits Snowden's formula: "the largest telecom works most closely with the government for surveillance." I asked Snowden: "Do you think that the Japanese telecoms are aware that this cable is being used by NSA?" He carefully responded:

> I don't have any specific understanding of a Japanese corporation cooperating directly with the American government, or NSA to spy on these things. However, I would be shocked if these corporations weren't cooperating with Japanese intelligence services to get exactly the same kind of information. It's simply a case of where they trade. The US feeds information from what they get to the Japanese, and the Japanese feed information from what they get to the US.

The NSA proudly declared in a top-secret document the establishment of "alliances with over 80 major global corporations supporting" its mission, as strategic partnerships.[27] Japanese collaborators have not been reported, but NTT has, at least unwittingly, cooperated with the NSA in constructing, operating, and maintaining submarine cables at the company's cost. The collaborative networks extend in a combination of witting and unwitting, and absorb data from the foreign communications infrastructure. It remains unknown whether or not the NSA's choke points are constructed only within the United States, but the NSA has been pushing the boundaries of dragnet surveillance outside US soil through unwitting relations with foreign ICT companies. Before the Internet became the main arena of mass surveillance, satellites were the major means of intercepting foreign communications, most famously known as ECHELON.[28] ECHELON started with the UKUSA Agreement in 1947, and soon came to be operated by the Five Eyes. It constructed satellite facilities outside the United States, such as the radomes in Menwith Hill, UK, and at the US airbase in Misawa, Japan. The NSA had already established international correspondence on these foreign sites, not only for Cold War tactics but also for corporate espionage against allied countries. Historically and legally, the NSA has had more of a free hand to access foreign citizens' information than that of American citizens.

Legalize the Illegal

The complex of witting and unwitting relationships also highlights foreign governments as another major group of NSA collaborators, besides ICT companies, as they deliver and exchange data with the NSA. To protect and enhance the surveillance networks, the NSA has been developing collaborative relations with foreign intelligence agencies and putting political pressure on foreign governments. This was the most eye-opening part of my interview with Edward Snowden, who worked as an NSA contractor at the American Yokota Airbase in Tokyo in 2009–11. With an insider's perspective, Snowden discussed the detailed, unknown background of a highly controversial law, the *Secrecy Act*, passed by the Japanese Diet in 2013, stating that "this new state secrets law was actually designed by the United States."

According to Snowden, the NSA has a group of roughly 100 lawyers who work for the Office of General Counsel. They partnered with a group called the Foreign Affairs Directory, which researches different countries' legal limits on collaboration with the NSA and how to get around the legal protections that prevent these countries from spying on their citizens or classifying the information. The legal experts' work includes hiding NSA mass surveillance from the public eye so that the NSA can further expand its surveillance networks. Japan's

Secrecy Act was needed in this respect, and was proposed to Japanese counterparts.

> Again, they are not doing this for [an] evil purpose. They see this as necessary for national defense. But the bottom line is, you start to get a group of countries, this Five Eyes network, that had been creating this system of spying and judicial run-arounds, legal runarounds for many years. And they start to export it to other countries. They go, if you pass these laws ... of course, you can rewrite it. You don't have to pass the law exactly as we say. But, in our experience, (we say,) this is what you should aim for, you should do this, you should do this. Those other countries go, well, hey, we should do this. And, this is exactly what happened with the state secrets law in Japan. When I was in Japan, we would have Japanese partners come over to our building at Yokota. They knew we were there. It was like the world's greatest secret, because we were sharing information that we were gaining from all this spying.

Characterizing them as typical NSA tactics, Snowden elaborated on how the NSA usually motivated its Japanese or foreign partners to legitimize their secret relationships:

> And, we would say we can only share information at this level of classification with you. We use it as sort of a carrot and a stick, where the Japanese military want this piece of information, or they want that piece of information. Then we say, well, we can't give you that because your laws aren't the way we want them to be. We'll give you this smaller piece of something else that might be helpful, just kind of a token gift to help them save face ... So we would share things at the secret level in Japan. We said, if you change your laws, we'll share things at the top-secret level with you.

These conversations all take place behind the curtain of intelligence agencies, which I had never heard of as a background of the *Secrecy Act*. I asked Snowden with suspicion how these conversations finally became law, what the diplomatic process was. He explained that the conversation normally began with division chiefs of intelligence agencies, then went up to the heads of the agencies and eventually to the Department of State to formalize the agreement at a policy level (this process was evidenced by an NSA document disclosed in April 2017).[29] The NSA is aware that conducting mass surveillance is illegal according to Japanese constitutional rights and judicial standards. "So it's in violation of the law. But, it doesn't really matter at this point because no one can find out, at least in terms of the government's political calculation." Secrecy, in this case about the diplomatic process, enables security agents and bureaucrats to discuss the unconstitutional bill against citizens:

> And, then, eventually, on the basis of this, if this program has been continuing for too long without legal authorization, we've proved that you need it. This is how they get their foot in the door, a kind of press government. And I'm talking about intelligence agencies in general, not just here in the States. In Japan, they get their foot in the door by saying we've already operationalized this policy and it allowed us to learn this, this, and do this and this, whatever, but we don't have the legal authorization we need to continue this program. So, if you don't force a law through your government that authorizes this, we'll have to shut the program down.

Then, according to Snowden, the NSA shows some examples of immediate "threats," such as that foreign agents are active in Japan, a terrorist attack is planned, or Japan is losing its advantage in trade negotiations. Whatever the stories are, these threats are used as "evidence" to convince not only the intelligence agencies but also lawmakers, who are not familiar with the realities of mass surveillance and how data are collected, retained, and used. Lawmakers tend to think that, though it's ambiguous how surveillance systems help them, the systems look valuable and can be useful. Apparently, there is no pushback against intelligence agencies' having more surveillance and control over information belonging to the citizenry.

The hidden processes Snowden described to me aptly correspond to recent studies about secret Japan-US treaties, negotiated at the Japan-US Joint Committee, which was established by Japanese bureaucrats and American *military* officers, not the government, after the Second World War.[30] We do not have space in this chapter to examine Japan-US relations further, but these historical . studies support Snowden's first-hand information that the United States pressured, if not forced, Japan's government to legitimize the hiding of American illegal surveillance in Japan, in order to maintain and enhance it. The *Secrecy Act* enabled the Japanese government to designate any administrative files as secret, upon which those files become immune to opening by the media, journalists, and citizens. Anyone who leaks secrets, and any journalist who reports on it, can be sentenced to up to ten years of penal servitude.

The harsh punishment secures the government's illegal practices from public view. A rapid chilling effect emerged among the Japanese media and caught international attention. The World Press Freedom Index, released by Reporters Without Borders in Paris, ranked Japan 72nd out of 180 countries in 2016 and 2017, rated for freedom of news access, transparency, and protection of journalists. This was an extreme drop from 11th place in 2010.[31] The index reflects the serious dampening influence of the *Secrecy Act,* which induced self-censorship in the media. The United Nations Special Rapporteur on Freedom of Expression, David Kaye, visited Japan in 2016 and also reported on the negative effects of the *Secrecy Act.*[32] The act has surely prevented the public from knowing about the government's illegal practices, including its support for the NSA's illegal surveillance. And this is not the end of the story.

After passing the *Secrecy Act* by an undemocratic procedure in the Diet, Prime Minister Shinzō Abe's government proposed and enacted two other surveillance laws. One is a revision of the *Wiretapping Act* of 2016 that greatly expanded the categories of crimes subject to police wiretapping investigations. The other is the 2017 *Conspiracy Act.* The *Conspiracy Act* had failed thrice in the Diet in the past because of its extreme stance against privacy and free speech. It criminalizes subjects for communications in which they agree on alleged crimes, whether or not they actually commit any criminal acts. It replaces Japan's postwar principle of criminal justice without declaration, under which no one is charged for a crime before taking action. It enables the police to tap potentially everyone's conversations, in order to identify who is talking about crimes.[33] We have not heard that the United States has been involved in crafting these two laws, but they obviously help both the Japanese and American governments enlarge their surveillance capacities. The *Wiretapping Act* legitimized the *means* of wiretapping in criminal investigations, and the *Conspiracy Act* created the new *reason* for the police to monitor everyone's conversations, including emails, text messages, video chats, and so on. The serial enactment of the three laws contributed first to protecting the NSA's operations and the Japanese government's collaboration in the first place, and then gave real teeth to their extension of mass surveillance legally. Together, the three laws vitiate the once established legal standards of privacy and right to confidential correspondence in the Japanese Constitution, and modify them to accommodate the illegal surveillance practices.[34] The previously illegal reality of mass surveillance has now been transformed into lawful data collection, where extra-judicial and judicial power are indistinguishable.

Significantly, retroactive immunity, the early means of collaborative surveillance to protect the NSA's private partners in the United States, has been developed to a more legitimate form in Japanese surveillance laws, to legalize illegal state surveillance. It is important to recognize this transformation because retroactive immunity is an exceptional measure particularly deployed to absolve the tech companies of violation of privacy. It had to be made retroactive, contrary to the legislative principle of non-retroactivity, otherwise those companies might have been found guilty in American courts. Retroactive immunity reveals the illegal origin of mass surveillance in once established legal standards, while governments try to blur the boundaries between legal and illegal surveillance, place practices in a "grey zone," and push the boundaries.

Taking into consideration Snowden's comments that the NSA first created the strategies in Five Eyes and began exporting them to other countries, the tendency to legalize illegal surveillance does not appear to be limited to Japan. For example, we can reconsider the backgrounds of Canada's Bill C-51 or the anti-terror measures enacted in France after 2015 in the state of emergency.[35] Although it is beyond the scope of this chapter whether this happens within the NSA's second or third parties, such practices would be highly problematic for the independence of the state and would show the United States as an imperial power that writes other nations' laws. Only whistle-blowers can reveal to us the political processes behind the scenes, just as Snowden disclosed the Japanese story. As he reiterated, the NSA has been using the same tactics in other countries, so some common explanation should be provided for its actions in different countries to bring about discrete changes in laws in the global War on Terror.

In this sense, the Council of Europe's *Convention on Cybercrime*, signed on 23 November 2001, can be seen as the first international move for surveillance legislation during the War on Terror.[36] Forty-three countries, including the non-member states of Canada, Japan, South Africa, and the United States, signed the convention, which requires participating nations to enact legislation that facilitates investigation and prosecution of crimes committed through the Internet. In the name of harmonizing national legislation and improving international cooperation, the signatories committed to granting law enforcement authorities "lawful access" to data traffic, which compels Internet service providers and telecoms to assist interceptions by the state. Similar legislation had been previously proposed in the United States and the United Kingdom but had been dropped because of public concerns about privacy.[37] Thus, the convention provided a "policy-laundering" detour for those governments[38] because, although it focused on particular crimes such as fraud, forgery, child pornography, and copyright infringement, it opened up a much larger sphere for state policing and intelligence gathering. Over time, compliance with the convention was invoked to justify legislation that significantly weakened the legal standards of data protection in each signatory country.[39]

Conclusion

In this chapter, I have described how the ICT industries have worked with the NSA to collect and deliver data worldwide, based on the accounts of two whistle-blowers. In summary, the NSA has developed a format of mass surveillance systems built into existing digital communications infrastructure, from telecoms' branches in populated areas to the landing sites of the transoceanic cables on remote shores. This format captured enormous amounts of big data, up to "60% of content" and "75% of metadata" in a data flow.[40] The alliance between security intelligence and ICT industries was constructed with "natural incentives," as Snowden calls them, for avoiding regulatory trouble with the government and expanding business on the business side, and for avoiding disputes in conformity with the existing organizational imperatives on the government/military side. These are the political economic ties, concealed and unprecedentedly expanded, between the two entities.

The political economic incentives were effectively developed in secrecy because giving consumers' data to the government without their consent would cause public outrage and damage business. Secrecy is vital to the functioning of political economic incentives. Then when the secret was uncovered, the government legitimized the companies' involvement in illegal surveillance by granting them retroactive immunity. It legalized the illegal surveillance practices, and enabled further alliance and cooperation for more secret surveillance by protecting the partners.

The NSA calls these relationships with the private sector "witting" relationships, and has also constructed "unwitting" relationships by secretly installing technological backdoors. With both witting and unwitting relationships, it has achieved a global network of mass surveillance incorporating American ICT companies, foreign governments, and foreign ICT companies.

As a result, my serious concern over expanding collaborations is the worldwide domino effect of legalizing the previously illegal surveillance by states over the population. Edward Snowden elaborated on the Japanese case in my interview, which revealed that foreign legislative change has been one of the goals of the NSA, to expand its surveillance networks. Japan's *Secrecy Act* first provided the NSA with official secrecy to cover illegal intelligence activities in Japan, and then allowed the NSA to maintain and enhance illegal data collection with support from the Japanese government. In turn, the law veiled the Japanese government's involvement with NSA surveillance, and its own illegal data collection, and enabled the government to punish any whistle-blowers or journalists who attempted to reveal these to the public. Two more surveillance laws followed the *Secrecy Act*. The revised *Wiretapping Act* and the *Conspiracy Act* legalized the previously illegal *means* and *reasons* of state surveillance over the last few years. The expansion of global surveillance networks has been pushing Japan to redraw the judicial borders of state surveillance and undermine the rights established by the Japanese Constitution – such as privacy, confidential correspondence, and freedom of expression – as a consequence of the invasive state surveillance against the population in the wars until 1945.

Situating the NSA's successful attempt in "designing" Japan's *Secrecy Act* of 2013 in a global context, we find a transformation of retroactive immunity, deployed by the US government and Congress in 2008, to protect the collaborators. Finding legal runarounds and eventually legalizing illegal surveillance are parts of the NSA's legal strategy to Partner It All and Collect It All that has been initially created and tested within Five Eyes, according to Snowden. The NSA's global strategy of expanding collaborative networks should be further researched and discussed in the context of different countries. As each country has different relations with the United States, it is important to reconsider surveillance legislation from the perspective of a country's relations with the United States. Together, we can identify the common dynamics involved in widening the circles of digitized mass surveillance, which nullifies legal protections for individuals, undermines constitutional rights, and presents itself as lawful afterwards. Defining borders between legal and illegal surveillance is important in order to resist the avalanche of illegal surveillance that seems to grow with every technological advancement.

With respect to the use of big data, the tech companies have taken more initiative than the intelligence agencies. It is the ICT companies that own the infrastructure to collect, use, and sell personal data, and that create new algorithms and exploit future markets based on collected data. Though big tech companies are unwilling to disclose their relationships with security intelligence, they are not shy to speak out about the predictive technologies generated by big data, which go beyond existing legal boundaries for a "better world."[41] Google co-founder Larry Page commented in 2013: "There are many, many exciting and important things we can do, but we can't, because they are illegal."[42] Illegal here refers to violations of human rights and regulations in democratic state systems. Marc Dugain and Christophe Labbé also refer to other tech business leaders, such as Facebook's Mark Zuckerberg or former Google CEO Eric Schmidt, showing their beliefs that technologies can draw out individual potential, achieve social equality, and overcome famine and unemployment.[43] Their comments represent not only the neoliberal ideologies of unlimited deregulation and marketization but also the view that big data is more efficient than politics in solving social problems. Democratic debates from various viewpoints seem just inefficient obstacles in their view of the world under the digital revolution. The algorithm is the new law governing this "exciting" era. Dugain and Labbé point out that traditional politics deals with causes of problems, whereas Silicon Valley deals only with results, ignoring causes, processes, and especially inconvenient facts for their businesses: "Big data is making politics unnecessary. This is an invisible coup, aimed at taking out the essence of democracy and leaving only the outline."[44] As a result, big data corporations have been changing citizens into consumers, purely and forcibly.

Thus, political and judicial standards to protect human rights are under attack from technological solutionism, in a larger picture of a data-driven society. The collaboration between security intelligence and big data corporations takes place outside official judicial institutions and takes over political spheres. There is a fundamental ideological sync between the two in transcending democratic oversight and subverting judicial rules. Big data is currently exploited in this depoliticized technological zone, where the two players (and other players too) envision controlling the future, without political and judicial interventions.

As a closing note, whistle-blowers are a very rare resource in unfolding the murky military/surveillance-industrial complex today. Their protection is an urgent matter for any society. On the other hand, Mark Klein told me that whistle-blowers are not sufficient to bring about political change: "What you really need is a combination of whistleblowers and a party that's determined to bring down the government. And, you need large masses of people angry and marching the streets." Even as I was nodding, I was curious about why *he* decided to begin this process alone. He answered in a husky voice, "I thought it [warrantless wiretapping by the NSA and AT&T] was illegal and immoral and dangerous, and I thought I had a chance to do it and get away with it ... Well, I had some principles." At least, democratic "principles" may offer everyone a starting point for holding the secretive collaborators of big data surveillance accountable and countering illegal state practices.

Notes

1 I have to admit with shame that I was part of the ignorant public despite having researched surveillance studies for several years.
2 Glenn Greenwald, *No Place to Hide: Edward Snowden, NSA, and the US Surveillance State* (Toronto: Signal, 2014), 97.
3 Midori Ogasawara, スノーデン、監視社会の恐怖を語る [Snowden talks about the horrors of the surveillance society: The complete record of an exclusive interview] (Tokyo: Mainichi Shimbun, 2016).
4 Canada, Bill C-51, *An Act to amend the Criminal Code and the Department of Justice Act and to make consequential amendments to another Act,* 2017, https://www.justice.gc.ca/eng/csj-sjc/pl/cuol-mgnl/c51.html; Ewen MacAskill, "How French Intelligence Agencies Failed before the Paris Attacks," *Guardian,* 15 November 2015, https://www.theguardian.com/world/2015/nov/19/how-french-intelligence-agencies-failed-before-the-paris-attacks; Kim Willsher, "France Approves 'Big Brother' Surveillance Powers despite UN Concern," *Guardian,* 24 July 2015, https://www.theguardian.com/world/2015/jul/24/france-big-brother-surveillance-powers; Angelique Chrisafis, "France Considers Extending National State of Emergency," *Guardian,* 22 January 2016, https://www.theguardian.com/world/2016/jan/22/france-considers-extending-national-state-of-emergency;

Lizzie Dearden, "Paris Attacks: France's State of Emergency Is Imposing 'Excessive' Restrictions on Human Rights, UN Says," *Independent*, 20 January 2016, http://www.independent.co.uk/news/world/europe/paris-attacks-frances-state-of-emergency-is-imposing-excessive-restrictions-on-human-rights-un-says-a6822286.html.

5 *Act on the Protection of Specially Designated Secrets*, Act No. 108 of 2013, Japanese Law Translation, http://www.japaneselawtranslation.go.jp/law/detail/?id=2543&vm=04&re=01 (*Secrecy Act*); *Act on Communications Interception during Criminal Investigations*, Act No. 137 of 1999, amended by Act No. 54 of 2016, https://elaws.e-gov.go.jp/search/elawsSearch/elaws_search/lsg0500/detail?lawId=411AC0000000137 (*Wiretapping Act*); *Revised Act on Punishment of Organized Crimes and Restriction of Criminal Profits*, Act No. 67 of 2017, https://www.sn-hoki.co.jp/article/pickup_hourei/ph728/ (*Conspiracy Act*).

6 Jeff Larson, Julia Angwin, Henrik Moltke, and Laura Poitras, "A Trail of Evidence Leading to AT&T's Partnership with NSA," *ProPublica*, 15 August 2015, https://www.propublica.org/article/a-trail-of-evidence-leading-to-atts-partnership-with-the-nsa.

7 I interviewed Mr. Klein for about two hours at his house in a suburb of San Francisco in May 2017.

8 Electronic Frontier Foundation, *Hepting v AT&T*, https://www.eff.org/cases/hepting.

9 Ibid.

10 Electronic Frontier Foundation, *Jewel v NSA*, https://www.eff.org/cases/jewel.

11 Mark Klein, *Wiring Up the Big Brother Machine ... and Fighting It* (Charleston, SC: BookSurge, 2009); Julia Angwin, Charlie Savage, Jeff Larson, Henrik Moltke, Laura Poitras, and James Risen, "AT&T Helped U.S. Spy on Internet on a Vast Scale," *New York Times*, 15 August 2015, https://www.nytimes.com/2015/08/16/us/politics/att-helped-nsa-spy-on-an-array-of-internet-traffic.html; Ryan Gallagher and Henrik Moltke, "The NSA's Hidden Spy Hubs in Eight U.S. Cities," *Intercept*, 25 June 2018, https://theintercept.com/2018/06/25/att-internet-nsa-spy-hubs/.

12 I interviewed Mr. Snowden for two and a half hours in May 2016, via an encrypted video channel from Queen's University, Ontario.

13 Greenwald, *No Place to Hide*.

14 "Newly Disclosed N.S.A. Files Detail Partnerships with AT&T and Verizon," *New York Times*, 15 August 2015, https://www.nytimes.com/interactive/2015/08/15/us/documents.html?_r=0.

15 Greenwald, *No Place to Hide*, 97.

16 Julia Angwin, Jeff Larson, Charlie Savage, James Risen, Henrik Moltke, and Laura Poitras, "NSA Spying Relies on AT&T's 'Extreme Willingness to Help,'" *ProPublica*, 15 August 2015, https://www.propublica.org/article/nsa-spying-relies-on-atts-extreme-willingness-to-help.

17 Paul Farrell, "History of 5-Eyes – Explainer," *Guardian*, 2 December 2013, https://www.theguardian.com/world/2013/dec/02/history-of-5-eyes-explainer.

18 Greenwald, *No Place to Hide*; Bruce Schneier, *Data and Goliath: The Hidden Battles to Collect Your Data and Control Your World* (New York: W.W. Norton, 2015).

19 Ryan Gallagher, "How Secret Partners Expand NSA's Surveillance Dragnet," *Intercept*, 18 June 2014, https://theintercept.com/2014/06/18/nsa-surveillance-secret-cable-partners-revealed-rampart-a/.

20 Kevin Rawlinson, "NSA Surveillance: Merkel's Phone May Have Been Monitored 'for Over 10 Years,'" *Guardian*, 26 October 2013, https://www.theguardian.com/world/2013/oct/26/nsa-surveillance-brazil-germany-un-resolution.

21 Julian Borger, "Brazilian President: US Surveillance a 'Breach of International Law,'" *Guardian*, 24 September 2013, https://www.theguardian.com/world/2013/sep/24/brazil-president-un-speech-nsa-surveillance.

22 WikiLeaks, "Target Tokyo," news release, 30 July 2015, https://wikileaks.org/nsa-japan/.

23 Larson et al., "A Trail of Evidence."

24 Ibid.

25 Ibid.

26 "Newly Disclosed N.S.A. Files."

27 Greenwald, *No Place to Hide*, 102.

28 Toshimaru Ogura, エシュロンー暴かれた全世界盗聴網 [ECHELON: The unveiled global tapping network] (Tokyo: Nanatsumori-shokan, 2002); Duncan Campbell, "GCHQ and Me: My Life Unmasking British Eavesdroppers," *Intercept*, 3 August 2015, https://theintercept.com/2015/08/03/life-unmasking-british-eavesdroppers/.

29 See the NSA document found in "The Story Behind the Move," *Intercept*, 24 April 2017, https://theintercept.com/document/2017/04/24/the-story-behind-the-move/, published as part of the article by Ryan Gallagher, "Japan Made Secret Deals with the NSA That Expanded Global Surveillance," *Intercept*, 24 April 2017, https://theintercept.com/2017/04/24/japans-secret-deals-with-the-nsa-that-expand-global-surveillance/.

30 Ukeru Magosaki, 戦後史の正体 [The true face of the postwar history] (Tokyo: Sougen-sha, 2013); Koji Yabe, 日本はなぜ、「戦争ができる国」になったのか [Why Japan became the country that can conduct war] (Tokyo: Shueisha International, 2015); Toshi-hiro Yoshida, 「日米合同委員会」の研究 [The research on the Japan–United States Joint Committee] (Tokyo: Sougen-sha, 2016).

31 Reporters Without Borders, "World Press Freedom Index," https://rsf.org/en/ranking.

32 Ogasawara, [Snowden talks about the horrors of the surveillance society].

33 Midori Ogasawara, "Surveillance at the Roots of Everyday Interactions: Japan's Conspiracy Bill and Its Totalitarian Effects," *Surveillance and Society* 15, 3/4 (2017): 477–85, https://ojs.library.queensu.ca/index.php/surveillance-and-society/article/view/6626/6442.

34 *The Constitution of Japan*, 1946, Japanese Law Translation, http://www.japaneselaw translation.go.jp/law/detail/?id=174.

35 Daniel Leblanc and Chris Hannay, "Privacy, Security and Terrorism: Everything You Need to Know about Bill C-51," *Globe and Mail*, 10 March 2015, https://beta.the globeandmail.com/news/politics/privacy-security-and-terrorism-everything-you-need -to-know-about-bill-c-51/article23383976/?ref=http://www.theglobeandmail.com&; MacAskill, "How French Intelligence Agencies Failed before the Paris Attacks"; Willsher, "France Approves 'Big Brother' Surveillance Powers"; Chrisafis, "France Considers Extending National State of Emergency"; Dearden, "Paris Attacks."

36 Kristin Archick, *Cybercrime: The Council of Europe Convention* (Washington, DC: Congressional Research Service, 2006); *Convention on Cybercrime*, 2001, ETS No. 185 (entered into force 1 July 2004), Council of Europe, https://www.coe.int/en/web/conventions/full-list/-/conventions/treaty/185.

37 Terry Palfrey, "Surveillance as a Response to Crime in Cyberspace," *Information and Communications Technology Law* 9, 3 (2000): 173–93.

38 American Civil Liberties Union, "ACLU Announces International Project to Stop 'Policy Laundering,'" 13 April 2005, https://www.aclu.org/news/aclu-announces-international -project-stop-policy-laundering?redirect=technology-and-liberty/aclu-announces -international-project-stop-policy-laundering; Colin J. Bennett, Kevin D. Haggerty, David Lyon, and Valerie Steeves, *Transparent Lives: Surveillance in Canada* (Edmonton: Athabasca University Press, 2014).

39 Laura Huey and Richard Rosenberg, "Watching the Web: Thoughts on Expanding Police Surveillance Opportunities under the Cyber-Crime Convention," *Canadian Journal of Criminology and Criminal Justice* 46, 5 (2004): 597–606; Colin J. Bennett and Charles

Raab, *The Governance of Privacy: Policy Instruments in Global Perspective* (Cambridge, MA: MIT Press, 2006).

40 "Newly Disclosed N.S.A. Files."

41 Greenwald, *No Place to Hide*.

42 Marc Dugain and Christophe Labbé, *L'homme nu: La dictature invisible du numérique* [ビッグデータという独裁者], trans. Kinuko Tottori (Tokyo: Chikuma shobo, 2017), 33.

43 Ibid.

44 Ibid., 101.

2

On Denoting and Concealing in Surveillance Law

Christopher Prince

> *Accumulate, then distribute.*
> *Of the mirror of the universe, be the part that is densest,*
> *most useful and least apparent.*
>
> — RENÉ CHAR, "LEAVES OF HYPNOS"

IN THE CONTEXT of security intelligence, three premises can usefully kick-start discussion of how the law operates. First, the law itself, as an instrument of policy, has generally grown more complex (and contested) in the past decade. At the same time, citizens, companies, and civil society groups stand ready to contest new laws before they even come into force. Second, surveillance provisions, as a substratum of law, can be labyrinthine. And, finally, when those authorities are exercised in a national security context, they tend towards the most opaque statutory powers of all.[1]

To be clear, long before preoccupation with counterterrorism, national security exceptions cast a long shadow over the law; in this domain, many aspects of law and its mechanics "went dark" at the very outset of the Cold War.[2] Governments today are still remedying those past excesses.[3] So, while official secrecy is nothing new, more recent criticism has begun to consider how law that is both covert and complex can not only impact individuals but also erode confidence in systemic notions of justice and rule of law as a whole.[4] Facts withheld are one thing, but fundamentals abandoned are a problem of another magnitude altogether.[5]

There are two separate but mutually reinforcing issues here. The first issue is secrecy. Laura Donahue, in her *Future of Foreign Intelligence* (2016), describes a whole legal corpus hidden from view, "a separate body of secret law" that has developed in the national security courts of the United States since the 1970s that few outside the classified legal system are able to grasp.[6] The second issue is complexity. David Anderson, in his 2015 review of British surveillance law, made a related observation when he described the legal provisions as so complex and entangled that probably only a dozen or so persons outside government truly grasped how they all fit together.[7] And finally, here in Canada, we have had two high-profile decisions from our national security court making pointed observations as to the lack of clarity and candour in the warrants they have authorized or the operations they have been called upon to review.[8]

In Canada, transparency and oversight are perennial issues. Risks labelled by security agencies as the *judicialization* of intelligence consumed an entire volume of the federal Commission of Inquiry into the role of the Canadian Security Intelligence Service (CSIS), the RCMP, and the Communications Security Establishment (CSE) in the 1984 bombing of Air India Flight 182.[9] This study made much (over 300 pages) of the inherent tension between openness and due process commitments (under the principle of open courts) and the clandestine requirements of intelligence sharing and source protection (that accompany highly classified national security operations).[10] More broadly, there are also rule-of-law questions concerning *justiciability* in the national security context, where it becomes unclear where the jurisdiction of a given court extends and where executive authority maintains.

This chapter does not aim to revisit these issues; the three studies just cited provide an extensive comparative view of open courts versus covert methods. Neither does it argue for any particular legal solution, because published statute does not definitively delimit surveillance practice as a whole.[11] Instead, it provides a sketch of the particular situation in Canada by mapping the array of federal law that intersects and combines when drawn into focus by a specific, complex investigation. Flowing from that, one can then ask how core legal principles (such as openness, intelligibility, or predictability) or privacy protections (such as accountability and accuracy) withstand the overarching framework of powers described. Finally, the rest of the contributions in this book are related to these core protections and principles.

Canadian Surveillance Law in Brief

Numerous, complex federal laws come into play in this domain. The *Security of Information Act* (*SOIA*), *CSIS Act, Customs Act,* and *Canada Evidence Act* can come into play early in investigations. As information gathering ramps up, the *Criminal Code, National Defence Act, RCMP Act, Personal Information Protection and Electronic Documents Act* (*PIPEDA*), and *Privacy Act* tend to be cited, either as sources of authority, as germane to issues flagged in legal opinions, or as provisions dictating relevant disclosures between organizations to produce evidence or advance investigations. Finally, where electronic data was conveyed over networks as part of the offence, certain foundational clauses of the *Radiocommunication Act* and *Telecommunications Act* could also be considered as part of the legal landscape.[12]

To be clear, these are just the laws implicated in authorizing specific electronic surveillance or forensic evidence gathering. The black-letter law alone provides an incomplete picture and the parameters that govern surveillance and intelligence gathering are nested in numerous other forms of regulation that operate alongside each statute: the *Solicitor General Enforcement Standards for Lawful Interception*,[13] CSE Ministerial Authorizations,[14] Canadian Radio-television and Telecommunications Commission (CRTC) Licensing Requirements, CSIS Operational Directives,[15] classified opinions and recommendations from the National Security Branch at the Department of Justice,[16] redacted jurisprudence from the Federal Court,[17] and reviews determined to be Secret or Top Secret previously conducted by the Security Intelligence Review Committee (SIRC) and the Office of the Communications Security Establishment Commissioner (OCSEC) and now conducted by the National Security Intelligence Review Agency (NSIRA). All such documentation can impact operations significantly, even though they flow beneath the visible surface of the law(s). For example:

- *Security of Information Act* – provisions on document-handling infractions [section 4(4)(b)] and offences for unauthorized entry of classified areas (section 6)
- *Criminal Code* – the investigative powers utilized in national security investigations, including production orders (section 487.014), tracking devices (section 492.1), wiretaps (section 186),[18] and/or search warrants (section 487)[19]
- *CSIS Act* – sections 21 and 21.1, providing authorities to investigate threats to Canadian systems[20] and/or alleged involvement of foreign powers
- *Customs Act* – section 99.2, providing for broad powers of inspection and/or seizure for any persons leaving or entering Canada
- *Canada Evidence Act* – section 38, providing for secrecy provisions and sealing of court records used to cover sensitive evidence revealed, as well as to conceal particular surveillance techniques
- *National Defence Act* – section 273.3, allowing CSE to provide specialized lawful access (SLA) assistance to other federal agencies [paragraph 273.64(1)(c)][21]
- *PIPEDA* – subparagraphs 7(3)(c.1)(i) or 7(3)(d)(ii), wherein companies such as airlines or telecommunications service providers (TSP) holding information relevant to an investigation bearing on Canada's national defence or security are given specific discretion to disclose information to authorities
- *Privacy Act* – paragraph 8(2)(c) or (e), whereby other government departments may also disclose information to investigators, either under a court order or in the enforcement of any law of Parliament[22]
- *Telecommunications Act* [section 15(1)] and *Radiocommunication Act* [section 5(1)(d)], which set out provisions[23] allowing agencies to specify through regulation or standards the maintenance of particular surveillance capabilities on networks.[24]

Any or all of the above-noted provisions may figure in the court orders, ministerial authorizations, supporting opinions, or warrant procedures tied to either initiating specific surveillance or laying the foundation for approving such activities. Arguably, they form the core legal parameters that responsible ministers, members of the judiciary, or both expect to review before they sign off on the particulars of intrusive surveillance or authorize broad collection of digital evidence.[25] Specific targets and suspected crimes may change from case to case, but the underlying legal ground rules should be fairly familiar to officials, even if they are not widely known outside security intelligence organizations.[26]

So while surveillance conducted in the context of security intelligence is almost always clandestine, it would be difficult to argue that these activities are somehow unmoored from the law.[27] Nor is it automatically malicious for government to keep secrets, if only to safeguard the lives of certain sources and citizens. In fact, in any given operation conducted in Canada, by the RCMP, CSIS, or CSE, the overlapping legal requirements accumulate quickly. Despite commentary to the contrary – that surveillance and security operations somehow unfold in a legal vacuum – the opposite argument can be made. The legal framework around national security investigations in Canada offers practical examples of *surveillance assemblage,* given the number of statutes that mutually reinforce and legitimize each other.[28] That theoretical term – developed by Kevin Haggerty and Richard Ericson – refers to the elaborate arrangement of technical, legal, personnel, and commercial systems required to operationalize ongoing, persistent surveillance.

Law as Context, Complexity, or Complacency

To outside observers, these interlaced authorities appear both opaque and daunting.[29] As we are all aware, however, urban life at this particular moment of modernity is very highly regulated. Ultimately, the qualitative difference in law around surveillance arises from the highly sensitive nature of state surveillance (for individuals) as well as the potential dangers posed to democracy (for society collectively). Certainly police often remark that even just a generation ago (before disclosure requirements and Charter issues) it was far simpler to conduct investigations and advance cases to court. One can debate this point in several ways; anyone reading Rebecca West's *New Meaning of Treason* – from the British espionage trials of the 1950s – might conclude it has in fact *never* been simple.[30] Many of the provisions cited above are exceptions and carve-outs specifically placed into newer statutes as they were drafted within government (or debated in Parliament) in order to maintain the efficacy of pre-existing tools and practices used by intelligence agencies or police.

To be more explicit, in the Canadian context, it is easy to forget that CSE had existed and operated for forty years *before* the first Charter jurisprudence began to emerge from the Supreme Court or the federal *Privacy Act* came into force.

Similarly, CSIS had been gathering information through Canadian telecommunications networks for fifteen years *before* Canada had a full-fledged commercial privacy law (albeit under a warrant scheme). As a result, the complex, interstitial nature of the laws outlined above can present some very puzzling, historical artifacts. Like layers of accrued sediment, the security apparatus of a government might well reach back decades or longer, but on such an extended timeline, new jurisprudence, new rights, new social practice, and new technologies also emerge and overlap. While cross-referential legal texts may not be an intentional product, they can produce confusion in language and interpretation that even seasoned lawyers and long-serving jurists struggle with.[31] Examples of these controversies in the surveillance and security context are well documented in subsequent chapters.

A skeptic might ask at this point whether it has not been ever thus: the British law establishing the Royal Mail three centuries ago carried an oblique loophole for the interception of letters and packets under the order of the minister of state.[32] What of it? Here a critical reader can turn back to the contemporary discussion around the re-emergence of "secret law," a line of discussion wherein constitutional scholars and international jurists remind us that our whole edifice of justice is defined by avoiding the secretive hallmarks of Star Chambers and general warrants.[33] As we have discovered in the past few years, in the United States, the United Kingdom, and Canada it is not simply that the legal machinery is complex (to a point approaching arcane).[34] It is not solely that the investigative authorities and government counsel have exceptionally nuanced interpretations and definitions for terms and techniques that can greatly stretch their legal powers.[35] It is not strictly speaking that much of the court oversight in the national security domain is conducted in camera and *ex parte,* allowing little openness to the public or adversarial challenge.[36]

These are all dangers in their own way, but what is of truly grave concern is that there is now in many countries an entire body of jurisprudence, administrative review, and legal interpretation of which the free press, Parliament, and the public are wholly ignorant.[37] If there is a singular bedrock principle nested in the term "rule of law," it is that courts be open so that their decisions are available for scrutiny and the law itself be accessible and predictable (granted, those are three principles, but they are related).[38] It is very difficult to see how any of these conditions hold at present.[39] So if we accept the premise that surveillance law is highly fragmented, where does this lead? How do those conditions impact conditions of fundamental justice? Besides the interpretative confusion and bafflement of the general public, what is the actual harm?

From Rights to Bare Harms

Canada has been through the experience of constraining wayward intelligence work – through an assessment of impacts upon rights and principles of justice – a good many times before. These questions have been the source of near-perennial inquiry – from the aftermath of Igor Gouzenko's defection[40] to the Munsinger spy scandal; from the RCMP's CATHEDRAL and CHECKMATE programs[41] to the Air India tragedy and the Arar Affair. Each generation has seen its own challenge and response to the question of how much discretion we as a citizenry are prepared to allow our security agencies in their use of intrusion and deception. The debate over Bill C-51 (2015) and the remedies offered by Bill C-59 (2017) are but the most recent echoes of that same indispensable question: How far to go?[42]

The complexity and opacity described above enormously affects how sensibly that question can even be asked or answered by the public, by parliamentarians, by civil society writ large.[43] The density of the material creates obvious procedural hurdles for participating in the debate.[44] Worse, over time, the inaccessibility created by those conditions produces a corrosive effect upon individuals and their rights.[45] Specifically, this occurs whenever we compromise the justiciability of government decision making, the clear accountability for errors and missteps, and the plain-language predictability of the law itself.[46] As these are significant ripple effects of the complexity inherent in surveillance law especially, it is better to examine them one at a time.

The principle of **justiciability** (i.e., court appeal or judicial review) mentioned at the outset of this chapter is a core element of due process within a system of justice tethered to rule of law.[47] Without this, systemic mistakes, political meddling, or simply arbitrary use of power go unchecked; that is point one.[48] The principle of **accountability** (i.e., state power overstepping its bounds will be answered for) within a rule-of-law framework requires some degree of ongoing openness or transparency for that process of questioning to even begin.[49] Without a channel for feedback and challenge, the security process leads effectively to a parallel system of justice that operates under different controls, categories, and conclusions; that is point two. Finally, such incoherence leads to a final compromise, by thwarting the principle of **predictability**.[50] When a classified system of complaint, review, and interpretation operates beneath the veneer of public law, practices and operations can be set in motion that would very likely fall by the wayside under more rigorous, open scrutiny.

The Foreign Intelligence Surveillance Court (FISC) in the United States produced just such an effect in its year-over-year endorsement of creative and expansive interpretations by the executive drawn from the *USA PATRIOT Act* provisions in the decade after 9/11.[51] The Independent Reviewer of Terrorism Legislation in the United Kingdom uncovered the same "creativity" in reading the statutes in his system. And, arguably, the irritation made clear in recent decisions by Justice Mosley[52] and Noël[53] (to say nothing of the basic-law-school tone of the *Spencer* decision by the Supreme Court of Canada)[54] also represented considerable reversals of securitized legal reasoning here in Canada. Either way, it is clear that for arbitration of security matters to be effective in an ongoing fashion, they must be wholly independent of government influence and the courts need to have all the facts beforehand (not just the arguments of the security authorities themselves).[55]

Those are the formalist "rule-of-law" objections to overclassification and muddying of complexity in security surveillance law. They are significant criticisms, if only because they affect not only the quality and resilience of our justice systems but also their global repute and influence. If that sounds abstract and idealist, there are other recent trends that indicate that the problems spelled out above will also tend to manifest not just in human rights cases and constitutional challenges – eventually these will overflow into the economic arena as well.

To cite one prominent example focused on Canada (well described by Gabe Maldoff and Omer Tene), recent developments in the European Union show a clear linkage between trade and commerce issues, on the one hand, and respect for basic human rights protections and clear channels for judicial review, on the other.[56] The courts and other legal authorities of the EU have been ruling along these lines for several years now, with the collapse of the US Safe Harbor privacy framework being just one recent instance.[57] The rejection in 2017 of the *EU-Canada Passenger Name Record (PNR) Agreement* is another.[58] To put it bluntly, where security and intelligence powers are at play, complexity quickly becomes a bug, not a feature.

At least within the EU model, when other countries are being examined for their commitments to core rights such as privacy and legal redress, one of the criteria courts are flagging as non-negotiable is accessibility. Another is independence. A third is transparency.[59] On those pillars alone, the measures in the United States and the United Kingdom to contain surveillance powers have been found wanting, which has in turn created considerable uncertainty for many companies. It is no coincidence that Silicon Valley firms lobbied very hard for Congress to speed passage of the *Judicial Redress Act* after EU authorities threatened to halt transfers of personal data on their citizens.[60] While it is difficult to accurately tally the costs for business and investment, certain sectors such as banking, transportation, and data services report contracting losses and higher operational costs in the billions of dollars.[61]

The Case for Openness

Accretion of secrecy and porosity of interpretation leads to a basic question: How well does law actually control surveillance, or conversely, does it simply facilitate it? Take a specific example like data analytics or machine learning: Where are the statutory limitations? Until very recently, at least in Canada, law was silent there. Mute is, after all, the default for security organizations when sources and methods are at play. For the past half-century, describing their capabilities, technologies, or techniques in published writing or public comment was strictly forbidden, a crime to describe unless authorized, carrying prison terms of ten years or more.

Yet most media-aware citizens are generally aware that security agencies, who are in the business of surveillance, have access to powerful tools, advanced technologies, massive computing power, and shared global information networks.[62] These have been treated in leaked documents, media coverage, and academic work around surveillance for the past decade.[63] Until quite recently, however, these capabilities were not specified through legislation.[64]

Recently, though, a federal government push towards big data has finally resulted in public law that actually bears scrutiny. We now have in Canada specific clauses in law passed by Parliament regarding the use of tracking devices, communications tracing, and transmission data recorders,[65] in addition to specific warrants to compel production of location data, transaction records, and communications metadata, all in the *Criminal Code*. We now even provide stand-alone authorizations in the law for frequency jammers, under the *Radiocommunication Act*.[66] All have come into force in just the past few years. More recently still, now before Parliament, are a bevy of new legal authorities governing how CSIS will obtain and analyze datasets as well as how the CSE will conduct a wide range of collection activities and cyber operations.[67]

It has taken over a decade to arrive at this point – where federal authorities see the general benefit of being ostensibly open about their surveillance activities versus the cost of too much information being set before the public – but it is heartening at last to be able to survey the legal landscape with more precision and less paranoia.[68] Canada has been through a protracted, trying debate these past fifteen years; academics, civil society, security officials, and the human rights community all grew deeply divided. Lawful access, metadata collection, Snowden, *Spencer*, the *Security of Canada Information Sharing Act* (*SCISA*) – each was a bruising argument on its own. What they in succession have produced, however, if nothing else, is a clarification of both the terms of art as well as the high stakes involved for all.[69]

And in this midst of these controversies, our courts have rightly maintained an independent skepticism towards surveillance solutionism; they have instead asked government to reconsider first principles. The Supreme Court of Canada treated these questions in recent cases such as *Tse, Wakeling, Spencer,* and *TELUS.*[70] Our Federal Court underscored related points through decisions of Justice Mosley and Noël.[71] The US Courts of Appeals did likewise in their review of mobile device tracing and *Jones.*[72] The European Court of Justice did so in annulling the *Safe Harbor Agreement.* Proper democratic practices and constitutional safeguards against intrusive state powers have been insisted upon, and that is, ultimately, the purpose of public law, underscored by the very due process discussions that courts around the world have been urging us to have.

Acknowledgments

The views presented are solely those of the author. Thanks to both Christopher Parsons and Lisa Austin for kind suggestions.

Notes

1 Henry A. Crumpton, *The Art of Intelligence Lessons from a Life in the CIA's Clandestine Service* (New York: Penguin, 2012), 7; Heidi Boghosian, *Spying on Democracy: Government Surveillance, Corporate Power and Public Resistance* (San Francisco: City Lights Books, 2013), 22.

2 Frederick A.O. Schwarz, *Democracy in the Dark: The Seduction of Government Secrecy* (New York: New Press, 2015), 36–37.

3 The most recent official apology and work towards compensation concerned the targeting and harassment of public servants and military staff who were gay, a practice that continued into the early 1990s; see John Paul Tasker, "Ottawa to Apologize Formally to LGBT Community for Past Wrongs," *CBC News,* 17 May 2017, http://www.cbc.ca/news/politics/ottawa-apologize-lgbt-community-past-wrongs-1.4120371.

4 For recent discussion of individual effects, see Fen Osler Hampson and Eric Jardine, *Look Who's Watching: Surveillance, Treachery and Trust Online* (Waterloo, ON: CIGI, 2016).

5 G.T. Marx, *Windows of the Soul: Privacy and Surveillance in the Age of High Technology* (Chicago: University of Chicago Press, 2016), 321.

6 Laura Donahue, *The Future of Foreign Intelligence: Privacy and Surveillance in the Digital Age* (New York: Oxford University Press, 2016), 145.

7 David Anderson, *A Question of Trust: Report of the Investigatory Powers Review* (London: The Stationery Office, 2015), https://terrorismlegislationreviewer.independent.gov.uk/wp-content/uploads/2015/06/IPR-Report-Web-Accessible1.pdf, 8, 148, 218.

8 2014 FCA 249, Federal Court of Appeal, https://www.canlii.org/en/ca/fca/doc/2014/2014fca249/2014fca249.pdf.

9 Commission of Inquiry into the Investigation of the Bombing of Air India Flight 182, *Air India Flight 182: A Canadian Tragedy,* vol 3, *The Relationship between Intelligence and Evidence and the Challenges of Terrorism Prosecutions* (Ottawa: Public Works and Government Services Canada, 2010), http://publications.gc.ca/collections/

collection_2010/bcp-pco/CP32-89-2-2010-3-eng.pdf; Kent Roach, "The Unique Challenges of Terrorism Prosecutions: Towards a Workable Relation between Intelligence and Evidence," in *Air India Flight 182: A Canadian Tragedy,* vol 4, *The Unique Challenges of Terrorism Prosecutions* (Ottawa: Public Works and Government Services Canada, 2010), http://publications.gc.ca/collections/collection_2010/bcp-pco/CP32-89-5-2010-4-eng.pdf.

10   *Canada (Citizenship and Immigration) v Harkat,* 2014 SCC 37, para 85, https://scc-csc. lexum.com/scc-csc/scc-csc/en/item/13643/index.do.

11   In support of that point (to cite just one example), there are by one estimate somewhere approaching a *thousand* informal arrangements, agreements, letters, memoranda of understanding, and formal treaties between the Five Eyes states alone governing exchange of information. See J.T. Richelson and D. Ball, *The Ties That Bind: Intelligence Cooperation between the UKUSA Countries, the United Kingdom, the United States of America, Canada, Australia, and New Zealand* (Boston: Unwin, 1985), 141–43, cited in Ashley Decks, "Intelligence Services, Peer Constraints and the Law," in *Global Intelligence Oversight,* edited by Z.K. Goldman and S.J. Rascoff (New York: Oxford University Press, 2016), 6.

12   *Security of Information Act,* RSC 1985, c O-5; *Canadian Security Intelligence Service Act,* RSC 1985, c C-23; *Customs Act,* RSC 1985, c 1 (2nd Supp.); *Canada Evidence Act,* RSC 1985, c C-5; *Criminal Code,* RSC 1985, c C-46; *National Defence Act,* RSC 1985, c N-5; *Royal Canadian Mounted Police Act,* RSC 1985, c R-10; *Personal Information Protection and Electronic Documents Act,* SC 2000, c 5; *Privacy Act,* RSC 1985, c P-21; *Radiocommunication Act,* RSC 1985, c R-2; *Telecommunications Act,* SC 1993, c 38.

13   Available at https://cippic.ca/uploads/ATI-SGES_Annotated-2008.pdf.

14   K. Walby and S. Anaïs, "Communications Security Establishment Canada (CSEC) Structures of Secrecy, and Ministerial Authorization after September 11," *Canadian Journal of Law and Society* 27, 3 (2012): 365–80, doi:10.1017/S0829320100010553; Wesley Wark, "CSE and Lawful Access after Snowden" (working paper, Centre for International Policy Studies, University of Ottawa, 2016), http://www.cips-cepi.ca/wp-content/uploads/2011/09/WWP-FINALfinal.pdf.

15   Public Safety Canada, "Ministerial Directions," https://www.publicsafety.gc.ca/cnt/trnsprnc/ns-trnsprnc/index-en.aspx.

16   Public Safety Canada, "Memorandum for the Minister: Next Steps on a Federal Court Decision on CSIS Warrant Powers," 13 December 2013, https://www.scribd.com/document/211668176/DIFTS-in-Jeopardy.

17   2016 FC 1105, https://decisions.fct-cf.gc.ca/fc-cf/decisions/en/item/212832/index.do.

18   "Section 186," in *Martin's Annual Criminal Code 2018,* edited by Edward L. Greenspan, QC, The Honourable Justice Marc Rosenberg, and Marie Henein, LLB (Toronto: Thomson Reuters Canada, 2017), 384–94.

19   "Section 487," in ibid., 928–39.

20   Robert W. Hubbard, Peter M. Brauti, and Scott K. Fenton, "Electronic Surveillance under the CSIS Act," in *Wiretapping and Other Electronic Surveillance: Law and Procedure* (Toronto: Canada Law Book, 2009), 12–13.

21   Stanley Cohen, "Communications Security Establishment," in *Privacy, Crime and Terror* (Markham, ON: LexisNexis, 2005), 226–28.

22   Craig Forcese, "Privacy Act," in *National Security Law* (Toronto: Irwin Law, 2008), 390–93.

23 Robert Howell, "Regulatory Structures and Features," in *Canadian Telecommunications Law* (Toronto: Irwin Law, 2011), 79–80.

24 In the case of use of radio-spectrum, in connection with standards developed with Public Safety Canada, these can entail identification, data capture, location, and electronic surveillance features on their networks, as a condition of licence. See Law Library of Congress, "Government Access to Encrypted Communications: Canada," https://www.loc.gov/law/help/encrypted-communications/canada.php; also Christopher Parsons, "Canada's Quiet History of Weakening Communications Encryption," Technology, Thoughts and Trinkets, 11 August 2015, https://christopher-parsons.com/canada-quiet-history-of-weakening-communications-encryption/.

25 Stanley Cohen, "The Administration of Justice, the Charter and Canada's National Security," in *In the Balance: The Administration of Justice and National Security in Democracies* (Toronto: Irwin Law, 2007), 99.

26 David K. Shipler, *The Rights of the People : How Our Search for Safety Invades Our Liberties* (New York: Knopf, 2011), 28.

27 Gary T. Marx, *Windows in the Soul: Surveillance and Society in the Age of High Technology* (Chicago: University of Chicago Press, 2016), 17. Note that despite all the criticisms and gaps noted above, it should be restated that at a certain level of granularity, surveillance in the intelligence and security context will of necessity remain secret. This must be so often – in point of fact, even largely – to protect the targets of surveillance as opposed to the technical tradecraft involved; the secrecy in that sense is not malicious but rather one that protects the reputation and livelihood of those under scrutiny.

28 K.D. Haggerty and R.V. Ericson, "The Surveillant Assemblage," *British Journal of Sociology* 51 (2000): 605–22. See also R.V. Ericson, *Crime in an Insecure World* (Cambridge: Polity, 2007).

29 Boghosian, *Spying on Democracy,* 118–19.

30 "The law should be at once the recognition of an eternal truth and the solution by a community of one of its temporal problems; for both conceived that the divine will was mirrored in nature, which man could study by the use of his reason. This is the faith which has kept jurisprudence an honest and potent exercise through the ages": Rebecca West, *New Meaning of Treason* (New York: Viking, 1964), 40.

31 Peter Gill, *Policing Politics: Security Intelligence and the Liberal Democratic State* (London: Cass, 1994), 64, 78.

32 Jon Moran and Clive Walker, "Intelligence Powers and Accountability in the UK," in *Global Intelligence Oversight,* edited by Z.K. Goldman and S.J. Rascoff (New York: Oxford University, 2016), 293.

33 Daniel Solove, *Nothing to Hide* (New Haven, CT: Yale University Press, 2011), 178–79; also Commission of Inquiry into Certain Activities of the Royal Canadian Mounted Police, *Second Report,* vol 1, *Freedom and Security under the Law* (Ottawa: Minister of Supply and Services Canada, 1981), 841, 881, http://publications.gc.ca/collections/collection_2014/bcp-pco/CP32-37-1981-2-1-1-eng.pdf.

34 Dorle Helmuth, *Counterterrorism and the State* (Philadelphia: University of Pennsylvania Press, 2016), 58–59.

35 Schwarz, *Democracy in the Dark,* 124–25.

36 Steven Aftergood, "Privacy and the Imperative of Open Government," in *Privacy in the Modern Age: Search for Solutions* (New York: New Press, 2015), 22–23.

37 David Wise and Thomas Ross, *Invisible Government* (New York: Random House, 1964), 6.

38 William Arkin, *American Coup: Martial Life and the Invisible Sabotage of the Constitution* (Boston: Little, Brown, 2013), 33.

39   Tamir Israel, "Foreign Intelligence in an Inter-Connected World," in *Law, Privacy, and Surveillance in Canada in the Post-Snowden Era*, edited by Michael Geist (Ottawa: University of Ottawa Press, 2015), 73, https://ruor.uottawa.ca/handle/10393/32424.

40   Stuart Farson and Mark Pythian, *Commissions of Inquiry and National Security* (Denver: Praeger, 2011), 35.

41   Greg Marquis, *The Vigilant Eye: Policing in Canada from 1867 to 9/11* (Black Point, NS: Fernwood, 2016), 96; see also Richelson and Ball, *The Ties That Bind*, 290–94; Morris Manning, *The Protection of Privacy Act: Analysis and Commentary* (Toronto: Butterworths, 1974), 78.

42   H.H. Ransom, "Can the Intelligence Establishment Be Controlled in a Democracy?" in *Surveillance and Espionage in a Free Society*, edited by Richard H. Blum (New York: Praeger, 1972), 215.

43   William W. Keller, *Democracy Betrayed: The Rise of the Security Surveillance State* (Berkeley, CA: Counterpoint, 2017), 19, 192.

44   David Tucker, *The End of Intelligence: Espionage and State Power in the Information Age* (Stanford, CA: Stanford University Press, 2014), 33.

45   Brian Tamanaha, *Laws as a Means to an End* (Cambridge: Cambridge University Press, 2006), 2; also Joseph Stiglitz, "Liberty, the Right to Know and Public Discourse" (1999), in *Government Secrecy: Classic and Contemporary Readings*, edited by Jan Goldman and Susan L. Maret (Westport, CT: Libraries Unlimited, 2009), 697–98.

46   F.A. Hayek, *Constitution of Liberty* (Chicago: University of Chicago Press, 2011), 239, 319–23.

47   Ian Kerr, "Prediction, Pre-emption and Presumption," in *Privacy, Due Process and the Computational Turn*, edited by Katja de Vries (New York: Routledge, 2013), 107–8; see also Peter W. Hogg and Allison A. Thorton, "The Charter Dialogue between the Courts and the Legislatures," in *Judicial Power and Canadian Democracy*, edited by Paul Howe and Peter H. Russell (Montreal and Kingston: McGill-Queen's University Press, 2001), 106.

48   Lisa Austin, "Lawful Illegality," in Geist, *Law, Privacy, and Surveillance in Canada*, 108.

49   Andre Nollkaemper, *National Courts and the International Rule of Law* (Oxford: Oxford University Press, 2011), 3–5.

50   Raymond Plant, *The Neo-liberal State* (Oxford: Oxford University Press, 2012), 16.

51   Gabriel Schoenfeld, *Necessary Secrets: National Security, the Media and the Rule of Law* (New York: Norton, 2010), 40; see also Donahue, *The Future of Foreign Intelligence*, 32, and Elaine Scarry, *Rule of Law, Misrule of Men* (Cambridge, MA: MIT Press, 2010), xvii.

52   2013 FC 1275, CanLII, https://www.canlii.org/en/ca/fct/doc/2013/2013fc1275/2013fc1275.pdf.

53   2016 FC 1105, https://decisions.fct-cf.gc.ca/fc-cf/decisions/en/item/212832/index.do.

54   *R v Spencer*, 2014 SCC 43, https://scc-csc.lexum.com/scc-csc/scc-csc/en/item/14233/index.do.

55   Law Reform Commission of Canada, *Electronic Surveillance* (Ottawa: Information Canada, 1986), 12, 17.

56   Gabe Maldoff and Omer Tene, "'Essential Equivalence' and European Adequacy after Schrems: The Canadian Example," *Wisconsin International Law Journal* 34 (2016): 211–83, SSRN, https://ssrn.com/abstract=2896825.

57   Michael Warner, *The Rise and Fall of Intelligence: An International Security History* (Washington, DC: Georgetown University Press, 2014), 263.

58   Gabriela Baczynska, "Deal to Share Passenger Info between EU and Canada Struck Down on Privacy Concerns," 26 July 2017, http://www.cbc.ca/news/business/airline-travel-deal-1.4222074.

59   Zachary K. Goldman and Samuel J. Rascoff, "The New Intelligence Oversight," in *Global Intelligence Oversight: Governing Security in the Twenty-first Century*, edited by Zachary K. Goldman and Samuel J. Rascoff (New York: Oxford University Press, 2016), xxix.

60 *Judicial Redress Act of 2015,* 5 USC.
61 Daniel Castro and Alan McQuinn, "Beyond the USA Freedom Act: How US Surveil-lance Still Subverts US Competitiveness," June 2015, Information Technology and Innovation Foundation, http://www2.itif.org/2015-beyond-usa-freedom-act.pdf?_ga=1. 114044933.369159037.1433787396; see also Claire Groden, "NSA Spying Is Going to Cost the Tech Sector Much More Than We Thought," *Fortune,* June 2015, http://fortune.com/2015/06/09/surveillance-tech-sector/.
62 David Omand, *Learning from the Secret Past: Cases in British Intelligence History* (Washington, DC: Georgetown University Press, 2011), 7.
63 Internet Archive, "Global Surveillance Disclosures," https://archive.org/details/nsia-snowden-documents; Electronic Frontier Foundation, "NSA Primary Sources," https://www.eff.org/nsa-spying/nsadocs; Snowden Surveillance Archive, https://snowdenarchive.cjfe.org; Technology, Thoughts and Trinkets, "Canadian SIGINT Summaries," Technology, Thoughts and Trinkets, https://christopher-parsons.com/writings/cse-summaries/; *Guardian,* "The NSA Files," https://www.theguardian.com/us-news/the-nsa-files; ACLU, "NSA Documents," https://www.aclu.org/nsa-documents-search. See also the related WikiLeaks, "The Spy Files," https://wikileaks.org/the-spyfiles.html, and National Security Agency Central Security Service, "Declassification and Transparency Index," https://www.nsa.gov/news-features/declassified-documents/.
64 Ian Leigh and Laurence Lustgarten, *In from the Cold: National Security and Parliamentary Democracy* (Oxford: Clarendon, 1994), 372–73.
65 Robert W. Hubbard, Peter M. Brauti, and Scott K. Fenton, "IMSI Catchers and MDI Devices," in *Wiretapping and Other Electronic Surveillance,* 96–100.
66 *Radiocommunication Act (Subsection 4(4) and Paragraph 9(1)(b)) Exemption Order, No. 2015-1,* SOR/2015-36, http://laws-lois.justice.gc.ca/eng/regulations/SOR-2015-36/page-1.html.
67 Canada, Bill C-59, *An Act respecting national security matters,* 1st Sess, 42nd Parl, 2017, http://www.parl.ca/Content/Bills/421/Government/C-59/C-59_1/C-59_1.PDF; see also "Spy Bill Allows Government Security Agency to Collect 'Publicly Available' Info on Canadians," *The Star,* 21 June 2017, https://www.thestar.com/news/canada/2017/06/21/spy-bill-allows-government-security-agency-to-collect-publicly-available-info-on-canadians.html.
68 Rahal Sagar, *Secrets and Leaks: The Dilemma of State Security* (Princeton, NJ: Princeton University Press, 2013), 184; see also Schwarz, *Democracy in the Dark,* 224. The next logical step would be to provide annual reporting and statistics on the use of all these new powers – as is already done for earlier forms of electronic surveillance such as wiretapping, hidden microphones, and covert video surveillance. This may not cure the complexity problem noted above, but it could bring a good deal more coherence to the understanding of the law and increase efficacy in the review of operations.
69 One can pick from the official nomenclature – "mass surveillance, bulk collection, unspecified acquisition" – but the real question is how the law can be said to operate in an environment respecting democratic norms. What the courts in the United States, Canada, and the European Union are saying (the highest courts in the land, one might add) has been rather chastening. Government collection of big data, metadata, bulk data, personal datasets, identity data have all met with stern rebuke from our most senior judges.
70 *R v Tse,* 2012 SCC 16, https://scc-csc.lexum.com/scc-csc/scc-csc/en/item/8002/index.do; *Wakeling v United States of America,* 2014 SCC 72, https://scc-csc.lexum.com/scc-csc/scc-csc/en/item/14439/index.do; *R v Spencer,* 2014 SCC 43, https://scc-csc.lexum.com/scc-csc/scc-csc/en/item/14233/index.do; *R v TELUS Communications Co.,* 2013 SCC 16, https://scc-csc.lexum.com/scc-csc/scc-csc/en/item/12936/index.do.

71   Canadian Press, "CSIS Slammed for End-Running Law to Snoop on Canadians Abroad,"
     CBC News, December 2013, http://www.cbc.ca/news/politics/csis-slammed-for-end
     -running-law-to-snoop-on-canadians-abroad-1.2472843.
72   "United States v. Jones," *SCOTUSblog* (blog), http://www.scotusblog.com/case-files/
     cases/united-states-v-jones/; "Police Use of 'Sting Ray' Cellphone Tracker Requires
     Search Warrant, Appeals Court Rules," *Washington Post,* 21 September 2017, https://
     www.washingtonpost.com/news/true-crime/wp/2017/09/21/police-use-of-stingray
     -cellphone-tracker-requires-search-warrant-appeals-court-rules.

3
Big Data against Terrorism

Stéphane Leman-Langlois

IN THE REALM of national security, big data analytics aim at two things. The first is *pre-emption,* or stopping an attack at the preparation stage. This might involve communications analysis or the recording of purchases of dangerous materials. It may also be possible to detect behaviour patterns that reveal the "casing" of particular targets. The second aim is *prevention,* which needs to occur further upstream, before violent action is being considered. Usual prevention tactics involve network disruption or the identification of persons "at risk."

The analytical tools used to extract "actionable" information from large datasets have yet to show results, however. Agencies tasked with maintaining order and with law enforcement have mostly tackled terrorism through traditional patrol and investigation techniques, and mostly starting with citizen reports. Such so-called low policing organizations are quickly adopting high-tech "predictive policing" approaches that make use of big data analysis, but those are most useful with common, high-frequency crimes. On the other hand, entities tasked with national security missions outside of officially defined crimes, or "high policing" organizations,[1] have enthusiastically embraced big data surveillance for the protection of the state, both in detection and interference missions. This also remains less than conclusive to date, for reasons listed below.

Meanwhile, since the data in question involve large numbers of citizens, collecting it has raised many questions about state power and individual autonomy. Despite the overwhelming costs and the fleeting benefits, however, big data approaches to terrorism flourish and are definitely here to stay. In this chapter, I review the problems and then the costs of big data for national security, concluding with the incentives that keep it alive.

Hurdles for Big Data Analytics in Terrorism Prevention

Rarity. Terrorism, even if one uses the widest possible definition, is vanishingly rare in the West. In Canada, it is rare enough to be considered statistically nonexistent. This of course means that there simply is no big data directly about terrorism, and that if trends continue, there never will be. There are three types of big data solutions to this "problem."

The first is to identify *patterns* of terrorist or "pre-terrorist" (early preparation) activity. Here, the method consists of matching observed sets of activity with known terrorist behaviour. In short, the analytical process rests on a distillation of what terrorists, in general, have done when planning past attacks. Unfortunately, this distillation is vulnerable in many ways. First, our knowledge of terrorist biographies is incomplete at best. Most were collected through statements given to police, court proceedings, and direct or indirect testimony. Each of these sources is weighted by different, but highly consequential, biases. So these biographies are reconstructions, framed by the demands of the circumstances in which they are produced. This is true of even the most factual aspects of the stories being told.

Second, much external data on terrorist activity comes from sources whose objectivity is overestimated. Official reports, stories in the media, and police reports are in fact filters that process and classify data according to common (usually wrong) knowledge about terrorism. In the case of police reports, we must also take into account the dozens of cases involving non-trivial intervention by undercover agents in the plotting.[2]

In Canada, the Korody-Nuttal case in British Columbia illustrates this problem. After months of investigation and trial, the court finally found that RCMP personnel were so closely involved in the plotting of the attack that the two defendants had been entrapped. Both were immediately freed. Intelligence reports are also commonly used in the building of terrorism or extremism models and are often taken as highly reliable. Yet they are often heavily flawed and rest on highly questionable sources. In reality, untold amounts of "intelligence" are based on show trials held in dictatorships around the world, security services manipulation, and politically expedient designations used to neutralize individuals, groups, and populations. For instance, the famous "returnees from Albania" show trial in Egypt in 1999 gave rise to hundreds of wrongful identifications in the West, including the issuance of security certificates in Canada. One Mohamed Mahjoub was held in custody for over twelve years as the head of the *Vanguards of Conquest* in Canada, an extremely dangerous Egyptian terror group, which also happens to have never actually existed, according to expert testimony in the case. Finally, even scientific, apolitical databases are coloured by politically loaded definitions of "terrorism." This is not a semantic problem: it can multiply or divide the number of cases in extreme proportions.[3] In turn, this variation is bound to affect any identification of possible "pre-terrorist" behaviours.

Originally, the next step was to use these historical sources to identify behaviours or sequences of behaviours that had preceded past terrorist acts. These, in turn, would become the red flags that automated search tools would look for in current masses of data. This is what the *Total* (later, *Terrorism*) *Information Awareness (TIA)* program at the US Defense Advanced Research Projects Agency (DARPA) had planned to achieve in the frantic months following 11 September

2001.[4] Current big data analytics are no longer looking for patterns in masses of data. The idea is to develop both the patterns and the search strategy in combination, in real time, one adjusting the other continuously. Though this solves the post facto problem, it does almost nothing to counter the "garbage in, garbage out" problem of unreliable data. At best, it can contribute in flagging particularly egregious unintentional or deliberate errors.

The second strategy is to look at statistically atypical clusters of data traces and transactions. The need for pre-established patterns disappears, as the target moves from the needle to the haystack and the goal is to filter out whatever is statistically normal. Of course, the parameters for "normal" behaviour are also far from consistent, but outliers are relatively easy to identify. Large amounts of fertilizer being ordered to a suburban bungalow, or multiple one-way airline tickets being purchased at the same time, can stand out.

One approach is to start by a clustering method, first sorting out the base rates for various behaviours in order to identify statistical outliers. Neural networks are especially adept at automatically forming and testing hypotheses about regularities, through machine learning. This takes many subjective, cultural, and simply erroneous assumptions, theories, and classifications out of the loop.

However, both terrorist and non-terrorist behaviours are extremely diverse and do not fall in clear categories, meaning that there is no way to identify the extent of the intersection between the "abnormal but acceptable" and the "terrorist" sets. Because of the rarity of terrorism, and the profusion of eccentric behaviours, the number of false positives is likely to skyrocket. The result could easily overwhelm policing organizations, who might be able to follow up only a very small minority of computerized notifications.

Finally, big data analytics may also seek to identify clandestine, or "dark" social networks. Such networks are different from those based on family, work or leisure, friendships, and the like, because they are attempting to evade detection. This means that their communication structure is significantly different, and therefore might be detected. At the moment, most link analysis approaches begin not with big data but with very small data: once a person is labelled a terrorist, his or her contacts are simply singled out within the masses of captured metadata (usually with a court-issued warrant). This is at once simpler and more reliable, but rests heavily on the trustworthiness of the initial labelling.

When successful, this approach significantly narrows down the populations that should be given additional attention by high policing, national security intelligence organizations. In that way it is far more efficient, but it is not big data analysis *per se*. Big data, or bottom-up/inductive graph analysis, has a different set of hurdles. One common strategy of network analysis is to daisy chain communications through metadata. When sender, recipient(s), time of day, duration of call, and frequency of communications are fed into the algorithm, various types of network analysis statistical techniques can be used. Combined with social psychology theory, this technique can reveal both the structure of the network and the role of individuals within it. The proper big data way to start the process is to access large amounts of bulk communications, and from the data attempt to identify the networks that have common characteristics not shared by most "normal" groups of telecom users (mostly time of day of the calls, duration, and locality; statistically, they also tend towards low link density, or fewer contacts among members). The problem with this analytical strategy is that there is no base rate of legitimate dark networks (of political dissidents, for instance). Each statistical study uses only confirmed illegitimate or criminal networks in its analysis (for instance, Jennifer Xu and Hsinchun Chen simply treat "dark" as *synonymous* with "illegitimate").[5]

Each of these strategies circumvents the rarity problem, but in so doing also generates new problems. There are two additional fundamental hurdles.

Math

Using big data analytics to prevent rare events is an overly optimistic scenario for two other, more fundamental reasons. The first one is the Bayes theorem, which simply uses basic probability calculations to underline the impracticality of such predictions. Simply put, and only considering false positives, even a near-magical 99 percent accurate algorithm would wrongly identify 1 percent, or 320,000 random Canadians, as suspects (out of 32 million adults). Again, this is not a realistic, practical scenario for policing. Of course, that still leaves false negatives, those whom the algorithm falsely labelled non-dangerous but who will in fact still commit crimes. Given this, it is difficult to detect any added value in the use of big data analytics in the so-called War on Terror. In fact, it is obviously not going to work as the proverbial "added layer" of security or as an additional tool. In practice, it would drain disproportionate resources away from the other layers into an effort that is extremely unlikely to pay off.

The other mathematical problem is the explosion of spurious correlations. It was first raised by data scientist Jeff Jonas[6] and has grown into a humour industry on the web.[7] Fortuitous or spurious correlations of variables increase rapidly with the amount of available data, become plentiful, and eventually form an entirely new type of haystack. They are not identifiable with statistical tools and can show extremely high statistical significance. Only human logic can tell that, for instance, the high correlation between the marriage rate in Kentucky and the number of drownings after falling out of a fishing boat in the last decade is probably meaningless (Tyler Vigen has an inventory of over 30,000 such examples).[8] Put another way, just as it has been said that 600 monkeys on 600 typewriters, given enough time, would eventually rewrite the works of Shakespeare, given enough data it seems that any hypothesis, however eccentric, can be proven (and, given enough data, in no time at all). Since much data mining is the identification of patterns and the algorithmic comparison of digital traces of behaviour, this problem is likely to become intractable with the ever-increasing mountains of data. This is sure to shatter hopes that big data is a direct path to reality: on the contrary, the more data, the greater the need for theory.

Civil Liberties

The acquisition and analysis of masses of private data is sure to raise more than a few eyebrows. It *may* spur resistance within the public, or at least within subgroups with sufficient political capital, who might successfully block or hamper efforts to exploit big data analytics. Such attacks may diminish the political and social capital of organizations that use or promote big data analytics as "moral entrepreneurs." Moral entrepreneurs establish themselves as "owners" of social problems, in the sense that they have the authority to define them and to elaborate, to suggest – if not to directly apply – corresponding solutions. Such organizations are facing a difficult dilemma. On the one hand, there is a risk that the occurrence of a terrorist attack could diminish the power of their claimed expertise in national security. On the other, aggressive surveillance and social control tactics might undermine their legitimacy with the public and increase their vulnerability to criticism.

Adverse Consequences of Big Data Analytics in Terrorism Prevention

Sources of data are already influenced by the intense cultural focus on selected populations of "terrorists." Most police forces, for instance, identify "Islamist" terrorism as the most important source of terrorist risk. The Canadian Security Intelligence Service (CSIS), which informs the federal government on risks to national security, has consistently rated Islamist extremists as the most important threat to Canada and Canadians, even when the actual number of related attacks and plots has remained very low for decades. It is no surprise, then, that Arab, Muslim, or Arab Muslim populations are overrepresented in any database, which in turn further skews the models towards the same populations.

Police reports produce much of the information included in databases, especially the confidential ones used by national security organizations. This creates a feedback loop where the data are collected and analyzed under a closed set of assumptions, expectations, and definitions dictated by police objectives. This problem is common to all crime statistics, but it is especially deep with terrorism cases because a significant proportion of the latter are the product of preventive investigations led by undercover police. From the start, such investigations tend to format situations with conventional categories. The resulting data, then, form a very specific type of social construction determined by policing objectives. It is difficult to see how any deep learning activated within this closed universe might avoid assimilating and reproducing the structural bias.

In the case of algorithmic profiling, we have seen that even the best-designed system will generate massive numbers of false suspects. This will certainly have the effect of swamping police and security forces, making them less, not more, efficient. The year 2014 was an unusually busy one for counterterrorism in Canada, with *two* separate "lone wolf" attacks. Michael Zehaf-Bibeau invaded the Canadian Parliament with a firearm and Martin Couture-Rouleau hit military personnel with his car. This prompted RCMP management to reassign hundreds of investigators who were working on organized crime to terrorism investigations. The case of Couture-Rouleau was particularly damaging for police, who had interviewed him many times in the weeks prior to his attack. This clearly indicates that a sudden influx of hundreds of leads would either destabilize the system or require massive new investments in policing.

The glut of false suspects would subject thousands of computer-selected persons to excessive scrutiny from police organizations. This scrutiny might extend to the international level. As shown by a recent Federal Appeal Court case (*X(Re)*, 2013 FC 1275), Canadian intelligence agencies have subcontracted the surveillance of Canadians to foreign Five Eyes partners, this without informing the court when obtaining the original interception warrants. The law has since been amended to *allow* the practice, which should make watching suspects around the globe much easier. Hundreds of Canadians will be travelling with secret "terrorism" labels affixed to their passports, the consequences of which are well illustrated by the cases of Canadians Maher Arar, Abdullah Almalki, Muayyed Nureddin, and Ahmed Abou-Elmaati. Each was the victim of torture abroad due to misidentification by Canadian police as a terror suspect.[9]

As David Lyon notes, data mining and especially clustering and network analysis amplify *social sorting*.[10] Neutral technology, once deployed in a socially stratified world, can only reinforce and exaggerate the stratification. Automated network analysis categorizes users according to their communication habits. This includes frequency of use, time of day, chain of contacts, duration of calls, attachments in emails, and so on, and produces a typology based on the estimated risk of belonging to a radical network.

Many chilling effects associated with mass surveillance will also appear. Research has shown that surveillance modifies the way we express ourselves, even if we are convinced we have "nothing to hide."[11] Elizabeth Stoycheff found that fewer of those polled were willing to discuss the power of the National Security Agency (NSA) once they were informed that the NSA might intercept their words.[12] Surveillance, even without intervention, affects our feeling of autonomy from the state apparatus. It lowers our ability, and in fact our *desire*, to speak freely. This reduced autonomy is certain to affect areas other than speech. For instance, geolocation may deter people from visiting urban areas associated with illegal or potentially embarrassing behaviours.

In principle, big data analytics are driven by algorithms: it is robotic surveillance. This form of machine watching is often presented as free from the potential for abuse. Machines are devoid of personal interest and are not prone to predatory behaviours such as blackmail. In the case of human-designed algorithms, there subsists a potential for misuse at the programming stage. But learning machines, such as neural networks, start with only basic programming and improve themselves. One hope is that this could neutralize any original bias built in at the programming stage, such as ethnic profiling, if it does not fit the data. As we have seen, however, most databases that have to do with terrorism contain structural biases. To the extent that robots "learn" from these data, they could exponentially increase the effects of the original bias.

Incentives for Adoption of Big Data Analytics in Terrorism Prevention

Given the hurdles and adverse consequences, the accelerated expansion of big data analytics in the context of national security is puzzling. The paradox is not unlike that which exists in the world of camera surveillance. Cameras are also accepted, if not defined, as the ready solution to almost any particular security problem, even when clear evidence of lack of results is available. Cameras flourish because of several important factors: their non-threatening appearance – they are sometimes called "protection cameras" in order to enhance their inoffensive aspect; their relatively low cost, especially since maintenance or operational costs are never taken into account; their "democratization," which lowers the perceived risk to privacy and autonomy through familiarity; their assumed objectivity in showing reality; the conviction that surveillance solves all misbehaviour problems – or, in fact, that undesirable behaviours are *caused* by deficient surveillance; the high-tech "disruptive," "innovative," "smart," and "connected" sales pitch; and the risk mitigation approaches promoted by the insurance industry, which often *require* the installation of cameras.

Many of the same general factors are at work with big data analytics. Though they are part of the suspicious, unfamiliar world of programmers, mathematicians, and cutting-edge computer science, they are not threatening because they are *invisible*. Second, they are usually sold as a low-cost replacement to the heavy manpower necessary to watch massive amounts of information. Third, automated systems and artificial intelligence are increasingly used in many devices in the consumer market, including toys, home appliances, and of course cellphones, which increases their familiarity and lowers the potential dread associated with non-human intelligence. Fourth, big data analytics are presented as the apex of pure objectivity, free from human desires, assumptions, personal and institutional agendas, and politics. Fifth, as physical surveillance solves problems in the real world, automated surveillance is seen as solving behavioural problems in cyberspace. There is much demand for monitoring behaviours such as bullying, terrorism, sexting, suicidal thoughts, and so on. Finally, the very word "algorithm" has come to symbolize progress, innovation, and "disruptiveness," as in "the Uber algorithm" or "the Amazon algorithm."

Practical Incentives

Beyond conventional wisdom, there are a few more tangible incentives for the adoption of massive data analytics in security policing. Most modern organizations, whether public, private, or hybrid, are already collecting large amounts of data on every facet of their day-to-day operations. With exponentially more to come in the near future, most are trying to keep afloat by improving their data centres or moving them to the cloud. And it so happens that every data centre management software vendor, as well as all cloud providers, now sell their services with "big data analytics" included in some way.

Policing organizations have not been immune to either the data glut or the sales pitch. They contribute to the latter by claiming that better analytics will lead to better security. This is taking place as most police organizations are in the course of adopting in part or in whole the language, the tactics, the analytical methodologies, the policies, and the management style associated with the "intelligence-led policing" (ILP) model. ILP rests heavily on the efficient use of the data available to police in order to maximize their impact on crime statistics. As such, it is made to measure for the world of big data.

One of the most powerful factors of acceptance of big data surveillance is its claimed security function. For the time being, however, this is more a promise than an actual result, as security successes are few and far between. The NSA claims that its massive interception and analysis capabilities were used in some fifty-four investigations since 2001. This seems like a rather meagre return on investment, considering the astounding resources engaged. On close scrutiny, the technology played what might charitably be called a peripheral role at best.[13] Of course, it could be argued that the data involved are simply not yet *big* enough: most of the NSA holdings are communications intercepts. The original concept of the *TIA* project was to gather all kinds of data, from *everywhere,* including financial institutions, utilities, transportation, hospitals, clinics and pharmacies, schools, large retail enterprises, distributors of specific services, goods (such as books, chemicals, tools, weapons), and information. With enough data, security would finally be attainable.

Meanwhile, the *"security"* provided by this colossal apparatus remains a rather vague concept. As adopted by police, intelligence agencies, politicians, and the media, the concept blurs the distinction between security *outcomes* and security-labelled *activities*. For instance, most of the debates about mass surveillance that followed the Snowden papers centred on "balancing" rights not with actual security outcomes but with (always increasing) security-labelled powers, budgets, and tactics. The effect of this blurring, other than wrapping unproven police tactics in the indisputable legitimacy blanket of "security," is to confuse the means and the goal and to transform the mere implementation of new strategies into security successes. This is politically and administratively useful because it depicts policing organizations as knowledgeable, diligent, and responsible, stable rocks in the morass of global uncertainty and insecurity.

What is more, massive data is often presented as freeing organizations from the equally murky world of the overly politicized social sciences.[14] This is especially important in this era of evidence-based policing. Under this view, the social sciences rest on a defective scientific model involving subjective theories, incomplete, cherry-picked observations, and, too often, the value judgment of the researcher. This scientific process should be replaced by the direct contact with reality and its workings that big data analytics now offer us. In other words, big data is defined not only by its size, speed, variety, and so on but by the way it bridges the gap between the data and the thing, between the map and the land. This seems like a rather obvious misunderstanding of the nature and function of theory in understanding the world, one that allows its replacement by the spurious correlations noted above.

Finally, it is often argued that big data brings us not a fearsome new era of total surveillance but one of renewed privacy. As noted above, the machine-led "privacy" protecting data from human misuse was a cornerstone of the defence of the *TIA* program. It was also an important response offered by the NSA to the Snowden revelations. When Director of National Intelligence James Clapper claimed that information was not being "collected," he merely meant that humans could never see it all. Only a small slice became visible, with court-issued permission – even though gargantuan flows of data were finding their way to NSA servers. Since the future of all forms of technical surveillance will in fact be big data analytics, machine-led privacy is bound to become the leading response to claims of loss of privacy or autonomy. Of course, one flaw is that machines tend to be programmed with human politics and agendas in the first place. Part of the promise of big data is to circumvent this shortcoming, and we should expect that it will soon be possible to argue convincingly that this has been achieved to a satisfactory extent. Then, in the near future, we will have to decide if we collectively feel that our privacy and autonomy are invaded or reduced by machines programmed for outcomes we have set ourselves.

Conclusion

It seems rather unlikely that national security will be better protected with the adoption of big data analytics. The extreme rarity of national security threats virtually ensures that unwanted consequences will outnumber prevention "successes." What it will achieve is always-on or *ambient* surveillance, where omnipresent robotic systems collect continuous, fine-grained information about our daily activities. The promise of complete security through machine analytics will become impossible to resist, especially if new signal crimes alert public opinion to the police complaint of "going dark" because of increasingly prevalent anonymization and encryption in communications.

Notes

1   Jean-Paul Brodeur and Stéphane Leman-Langlois, "Surveillance-Fiction: High and Low Policing Revisited," in *The New Politics of Surveillance and Visibility*, edited by Kevin Haggerty and Richard Ericson (Toronto: University of Toronto Press, 2006), 171–98.
2   John Mueller, *Terrorism since 9/11: The American Cases* (Columbus, OH: Mershon Center for International Security Studies, Ohio State University, 2011).
3   Stéphane Leman-Langlois and Jean-Paul Brodeur, *Terrorisme et antiterrorisme au Canada* (Montreal: Presses de l'Université de Montréal, 2009).
4   Jean-Paul Brodeur and Stéphane Leman Langlois, "Surveillance-Fiction," 171–98.
5   Jennifer Xu and Hsinchun Chen, "The Topology of Dark Networks," *Communications of the ACM* 51, 10 (2008): 58–65.
6   Jeff Jonas and Jim Harper, "Effective Counterterrorism and the Limited Role of Predictive Data Mining," *Policy Analysis* 584 (2006), https://www.cato.org/sites/cato.org/files/pubs/pdf/pa584.pdf.
7   For instance, "Spurious Correlations," tylervigen.com, http://www.tylervigen.com/spurious-correlations.
8   Ibid.
9   The Honourable Frank Iacobucci, *Internal Inquiry into the Actions of Canadian Officials in Relation to Abdullah Almalki, Ahmed Abou-Elmaati and Muayyed Nureddin* (Ottawa: Public Works and Government Services Canada, 2008).
10 David Lyon, "Surveillance, Snowden, and Big Data: Capacities, Consequences, Critique," *Big Data and Society* 1, 13 (2014), https://doi.org/10.1177%2F2053951714541861.
11 See Elizabeth Stoycheff, "Under Surveillance: Examining Facebook's Spiral of Silence Effects in the Wake of NSA Internet Monitoring," *Journalism and Mass Communication Quarterly* 1, 16 (2016), https://doi.org/10.1177%2F1077699016630255; Jonathon Penney, "Chilling Effects: Online Surveillance and Wikipedia Use," *Berkeley Technology Law Journal* 31,1 (2016): 117–83, https://papers.ssrn.com/sol3/papers.cfm?abstract_id=2769645.
12 Stoycheff, "Under Surveillance."

13 Bailey Cahall, David Sterman, Emily Schneider, and Peter Bergen, "Do NSA's Bulk Surveillance Programs Stop Terrorists?" (policy paper, *New America,* Washington, DC, 2014), https://www.newamerica.org/international-security/do-nsas-bulk-surveillance-programs-stop-terrorists/.
14 Chris Anderson, "The End of Theory: The Data Deluge Makes the Scientific Method Obsolete," *Wired,* 27 June 2008, https://www.wired.com/2008/06/pb-theory/.

4

Algorithms as Suspecting Machines
Financial Surveillance for Security Intelligence

Anthony Amicelle and David Grondin

> *The concept of mobilities encompasses both the large-scale movements of people, capital and information across the world, as well as the more local processes of daily transportation, movement through public space and the travel of material things within everyday life ... Fears of illicit mobilities and their attendant security risks increasingly determine logics of governance and liability protection within both the public and private sectors.*
> – Kevin Hannam, Mimi Sheller, and John Urry, "Mobilities, Immobilities and Moorings"

Mobilities raise security concerns, and technology is seen as crucial to ensuring the everyday securing of mobilities in the digital age. Technological innovations in digital computing and big data analytics now play a central role in managing the security/mobility nexus, the "dynamic tension between freedom of mobility and the provision of security."[1] Controlling mobility increasingly involves "new" technologies to deal with what is presented as the dilemma of how to facilitate movements of people, money, and data while enforcing the laws against illicit mobilities. Despite its importance, however, little is known about the set of problems posed by the choice and use of the new technologies that make mobility controls operational for law enforcement and counterterrorism purposes.

This chapter examines what it means to govern through algorithms in the age of big data surveillance. To that end, we look at how algorithms work as logistical media to monitor mobilities for crime control and national security purposes. We then introduce our case study of security intelligence and big "dataveillance" in relation to financial mobilities. We propose the idea of "suspecting machines" to explore the use of algorithmic devices that produce alerts regarding suspicious financial flows and conduct, which are usually focused on money laundering and terrorism. Our case study involves document analysis and over thirty interviews with a representative sample of officials from domestic banks in Canada as well as Financial Transactions and Reports Analysis Centre of Canada (FINTRAC) officials in Ottawa, Toronto, and Montreal in 2015 and 2016.

Policing Financial Flows with the Security/Mobility Nexus

We use the term "security/mobility nexus" to suggest how security and mobility have been increasingly stitched together to function as part of a governmental regime that manages and polices mobility flows through digital technologies and surveillance configurations.[2] The mobility regimes of people, money, and data, while often distinguished heuristically for analytical purposes, are in fact closely related, and we contend that analysis should acknowledge their connection and interdependence in security discourses and practices. It is no accident that security programs with dataveillance capabilities – such as the US terrorist finance tracking program[3] – are officially promoted for their ability to recognize interconnecting mobilities. According to the US Treasury Department and the European Commission:

> Terrorist finance tracking program-derived information may be used to provide leads that assist in identifying and locating persons involved with terrorist networks and providing evidence of financial activities in aid of terrorist attacks. For example, it is possible to locate a suspect by checking when and where the suspect closed and/or opened a new bank account in a city or country other than his or her last known place of residence. This is a clear indicator that the person may have moved. However, even when a suspect does not change bank accounts but rather moves and continues using the "old" account (e.g., through e-banking), it has been possible to detect the change of location by, for example, identifying payments for specific goods or services (e.g., for repairs or maintenance or other activities which are usually carried out where a person lives) ... The terrorist finance tracking program can provide key information about the movements of suspected terrorists and the nature of their expenditures.[4]

The surveillance-related connection to mobilities is explicit in this context. On the basis of digital data about financial transactions, this security program traces the movement of money to track terrorist suspects. In other words, it relies on the digital traces of financial mobilities to find and follow the physical traces of human mobilities.

Governing Finance with Algorithmic Infrastructures of Security

In this chapter, we are specifically interested in the policing of financial flows to understand how people and data are governed and controlled through algorithmic infrastructures of security. Using the "haystack metaphor" at the core of current security intelligence discourses,[5] providers of surveillance devices describe the detection of illicit financial flows as the "ultimate search for the needle in the haystack."[6] To see how that goal is achieved, we investigate the policies and practices involved in financial surveillance as well as the detection and reporting of "suspicious transactions." But who is in charge of finding the needle of dirty money in the Canadian financial haystack? As Jef Huysmans suggests in his work on contemporary policing, financial policing is partly detached from the institution of the police as it deals with the more general associative practices found in networks of risk knowledge, technologies, and agencies.[7]

In Canada, over 31,000 businesses – from the real estate sector to the banking industry – must comply with legal obligations dealing with dirty money, including reporting suspicious transactions to the relevant state authority, namely, FINTRAC. As Canada's financial intelligence unit, "FINTRAC receives reports from financial institutions and intermediaries, analyzes and assesses the reported information, and discloses suspicions of money laundering or of terrorist financing activities to police authorities and others as permitted by the Act. FINTRAC will also disclose to CSIS [Canadian Security Intelligence Service] information that is relevant to [a] threat to the security of Canada."[8] FINTRAC receives over 200,000 reports of suspicious transactions annually, mainly from banks, which have become the main source of denunciation to the state,[9] practising financial dataveillance in the name of security through "the systematic use of [financial-related] personal data systems in the investigation or monitoring of the actions or communications of one or more persons."[10]

In an attempt to meet their legal responsibilities regarding anti–money laundering and counterterrorism financing, numerous banks have implemented algorithmic infrastructures to monitor suspicious activity and help make sense of the daily avalanche of transaction-related digital data. Our aim in discussing the seemingly invisible work of these security/mobility infrastructures is to shed some light on the impact and productive power of governing with algorithms in an era characterized by big data surveillance. We seek to show how doing so changes former practices, highlighting how socio-technical devices have become part of security apparatuses, as we explore financial big dataveillance practices through the algorithmic instrumentation that makes everyday surveillance and denunciation possible and stable over time.

Making Sense of Algorithms as Logistical Media of Big Financial Dataveillance

"Logistical media – as technologies, infrastructure, and software – coordinate, capture, and control the movement of people, finance and things. Infrastructure makes worlds. Logistics governs them."[11] This quotation captures Ned Rossiter's logistical media theory of infrastructures and suggests how thinking about algorithms and security brings the issue of infrastructures to the fore.[12] To understand security/mobility, we must understand what infrastructures do in the background – what they "do" when they work. As Keller Easterling says, infrastructures actually *do* something: they make "certain things possible and other things impossible."[13] To grasp how mobilities of people, money, data, or objects are governed according to an algorithmic security rationality,[14] we must be keenly attentive to the power of infrastructures, particularly to algorithms as *digital infrastructures* acting invisibly while governing mobilities through the digital socio-technical environment.

"Infrastructure is defined by the movement or patterning of social form. It is the living mediation of what organizes life: the lifeworld of structure."[15] This relational understanding echoes Susan Leigh Star's groundbreaking framing of "infrastructure [a]s a fundamentally relational concept, becoming real infrastructure in relation to organized practices."[16] As John Durham Peters points out, infrastructures set the terms for operations: "The job of logistical media is to organize and orient, to arrange people and property, often into grids. They both coordinate and subordinate, arranging relationships among people and things."[17] Algorithms, understood as logistical media governing mobilities, act as infrastructures that organize life. Recognizing this underscores the importance of understanding how governance is achieved through algorithms. As argued by Rob Kitchin:

> Algorithms cannot be divorced from the conditions under which they are developed and deployed ... What this means is that algorithms need to be understood as relational, contingent, contextual in nature, framed within the wider context of their socio-technical assemblage. From this perspective, "algorithm" is one element in a broader apparatus which means it can never be understood as a technical, objective, impartial form of knowledge or mode of operation.[18]

Louise Amoore and Rita Raley construe the algorithm "as both technical process and synecdoche for ever more complex and opaque socio-technical assemblages."[19] To put it simply, an algorithm is a mathematical formula or a set of instructions or rules that enable its users to obtain a specific result using its computational ability to sift through large amounts of data and accomplish tasks that human agents could not perform in a timely manner.[20] More tellingly, algorithms have become highly publicized artifacts that populate our everyday life, with their logic woven "into the very fabric of all social processes, interactions and experiences that increasingly hinge on computation to unfold."[21]

Looking at the security/mobility nexus enables us to analyze surveillance and infrastructure in the digital world. As part of a secretive security infrastructure, algorithms operate in the background, not unlike the "black box society" that Frank Pasquale describes in relation to the hidden algorithms that control money and information, affecting decisions made on the mistaken assumption that the information they are based on is neutral and technical. Pasquale uses the black box to recognize both its function as a recording device for monitoring technical data in transportation (cars, planes, and trains) and its metaphorical use suggesting the obscurity and opacity of complex systems whose inner workings we cannot easily decipher or reveal.[22] Thinking about what algorithms do with dataveillance means taking into account how vast streams of digital data about people's life, conduct, and mobility are sifted and sorted.

On Suspecting Machines: Surveillance in the Canadian Financial System

Our case study of security intelligence and big financial dataveillance in Canada provides clear examples of the critical importance of algorithms in contemporary "modes of policing that combine risk communication and surveillance to technologically assemble and circulate suspicion."[23] We introduce the expression of "suspecting machines" to account for the pivotal role played by technologically driven digital surveillance devices in monitoring, detecting, and reporting suspicious activity. Financial technology providers sell financial institutions what they describe as "suspicious activity monitoring" solutions, using advertisements such as this:

> The Actimize Suspicious Activity Monitoring (SAM) solution combines cutting-edge technology with years of anti money laundering human-expertise, helping to ensure accurate alert detection, increased team productivity and lowered compliance program costs. Anti-money laundering automation brings together AI, machine learning and robotic process automation, the solution enables end-to-end coverage for the detection, scoring, alerting, workflow processing and suspicious activity reporting. As a result, anti-money laundering departments can more effectively monitor suspicious activities, be confident they're focusing on the right issues and risks, and automate processes while retaining the power to make the final decision.[24]

Before examining the algorithms in action and looking at their specific findings beyond those described in the promotional material, let us briefly paint a rough picture of our case study.

The Context for the New Financial Intelligence Systems

On one side, we have 31,000 reporting entities, which include banks as well as life insurance providers, dealers in precious stones, real estate brokers and developers, accountants, casinos, and securities dealers. These entities are responding to legal requirements regarding anti–money laundering and counter-terrorism. The banks, for example, wish to be seen as compliant with their specific security-related obligations but, as for-profit providers of financial services, not security services, they also wish to remain profitable. On the other side is FINTRAC. "As Canada's financial intelligence unit and anti-money laundering and anti-terrorist financing regulator, FINTRAC plays a critical role in helping to combat money laundering, terrorism financing and threats to the security of Canada."[25] FINTRAC relies first and foremost on non-security-oriented businesses (the reporting entities), which act as the eyes and ears of the state in the field of finance. As summed up by a FINTRAC spokesperson, "the reporting to us is absolutely critical. Without those reports, FINTRAC is out of business."[26]

Banks report both suspicious and certain transactions to FINTRAC. According to official guidelines at the time of our study, suspicious transactions are financial transactions that reporting entities have "reasonable grounds to suspect" are related to the commission or attempted commission of a money laundering offence and/or the commission or attempted commission of a terrorist activity financing offence.[27] According to FINTRAC, "'reasonable grounds to suspect' is determined by what is reasonable in your circumstances, taking into account normal business practices and systems within your industry. While the Act and Regulations do not specifically require you to implement or use an automated system for detecting suspicious transactions, you may decide that such a system would be beneficial to your business."[28] While the last sentence suggests that using an automated system is voluntary, a FINTRAC officer stated in an interview: "They have no choice. Listen, all the big banks I know, they have an IT system for that."[29] The legal framework creates a context of practice that pressures institutions such as banks to rely on suspecting machines to meet compulsory security demands. The regulator wants those regulated to comply with the law, while recognizing that a small real estate agency does not need – and cannot afford – the apparatus used by the biggest banks in the country to identify clients, keep records, monitor financial conducts, and, ultimately, report suspicious transactions. Faced with a daily avalanche of transaction-related digital data – over 150 million transactions per month at each of the top six financial institutions in Canada – institutions hoping to make sense of the totality of digital noise generated by business relationships and account activities have no choice but to implement technologically mediated "solutions" if they wish to be stamped compliant. As a result, the non-binding nature of the formal reference to automated surveillance devices becomes, in practice, a categorical obligation for banks in particular, both in Canada and internationally:

"Regulators are pressuring smaller financial institutions to adopt more automated solutions while pushing larger financial institutions to upgrade their current solutions' sophistication."[30]

This process has created tensions within the banking sector at two levels: (1) internal debates about the conflicting demands of security versus profit, especially over the costs of meeting the financial surveillance requirement; and (2) the actual socio-technical challenges posed by suspecting machines and their interaction with human resources. As with any informational infrastructure, this requires "making visible an infrastructure that, in other contexts, has been rendered invisible" *and* making it meaningful and useful for "radically different users."[31] Meeting these requirements is a challenge as much for researchers as it is for financial and security practitioners; our findings highlight the tensions and difficulties in big financial dataveillance. We show that looking at how logistics govern "practice" makes clear how algorithmic infrastructures, as logistical media, are part of governance. Only when we focus on how these socio-technical devices are called upon, enlisted, solicited, and made part of security infrastructures can we recognize the "human and institutional choices [as well as the science, rationalities, and technologies] that lie behind these cold mechanisms."[32]

Between the Hammer of Defensible Compliance and the Anvil of Financial Burden

Regardless of their degree of willingness to help combat crime and terrorism, banks are, above all, for-profit organizations. Trying to reconcile these two goals has contradictory consequences for their use of financial surveillance equipment. On the one hand, as extensively discussed in the academic literature, bank representatives are very sensitive about their reputation in relation to organized crime and terrorism issues.[33] "Protect your reputation" is still one of the main advertising slogans used by vendors to promote financial surveillance devices. As one bank's chief anti–money laundering officer reported:

I think the motivation to be compliant is, you know, you want to protect the bank's brand. And you want customers and the shareholders to feel as if their bank is a safe bank in which they can conduct transactions and they go without having to worry about. You know, is this bank going to be open tomorrow? Are there issues associated with whom they are lending money to? Do they have good business practices? And to comply allows us to give that type of confidence to our customers, internally to our employees and also to our shareholders. We look at it as a value proposition whereas before compliance was looked as a cost of doing business or an expense. But, you know, we treat compliance as our ability to contribute to the brand and to the safety and soundness of the organisation. We think it is a competitive advantage to comply.[34]

The focus on possible fines and criminal or administrative penalties associated with non-compliance complements the selling point of reputational protection. Chief anti–money laundering officers also mention the fear of losing part or all of their banking licences and the possibility of losses due to the reaction of the other financial institutions – the critical business partners of correspondent banks – if they are sanctioned for regulatory breaches. Public penalties for non-compliance have a large impact on a bank's reputation and risk score within the industry. Indeed, any bank sanctioned for non-compliance with surveillance and reporting obligations will be seen as high-risk across the industry, which has tremendous financial consequences for maintaining or building vital relationships with other banks.

The internalization of compliance requirements as an integral part of business in finance means that these requirements are seen as an inevitable regulatory burden at worst and a competitive advantage at best. The irony of this internalization is that *the main concern of financial institutions is related to non-compliance* rather than money laundering and terrorist financing. Surveillance technology, however necessary it may be for defensible compliance,[35] is seen as a costly investment that is not expected to provide a fair return to for-profit organizations whose core businesses are clearly not involved with crime control and national security issues. In this context, the distinction between saving money (i.e., avoiding sanctions and reputational damage) and making money (i.e., business as usual) is often mentioned to qualify and clarify the role of technological developments:

There is still ... hum ... a bit of push back in cost. There is always a bottom line cost in that, the requirement is you have to do X, Y and Z, now they have to adjust their system and internal technology in order to meet that requirement ... And they say, "you know, we cannot just go and do so many technological changes plus we have a business to run. So, it is not all about you [the regulator] all the time." So, it is always about money and it is always about the time to do it [technological improvement]. And they say, "we can't do it now, then we will do it in a year." Well, a lot can happen in a year. Right? So, they push back on us, and their technology department pushes back on them, because the priority is making money. For instance, they have to put a system in to collect service fees. That probably takes priority over what we want them to do, because it is going to affect their bottom line. We are costing them money. We don't make them money. We can save their reputation or risk, right! But they don't see it that way. They don't see it that way at all, every time. And it is always, and it is not just the banks. It is all of them [reporting entities]. They all push back because of the finance, the financial burden. Burden. That's what it is: a financial burden.[36]

The work of surveillance is also a cost challenge in a different way for bank tellers who are the other main – and the traditional – source of internal alerts in any financial institution. As a former compliance officer interviewed noted:

> The bottom line is always the dollar. So, at the branch level, the customer service representatives, or the loan manager, their major focus is to make money. To sell by opening up accounts, sell credit cards, sell mortgages, sell loans, sell this ... that is their job. It is to make that money. So, they have quota. They will say to their tellers in one day-time you have to do X amount of loans or X amount of mortgages, or X amount of credit cards. They push from the top. So you don't spend the time that you need to the KYC [Know Your Customer compliance obligations] because the requirement of making money comes first again. So, if as a teller I can sell a mortgage, if I can do two deals or sell a credit card in half an hour that would be great, as oppose [sic] to doing one in an hour because I have taken the time to have a conversation, do the KYC, file out everything properly. The branches don't have the time to do it. They are just under the gun of making more revenue.[37]

The emphasis on making money also explains the diversity in complexity of algorithmic infrastructure in the banking industry, with the level of technological involvement widely dispersed on a continuum of financial surveillance equipment that ranges from a minimalist high-tech setting to a maximalist one.

Uneven Distribution of Technological "Solutions" with Suspecting Machines

The Minimalist High-Tech Version

Certain financial institutions have not fully implemented suspicious activity monitoring devices. Their first technological investment has been in automated devices to help comply with reporting obligations for monetary thresholds and targeted sanctions rather than those for suspicious financial conduct.

For financial transactions that must be reported on the basis of monetary threshold, such institutions have implemented software that is designed to detect electronic fund transfers "of $10,000 or more out of or into Canada in a single transaction or in two or more transactions totalling $10,000 or more made within 24 consecutive hours by or on behalf of the same individual or entity, through any electronic, magnetic or optical device, telephone instrument or computer."[38] In 2018–19, FINTRAC received over 17 million electronic cross-border fund transfer reports.[39]

For financial transactions that must be reported on the basis of national and international sanctions of particular regimes, the financial institutions' priority has been to create consolidated digital lists of targeted entities using screening and watch-list filtering devices that can compare customers and their financial relations to the listed parties.[40] In particular, banking actors must submit "terrorist property reports" when they know or believe that financial assets are related to a designated terrorist group or a listed person suspected to be associated with entities such as the Taliban, al-Qaeda, or ISIL (Islamic State of Iraq and the Levant). A routine part of surveillance and filtering practices, with or without dedicated technology, also consists in looking at news and open-source information.[41]

Finally, with regard to suspicious financial transactions, most financial institutions without fully operational suspicious activity monitoring devices have begun implementing such procedures but they take time to complete, as noted by one chief anti–money laundering officer we interviewed:

> Initially it took three years just getting all the data feeds right, and going through the banking system, data and figuring ... and I know we are not the only one that has this issue ... but actually figuring where all the data is, and how to get it into the right format, and be able to identify the type of transaction ... So there is a lot of manipulation that goes on in the background to get the data that you need in the transaction monitoring system, to be able to effectively get meaningful alerts.[42]

The idea that technologically mediated suspicious activity monitoring is the culmination of a long implementation process is accepted by FINTRAC officials:

> Two years, you are very optimistic! We are talking about banks, they have millions of customers, whether involved individuals, corporations, trusts, and so on. And it is even worse when we talk about big financial institutions. The IT system is not only for the bank but for all the subsidiaries of the group, insurance, life insurance, investment activity and many more, in Canada and abroad. Thus, the system often begins with the bank and it is gradually extended to the other subsidiaries too. The task is enormous. It is a work in progress. Even when you are there, you are still in the process of calibration because there are new financial products, you have bought a competitor or you have forgotten a market and so on.[43]

Before or during the implementation of the algorithmic device, the socio-technical process of suspicion production requires much more manual labour to generate internal alerts on financial conducts. Consider the example of a financial institution with 10 million clients. Before implementation, surveillance of financial conduct and production of related internal alerts must be largely hand-done in two main ways.

First, bank tellers and bank advisers are in direct contact with clients. In addition to the commercial objectives at the core of their work, they are encouraged to report any "unusual transaction" to their line manager or to the bank's anti–money laundering/counterterrorism financing compliance department. Financial surveillance and internal reporting is thus largely focused on transactions that depend on face-to-face interaction in a bank branch. Furthermore, it relies on banking employees whose main tasks, priorities, and training are not related to the fight against dirty money. Internal alerts are normally based on specific behavioural indicators, although FINTRAC's official guidelines note that gut feelings matter: "As a general guide, a transaction may be connected to money laundering or terrorist activity financing when you think that it (or a group of transactions) raises questions or gives rise to discomfort, apprehension or mistrust."[44] Unusual transaction reports, as internal alerts, are assigned to dedicated analysts within the compliance department for further investigation. This investigative process "results in [one of] two opposite outcomes with the translation of the detected abnormality into a false-alert or a suspicious behaviour that must be reported" to the state authorities.[45]

Second, in addition to vigilance over direct business, one unit of the bank compliance department is dedicated to monitoring the transactions and account activities of clients "scored" as high-risk on a regular basis. According to one bank's risk-scoring practices, about 20,000 clients out of 10 million are considered high-risk in relation to money laundering and/or terrorist financing.[46] Such financial surveillance and internal reporting is thus focused on a rather small percentage of customers, i.e., the predefined high-risk minority. Looking at the process after the implementation of a suspicious activity monitoring device highlights how the new algorithmic infrastructure makes a difference in everyday financial surveillance.

The Maximalist High-Tech Version

In the maximalist high-tech version of a suspicious monitoring device, previous methods of surveillance of financial conduct and internal reporting of suspicious activity still exist. However, the implementation of a dedicated algorithmic device transforms the scope and systematization of financial surveillance. In addition to filtering based on monetary threshold and watch lists, every single financial transaction by each of the bank's clients is now technologically monitored on an everyday basis, leading to internal alerts about potentially suspicious actions. These alerts are produced automatically overnight, ready for human analysis the next morning. This blanket, technologically driven surveillance of financial conduct does not mean that risk scoring no longer matters, as behavioural and transactional indicators are weighted according to risk indicators. In other words, risk score affects the production of alerts to the extent that, depending on clients' risk scores, the same financial conduct will or will not generate an automated alert. More generally, suspicious activity monitoring relies on a combination of indicator-related scenarios and analytics, plus additional features. In this respect, algorithmic devices, acting as suspecting machines, rely on the deductive and/or inductive determination of abnormality, unusualness, and, ultimately, suspicion.

Suspicious activity monitoring occurs automatically based on one of two sets of algorithms. In the first set, the algorithms of detection are designed to uncover transactions that match a predefined set of scenarios. These scenarios – also called rules – are based on a combination of indicators from internal and external sources, beginning with those provided by FINTRAC, which are intended

to help assess whether or not transactions might give rise to reasonable grounds for suspicion. They are examples of common and industry-specific indicators that may be helpful when evaluating transactions, whether completed or attempted. They include indicators based on certain characteristics that have been linked to money laundering or terrorist activities in the past. These indicators were compiled in consultation with reporting entities, law enforcement agencies and international financial intelligence organizations.[47]

FINTRAC's hundreds of indicators are selected, combined with others, and then tested – including fine-tuning or deletion – on a more or less regular basis either by the technology providers or by individuals on the site where they will be used:

There is continuous feedback from the triage group [which receives the automatically generated alerts] to the analytics people [who deal with tuning on-site scenarios]. They say, "You know, we keep seeing this and we keep seeing this. It is nothing, it is nothing. Can we optimize the rules?" That, as a process, continually takes place from that perspective, in order to optimize the rules while, at the same time, through typologies and other things, we build new rules to bring in new alerts. It is a continuous process to maintain and keep your rules up to date.[48]

In the second set, suspicious activity monitoring is automatically driven by algorithms designed to uncover unusual and potentially suspicious transactions rather than using comparison with a predefined set of information. This second production-alert generation process is based on recognizing a customer's deviation from peer-group behaviour and/or historical and expected individual behaviour. Such an alert is a by-product of social and behavioural sorting strategies as well as comparison with historical data for account activity. Link analysis is also used to explore a bank's databases to identify associations among clients (both individuals and businesses), bank accounts, and transactions (electronic fund transfers, cash deposits, and so on). This social network approach both supplements analysis of already detected suspicious financial conduct or discovers new cases. The work of suspicious activity monitoring devices (and link analysis) can be combined with the technologically mediated analysis of unstructured data sources such as websites (media, social networks, and so on) or "free-text" narratives related to previous suspicious transaction reports.

Ultimately, it goes without saying, there is wide variation between financial institutions along the continuum from the minimalist version to the maximalist version of financial surveillance equipment. Despite the technological asymmetries, however, every bank faces the same challenge in attempting to find a way to make money while avoiding the pain of being caught between the hammer of defensible compliance and the anvil of financial burden resulting from false-positive alerts.

Managing False Positives

"[Five percent] to 10% of all alerts actually turn into cases. So, 90% to 95% are false positives. And then, from a case to a suspicious transaction report, it is less than 10% ... less than 10% of the cases actually turn into suspicious transaction reports."[49] According to this chief anti–money laundering officer (working with a system close to the maximalist version of high-tech equipment), at best 1 alert out of 100 leads to a suspicion-based denunciation from his financial institution, which still results in thousands of suspicious transaction reports being sent to FINTRAC per year. The most time-consuming task for any bank compliance unit is related to the "triage" of alerts – annually from tens of thousands to millions for the largest financial institutions – most of which are generated by automated surveillance devices. One chief anti–money laundering officer underscored the challenge facing all bank compliance units in trying to reduce the rate of "obvious" false alerts as much as possible:

It is still the big issue, there is a lot of false positives, and there is always the balance between spending money on improving this system and also the resources available on improving the system, versus going through the false positives and spending the time to go through the false positives, so that is an issue and it is always going to be an issue until I can find someone to give me more money [laughs]. Anyway, false positives will always stay but the number of false positives, to get that down to a reasonable size so that you are getting alerts on what you should be getting alerts on, and covering off the activity without just getting a lot of noise and having to go through that noise, because once the alert is generated, you have to at least look at it. And every single one takes time.[50]

Looking at suspecting machines and the management of the problem of false positives helps us understand how algorithms act as a logistical media of technological financial surveillance. To paraphrase Evelyn Ruppert, alerts do not simply pop up but are the result of multiple socio-technical arrangements between technological and human actors that configure agency and action.[51] As with other contemporary policing practices, the capacity to produce alerts emerges from the relationships – the connections – between a range of equipment and social actors, from the designers of surveillance devices to their end-users.[52] While "the internal characteristics (technical, logical, and cognitive) of devices both constrain and enable the action of their users,"[53] it is critical to recognize the variable features of suspicious activity monitoring devices in order to understand how they are appropriated within banks. Specifically, how do banking actors fine-tune their surveillance and detection practices according to the specific characteristics of their technological "solutions"? Part of the answer to this question requires looking at banking actors' relationships with vendors of surveillance devices, which range from high dependency to relative autonomy. It is also where we see power relations at work, revealing that the choices made are contingent, based on human decisions. Returning to the black box metaphor, the critical issue is to know who – as well as how and to what extent – is in favour of preserving the black box rather than opening it.

High dependency refers to cases in which algorithmic devices remain largely a black box to the banking actors themselves, with few customized elements. Actors must rely on the vendors for any changes, especially for the creation and modification of scenarios:

The problem with actually changing the algorithms is that every time you engage the vendor it costs money, and the organisation is not willing to pay for extras ... And that is how the technical model [of the vendors] is set up. It is set up so that once they become your provider, that is when they start charging you the extras because they know that you cannot go anywhere else. And to implement a new system is not cost-effective, especially every couple of years when you really need to upgrade because the technology is changing. Once you have decided on one provider, you pretty much are going to stay with them unless there is something really significant that takes place.[54]

Relative autonomy refers to cases in which the ability to conduct fine-tuning operations such as scenario authoring is done primarily through in-house expertise using dedicated human resources (the "data junkies"):

> The analytics people, this is where we develop the rules, the thresholds, where we basically identify alerts that could be cases that could be suspicious transactions. They actually are the ones who are programming our transactions monitoring rules, the algorithms. The stats and the math guys who develop the algorithms for transactions, sanctions, names matching, everything ... My analytics people are all, not all but most of them, masters of science or PhD analytics, so they grew either in the computer science or the quantitative sciences world. They are the data junkies. They love the data, they love to work with the data.[55]

The "data junkies" are hired to connect with "data-hungry beasts" (i.e., algorithmic devices)[56] and refine algorithmic monitoring in accordance with testing sessions, internal feedback, and new indicators. Although the "white box" or "open box [transparent] environment" approach is more expensive than black-box algorithms, its selling point is still about "saving money": "Can you really afford a bigger staff to handle growing alert volumes?"[57] In either case, the reduction of false positives often becomes an end in itself, thus obscuring the original financial surveillance mission for security intelligence.

Conclusion

Ultimately, the automated production of alerts turns out to be more negotiated than automated, given the competing objectives of making money and fighting crime and terrorism. The outcome of these negotiations in terms of alerts and false positives not only is based on the algorithmic design used in transaction monitoring but depends equally on the quality and verifiability of the data being processed. The changes that algorithms as logistical media lead to in the inner workings of financial surveillance are significant.

The algorithmic production of alerts differs from bank tellers' alerts in many ways, one of which deserves further attention. In both cases, knowledge about the client is part of the process of alert production, but there is a difference in the type of knowledge that can be used. With regard to clients, the form and content of knowledge may vary from one bank to another, from one type of clientele or business relationship to another, and from one type of bank employee to another (i.e., bank tellers in bank branches versus data analysts in headquarters). According to Lyn Loftland and John Dewey, human beings can develop a knowledge of people (acquaintance-knowledge) or a knowledge about people (knowledge-about).[58] Clive Norris sums up the importance of this distinction in connection with surveillance and control by noting that the "basis of knowing of, rather than about, people is face-to-face interaction. When we only know about people our knowledge is second-hand."[59] De facto, analytics and data analysts are further removed from the local branch context than the front-line staff – acting on the basis of face-to-face interaction and face-to-face knowledge is no longer an option. The resulting surveillance at a distance through data can be seen either as a critical lack of knowledge or as a key element of objectivity in controlling mobility.

The first interpretation highlights the inability of analytics "to look at somebody and understand if they are avoiding eye contact, if they are being really fidgety, or if they are hurrying you along. Those are indicators that something is not quite right."[60] The second interpretation highlights the connivance bias that may be introduced by face-to-face interactions:

> That is often the case, especially if, in some cases, the managers have more a relationship model with the clientele. So if you get into, like, wealth management businesses where the whole nature of the business is the relationship, then they may take a more personal view, you know, I know the client, the client is good, I have known him for ten years, blah-blah-blah, there should not be anything wrong with what they are doing. So you always got to balance that aspect with what you see and sometimes stark realities have to come out depending on what you find.[61]

More generally, these two interpretations illustrate the tension between "Ancients" and "Moderns" in policing financial conduct and mobility, with the process for identifying cases that trigger suspicion and denunciation oscillating between a focus on human hunches or on technological processing of numbers and big data. In practice, human hunches and big data devices are often entwined, in everything from the tuning of suspicious activity monitoring devices to the finalization of suspicious activity reporting.

The changes in the inner workings of big (financial) dataveillance created by algorithms as logistical media are significant, particularly in normalizing the use of financial surveillance as a way to protect banks' reputations and business relationships. However, the imbalance created by the resulting number of false-positive alerts, which must be analyzed by human agents, suggests that we need to go further down a more sociological path and consider the security practices of both technologies and agents. It also reveals the need to reconcile a technical problem – i.e., the work of suspecting machines – with a business rationale that seeks to minimize as much as possible the costs of using such machines (as banks, after all, want to make money). The challenge we faced in this chapter was making visible the complex process of algorithms as logistical media, in a context in which they govern data. Doing so also involved understanding how this process is part of a human/non-human assemblage, a socio-technical infrastructure in which the algorithm is embedded. Looking at how suspecting machines operate enables us to see where power relations and preferences play a role in what may appear to be neutral technical operations, through human decisions.

Notes

1 Louise Amoore, Stephen Marmura, and Mark B. Salter, "Smart Borders and Mobilities: Spaces, Zones, Enclosures," *Surveillance and Society* 5, 2 (2008): 96–101.
2 This chapter is drawn from a larger project funded by an Insight Social Sciences and Humanities Research Council (SSHRC) grant on the central role of algorithms in the governance of North American borderlands (NAB) and the related policing of mobilities in the digital age of big data. The project deals with the question of how algorithms "act" and make a difference in the security process, specifically to what extent algorithms have come to serve as critical operators and "gatekeepers" given the security/mobility nexus that has come to define how security is processed and delivered in the digital era.
3 Marieke de Goede and Mara Wesseling, "Secrecy and Security in Transatlantic Terrorism Finance Tracking," *Journal of European Integration* 39, 3 (2017): 253–69; Anthony Amicelle, "The Great (Data) Bank Robbery: The Terrorist Finance Tracking Program and the Swift Affair," *CERI Questions de recherche/Research Questions* 36 (2011): 1–27.
4 European Commission, *Joint Report from the Commission and the U.S. Treasury Department regarding the Value of TFTP Provided Data* (Brussels, 2013), 5.
5 Claudia Aradau, "The Signature of Security: Big Data, Anticipation, Surveillance," *Radical Philosophy* 191 (2015): 1–8.
6 Julie Conroy, *Global AML Vendor Evaluation: Managing Rapidly Escalating Risk* (Boston: Aite, 2015), https://www.aitegroup.com/report/global-aml-vendor-evaluation-managing-rapidly-escalating-risk.
7 Jef Huysmans, *Security Unbound: Enacting Democratic Limits* (Abingdon, UK: Routledge, 2014).
8 FINTRAC, "What Is FINTRAC?" 16 August 2019, http://www.fintrac-canafe.gc.ca/questions/FAQ/1-eng.asp.
9 FINTRAC, *FINTRAC Annual Report 2018–19* (Ottawa: FINTRAC, 2019), 37, https://www.fintrac-canafe.gc.ca/publications/ar/2019/ar2019-eng.pdf.
10 Roger Clarke, "Information Technology and Dataveillance," *Communications of the ACM* 31, 5 (1998): 498–512.
11 Ned Rossiter, *Software, Infrastructure, Labor: A Media Theory of Logistical Nightmares* (New York: Routledge, 2016), 4–5.
12 Joseph Masco, *The Theater of Operations: National Security Affect from the Cold War to the War on Terror* (Durham, NC: Duke University Press, 2014); Brian Larkin, "The Politics and Poetics of Infrastructure," *Annual Review of Anthropology* 42, 1 (2013):

327–43; Gabrielle Hecht, "Introduction," in *Entangled Geographies: Empire and Techno-politics in the Global Cold War*, edited by Gabrielle Hecht (Cambridge, MA: MIT Press, 2011), 1–12; Claire Waterton, "Experimenting with the Archive: STS-ers as Analysts and Co-constructors of Databases and Other Archival Forms," *Science, Technology, and Human Values* 35 (2010): 645–76; Susan Leigh Star, "The Ethnography of Infrastructure," *American Behavioral Scientist* 43, 3 (1999): 377–91.

13 Keller Easterling, *Extrastatecraft: The Power of Infrastructure Space* (London: Verso, 2014), 14.

14 David Grondin., "Mobilité, vie algorithmique et société de surveillance dans Person of Interest: La traque du national security state cyberspatial," in *Représentations politiques, luttes de pouvoir et science-fiction*, edited by Isabelle Lacroix and Karine Prémont (Quebec City: Presses de l'Université du Québec, 2016), 165–202; Frank Pasquale, *The Black Box Society: The Secret Algorithms That Control Money and Information* (Cambridge, MA: Harvard University Press, 2015); David Lyon, "Surveillance, Snowden, and Big Data: Capacities, Consequences, Critique," *Big Data and Society* 1 (2014): 1–13; Antoinette Rouvroy and Thomas Berns, "Gouvernementalité algorithmique et perspectives d'émancipation: Le disparate comme condition d'individuation par la relation?" *Réseaux* 177, 1 (2013): 163–96.

15 Lauren Berlant, "The Commons: Infrastructures for Troubling Times," *Environment and Planning D: Society and Space* 34, 3 (2016): 39.

16 Star, "The Ethnography of Infrastructure," 388.

17 John Durham Peters, *The Marvelous Clouds: Toward a Philosophy of Elemental Media* (Chicago: University of Chicago Press, 2015), 37.

18 Rob Kitchin, "Thinking Critically about and Researching Algorithms," *Information, Communication and Society* 20, 1 (2016): 18.

19 Louise Amoore and Rita Raley, "Securing with Algorithms: Knowledge, Decision, Sovereignty," *Security Dialogue* 48, 1 (2016): 1.

20 Dominique Cardon, "Deconstructing the Algorithm: Four Types of Digital Information Calculations," in *Algorithmic Cultures: Essays on Meaning, Performance and New Technologies*, edited by Robert Seyfert and Jonathan Roberge (New York: Routledge, 2016), 95–110.

21 Seyfert and Roberge, *Algorithmic Cultures*.

22 Pasquale, *The Black Box Society*.

23 Huysmans, *Security Unbound*, 91.

24 NICE Actimize, "Transforming Transaction Monitoring and Reporting of Suspicious Activity," https://www.niceactimize.com/anti-money-laundering/suspicious-activity-monitoring.

25 FINTRAC, *FINTRAC Annual Report 2017–18*, 2.

26 Jim Bronskill, "Canadian Bank Fined $1.1M for Failing to Report Suspicious Transaction, Money Transfers," *The Star*, 5 April 2016, https://www.thestar.com/business/2016/04/05/canadian-bank-fined-11m-for-failing-to-report-suspicious-dealings.html.

27 FINTRAC, "Guideline 2: Suspicious Transactions," June 2017, http://fintrac-canafe.gc.ca/guidance-directives/transaction-operation/Guide2/2-eng.asp.

28 Ibid.

29 Interview with a FINTRAC official, Canada, 2015.

30 Conroy, *Global AML Vendor Evaluation*.

31 Patrice Flichy, "Rendre visible l'information," *Réseaux* 178–79 (2013): 55–89.

32 Tarleton Gillespie, "The Relevance of Algorithms," in *Media Technologies: Essays on Communication, Materiality, and Society*, edited by Tarleton Gillespie, Pablo Boczkowski, and Kirsten Foot (Cambridge, MA: MIT Press, 2014), 167–94.

33 Anthony Amicelle, "Towards a 'New' Political Anatomy of Financial Surveillance," *Security Dialogue* 42, 2 (2011): 161–78; Kirstie Ball, E. Daniel, S. Dibb, A. Canhoto, M.

Meadows, and Keith Spiller, *The Private Security State? Surveillance, Consumer Data and the War on Terror* (Frederiksberg: Copenhagen Business School Press, 2015); Gilles Favarel-Garrigues, Thierry Godefroy, and Pierre Lascoumes, "Reluctant Partners? Banks in the Fight against Money Laundering and Terrorism Financing in France," *Security Dialogue* 42, 2 (2011): 179–96; Lyliya Gelemerova, "On the Frontline against Money-Laundering: The Regulatory Minefield," *Crime, Law and Social Change* 52 (2009): 33–55; Eric Helleiner, "State Power and the Regulation of Illicit Activity in Global Finance," in *The Illicit Global Economy and State Power,* edited by Peter Andreas and Richard Friman (Lanham, MD: Rowman and Littlefield, 1999), 53–89; Béatrice Hibou, *The Bureaucratization of the World in the Neoliberal Era* (London: Palgrave Macmillan, 2015).

34 Interview with a compliance officer, Canada, 2016.

35 Richard Ericson, *Crime in an Insecure World* (London: Polity, 2007).

36 Interview with a FINTRAC official, Canada, 2015.

37 Interview with a former compliance officer, Canada, 2015.

38 FINTRAC, "Financial Transactions That Must Be Reported," 2020, https://www.fintrac-canafe.gc.ca/reporting-declaration/rpt-eng.

39 FINTRAC, *FINTRAC Annual Report 2018–19.*

40 Anthony Amicelle and Elida Jacobsen, "The Cross-Colonization of Finance and Security through Lists: Banking Policing in the UK and India," *Environment and Planning D: Society and Space* 34, 1 (2016): 89–106.

41 Anthony Amicelle and Vanessa Iafolla, "Suspicion-in-the-Making: Surveillance and Denunciation in Financial Policing," *British Journal of Criminology* 58, 4 (2018): 845–63.

42 Interview with a bank compliance officer, Canada, 2015.

43 Interview with a FINTRAC official, Canada, 2015.

44 FINTRAC, "Financial Transactions That Must Be Reported," item 6.1.

45 Amicelle and Iafolla, "Suspicion-in-the-Making."

46 Ibid.

47 FINTRAC, "Guideline 2: Suspicious Transactions," item 6.3.

48 Interview with a compliance officer, Canada, 2015.

49 Ibid.

50 Interview with a bank compliance officer, Canada, 2015.

51 Evelyn Ruppert, "The Governmental Topologies of Database Devices," *Theory, Culture and Society* 29, 4–5 (2012): 116–36.

52 Anthony Amicelle, Claudia Aradau, and Julien Jeandesboz, "Questioning Security Devices: Performativity, Resistance, Politics," *Security Dialogue* 46, 4 (2015): 293–306.

53 Ibid., 294.

54 Interview with a bank compliance officer, Canada, 2015.

55 Interview with a bank compliance officer, Canada, 2015.

56 Conroy, *Global AML Vendor Evaluation.*

57 SAS, "SAS Anti-Money Laundering" (fact sheet, 2016), 2, https://www.sas.com/content/dam/SAS/en_us/doc/factsheet/sas-anti-money-laundering-105623.pdf; BAE Systems, "Net-Reveal AML Transaction Monitoring," https://www.baesystems.com/en/cybersecurity/product/aml-transaction-monitoring.

58 Lyn H. Lofland, *A World of Strangers: Order and Action in Urban Public Space* (New York: Basic Books, 1973); John Dewey, *Logic: The Theory of Inquiry* (New York: Holt, 1938).

59 Clive Norris, "From Personal to Digital: CCTV, the Panopticon, and the Technological Mediation of Suspicion and Social Control," in *Surveillance as Social Sorting: Privacy, Risk, and Digital Discrimination,* edited by David Lyon (New York: Routledge, 2003), 251.

60 Interview with a bank compliance officer, Canada, 2015.

61 Ibid.

Part 2
Big Data Surveillance and Signals Intelligence in Canadian Security Organizations

5

From 1967 to 2017
The Communications Security Establishment's Transition from the Industrial Age to the Information Age

Bill Robinson

CONCERN ABOUT THE possibility of domestic surveillance has long surrounded the Communications Security Establishment (CSE), Canada's signals intelligence (SIGINT) agency. The validity of this concern has been difficult to assess, however, as information about the highly secretive agency is hard to find. This chapter pulls together scattered, little-known, and recently released information on the history of CSE to provide for the first time a detailed – although still incomplete – overview of the evolution of the agency and its operations over the last half-century. At the beginning of the period covered by this chapter, the Communications Branch of the National Research Council (CBNRC), as CSE was then called, paid almost no attention to Canadians. In the years since 1967, however, changes in intelligence priorities, budget resources, legal authorities, and, most important, communications and computing technologies have led to a growing overlap between the lives of Canadians and the operations of CSE. Today, CSE remains primarily a foreign intelligence agency, but its operations take place in a context where the communications of Canadians and non-Canadians are thoroughly intermixed, targets and non-targets are often difficult to distinguish, counterterrorism concerns make communications involving individuals in Canada some of the agency's highest collection priorities, and CSE's analysts increasingly look to a wide range of big data pertaining to both Canadians and non-Canadians to help answer the agency's intelligence questions. These changes have fundamentally altered the relationship between the agency and Canadians.

CBNRC at the End of the 1960s
In the summer of 1967, as Canadians celebrated the centennial of Confederation, the Soviet Union conducted the largest strategic nuclear forces exercise ever detected by the West,[1] the Six-Day War threw the Middle East into turmoil, and French president Charles de Gaulle, visiting Expo 67, delivered his notorious *Vive le Québec libre* speech and was promptly invited to go home. CBNRC had spent most of its twenty-one years of existence focused primarily on monitoring the Soviet Union. For the last ten of those years, its collection and processing activities had been directed principally at the Soviet Arctic, providing

intelligence to the National Security Agency (NSA) and Government Communications Headquarters (GCHQ), CBNRC's American and British partners, as well as to Canadian intelligence customers. In addition to its own reporting, the agency served as the funnel through which the Canadian government received the voluminous SIGINT reporting produced by those partners. SIGINT on the Middle East crisis flooded the agency's communications centre that summer.[2] Domestic Canadian communications, by contrast, were almost entirely ignored. The agency did monitor the cross-border communications of foreign delegations in Ottawa and the clandestine radio communications of foreign intelligence agents, but otherwise paid little attention to communications originating or terminating in Canada.[3]

About 80 percent of CBNRC's 600 employees were engaged in SIGINT-related activities, while the remaining 20 percent worked on the Communications Security (COMSEC) side of the agency.[4] Although a member of the five-country UKUSA (UK-USA agreement) SIGINT partnership (now commonly called the Five Eyes), CBNRC worked almost exclusively with NSA and GCHQ, with only occasional contact with its Australian and New Zealand partners. Canadian documents from the period refer mostly to "Tripartite" or "CANUKUS" SIGINT arrangements.

Soviet high-level encryption systems had been almost entirely resistant to cryptanalysis since the late 1940s,[5] and thus Canadian SIGINT activities focused on low-echelon military and civilian communications, which could still provide important information when collected in bulk and analyzed in conjunction with the "external" data (originator, destination, date, time, etc.) that accompanied both encrypted and unencrypted communications. (Today we call these externals "metadata.") Monitoring the movements of Soviet aircraft, for example, could provide vital information about the status of Soviet nuclear forces, including changes in their level of alert and preparations for possible operations.

By the 1960s, however, many Soviet communications were migrating away from long-range high-frequency (HF) radio circuits to shorter-range VHF and UHF circuits, or in the case of fixed installations, to highly directional microwave and troposcatter systems, satellite links, and domestic cable systems, none of which were accessible from Canada. CBNRC was facing the prospect of going dark.[6] Between 1971 and 1975, the number of Canadian SIGINT reports issued per year fell from 6,813 to 4,591. The small scale of the Canadian contribution is illustrated by the fact that in 1972 the five UKUSA partners produced in total approximately 167,000 reports.[7] The drop in the already small Canadian contribution did not go unnoticed.

Other kinds of change were also in the air as the 1960s came to an end. The capacity of transoceanic telecommunications cables was expanding rapidly, with an increasing number of voice circuits being carried.[8] Communications satellites had begun to populate the skies. In 1965, INTELSAT's Early Bird, the first commercial transatlantic communications satellite, was placed into orbit. Just four years later, in 1969, an even more momentous event occurred: the first packet-switched message transited the Advanced Research Projects Agency Network (ARPANET), marking the birth of what would eventually become the Internet.

Canadian intelligence priorities were under examination as well. Pierre Trudeau, who succeeded Lester Pearson as prime minister in April 1968, came into office determined to increase Canada's independence from the United States. Greater production of political and economic intelligence might have a part to play in that program. The Trudeau government also faced growing domestic tensions. The Front de libération du Québec (FLQ) was becoming increasingly active, and student radicalism was spreading on the country's university campuses. In October 1968, the Royal Commission on Security (the Mackenzie Commission) reported that "the most important communist activities in Canada are largely directed from abroad, although domestic adherents of and sympathizers with communism pose considerable problems in themselves; the separatist movement is primarily of domestic origin, although there has been some indication of foreign involvement."[9] Resolving the question of foreign influence was also an area where the Canadian intelligence program might have a contribution to make.

The Ears Turn Inward

In November 1969, Clerk of the Privy Council Gordon Robertson suggested to the Intelligence Policy Committee that "there was a need to formulate new Objectives and Priorities for the Intelligence Program, since the present program did not seem to be meeting governmental requirements adequately." A senior public servant, Claude Isbister, was subsequently appointed to act as an "outside examiner" of the Canadian intelligence program.[10] Isbister's report, delivered in November 1970, endorsed the main elements of the existing program, but also backed Robertson's concerns, recommending that "an effort be made ... to give more emphasis to areas of direct interest to Canada."[11] Submitted in the immediate wake of the October Crisis, the report reinforced the government's interest in better utilizing the foreign intelligence program to address domestic security questions.

Cross-border cable traffic was one potential source of intelligence. NSA and GCHQ had long monitored the communications carried by commercial telecommunications companies (International Licensed Carriers, or ILCs) on the world's transoceanic cable systems, most of which made landfall on the territory of one or both of the partners,[12] and some of that material was already being made available to Canada. But the question remained whether more specific Canadian intelligence needs might be served by direct Canadian intelligence collection.

By April 1972, a survey was underway to "determine the value of arrangements with the Canadian Overseas Telecommunications Corporation (COTC) by which we would have the opportunity to examine messages between Canada and locations abroad which would (1) clarify links between revolutionary activities abroad, (2) provide information concerning known revolutionary elements, and (3) contribute intelligence about foreign and economic affairs of direct interest to Canada."[13] The location of the test operation was the COTC's Montreal office,[14] which served as the gateway for all Canadian transatlantic telecommunications.

Later in 1972, CBNRC sought the budget authority to place the COTC operation on a full operational footing beginning in fiscal year 1973–74.[15] The proposal was put on hold, however, when cabinet froze the entire Canadian intelligence program at its existing level pending completion of a review of the program.[16] Not long afterwards, passage of the *Protection of Privacy Act* made the interception of "private communications" (communications with one or more ends in Canada) illegal except under specific defined circumstances, quashing the CBNRC's cable-monitoring plan in the process. Nobody had asked the agency what effect the new act might have on SIGINT collection:

> The Department of External Affairs queried some aspects of the draft bill which might affect legitimate intelligence interests adversely. Copies of the queries, which went out over the signature of the Under-Secretary of State for External Affairs (USSEA), went to the Cabinet Secretary, the Chief of the Defence Staff (CDS) and the Director General of the Security Service (DGSS) in the RCMP, but not to Director CB. After receiving answers from Justice, the USSEA told his Minister in June [1971] that "radio communications would not come within the prohibition" against the interception of "private communications." Also, the "use or disclosure" of communications intercepted outside Canada would not constitute an offence, because such an act would not be "wilful," as being based on selection from a mass of material picked up without any "mens rea." He also told his Minister that relevant information would be made available to intelligence authorities (presumably including CB), even if obtained for specifically security purposes under a warrant issued by the Solicitor General. However, these did not all turn out to be the interpretations of several subsequent Solicitors General and Ministers of Justice.[17]

Among its other effects, the *Protection of Privacy Act* denied CBNRC access to telephone, telegraph, and telex messages transmitted by cable if one or both ends were in Canada, as these were by definition private communications. CBNRC was prohibited both from collecting the messages itself and from asking its partners to collect the traffic. "The effect on RCMP interests such as terrorism, drug trafficking and illegal immigration could be judged by the angry reaction of the DGSS to the cutting off of the UK and US intercepted cable traffic."[18]

CBNRC Becomes CSE

On 1 April 1975, CBNRC was transferred to the Department of National Defence and renamed the Communications Security Establishment. Cross-border telecommunications traffic continued to grow as cable and satellite connections improved, but CSE's exploitation of ILC traffic remained stalled by the effects of the *Protection of Privacy Act*. During 1977 and 1978, CSE and the RCMP pushed within the Intelligence Advisory Committee (IAC) for approval of a special collection project apparently focused on ILC traffic. But the fraught politics of national unity following the election in November 1976 of the first Parti Québécois government, compounded by revelations of RCMP wrongdoing in Quebec, made the timing poor for a new intelligence operation centred on that province. Commenting on the project in March 1977, IAC chair John Hadwen wrote:

> I doubt if we can get everything the RCMP and CSE want, but we can certainly get something if we come up with a practical proposal. My own assessment is that we could get permission at least to tap the US and UK data banks and lately I have been wondering whether we could not take some action in Toronto and Vancouver which would be less difficult to organize and explain than action in Montreal.[19]

(Toronto and Vancouver were the locations of the COTC's other gateways for cross-border telecommunications.) Within a few months, however, both the Keable Inquiry and the McDonald Commission had been launched to investigate the RCMP's misdeeds.[20] In January 1978, the IAC "generally agreed the present atmosphere associated with the McDonald Commission and the Keable Inquiry is not conducive at this time for government approval of the [special collection] project."[21] Nevertheless, it remained on the wish list. Just one month later, in its *Review of 1977 and Forecast for 1978*, the IAC put the Interdepartmental Committee on Security and Intelligence on notice that a proposal would likely be forthcoming: "At present very little intelligence is available which would lend itself to the production of analyses on foreign attitudes, intentions and activities relating to Canadian unity. A special collection project may be required to improve prospects in this regard, and it is anticipated that a specific proposal concerning the project will be submitted later."[22]

Renewed access to US and UK ILC collection was probably secured over the next few years,[23] but the politics of establishing a Canadian cross-border collection ability remained unfavourable throughout the rest of the 1970s and early 1980s. The May 1980 referendum on sovereignty-association and the reports of the Keable Inquiry (1981) and the McDonald Commission (one in 1979 and two in 1981) ensured that questions of intelligence gathering in Quebec remained politically delicate, and the effort to draft and then pass legislation to replace the RCMP Security Service with the Canadian Security Intelligence Service (CSIS) took priority during the remaining years of the Trudeau government.

One section of the resulting *CSIS Act* did, however, pertain to the collection of foreign intelligence within Canada. Section 16 was probably intended primarily to provide legal authority for foreign-intelligence monitoring of the communications of foreign diplomats and diplomatic premises in Canada, but it may also have been intended to enable the collection of economic and other intelligence in communications crossing Canada's borders. The volume of "transit traffic" – ILC traffic that passed *through* Canada during transmission between foreign originators and foreign recipients – was growing rapidly during this time. Transiting telephone traffic, for example, more than doubled between 1982 and 1986, totalling nearly 150,000 hours in 1986.[24] In August 1987, the minister of national defence, the secretary of state for external affairs, and the solicitor general signed a memorandum of understanding governing the use of section 16. However, few section 16 operations were conducted prior to 1990. The Security Intelligence Review Committee commented in its 2001–02 Annual Report:

> Since 1990, collection activities under section 16 have gradually increased. The Committee believes several factors are behind this trend. First, the notion of collecting foreign intelligence in the early years of the Act was novel and untested. It was only after the signing of the Tri-Ministerial MOU that the details of exactly how to proceed were established. Second, there has been a growing awareness within government of the utility of the kind of information that tasking under section 16 can generate.[25]

Thus, Canadian foreign-intelligence exploitation of cross-border ILC traffic, first explored at the beginning of the 1970s, is likely to have begun, if at all, only in the 1990s. By that time, the Berlin Wall had fallen, and CSE was already a much different agency than it had been at the beginning of the 1970s.

Collection Goes Global

Despite fears of going dark, the continuing effects of budget and resource pressures, and a series of embarrassing public disclosures, the 1970s were good to the UKUSA SIGINT agencies. The CANYON and RHYOLITE families of geosynchronous SIGINT satellites, first orbited in 1968 and 1970, respectively, gave NSA better access to Soviet communications, including internal microwave and troposcatter networks, than the agency had ever had before. In 1971, the CIA, which controlled access to the data collected by the RHYOLITE satellites, agreed to bring Canada into the program; by 1974, 109 "slots" had been allotted to CSE voice transcribers and analysts.[26] Additional slots were provided to analysts in the Department of National Defence's Directorate of Scientific and Technical Intelligence to process Soviet missile telemetry intercepted by the satellites.[27] NSA had been an especially strong proponent of bringing Canada into the program. In a meeting of the US Intelligence Board in November 1970, NSA's long-serving deputy director, Lou Tordella,

> discussed the contribution that could be made by Canada, under the CAN-UKUS agreement, in support of NSA processing of "R" take. He covered the following points: a. Canadian responsibilities under the CANUKUS agreement are to process all raw voice intercepts in the Soviet Arctic and the northern military districts. In order to accomplish this, the Canadians use linguists, transcribers and analysts. At the present time, with the switch of the Soviets away from HF, this Canadian capacity is not being used. b. The "R" system is now intercepting the troposcatter system in the Soviet Arctic. NSA, therefore, proposes that Canada be authorized to process this in order to take up the slack resulting from the HF dry-up.[28]

CSE probably also helped to process traffic from the CANYON satellites, which were controlled by NSA.[29]

Meanwhile, the advent of the supercomputer, heralded by the arrival of the Cray-1 in 1976, revolutionized UKUSA cryptanalysis. Within a year, NSA began breaking into high-echelon Soviet encryption systems, obtaining a degree of access not seen since the end of the Second World War. NSA historian Thomas R. Johnson wrote that "for the cryptologists, it was their finest hour since 1945."[30] Access to the encryption systems of other countries was even more complete: a 1979 assessment of NSA's G Group, which was responsible for non-Soviet targets, concluded that its cryptanalytic achievements were "at an all-time peak."[31]

CSE and the other partners in the UKUSA community were the beneficiaries of NSA's successes. But the shrinking importance of their own contributions also placed the partners under pressure to justify their privileged access to the output of the US intelligence system. US pressure probably contributed significantly to the decisions made at the end of the 1970s and beginning of the 1980s to revitalize and expand Canadian SIGINT capabilities. Other factors that may have played a role include the deteriorating state of East-West détente, especially in the wake of the Soviet intervention in Afghanistan; significant increases in the budget of the Department of National Defence, which opened space for comparable increases in the CSE budget; and the government's continuing interest in expanding the range of Canadian foreign intelligence targets, including its desire to collect more economic-related intelligence. Whatever the relative weights these and other factors may have had, it is clear that major new initiatives began to be approved around 1980.

These initiatives included a series of increases in CSE's authorized establishment that enabled the agency to grow from approximately 600 employees at the end of the 1970s to 900 at the beginning of the 1990s; approval in 1980 to conduct site surveys to determine the best locations for embassy-based intercept sites (Project PILGRIM);[32] and the first steps, also taken in 1980, towards the revitalization of CSE's cryptanalytic capabilities, which led to acquisition in 1985 of a Cray X-MP/11, Canada's first cryptanalytic supercomputer.[33] The cryptanalysis initiative seems to have been part of a UKUSA-wide effort, as the Australian SIGINT agency obtained its first supercomputer, also a Cray, in 1986,[34] and New Zealand's agency established its first cryptanalysis unit around the same time.[35]

Another collection initiative involved satellite communications. Around 1985, CSE began installing satellite monitoring dishes at Canadian Forces Station Leitrim, just south of Ottawa. Four dishes, all covered by radomes, were in place by 1990.[36] Some of the dishes seem to have been targeted on the Atlantic INTELSAT satellites as part of the UKUSA agencies' ECHELON program. The specific users targeted may have been located in Latin America or the Caribbean. Other satellites, such as the Brazilian and Mexican domestic communications satellites and the INMARSAT maritime satellites, may also have been monitored at various times.

In December 1987, External Affairs reported that legal concerns threatened to block CSE's participation in the program:

ECHELON is a CSE project which was designed to collect Intelsat communications but which has been stopped by a legal opinion from Justice which states that such collection activity would be, if not illegal, at least "imprudent." We understand that [CSE Chief Peter] Hunt wishes to brief the [Security and Intelligence Consultative Meeting] on the project and the problems it encountered with Justice. Basically Mr. Hunt will emphasize that there appears to be no real awareness in the legal system of the needs of the S&I community and there may be implications down the road for other projects (e.g., PILGRIM, MADRIGAL). Our position on ECHELON has been to support the project as a valuable contribution to the overall Canadian and allied effort. We regret that it appears it will not go forward.[37]

The Department of Justice's concerns, probably related to the possibility that Canadian private communications would inadvertently be intercepted, were evidently resolved not too long afterwards, as a June 1988 memo noted that the project was "going forward" after all.[38] Satellite monitoring activities continue at the Leitrim station today.

In October 1987, CSE's workforce was augmented by the creation of 771 Communications Research Squadron,[39] a military unit whose members were integrated into CSE's SIGINT directorate, boosting the combined workforce at CSE to as many as 1,000 by the end of the decade, about 800 of whom worked on the SIGINT side of the house. The increase in collection and processing resources during the 1980s led to a noticeable increase in SIGINT output. By 1990, Canada was producing about 10,000 end product reports per year, more than double its 1975 figure. By comparison, the total number of reports available to Canada in 1990 was about 200,000, or about 20 percent more than the number produced in the early 1970s.[40]

New Targets and New Technology

CSE had just about completed its decade-long buildup when its primary target, the Soviet Union, disintegrated. The end of the Cold War did not eliminate all interest in events in Russia and other former Soviet republics, but it did wipe out much of the operational military traffic that CSE had formerly monitored, and it reduced the apparent importance of the traffic that remained, both to Canada and to its UKUSA partners. Canadian foreign intelligence priorities were revisited from the ground up. Political and economic intelligence concerning other parts of the world had already begun to be collected through the PILGRIM and ECHELON programs, and these subjects quickly grew in importance. The 1990s also saw the growth of *CSIS Act* section 16 collection. Former CSE analyst Jane Shorten revealed in 1995 that section 16 targets included the Japanese, Mexican, and South Korean embassies in Canada,[41] but as noted above, such operations may also have targeted foreign transit traffic. Economic intelligence was a major goal of these activities. CSE chief John Adams confirmed in 2007 that "in the time between the end of the cold war and 2001, CSE's reporting concentrated mostly on prosperity issues."[42] Monitoring the activities of the fishing fleets off Canada's East Coast also remained important,[43] and international narcotics smuggling became a significant target. In 1996, Canada formally joined the US SANDKEY program, which provided SIGINT support to the US War on Drugs in the Caribbean and Latin America.[44] Support to peacekeeping and other military operations also featured in the priorities list. Counterterrorism and other security issues were on the list too, but accounted for only 3 percent of reporting at the end of the 1990s.[45]

The 1990s also saw the arrival of the Internet as a significant phenomenon. Initially, the volume of email, file-sharing, and web traffic was tiny in comparison to traditional teletype, fax, and, especially, telephone services. The UKUSA partners began hacking into network-connected computers to acquire information (computer network exploitation, or CNE), but collection and processing of the still-growing volume of voice traffic remained the main challenge facing the UKUSA community in the mid-1990s. CSE and its partners focused a lot of attention on developing better computer technology for speaker recognition, language recognition, and speech recognition for keyword and topic spotting.[46]

By one set of estimates, voice traffic represented 98 percent of the volume of global telecommunications in 1993, while Internet traffic represented just 1.3 percent. By the year 2000, however, the figures were 44 percent and 51 percent, respectively, and by 2007 voice traffic accounted for just 2 percent of global telecommunications while the Internet accounted for 97 percent. This reversal was not the result of a drop in voice traffic, which more than tripled during the intervening fourteen years; rather, it was a consequence of the explosive growth in Internet traffic over that period.[47] Towards the end of the 1990s, it had become clear that the Internet was the future of telecommunications. The NSA's *Transition 2001* report, published in December 2000, declared the agency's determination to "master and operate in the global net of tomorrow":[48]

SIGINT in the Industrial Age meant collecting signals, often high frequency (HF) signals connecting two discrete and known target points, processing the often clear text data and writing a report. eSIGINT in the Information Age means seeking out information on the Global Net, using all available access techniques, breaking often strong encryption, again using all available means, defending our nation's own use of the Global net [sic], and assisting our warfighters in preparing the battlefield for the cyberwars of the future. The Fourth Amendment is as applicable to eSIGINT as it is to the SIGINT of yesterday and today. The Information Age will however cause us to rethink and reapply the procedures, policies and authorities born in an earlier electronic surveillance environment ... senior leadership must understand that today's and tomorrow's mission will demand a powerful, permanent presence on a global telecommunications network that will host the "protected" communications of Americans as well as the targeted communications of adversaries.[49]

The term "eSIGINT" fortunately never caught on, but the transition to Information Age SIGINT certainly did. In 2000, CSE "embarked upon an important strategic exercise to identify alternative approaches to delivering its mandate. As a starting point, it defined its vision thus: 'to be the agency that masters the global information network to enhance Canada's safety and prosperity.'"[50] But its efforts remained hamstrung by a lack of suitable legal authorities. Internet traffic could be monitored for foreign intelligence purposes, but CSE had to ensure that no private communications were intercepted by its systems. The difficulty of determining whether a particular Internet user was in Canada at the moment of communication made this an extraordinarily challenging task. The occasional inadvertent intercept might be forgiven, but any lapse in diligence would open the agency to the charge of violating the ban on wilful interception.[51] Moreover, if a private communication did end up inadvertently intercepted, the information in it could be neither used nor disclosed, even if it concerned the proverbial ticking time bomb. A new watchdog position, the CSE Commissioner, was created in 1996 to keep CSE's compliance with the law under continuing review. Successive commissioners demonstrated little inclination to declare CSE in non-compliance,[52] but their activities certainly forced the agency to tighten up its privacy-related practices. Behind-the-scenes work was begun to draft an Information Age legal regime for CSE, but no bill was put before Parliament.

In the meantime, budget resources had become tight. Despite having lost its primary target at the end of the Cold War, CSE avoided the major program cuts that swept through Ottawa in the mid-1990s, but it did suffer minor cuts. "Program integrity" top-ups for fiscal years 2000–01 and 2001–02 enabled the agency to grow to nearly 950 personnel by mid-2001.[53] However, this increase probably served only as partial compensation for the loss of 771 Communications Research Squadron, which was disbanded shortly afterwards.[54]

According to CSE chief Keith Coulter, by the end of the 1990s the agency was facing a serious erosion of its SIGINT capabilities:

[When] the events of 9/11 took place, CSE was ... facing a tough scenario. Simply put, in a kind of perfect storm situation, the 1990s saw the global revolution in communications technologies, resource shortages and the lack of an updated authority framework combine to create a serious erosion of CSE's SIGINT capabilities.[55]

9/11 Changes Everything

All of that changed following the terrorist attacks of 11 September 2001. Within months, CSE's technological capabilities, staff and budget resources, legal authorities, and target priorities were all transformed. The government of Jean Chrétien took the broader CSE powers that had been under discussion within the bureaucracy and bundled them into an omnibus *Anti-terrorism Act* (Bill C-36) that was quickly pushed through Parliament, receiving royal assent just nine weeks after first reading.[56] Bill C-36 amended the *National Defence Act* to give CSE a statutory mandate for the first time and create a ministerial authorization regime that enabled the agency to intercept private communications during its foreign intelligence and IT security activities. This made it legal for CSE to intercept, use, and disclose the communications of foreign targets even when the other end of the communication was located in Canada. However, the agency remained prohibited from directing its activities *at* persons in Canada or Canadians anywhere, except when providing support to a federal law enforcement or security agency, when it would be subject to that agency's legal authorities, including the requirement for judicial warrants to intercept private communications. Passage of the bill also gave CSE the power to engage in computer network exploitation activities; the ministerial directive issued on 14 January 2002 was probably the order that formally established the agency's CNE program.

The doors to the treasury were thrown open at the same time. In October, CSE's $100 million fiscal year 2001–02 budget was boosted by an immediate injection of $37 million, $31 million of which was for computer purchases and other technology upgrades.[57] The final amount CSE spent that year was even higher, totaling $189 million. The budget for the following year, fiscal year 2002–03, increased CSE's baseline funding to $175 million and authorized the agency to boost its workforce by 35 percent, to about 1,300 employees.

CSE's intelligence priorities were also transformed. Overnight, counterterrorism became its top priority. In October 2001, the agency's Office of Counter Terrorism was created "to centralize foreign signals intelligence efforts relating to international terrorism threats."[58] Counter-proliferation, defence against cyber threats, and support to military operations also moved up on the priorities list. In 2003, CSE informed the NSA that it planned to "dedicate 40 percent of its SIGINT resources to security initiatives,"[59] and in 2005 Coulter testified that security issues, broadly defined, accounted for over 80 percent of the agency's activities.[60] By 2006, with Canadian combat operations heating up in Afghanistan, over one-quarter of CSE security reporting was said to be related to that country.[61]

One consequence of CSE's reshuffled intelligence priorities and new legal authorities was that Canadians began to show up a lot more in CSE reporting.

Canadian identity information is normally "suppressed" (replaced by a generic reference such as "a named Canadian") in end product reports derived from CSE's foreign intelligence activities, but those identities can subsequently be released to customers who affirm a need for the information and can show that it is relevant to the customer's mandate and operational program. An indication of the degree to which communications concerning Canadians had come to figure in CSE's operations can be found in the fact that during the first six months of 2005, 300 to 400 Canadian identities, or about two a day, were released to CSE customers.[62]

The aftermath of 9/11 also transformed information-sharing arrangements within the Five Eyes community: "Canada had always benefitted from sharing arrangements with the US, but after 9/11, Canada was told that 'the taps were being opened.' The increased flow of foreign intelligence reporting and the volume of US assessments was so immense that a special capacity had to be created to handle it."[63] The principle of "need to know," which had dominated access to SIGINT during the Cold War, was augmented by "need to share." With minor exceptions for especially sensitive topics or accesses, all SIGINT reporting became shared by default among the Five Eyes partners. A push was made to share raw traffic, including metadata, much more extensively as well.[64]

Data Gets Big

In the years that followed, CSE and its partners struggled to take advantage of the growing torrent of data flooding through the world's communications networks. In March 2004, CSE received a 25 percent increase in its baseline budget and personnel establishment, enabling it to expand its workforce to 1,650 employees. A new ministerial directive, signed in the same month as the budget increase, probably provided new guidance on Internet collection activities. It also provided the agency with its first ministerial guidance on the use of communications metadata.[65] It may have marked the beginning of CSE's EONBLUE program, which would eventually see over 200 intercept and forward-processing systems deployed around the world.[66] Chief Coulter was probably referring to that program when he testified in 2005 that "we are trying to go out there into those haystacks and electronic highways outside our borders and find information that is of value to government decision makers."[67]

A similar evolution was underway around the same time at NSA, which cancelled its troubled TRAILBLAZER program in mid-2004 and in 2005 launched a replacement program called TURBULENCE.[68] By late 2006, NSA was anticipating the imminent deployment of TURBULENCE's TURMOIL subsystem, which would improve the agency's Internet filtering and selection processes and move them to forward intercept points to help save its analysts from the "tsunami of intercept" threatening to overwhelm them.[69] That tsunami was still building. Between 2000 and 2007, the spread of broadband Internet "effectively multiplied the world's telecommunication capacity by a factor of 29, from 2.2 exabytes in 2000 to 65 in 2007."[70] And it had only just begun. In 2016, annual Internet traffic surpassed 1,000 exabytes (one zettabyte). Much of that traffic consisted of streaming video and other feeds of little or no interest to SIGINT agencies, but the flood still had to be filtered and processed in order to find the traffic that was of interest.

In April 2007, John Adams, who became CSE chief in 2005, declared his agency's intent to "master the Internet" in partnership with the other Five Eyes agencies:

> That is a challenge that no one institution – be it ours or the National Security Agency, NSA, for that matter – can manage on their own. We try to do that in conjunction with our allies. At the same time, we have a threat that is very diverse, very distributed around the world – similar to needles in haystacks. We have the combination of the technology and the threat that, together, make it virtually impossible for any one organization to manage it on its own ... If we are to master that Internet, we will have to do it together; and we are focusing on that.[71]

GCHQ announced its own "Mastering the Internet" project during the same year,[72] and NSA's *SIGINT Mission Strategic Plan FY2008–2013*, promulgated in October 2007, declared that it too sought "to utterly master the foreign intelligence implications of networks and network technology."[73] One way NSA sought to do so was to collect target communications at the Internet companies that handled them, through the PRISM program, instead of intercepting them in the wild. In September 2007, Microsoft became the first participant in PRISM. Yahoo, Google, Facebook, and others quickly followed.[74] Within a few years, data obtained through PRISM appeared in nearly one in seven of the first-, second-, and third-party reports produced or received by NSA.[75] The NSA vision also called for improved "collection operations around the globe" to identify and collect the most important traffic wherever it could be found, using "fast, flexible, front-end processors [to] spot targets based on patterns, events, or metadata rather than pre-defined selectors or brute force scanning of content."[76]

The key to understanding and managing the deluge of data streaming through the Five Eyes worldwide monitoring systems was the collection and analysis of telephone and Internet metadata, which could be used both to monitor specific targets and, at least potentially, to identify previously unknown individuals and activities of intelligence interest. In 2004, CSE began working with the Mathematics of Information Technology and Complex Systems (MITACS) consortium, a Canadian network of academia, industry, and the public sector, to improve the agency's ability to exploit metadata. A 2006 description of the MITACS Semi-Supervised Learning in Large Graphs project provides a rare public look into CSE's interests:

> As part of ongoing collaborations with the Communications Security Establishment (CSE), we are applying unsupervised and semi-supervised learning methods to understand transactions on large dynamic networks, such as telephone and email networks. When viewed as a graph, the nodes correspond to individuals that send or receive messages, and edges correspond to the messages themselves. The graphs we address can be observed in real-time, include from hundreds to hundreds of thousands of nodes, and feature thousands to millions of transactions ... For reasons of efficiency, we have restricted our attention to meta-data of message transactions, such as the time, sender, and recipient, and ignored the contents of messages themselves. In collaboration with CSE, we are studying the problem of counter-terrorism, a semi-supervised problem in which some terrorists in a large network are labeled, but most are not ... Another common feature of counter-terrorism problems is the fact that large volumes of data are often "streamed" through various collection sites, in order to provide maximal information in a timely fashion. A consequence of efficient collection of transactions on very large graphs is that the data itself can only be stored for a short time. This leads to a nonstandard learning problem, since most learning algorithms assume that the full dataset can be accessed for training purposes. Working in conjunction with CSE, we will devise on-line learning algorithms that scale efficiently with increasing volume, and need only use each example once.[77]

Much of this research was later placed under the aegis of the Cryptologic Research Institute (now called the Tutte Institute for Mathematics and Computing), which was created in 2009 to help CSE bring outside mathematical expertise to bear on cryptanalytic and data-mining questions. The agency acquired a Cray XMT, a supercomputer optimized for data-mining operations, around the same time.[78] The XMT excels at two types of problems: "The first is the finding-the-needle-in-a-haystack problem, which involves locating a particular piece of information inside a huge dataset. The other is the connecting-the-dots problem, where you want to establish complex relationships in a cloud of seemingly unrelated data."[79]

CSE also sought big data analysis techniques that could run on "non-extraordinary" hardware. In late 2012, it began implementing what it called a New

Analytical Model designed to help its intelligence analysts keep up with and better exploit the metadata and other target-related information, such as financial and travel data, increasingly available to them.[80]

Additional growth in CSE's workforce was also on the agenda. Between 2009 and 2014, the agency grew from 1,650 employees to roughly 2,200, an increase of 33 percent over five years.[81] CSE's Long-Term Accommodation Project (LTAP) saw the construction of a brand-new headquarters complex located next to the CSIS headquarters over the same period. CSE asserts that the Edward Drake Building contains both the "largest concentration of supercomputers in Canada"[82] and the "largest volume databases in the country."[83]

Future Prospects

Whether the Five Eyes partners can truly be said to have "mastered" the Internet is open to question. In February 2012, however, the NSA felt justified in declaring it had successfully made the transition to the Information Age: "As the world has changed, and global interdependence and the advent of the information age have transformed the nature of our target space, we have adapted in innovative and creative ways that have led some to describe the current day as 'the golden age of SIGINT.'"[84]

The gradual spread of encryption in email, web browsing, and messaging apps – almost certainly accelerated to some degree by the Snowden leaks in 2013 – may have taken some of the lustre off the gold in the years since that statement. CSE maintains that Edward Snowden's "unauthorized disclosures have diminished the advantage that we have had, both in the short term but more worryingly in the long term."[85] It is certainly the case that encryption is becoming more common. In 2016, the United Kingdom's Independent Reviewer of Terrorism Legislation reported that "about 50% of Internet traffic was now encrypted, and 100% of emails from major email providers."[86] In June 2017, Australian attorney-general George Brandis lamented that over 40 percent of counterterrorism investigations were encountering encrypted communications, compared with less than 3 percent in mid-2013: "Within a short number of years, effectively, 100 per cent of communications are going to use encryption ... This problem is going to degrade if not destroy our capacity to gather and act upon intelligence unless it's addressed."[87]

Such claims are almost certainly exaggerated, however. Depending on when and in what form quantum computing makes its appearance, existing Internet encryption technologies could be rendered obsolete in less than a decade.[88] In the meantime, the continuing migration of Internet traffic to mobile devices, the pervasive vulnerability of existing software, and the growth of the Internet of Things may be making targeted surveillance even more difficult to evade – as long as you can identify your target. The Five Eyes agencies were already working hard on smartphone exploitation techniques in 2010, and they are likely to have made progress in the years since.[89] As ubiquitous computing becomes ever more deeply embedded in daily life, and governments and corporations collect the growing data trails thus generated, big data analysis is also likely to take on increasing importance, both as a means of identifying and tracking individual targets and for generating unique intelligence on target activities and connections.

Between June 2011 and May 2012, NSA and its partners shared approximately 180,000 end product reports, not much lower than the approximately 200,000 shared in 1990. Of those 180,000, 7,511 were issued by Australia, 11,257 were issued by the United Kingdom, and approximately 150,000 were issued by the United States.[90] A Canadian figure was not provided, but the number was probably somewhat lower than the 10,000 Canadian reports issued in 1990.[91] However, more recent documents suggest that the Canadian total has returned to the five-digit range.[92] On their face, these numbers do not support the suggestion that Canada's SIGINT output has suffered in the post-Snowden era, but it is possible that their continuing quantity masks a decline in quality.

An Agency Transformed

Today's CSE is very different from the CBNRC of 1967. It has more than four times the workforce it had fifty years ago, a much larger budget, and immeasurably greater information collection, storage, and processing capabilities. Its SIGINT activities remain focused on foreign intelligence, but the agency now has a much larger role in support of domestic law enforcement and security agencies than it had in the past. It also has a much more extensive role in information security than it had in 1967. CSE is even more tightly bound into the Five Eyes transnational SIGINT partnership, and it considers that partnership to be more valuable now than it has ever been.[93] The agency has evolved from a passive collector of radio signals received in Canada to an active hunter of data stored on information systems or passing through the air or fibre-optic cables at locations far removed from Canadian soil. It now has legal authority to intercept Canadian communications during its operations, although it can target Canadians or persons in Canada only when operating under the aegis of judicial warrants obtained by the law enforcement and security agencies to which it provides support. In the course of its activities, it collects and processes vast amounts of metadata pertaining to Canadians. And, perhaps most important, it now operates in a domain where foreign communications and Canadian communications are deeply and inevitably intermixed, its desired targets are frequently difficult to distinguish from non-targets, and activities such as terrorism that have an important nexus with Canadian domestic life are much higher on its intelligence priorities. It also operates under the eyes of a watchdog agency to ensure that CSE complies with the law and, since 2017, a new parliamentary review body, the National Security and Intelligence Committee of Parliamentarians (NSICOP). Further change came in June 2019 with the passage of Bill C-59, which gave CSE the authority to conduct Computer Network Attack operations for both defensive and offensive purposes, extended its cybersecurity mandate to the protection of Canadian private sector infrastructures (subject to request by those entities), and created an entirely new oversight and review structure for the agency.[94] These changes in priorities, budget resources, legal authorities, and worldwide communications and information technologies have transformed the relationship between CSE and Canadians. As this chapter has demonstrated, early concerns about domestic surveillance by CSE were largely unfounded, but the potential for Canadians to be drawn into the agency's dragnet is now much greater, highlighting the importance of oversight, review, and transparency measures for preventing abuse of the agency's extraordinarily intrusive capabilities.

Notes

1 Matthew Aid, *Secret Sentry: The Untold History of the National Security Agency* (New York: Bloomsbury Press, 2009), 139.

2 Kevin O'Neill and Ken Hughes, "History of CBNRC," Communications Security Establishment, August 1987, vol 4, ch 14, 43–45, released in redacted form under Access to Information Request Number A-2015-00045.

3 "The Current Canadian Intelligence Program – Objectives and Activities," attachment to draft memorandum to the Cabinet Committee on Security and Intelligence, 20 April 1972, Library and Archives Canada (LAC), RG 25, box 10, file 1-3-12-1. I am indebted to the Canadian Foreign Intelligence History Project for access to this and the other LAC documents cited in this chapter.

4 O'Neill and Hughes, "History of CBNRC," vol 6, ch 25, 8.

5 Aid, *Secret Sentry,* 17–18.

6 "Supplementary Radio Activities Consolidation Plan," Department of National Defence, 30 May 1966, released in redacted form under an Access to Information request.

7 O'Neill and Hughes, "History of CBNRC," vol 1, ch 4, 16–17.

8 Prior to 1956, all Canadian overseas telephone calls were transmitted by high-frequency radio; the last overseas call transmitted from Canada by commercial radio was made in 1975.

9 *Report of the Royal Commission on Security (Abridged)* (Ottawa: Queen's Printer, June 1969), 5.

10 O'Neill and Hughes, "History of CBNRC," vol 1, ch 2, 24.

11 Claude M. Isbister, "Intelligence Operations in the Canadian Government," Privy Council Office, 9 November 1970, 51, released in redacted form under Access to Information Request Number A-2011-00010.

12 GCHQ alone processed about 1 million ILC messages a month at this time: O'Neill and Hughes, "History of CBNRC," vol 3, ch 13, 16–17. NSA's effort was similar in scale

– in 1975 it was estimated that 2.8 million of the 2 billion telegrams that passed over ILC channels every month were forwarded to NSA headquarters, where analysts processed about 1 million of them: Letter from Frederick A.O. Schwarz to Thomas Latimer, Tab A, 16 September 1975, 5, National Security Archive, http://nsarchive2.gwu.edu//dc.html?doc=4058229-Document-10-Letter-from-Frederick-A-O-Schwarz-to.

13 "The Canadian Intelligence Program," draft memorandum to the Cabinet Committee on Security and Intelligence (CCSI), 20 April 1972, 13–14, LAC, RG 25, box 10, file 1-3-12-1. The final version of this document was considered by the CCSI in May 1972. The Canadian Overseas Telecommunications Corporation was a Crown corporation that had a monopoly on overseas telephone, telex, and telegraph services from Canada. It was renamed Teleglobe Canada in 1975 and was later privatized, eventually becoming part of Tata Communications.

14 A.F. Hart, "Meeting of Interdepartmental Committee on Security and Intelligence (ICSI) – Tuesday, May 2, 2:30 pm," 27 April 1972, LAC, RG 25, box 10, file 1-3-12-1.

15 Ibid.

16 O'Neill and Hughes, "History of CBNRC," vol 6, ch 25, 13.

17 Ibid., vol 6, ch 26, 44–45. See also vol 1, ch 2, 30.

18 Ibid., vol 6, ch 26, 45–46.

19 Memorandum from John Hadwen to Major-General Reg Weeks, 25 March 1977, LAC, RG 25, vol 29022, file 29-4-IAC, pt 2.

20 The Quebec government's Keable Inquiry was announced on 15 June 1977, and the federal government's McDonald Commission followed on 6 July 1977.

21 "Extract of the Minutes of the 1th [sic] Meeting of the Intelligence Advisory Committee Held on Wednesday, 11 January 1978," Intelligence Advisory Committee, LAC, RG 25, vol 29022, file 29-4-IAC, pt 3.

22 *Intelligence Advisory Committee (IAC) Review of 1977 and Forecast for 1978*, Intelligence Advisory Committee, 22 February 1978, LAC, RG 25, vol 29022, file 29-4-IAC, pt 3.

23 The current Department of Justice view is that it is legal for CSE to receive one-end Canadian traffic intercepted by Canada's allies. However, it is not permitted to ask those allies to target the communications of specific Canadians or persons in Canada except at the request of a federal law enforcement or security agency operating under a suitable warrant. Access to second- and third-party intercepts might explain former CSE employee Mike Frost's claim that there was a "French problem" section within CSE during the 1970s. See Mike Frost and Michel Gratton, *Spyworld: Inside the Canadian and American Intelligence Establishments* (Toronto: Doubleday, 1994), 96.

24 Teleglobe Canada, *37th Annual Report, for the Year Ended December 31, 1986* (Ottawa: Teleglobe Canada, 1987), 24.

25 Security Intelligence Review Committee, *SIRC Report 2001–2002: An Operational Audit of the Canadian Security Intelligence Service* (Ottawa: Public Works and Government Services Canada, 2002), 14–15, http://www.sirc-csars.gc.ca/pdfs/ar_2001-2002-eng.pdf.

26 O'Neill and Hughes, "History of CBNRC," vol 3, ch 11, 87; vol 6, ch 26, 43.

27 Ibid., vol 1, ch 4, 20–21.

28 Lieutenant General Donald Bennett, "Executive Session of USIB [US Intelligence Board], Thursday, 5 November 1970," Memorandum for the record, 9 November 1970. I am grateful to the late Jeffrey Richelson for providing a copy of this document to me.

29 According to Jeffrey Richelson, both Canada and the United Kingdom assisted in processing CANYON traffic: Jeffrey Richelson, "Eavesdroppers in Disguise," *AIR FORCE Magazine*, August 2012, 58–61, http://www.airforcemag.com/MagazineArchive/Documents/2012/August%202012/0812eavesdroppers.pdf.

30 Thomas R. Johnson, "A Cryptologist Encounters the Human Side of Intelligence," *Studies in Intelligence,* 8 February 2007, 2, https://www.cia.gov/library/readingroom/docs/DOC_0001407027.pdf.

31 Thomas R. Johnson, *American Cryptology during the Cold War 1945–1989* (Fort Meade, MD: National Security Agency, 1998), bk. III, 223. A large part of this success was due to secret US/West German control over Crypto AG, the company that supplied the encryption machines used by many non-Soviet Bloc countries: Greg Miller, "The Intelligence Coup of the Century," *Washington Post,* 11 February 2020.

32 Frost and Gratton, *Spyworld,* 112.

33 Bill Robinson, "The Fall and Rise of Cryptanalysis in Canada," *Cryptologia* 16, 2 (1992): 23–38.

34 Defence Signals Directorate, "DSD and Supercomputers," Internet Archive, http://web.archive.org/web/20020103063013/http://www.dsd.gov.au:80/dsd/supercomp.html. DSD was renamed the Australian Signals Directorate in 2013.

35 Nicky Hager, *Secret Power: New Zealand's Role in the International Spy Network* (Nelson, NZ: Craig Potton, 1996), 110–11.

36 Personal observations.

37 John M. Fraser, "S&I Consultative Meeting: December 18," 17 December 1987, LAC, RG 25, file 29-4-ICSI, pt 5. MADRIGAL was the section 16 project.

38 P.R. Anderson, "ICSI Meeting June 28 15:00 hrs.: Agenda Items," 28 June 1988, LAC, RG 25, file 29-4-ICSI-2, pt 4.

39 Lynn Wortman and George Fraser, *History of Canadian Signals Intelligence and Direction Finding* (London: Nanlyn Press, 2005), 15.

40 "The Canadian Intelligence Community," 16 March 1990, app. C, LAC, RG 25, BAN 2016-0149, box 2, file 3-5-5, pt 1.

41 "Canada Spied on Allies, Former CSE Agent Says: Embassies Said to Be Subjects of Surveillance," *Globe and Mail,* 13 November 1995.

42 John Adams, "CCSE Speech to Université Laval Students," 6 February 2007. On file with author.

43 Colin Freeze, "How CSEC Became an Electronic Spying Giant," *Globe and Mail,* 30 November 2013.

44 Dave Pugliese, "Canadian Spies Join U.S. Drug War," *Ottawa Citizen,* 17 May 2001.

45 "Integrated SIGINT Operational Model (ISOM)" presentation, slide 8, 652 in *CSEC Foundational Learning Curriculum* (Ottawa: Communications Security Establishment, January 2013), released in redacted form to journalist Colin Freeze under an Access to Information request.

46 Duncan Campbell, "Development of Surveillance Technology and Risk of Abuse of Economic Information" (working document for the STOA Panel, European Parliament, Luxembourg, October 1999), http://www.duncancampbell.org/menu/surveillance/echelon/IC2000_Report%20.pdf.

47 Martin Hilbert and Priscila López, "The World's Technological Capacity to Store, Communicate, and Compute Information," *Science,* 1 April 2011, 60–65, and supporting online material.

48 *Transition 2001* (Fort Meade, MD: National Security Agency, December 2000), 3.

49 Ibid., 32.

50 Office of the Communications Security Establishment Commissioner, *Annual Report 2000–2001* (Ottawa: Public Works and Government Services Canada, 2001), 7, https://www.ocsec-bccst.gc.ca/a83/ann-rpt-2000-2001_e.pdf.

51 The CSE Commissioner commented in 2001 that "CSE is well aware that it must continually upgrade its capabilities to screen out Canadian communications or risk acting unlawfully if it does not make every effort to do so": ibid., 13.

52 But it has happened on one occasion. See Bill Robinson, "CSE Commissioner: CSE Violated Law," *Lux Ex Umbra* (blog), 28 January 2016, https://luxexumbra.blogspot.ca/2016/01/cse-commissioner-cse-violated-law.html.

53 Keith Coulter, "CSE's Post-9/11 Transformation" (speech to the Canadian Association of Security and Intelligence Studies conference, 15 October 2004), Internet Archive, https://web.archive.org/web/20060502140839/http://www.cse-cst.gc.ca:80/documents/publications/casis-speech.pdf.

54 Wortman and Fraser, *History of Canadian Signals Intelligence and Direction Finding*, 131. 771 Communications Research Squadron was disbanded in December 2002: Christine Grimard, "15 Years of Service Remembered," *Maple Leaf*, 9 April 2003.

55 Coulter, "CSE's Post-9/11 Transformation."

56 Canada, Bill C-36, *An Act to amend the Criminal Code, the Official Secrets Act, the Canada Evidence Act, the Proceeds of Crime (Money Laundering) Act and other Acts, and to enact measures respecting the registration of charities in order to combat terrorism*, 1st Sess, 37th Parl, LEGISinfo, http://www.parl.ca/LegisInfo/BillDetails.aspx?Language=en&Mode=1&billId=73328.

57 Canadian Press, "Secretive Federal Spy Agencies Get $47 Million for New Technology," 19 October 2001.

58 Office of the Communications Security Establishment Commissioner, *Annual Report 2013–2014* (Ottawa: Public Works and Government Services Canada, 2014), 32, https://www.ocsec-bccst.gc.ca/a37/ann-rpt-2013-2014_e.pdf.

59 "Communications Security Establishment (CSE) – Our Good Neighbor to the North," 7 August 2003, *SIDtoday* (internal NSA publication), https://theintercept.com/snowden-sidtoday/3008306-communications-security-establishment-cse-our/.

60 Keith Coulter, testimony to Special Senate Committee on the Anti-terrorism Act, 11 April 2005, Senate of Canada, https://www.sencanada.ca/en/Content/SEN/Committee/381/anti/07evb-e. In later testimony, he used the figure "over 75%" and included counter-intelligence activities in the count: Coulter, testimony to Subcommittee on Public Safety and National Security of the Standing Committee on Justice, Human Rights, Public Safety and Emergency Preparedness, House of Commons, http://www.ourcommons.ca/DocumentViewer/en/38-1/SNSN/meeting-11/evidence. In both cases, the figure likely included the 20–25 percent of the CSE budget then spent on the IT Security program.

61 John Adams, testimony to the Standing Senate Committee on National Security and Defence, 30 April 2007, Senate of Canada, https://sencanada.ca/en/Content/Sen/committee/391/defe/15evb-e.

62 Office of the Communications Security Establishment Commissioner, "Role of the CSE's Client Relations Officers and the Operational Policy Section (D2) in the Release of Canadian Identities," 30 March 2007, 7, released in redacted form. The actual number was redacted from the document, but it can easily be seen that it consists of three digits and begins with a three.

63 Greg Fyffe, "The Canadian Intelligence Community after 9/11," *Journal of Military and Strategic Studies* 13, 3 (Spring 2011): 6.

64 "The Global Network Forum (Update #1)," 22 October 2004, *SIDToday*, https://theintercept.com/snowden-sidtoday/3676087-the-global-network-forum-update-1/; see also "Coming Soon: A SID Classification Guide," 1 March 2005, *SIDToday*, https://theintercept.com/snowden-sidtoday/3991126-coming-soon-a-sid-classification-guide/.

65 The directive was signed on 15 March 2004. The first ministerial directive specifically on metadata was signed on 9 March 2005. According to the latter directive, "metadata is defined as information associated with a telecommunication to identify, describe,

manage or route that telecommunication or any part of it as well as the means by which it was transmitted, but excludes any information or part of information which could reveal the purport of a telecommunication, or the whole or any part of its content."

66 Communications Security Establishment (CSE), "CSEC SIGINT Cyber Discovery: Summary of the Current Effort" (slide deck, November 2010), 13, https://christopher-parsons.com/Main/wp-content/uploads/2015/02/cse-csec-sigint-cyber-discovery.pdf.

67 Keith Coulter, testimony to the Special Senate Committee on the Anti-terrorism Act, 11 April 2005, Senate of Canada, https://www.sencanada.ca/en/Content/SEN/Committee/381/anti/07evb-e.

68 Fred Kaplan, *Dark Territory: The Secret History of Cyber War* (New York: Simon and Schuster, 2016), 156–57.

69 "Dealing with a 'Tsunami' of Intercept," *SIDtoday*, 29 August 2006, https://www.eff.org/files/2015/05/26/20150505-intercept-sidtoday-tsunami-of-intercept-final.pdf.

70 Hilbert and López, "The World's Technological Capacity," 63.

71 John Adams, testimony to the Standing Senate Committee on National Security and Defence, 30 April 2007, Senate of Canada, http://www.parl.gc.ca/Content/SEN/Committee/391/defe/15evb-e.htm.

72 Christopher Williams, "Jacqui's Secret Plan to 'Master the Internet,'" *The Register*, 3 May 2009.

73 National Security Agency (NSA), "SIGINT Mission Strategic Plan FY2008–2013," 3 October 2007, 4, https://www.eff.org/files/2013/11/15/20131104-nyt-sigint_strategic_plan.pdf.

74 NSA, "PRISM/US-984XN Overview" (slide deck, April 2013), 6, https://snowden archive.cjfe.org/greenstone/collect/snowden1/index/assoc/HASH01f5/323b0a6e.dir/doc.pdf.

75 NSA, "PRISM Expands Impacts: FY12 Metrics," 19 November 2012, https://www.aclu.org/foia-document/prism-expands-impacts-fy12-metrics.

76 NSA, "SIGINT Mission Strategic Plan FY2008–2013," 8.

77 "Mathematics of Information Technology and Complex Systems: Research," Internet Archive, https://web.archive.org/web/20070519133815/http://www.iro.umontreal.ca:80/~bengioy/mitacs/Research.htm.

78 CSE, "CSEC ITS/N2E: Cyber Threat Discovery" (slide deck, 2010), 47, https://christopher-parsons.com/Main/wp-content/uploads/2015/03/csec-its-dsco-2010-20101026-final.pdf.

79 Michael Feldman, "Cray Pushes XMT Supercomputer into the Limelight," *HPCwire*, 26 January 2011, https://www.hpcwire.com/2011/01/26/cray_pushes_xmt_supercomputer_into_the_limelight/.

80 For further discussion of the New Analytical Model, see Chapter 6.

81 As of 2020, the total had grown to approximately 2,900.

82 "Introduction to CSE Deck," CSE, November 2015, 3, released in redacted form under Access to Information Request Number A-2015-00067.

83 CSE, "Experienced Professionals and New Graduates," 24 April 2012, Internet Archive, https://web.archive.org/web/20130527193541/http://www.cse-cst.gc.ca/home-accueil/careers-carrieres/professionals-professionnels-eng.html.

84 *SIGINT Strategy 2012–2016* (Fort Meade, MD: National Security Agency, 23 February 2012), 2, https://www.eff.org/files/2013/11/25/20131123-nyt-sigint_strategy_feb_2012.pdf.

85 "Unauthorized Disclosures," CERRID #20084275, CSE, contained in briefing binder prepared for the Chief of CSE in March 2015, released under Access to Information Request Number A-2015-00021.

86 David Anderson, *Report of the Bulk Powers Review* (London: Williams Lea Group, August 2016), 105.

87 David Wroe, "How the Turnbull Government Plans to Access Encrypted Messages," *Sydney Morning Herald*, 11 June 2017.

88 Ian MacLeod, "Quantum Computing Will Cripple Encryption Methods within Decade, Spy Agency Chief Warns," *Ottawa Citizen*, 23 September 2016.

89 Government Communications Headquarters, "Mobile Theme Briefing: May 28 2010" (slide deck, 28 May 2010), 2, https://christopher-parsons.com/Main/wp-content/uploads/2014/12/gchq-mobile-theme-briefing.pdf.

90 NSA, "PRISM Based Reporting June 2011–May 2012" (slide deck, 13 June 2012), https://www.aclu.org/foia-document/prism-based-reporting-june-2011-may-2012. See also NSA, "PRISM Expands Impacts."

91 A briefing note produced by CSE appears to show that a four-digit number of reports were produced in FY 2011–12, i.e., from April 2011 to March 2012: "CSEC Metadata Collection," CSEC ref: 1327209, 18 June 2013, released in redacted form under Access to Information Request Number A-2013-00058.

92 For example, "In 2013–14, CSE issued [redacted five-digit number] intelligence reports (known as End Product Reports, or EPRs) in line with GC intelligence priorities." *Annual Report to the Minister of National Defence 2013–2014* (Ottawa: Communications Security Establishment, 2014), 2, released in redacted form under Access to Information Request Number A-2015-00086.

93 CSE, "Risk Assessment: Information Sharing with the Second Parties" (draft, 18 December 2015), 3, released in redacted form under Access to Information Request Number A-2015-00052.

94 For more on Bill C-59 as it pertains to CSE, see Christopher Parsons, Lex Gill, Tamir Israel, Bill Robinson, and Ronald Deibert, "Analysis of the *Communications Security Establishment Act* and Related Provisions in Bill C-59 (*An Act respecting national security matters*), First Reading (December 18, 2017)" (Citizen Lab/Canadian Internet Policy and Public Interest Clinic report, December 2017), https://citizenlab.ca/wp-content/uploads/2018/01/C-59-Analysis-1.0.pdf.

6

Pixies, Pop-Out Intelligence, and Sandbox Play
The New Analytic Model and National Security Surveillance in Canada

Scott Thompson and David Lyon

"EVERYTHING HAS CHANGED," proclaims a Canadian Communications Security Establishment (CSE) document, obtained using an Access to Information and Privacy (ATIP) request. It refers to the remarkable shift from older intelligence-gathering methods that had evolved steadily since the agency's founding in 1946 to an embrace of big data as a fresh set of practices. The new practices, collectively described as a "New Analytic Model (NAM)," include data mining – for example, interception from deep packet inspection devices (see Chapter 7), posted material from social media, apps, and the "mountains of raw data" stored or generated from Internet-connected devices[1] – and machine learning, in which both modes of data capture and modes of analysis are radically different from those of the past. Drawing on internal CSE documents obtained though ATIP requests,[2] this chapter demonstrates a significant shift in how CSE approaches knowledge production and speaks to the broader implications of a big data approach to national security work.

Sometimes history moves in a steady arc where the trajectory remains more or less the same over many decades or even centuries. From time to time, however, a historical turn occurs in which past practices are abandoned or allowed to shrink in importance, to be replaced with new practices that come to dominate the scene and, cascade-like, have effects in a broad range of other areas. A historic turn has been made at CSE. Some aspects of this are plain to see, such as the iconic multibillion-dollar Edward Drake Building in Ottawa and the partnership with the Tutte Institute for Mathematics and Computing (TIMC). Others are closely guarded secrets – there is notable continuity rather than rupture here – that may be gleaned only from non-redacted sections of documents released in response to specific requests.

Several other factors might lead one to suspect that there is a new modus vivendi at CSE. The Snowden scandal in 2013 prompted serious questions about how exactly the Canadian partner of the US National Security Agency (NSA) conducted its intelligence gathering. Two questions preoccupied journalists and others after the disclosures about the NSA: (1) were Canadians being targeted despite CSE's mandate to deal with foreign intelligence? and (2) how was metadata treated, as personal data or as something else, not covered by any privacy legislation? There was a recognition that massive amounts of data were becoming available, especially following the rapid development of Web 2.0, and that CSE was working towards exploiting those new data sources[3] (see also Chapter 14).

What was not fully recognized, however, was that a wholesale shift to big data practices was underway, creating a watershed in data handling. As Carrie Sanders and James Sheptycki put it (in relation to policing), this new development amounts to the "algorithmic administration of populations and territory ... based on morally neutral technology."[4] This is a new mode of doing intelligence gathering and analysis, based in fact on global neoliberalism, seen, for instance, in the public-private partnerships that help to drive the direction of the agency. The disclosures by Edward Snowden in 2013 and later make it very clear that among national security agencies, and especially at the NSA, there is a shift to big data practices.[5] The attempts to legalize certain data-gathering activities in Canada, notably in the *Anti-terrorism Act,* known generally as Bill C-51, display a desire to normalize big data in this realm.[6] While these two factors of data handling and public-private partnerships are clearest, there are others.

The establishment of the Tutte Institute for Mathematics and Computing in 2009 and its partnership with CSE are a reminder of a long-term association with top researchers. CSE was created as such in 1975, from the former Communications Branch of the National Research Council. Computer scientists, mathematicians, engineers, linguists, and analysts are all found at CSE. Hints of a new approach were available a few years ago. For example, Colin Freeze found that new recruits at CSE were told not to emulate Hollywood's James Bond style of secret agents. Rather, they should act like the "traffic fairy," a "tiny pixie who apparently flits through computer traffic in search of secrets."[7]

Here we comment first on the nature of the shift from the evolutionary approach since 1946 to the big data turn starting in 2012. From the 1940s to 1974, the existence of what became CSE was secret, but it is now known that signals intelligence (SIGINT) was its main mandate from the Second World War onward. This meant telephone, radio ("wireless"), and telegraph – indeed any system of communication used to send classified, and thus encoded or encrypted, information. The primary user of SIGINT was the Department of National Defence, although various leaks and scandals showed that sometimes Canadian citizens, including prominent ones, could be in view.

The shift to big data practices depends heavily on very large-scale computing facilities as well as technical, mathematical, and statistical expertise – hence CSE depends not on the tens of workers with which it began in the 1940s but now on more than 2,000 operating staff. At CSE, as elsewhere, big data is not so much suspicion-driven as data-driven. That is, rather than a process of targeted scrutiny of groups and individuals, big data engages in what was called after Snowden "mass surveillance," that is monitoring of communications to discern patterns of relationship that may be deemed "actionable intelligence." It should of course be recalled that the kinds of data sought and analyzed are millions or billions of bits of data generated by everyday transactions and communications; numbers, text, graphics, videos, images, and sensor information. This is what the "pixie" is trained to sift through.

Second, we note some key features of CSE big data practices and comment on their broader meanings. The term "big data" usually refers to the *volume* of data in use, which can now be handled by large-scale computing facilities that contribute to the *velocity* of calculation and analysis possible, along with the *variety* of datasets that may be drawn into any given analysis. Each of these characteristics is visible in the New Analytic Model. Although this name seems to lend weight to the analytical dimensions of big data, it is no less the case that CSE depends on new modes of data capture, especially those associated with "data exhaust" from everyday communications and transactions and so-called user-generated content from massive social media sources.

Third, we observe that the changes at CSE are not by any means limited to that body. Rather, some deliberate strategies indicate a plan to influence many or even all government departments to use big data methods, with which CSE expertise will be available to assist. Moreover, through potential legal changes and alteration of the protocols of data management policy, the idea is to catalyze a cascading effect of these new practices throughout government.

In what follows, we show what sorts of pressures and opportunities produced the radical shift to big data at CSE, the discernible patterns of development of big data that are becoming visible, and the likely consequences of the adoption of big data practices in intelligence services in Canada. This final item has a necessarily critical edge, but is intended to prompt those engaged with CSE's mission to reflect more deeply on certain matters that have to do with ethics, citizenship, and democratic oversight of which CSE is already aware, as seen in the ATIP documents made available to us.

The CSE's "New Analytic Model"

A significant shift in how intelligence work is done within CSE is described in internal documents as resulting from the new production, availability, and institutional ingestion of large, machine-readable datasets. In the "New Analytic Environment" (NAE), CSE documents from 2012 specifically identified a spike and shift in the volume and type of data ingested.[8] In response, the latter part of 2012 saw the radical adoption of new analytics-based methods and applications under a new initiative described as the "New Analytic Model." In its application, the model put aside the traditional "target, translate, report" approach and replaced it with one in which CSE analysts would be "rebuilt" to take up "new tasks" in a new "working environment" with an expanded skillset.[9] In short, analysts were to become data scientists – to "compose tests (tradecraft) through the composition of analytics."[10]

With changes in how national security knowledge development was defined in order to place a primary focus on data analytics, work at CSE would have to change as well. The NAM policy documents assert that "to address this challenge requires CSE and DGI [the Director General for Intelligence] to improve our skills, and shift our SIGINT systems development focus toward a new form of architecture and environment."[11] As these internal policy documents note, the shift in approach to SIGINT would be significant and fundamentally reshape the work done at CSE: "to be clear what we're talking about here is a revolution in the field of SIGINT analysis," as the NAM called for "a departure from the old way of doing things and there are tremendous implications for all of us."[12]

In taking up this data-driven, fluid, and flexible model, program designers identified six key benefits to SIGINT data collection and analysis from the NAM:

1) Provide a greater visibility into all collected data that w[ould] allow for the rapid development of analytical capabilities to enrich, discover and to analyze trends and anomalies across all relevant repositories at once; 2) Ensure that the technological evolution supports the analysts' quest to explore, experiment, discover, analyse and assert findings; 3) [REDACTED]; 4) Enable more effective and efficient implementation and performance of analytic methods by leveraging computer automation and machine learning in order to aid in the formulation of reasonable and actionable conclusions from sometimes conflicting information; 5) Evolve the deliverables beyond static one-way interface and aim towards an interactive mechanism through cutting edge interactive visualization that present valuable insights in impactful ways; 6) Provide the ability to plan, share and collaborate, monitor and measure performance, analyze results, predict outcomes and strategize among peers, across teams, across units and, ideally, set the stage for continued extension of these features.[13]

Where previously a single analyst or team would work to target, translate, and report on identified targets, acting in more siloed, specialist areas, the NAE would call for "a complete reworking of the DGI analyst's task, working environment, and skill set," acknowledging "that the role of analysis needs to undergo a revolution of sorts, focused on innovation and sharing and collaboration."[14] Analysts would shift "from being a unique service provider, to being just one tool in the box, from being a collector of facts, to an assessor or creator of information."[15]

Ultimately, the goal of the shift at CSE was to "re-build the intelligence analyst through the NAM and the NAE" by shifting from a specialized research area, with a targeted focus and specialty, to one that instead engaged with a sandbox of available data, moving flexibly from project to project exploring, experiencing, testing, and predicting, with machine learning and big data analytics tools.[16]

The New Analytic Model, Big Data, Machine Learning, and Data Sandbox Analysts

As noted above, CSE's response to the availability and ingestion of new types and massively increased volumes of machine-readable data was the development and adoption of the New Analytic Model policy initiative. This "analytical revolution," which significantly shifted the work of national security intelligence analysts, also reshaped the forms of knowledge being produced as part of SIGNIT.[17] What did these new analytic practices do to shift the expectations of analysts? How did they change the work done within CSE?

The NAM initiative started in late 2012, though as of 2014 "the initiative continue[d] to be informed by changes in ... priorities, client requirements, access, operations and technology environment."[18] The initiative's stated goals are "to use the model to develop an environment to fulfill CSE's mandate through cutting edge analysis," which would "ensur[e] an ability to detect, prevent, predict and respond to events crucial to Canada's security and sovereignty at scales consistent with our evolving data collection."[19] In envisioning what the NAM would look like in practice, its designers established "the solution aim" as being able to "ensure the creation of an agile, scalable and sustainable dynamic environment that can be easily stood up, torn down, shared, [and] modified."[20]

NAM policy was designed to achieve three central goals: (1) to "take advantage of the increasing volume of available data"; (2) to "facilitate the growth of analytic capacity"; and (3) to "better enable the full spectrum of analysis underway across the organization."[21] In establishing how intelligence work would change under the NAM, internal documents identify a required shift in technological and methodological approaches at CSE. At a technological level, work would be reconceptualized into an "Infrastructure Layer, Data Management Layer, Analytics and Service Layer, and Human Insights and Visualization Layer," while methodologically, the shift would reorganize SIGINT knowledge production into "interactive cycles of data gathering and examination through which meaning [would be] derived and questions answered, culminating in higher order understanding."[22] For analysts, this meant an emphasis on big data analytics and the adoption of machine learning initiatives into their development of actionable intelligence.[23]

Internally, CSE defines big data as "the amount of data that exceeds the processing capacity and analytic capabilities of conventional systems," while characterizing the classification of big data through the dimensions of the four Vs: Volume, or "quantities of collected data"; Variety, "encompass[ing] the many different data types and sources"; Velocity, or "the speed at which the data is created, collected and processed"; and finally, Veracity, "the level of reliability associated with a given type of data" – this final dimension being noted by CSE as the "least researched" aspect of big data.[24] As part of the NAM, big data was understood as providing "a new way of asking questions" and "organizing data," as well as providing "new tools to use" for analysts; more importantly, big data would initiate "a different way of thinking, since you learn to understand from summaries of data rather than individual items."[25] That is, "intelligence may 'pop out' of exploratory analysis, rather than being prompted by specific analytics questions."[26] In very plain language, big data analytics would work by enabling analysts to "understand what is 'normal' for [their] data set (which is some information in itself)," and "what is 'abnormal' (doesn't fall within the range of what is normal)."[27]

In this way, the NAM would shift the work of analysts into a type of virtual data sandbox, through which they would build, test, assess, and engage with big data and machine learning tools in order to develop actionable SIGNIT knowledge. As a 2012 internal document that explains this data-sandbox-type research environment notes, CSE under the NAM

> can be conceptualized as a virtual world for exploration and development by analysts. It's not unlike one of the more popular online games right now. In MINECRAFT, users have their own universe to explore, develop and survive in. Players start off with a completely blank slate. They are free to explore, mine for minerals, build their own tools, buildings, cities, sculptures etc. The environment is contained, operates according to the rules of physics etc. and players are free to do whatever they want within those bounds, without fear of breaking the system.[28]

In addition to opening up frictionless interactions with data, the quick assembly and disassembly of teams, fluid organizational nature at CSE, and incorporation of elements of play associated with the new analyst of the NAM were each built directly into the new architecture of CSE's new Cdn$1.2 billion dollar headquarters, the Edward Drake Building.[29] The building was specifically designed to "promote efficient workflow while being adaptable to enable a sense of collaboration so communities of interest can flourish without impacting on overall coherence."³⁰ In a practical sense, this meant modular workspace designs, the inclusion of special-purpose spaces, and a capacity to reorient how workspaces are laid out within the building.

Big Data and Machine Learning at CSE, 2012–14

The New Analytic Model was formally adopted at CSE in late 2012 and was to be implemented incrementally in a series of stages – from the internal identification of educational needs of CSE personnel to the application of big data and machine learning analytical practices in operational settings. This section reviews the phases in which the NAM was implemented and identifies within CSE internal documents what can be known about the current use of big data and machine learning in national security work at CSE.

By 2014, internal documents had already asserted the centrality of big data within CSE's national security intelligence work. As noted in a presentation to other Canadian government departments on big data, "CSE can be seen as one of the biggest consumers of 'big data' in Canada," and "'Big Data' is critical to everyday CSE operations," from how "CSE collects, manages, samples and analyses [REDACTED] volume of data on a regular basis," to how, by 2014, "this data [wa]s the primary feed for CSE's reporting on intelligence and cyber security."³¹ When approached by other Canadian government departments interested in adopting big data practices in 2014, CSE presented itself as an expert organization, explaining that it "has significant experience in the use of Big Data and Machine Learning to fulfill its operational requirements" and that "there is the potential for CSE to leverage Big Data beyond operations to other areas such as policy and reporting."³² Although precise operational details regarding the current use of big data at CSE remain redacted in ATIP release documents, overarching NAM policy, CSE presentations, reports to other departments, and public leaks do provide some details on how big data and machine learning work is being done at CSE.

At a more general level, CSE's work regarding big data and machine learning under the NAM policy initiative does retain a central role for the specialized knowledge of analysts and stresses the need for human actors within data-driven knowledge production. In particular, internal documents explain that "it is important for subject-matter experts to be involved with the entire process and interpretation as much as possible," in order "to make sure the questions are meaningful."³³ Interestingly, the analyst within the NAM is also to play a role in the identification and selection of relevant data, as "using 'convenient' data, may actually lead you astray and to incorrect conclusions," while analysts are also to manually review outputs since datasets "are not 'clean' (decision tree is not perfect; will classify some incorrectly)" – with the NAM approach, the importance of the analyst is highly stressed, as "one needs to start from the types of questions we want to answer, then obtain the relevant data, even if it seems expensive to do this at the beginning of the project."[34] Beyond simply involving the analyst, CSE internal documents on big data and machine learning specifically assert that fully automated approaches are incompatible with effective knowledge development, noting that

> by themselves, data analysis tools will not be useful unless there are analysts who understand both the tools and the data ... Instead the tools will be part of a process, which includes people analyzing the results produced by the tools and using their own knowledge of the business and data to draw conclusions. This analysis will include using good data visualization and other techniques to better understand the results. Usually those conclusions will be hypotheses which will need to be further tested in an ongoing process where the users continuously refine the results. In CSE's experience, pursuing the "Star Trek" vision has consistently led to a dead end.[35]

Consequences and Critique

Having established that, in their own words, "everything has changed" in terms of data analysis at CSE, it is important that the consequences of this shift be exposed and examined. Given the unlikelihood of obtaining any kind of account of the ongoing critical assessment of the New Analytic Method at CSE, we turn to the kinds of likely outcomes at CSE and the questions that are prompted by the use of big data practices in other fields. The language used in the documents obtained makes clear that (1) the shift to new methods is decisive and far-reaching; (2) its catalyst comprises developments taking place among partner organizations, especially with the NSA and Five Eyes, which in turn is predicated on (3) the veritable explosion of data availability from the exponential expansion of digital communications in the early twenty-first century. The continuity suggested by naming the new CSE building for Edward Drake, pioneer of the Canadian signals intelligence community from 1945, is ironically belied by the wholesale shift to methods that abandon Drake's approach.

The widespread public realization that security agencies rely extensively on big data occurred in 2013 with the publication of the first documents copied by Edward Snowden, subcontractor to the NSA, with Booz Allen Hamilton.[36] But had that public read James Bamford's account of the NSA's Utah Data Center in 2012, this was already evident. One of the key purposes of the Utah Data Center is cryptanalysis, for breaking complex encryption. Bamford explained its effects as "everybody is a target; everyone with communication is a target."[37] In Bamford's account, having been caught off guard by a series of terrorist attacks culminating in 9/11, the NSA was "quietly reborn" and the massive new data centre in Bluffdale, Utah, was the symbol of that rebirth.[38]

At Bluffdale and CSE, in intelligence *production,* big data is named and validated as the New Analytic Model in conjunction with machine learning and new forms of reliance on statistical techniques. It is important to recall, with danah boyd and Kate Crawford, that "Big Data is less about data that is big than it is about a capacity to search, aggregate, and cross-reference large data sets."[39] It is precisely that capacity that CSE was establishing with its shift to NAM. As boyd and Crawford also argue, big data is a combination of *technology,* for gathering, analyzing, and linking datasets; *analysis,* drawing on datasets to identify patterns, such that new claims can be made; and *mythology,* that large datasets offer a higher form of knowledge, accurately generating insights that were previously impossible.[40] As noted above, CSE compares the NAM shift to a "scientific revolution." In this case, NAM challenges the classic deductive scientific method that underlay the prior CSE approach.[41]

As a result, new types of knowledge are created from the data-driven approach, the likely direction of which is from a targeted causal logic to a bulk, correlational logic. The quest is for patterns, insights, and, as shown in CSE documents, intelligence that "pops out" of exploratory analysis. This is in effect a new form of empiricism that downplays theory and claims that meaningful knowledge may be produced from patterns in so-called raw data.[42] In this view, one no longer needs to test hypotheses, because the correlations generated by new computational, machine learning, algorithmic, and statistical methods produce superior knowledge when datasets are mined for patterns. From there, without human framing one may move forward to prediction, rather than backward to explanation. Anyone with some statistical sense or the means to visualize data can interpret the patterns.

The problems associated with this approach are manifold, including the following:[43]

- The data will always remain no more than a sample, taken from a certain vantage point.
- The newly developed systems are designed to capture certain kinds of data, and the analytics and algorithms must already have been scientifically tested in specific ways.
- Data never speak for themselves without being framed in some way and are not inherently meaningful – the correlations may well be random.[44]
- Information that "pops out" of the data is inadequate insofar as it lacks contextual and domain-specific knowledge.

This suggests that the hesitations hinted at in the ATIP documents are appropriate. Deep knowledge of prior modes of intelligence gathering would appear to be vital for correctly interpreting data generated by the NAM.

Surveillance is always and everywhere a means of making visible certain individuals or groups such that, in the case of national security intelligence-gathering operations, they may be assessed for their possible connections with criminal, violent, or terrorist activities. The shift to the NAM at CSE means that new kinds of visibility emerge, different from older targeted methods and involving "bulk" data. This is where the often missing "V" of big data – vulnerability – becomes acutely significant.[45] Evidence from many other areas of big data practice suggests that unless extreme care is taken, big data practices can make some already marginalized or disadvantaged groups more vulnerable than others.[46]

In the *organization* of intelligence work, the shift to big data practices may be seen in the use of new gaming metaphors, new partnerships, and, significantly, new concerns about whether the NAM will completely eclipse older practices. Again, these kinds of shifts are not uncommon in big data practices, especially in their corporate settings. Gaming is seen as a way of organizing teams of workers and as a model of how progress is made in the search for actionable data. This in turn plays into the kinds of partnerships evident among a variety of players, especially among those who on their own would lack the resources to mount big data centres of analysis on their own account. Universities and technology companies frequently form such alliances in order to share ideas and expertise. Lastly, while there is much hype surrounding big data practices, some sober assessments acknowledge the need to combine older with newer methods in order to make reliable claims about what the data indicate.

The gaming metaphors are significant. Those highlighted in the ATIP documents include the "sandbox" and the "Minecraft" models. Based originally on a children's exploratory playspace, the idea of a sandbox in software development is for production development, for learning, testing, and experimenting. But the sandbox also hints at limits, the ways in which certain kinds of experimentation may be constrained to protect items such as data, code, and servers from potential damage resulting from changes to the system. So while play is present, in this case it is clearly purposeful play that is in view. The same is true of the Minecraft analogy, where, in the SIGINT lab, "starting with a blank slate," analysts have opportunities to "experiment, explore, create and innovate in this universe." The documents state, curiously, that the analysts are bound "by the rules of physics" (really, no others?) and that within the "Minecraft" lab they are free to innovate at will without fear of doing damage.

Another crucial factor is the public-private partnerships that are evident in the very building now housing CSE and the academic-corporate connections visible in the relationship with the Tutte Institute. The latter has the focus of "research in fundamental mathematics and computer science" and is "continually working to strengthen and develop partnerships with research institutes, governmental agencies, industry and universities."[47] It works with the Institute for Defense Analyses in the United States, associated with universities including Princeton, and the Heilbronn Institute for Mathematical Research in the United Kingdom. It is formally partnered with the University of Calgary and with Carleton University in Ottawa. The participants in the Tutte programs are from the fields of mathematics, computing science, and engineering. There is no mention of whether these persons or partners involve legal scholars or persons from the social sciences, such as political science or international relations, or from the humanities, such as history.

All the emphasis at present appears to be on the mathematics, computing, and engineering aspects of surveillance, intelligence gathering, and analysis. For CSE, a shift of this magnitude means that new analysts must be found and trained to read the outputs of big data and machine learning. Some residual questions need to be addressed about whether older forms of expertise will be lost, and if so, whether or not this loss will reduce the capacity of CSE to do its work appropriately and efficiently. This does not seem to be a key priority of CSE and the NAM, however. While CSE says that they resist a fully automated system, which is why they want analysts to direct aspects of the process of intelligence gathering and analysis, the analysts appear to be drawn almost exclusively from disciplines that are unlikely to include expertise relating to classic intelligence gathering for national security purposes.

Conclusion

From the evidence presented here, everything has changed at CSE in the wake of decisions to switch to big data practices, known at CSE as the New Analytic Model. The aim is to improve national security in an age of exploding communications media. While some aims of the NAM are worthy ones, given the urgency of dealing with global crime, violence, and terrorism, the methods and modes of expertise chosen are very heavily weighted towards mathematics, computing, and engineering. While this is appropriate for grappling with the immense quantity of data available, it is not clear that sufficient attention is being paid to the quality of the intelligence thus gleaned. The problem with abandoning old methods in favour of new is that the risk of threatening situations may be misconstrued, with negative consequences for individuals and groups. In CSE's zeal to avoid human framing and "bias," blinkers appear around the very nature of the data and the inevitability that they are "framed" from the outset.

Along with this – and possibly CSE is aware of the problem, however dimly – is the ironic fact that without human involvement in the process of data analysis, the likelihood of successful utilization of big data for security intelligence and surveillance will remain slim. The focus on algorithms and machines precisely takes attention away from the crucial matters of context. As a 2017 article states, "these tools cannot replace the central role of humans and their ability to contextualize security threats. The fundamental value of big data lies in humans' ability to understand its power and mitigate its limits."[48] And, we might add, not just any humans will do. While those trained in mathematics, computing, and engineering are essential to the task, if these skills are not complemented with ones from, for example, law, the social sciences, and humanities, the essential task of contextualizing analysis not only will be poorer but could raise human rights, civil liberties, and privacy problems for vulnerable individuals, for whole classes of persons, and indeed for everyone.

Notes

1 Communications Security Establishment (CSE), "Opportunities for Professionals – Foreign Language Intelligence Analysts," 1 September 2017, https://web.archive.org/web/20170825040050/https://cse-cst.gc.ca/en/node/1402.

2 Under Canada's federal *Access to Information Act* or *Privacy Act,* individuals (either citizens, permanent residents, or those currently present in Canada) and corporations are able to make requests to federal government departments and organizations to obtain documents relating to a given subject (the provinces also have similar legislation to cover their departments and organizations). The acts do place some limitations regarding what kinds of information can be released, and it is at times challenging to obtain documents on subjects like national security or policing. Requests need to be written in such a way as to avoid asking for current practices or ongoing investigations; they also need to be made with the proper language or keywords of the institution. The language for the request upon which much of this chapter is based (#A-2016-00068), for example, was for all "high level briefing notes, presentations, policy framework documents or reports specifically related to CSE's definition of 'Big Data,' 'Knowledge Discovery,' and/or 'Data Mining' and their impact on the mission." The collected volume by Jamie Brownlee and Kevin Walby, *Access to Information and Social Justice: Critical Research Strategies for Journalists, Scholars, and Activists* (Winnipeg: ARP Books, 2015), is an excellent starting point for those looking to better understand the use of Access to Information and Privacy (ATIP) legislation for research, journalism, or social activism in Canada. ATIP requests can be made online (https://atip-aiprp.apps.gc.ca/atip/welcome.do), and the preceding two years of completed requests are also catalogued. The Surveillance Studies Centre, along with Queen's University, is currently working to develop a repository where the full texts of completed ATIP requests will be made available to researchers and the general public, including those used in this chapter.

3 CSE, "NAM Episode II: Rise of the New Analytical Environment, CSE PowerPoint Presentation Deck," 193, released under Access to Information Request Number A-2016-00068 (2016).

4 Carrie Sanders and James Sheptycki, "Policing, Crime and 'Big Data': Towards a Critique of the Moral Economy of Stochastic Governance," *Crime, Law and Social Change* 68, 1–2 (2017): 1–15.

5 David Lyon, "Surveillance, Snowden, and Big Data: Capacities, Consequences, Critique," *Big Data and Society* 1, 2 (2014): 1–13.

6 Craig Forcese and Kent Roach, *False Security: The Radicalization of Canadian Anti-Terrorism* (Toronto: Irwin Law, 2016).

7 Colin Freeze, "Canadian Spy Manual Reveals How New Recruits Are Supposed to Conceal Their Identities," *Globe and Mail,* 22 December 2013.

8 CSE, "NAM Episode II," 193.

9 CSE, "[REDACTED TITLE], CSE PowerPoint Presentation Deck," 175, released under Access to Information Request Number A-2016-00068 (2016); Communications Security Establishment, "NAM Episode II," 193.

10 CSE, "[REDACTED TITLE]," 184.

11 CSE, "Analytic Environment for DGI: Business Case Proposal – Draft," 98, released under Access to Information Request Number A-2016-00068 (2016).

12 CSE, "NAM Episode II," 191.

13 CSE, "Analytic Environment for DGI," 100–1.

14 CSE, "NAM Episode II," 193.

15 CSE, "[REDACTED TITLE]," 174.

16 CSE, "NAM Episode II," 205.

17 CSE, "[REDACTED TITLE]," 189.

18 CSE, "Analysis and Production Evolution: A Simplified Take on the NAM, CSE PowerPoint Presentation Deck," 162, released under Access to Information Request Number A-2016-00068 (2016).

19 Ibid.; CSE, "Analytic Environment for DGI," 96.

20 Ibid., 100.

21 CSE, "NAM Episode II," 205.

22 Ibid.

23 CSE, "[REDACTED TITLE]," 189.

24 CSE, "Analytic Environment for DGI," 97.

25 CSE, "Machine Learning, CSE PowerPoint Presentation Deck," 142, released under Access to Information Request Number A-2016-00068 (2016).

26 Ibid.

27 Ibid.

28 CSE, "NAM Episode II," 197–98.

29 Greg Weston, "Inside Canada's Top-Secret Billion-Dollar Spy Palace," *CBC News,* 8 October 2013, http://www.cbc.ca/news/politics/inside-canada-s-top-secret-billion-dollar-spy-palace-1.1930322.

30 Canadian Council for Public-Private Partnerships, *The Canadian Council for Public-Private Partnerships 2011 National Award Case Study Silver Award for Project Financing: Communication Security Establishment Canada Long-Term Accommodation Project* (Ottawa: Canadian Council for Public-Private Partnerships, 2011), 8.

31 CSE, "Big Data for Policy Development 2014, CSE PowerPoint Presentation Deck," 30, released under Access to Information Request Number A-2016-00068 (2016); CSE, "Big Data Discussion Paper," 4–5, released under Access to Information Request Number A-2016-00068 (2016).

32 CSE, "Big Data Discussion Paper."

33 CSE, "Machine Learning, CSE PowerPoint Presentation Deck," 142, released under Access to Information Request Number A-2016-00068 (2016).

34 Ibid., 129, 142.

35 CSE, "Big Data Discussion Paper," 6–7.
36 David Lyon, *Surveillance after Snowden* (Cambridge: Polity, 2014).
37 James Bamford, "The NSA Is Building the Country's Biggest Spy Center," *Wired*, 15 March 2012, https://www.wired.com/2012/03/ff_nsadatacenter/.
38 Ibid.
39 danah boyd and Kate Crawford, "Critical Questions for Big Data," *Information, Communication and Society* 15, 5 (2012): 663.
40 Ibid.
41 Rob Kitchin, "Big Data, New Epistemologies and Paradigm Shifts," *Big Data and Society* 1, 1 (2014): 1–12.
42 Geoff Bowker, *Memory Practices in the Sciences* (Cambridge, MA: MIT Press, 2005); Lisa Gitelman, ed., *Raw Data Is an Oxymoron* (Cambridge, MA: MIT Press, 2013).
43 Kitchin, "Big Data, New Epistemologies," 1–12.
44 One sees this even in non–big data contexts, such as the National Security actions taken against Ahmad Abou El-Maati, based on, *inter alia*, a map of government buildings in Ottawa. He was tortured in Syria as a result, but the simple explanation of the correlations between his driving a truck in Ottawa and a map showing government buildings was that he was on a delivery run for a company.
45 David Lyon, "The Missing 'V' of Big Data: Surveillance and Vulnerability," in *Reading Sociology: Canadian Perspectives*, edited by Patrizia Albanese, Lorne Tepperman, and Emily Alexander (Toronto: Oxford University Press, 2017), 324–27.
46 Neil Richards and Jonathan King, "Three Paradoxes of Big Data," *Stanford Law Review* 41 (2013): 41–46; Oscar Gandy, *Coming to Terms with Chance: Engaging Rational Discrimination and Cumulative Disadvantage* (Farnham, UK: Ashgate, 2009).
47 CSE, "Tutte Institute for Mathematics and Computing – About the Institute," 8 May 2020, https://www.cse-cst.gc.ca/en/tutte-institute.
48 Damien Van Puyvelde, Stephen Coulthart, and M. Shahriar, "Beyond the Buzzword: Big Data and National Security Decision-Making," *International Affairs* 93, 6 (2017): 1397–1416, https://academic.oup.com/ia/article-abstract/doi/10.1093/ia/iix184/4111109/Beyond-the-buzzword-big-data-and-national-security.

7

Limits to Secrecy
What Are the Communications Security Establishment's Capabilities for Intercepting Canadians' Internet Communications?

Andrew Clement

The largest, most significant big data surveillance operations are arguably the global Internet interception and analysis activities of the Five Eyes security alliance. Consisting of the US National Security Agency (NSA) and its signals intelligence partners in the United Kingdom, Canada, Australia, and New Zealand, this alliance is capable of intercepting and analyzing much of the world's Internet communications as they flow through major switching centres. While the public has learned a great deal from whistle-blowers such as Edward Snowden about how the American and British agencies conduct surveillance within their domestic networks, Canadians know relatively little about similar operations by Canada's own Communications Security Establishment (CSE).

Even at the best of times, secretive security agencies like CSE pose an inherent dilemma for liberal democracies. Public transparency and accountability of state institutions are fundamental tenets of democratic governance. This inevitably creates tension with the secrecy that such agencies require to be effective in their missions around national security. Central to achieving national security is upholding the democratic rights upon which the integrity of the nation ultimately depends. If citizens fear that their personal communications may be intercepted unjustifiably and feel at risk of being treated more as threats than rights holders, they are more likely to withdraw from the public sphere, withhold support for government initiatives, or even subvert them. Pursuing total secrecy is not a viable long-term option. Security agencies need to be sufficiently open about their activities to demonstrate that they respect the privacy, freedom of expression, and other rights of individuals. With an implicit duty of public candour, the onus is on them to hold themselves accountable and thereby earn public trust. Achieving an appropriate balance of secrecy and transparency is thus difficult and contingent.

Being publicly transparent is especially important when there are clear indications that an agency has violated public trust. The Snowden revelations of 2013 together with the recently legislated expansion of CSE's mandates make questioning CSE's highly secretive posture as well as its dubious surveillance practices particularly urgent. Yet when leaked documents have indicated that CSE is conducting domestic Internet surveillance comparable to that of its Five Eyes partners, its official responses generally go no further than bland assertions of legal compliance:

> CSE is prohibited by law from directing its activities at Canadians anywhere or at anyone in Canada.[1]

> Our activities are guided by a robust framework of Ministerial Directives and operational policies. CSE's activities, as well as its operational directives, policies and procedures, are reviewed by the CSE Commissioner, to ensure they are lawful.[2]

In the context of its partner agencies caught lying publicly about their domestic surveillance activities, stretching legal definitions and mandates far beyond conventional interpretations and engaging in activities that in Canada could arguably be considered unconstitutional, CSE's vague statements provide little reassurance. Without being more open and offering persuasive details, CSE invites questions about its integrity as well as whether existing laws and other regulatory measures are sufficiently robust to keep such a powerful agency within established democratic norms.

Canadians have shown a keen interest in issues of privacy, freedom of expression, and other democratic rights in relation to domestic surveillance, law enforcement, and national security. Recent legislative initiatives around lawful access (2011) and anti-terrorism (2015) triggered politically potent controversies. In 2017, Bill C-59 (*An Act respecting national security matters*)[3] raised new concerns and reinvigorated the public debate. At that time CSE exercised secret powers based on three broad mandates:

A. to acquire and use information from the global information infrastructure for the purpose of providing foreign intelligence, in accordance with Government of Canada intelligence priorities;
B. to provide advice, guidance and services to help ensure the protection of electronic information and of information infrastructures of importance to the Government of Canada;
C. to provide technical and operational assistance to federal law enforcement and security agencies in the performance of their lawful duties.[4]

Bill C-59 expanded these already formidable powers, adding two mandates that give CSE brand-new offensive and defensive cyber authorities. It also created the National Security and Intelligence Review Agency (NSIRA) and the Intelligence Commissioner. With these novel review and oversight bodies, passage of Bill C-59 in 2019 far from ended the national security debate but shifted it to a new, promising phase.

Much of the debate reasonably revolves around legal principles, democratic rights, and governance mechanisms. But in the absence of concrete insights into how they apply in practice to CSE operations, the debate remains relatively abstract. It is very difficult for people to relate CSE activities to their lived experience as individuals within a national community without knowing more about whether CSE may be intercepting their communications, and if so how, where, when, and with what legitimate justification. With CSE insistently shrouding every feature of its operations in obscurity, public dialogue regarding what it actually does and how its activities are relevant to personal Internet communications has been largely non-existent.

More specifically, CSE's meagre provision of public information about its surveillance techniques and practices hinders consideration of such essential policy questions as:

- Is mass surveillance of domestic electronic communication an appropriate means of ensuring national security and is it in the public interest?
- What is a reasonable scope for CSE secrecy?
- Where secrecy and surveillance may be justifiable, what mandates and oversight measures can ensure that authorized agencies operate this surveillance infrastructure within the civil liberties and governance norms fundamental to the integrity of Canada's "free and democratic society"?

For insight into these questions, and more generally in order for Canadians to participate meaningfully in the national security debate, a deeper understanding of CSE's practical capabilities is needed.

This chapter seeks to equip Canadians more fully for this ongoing debate.[5] The broad aim is to articulate "capability transparency" as a principle that security agencies such as CSE should be held to as a core feature of their democratic accountability. It makes the case that CSE has the capability to intercept Canadians' domestic Internet communications in bulk. It does not seek to establish this claim "beyond a reasonable doubt," as might be expected of conventional scholarly writing or in a criminal prosecution. Given the current degree of secrecy and obfuscation, this claim cannot be settled one way or another solely with publicly available information. Rather, the immediate goal is more modest – to reach the lower standard of "reasonable suspicion." This means that where evidence of mass surveillance is ambiguous, the benefit of the doubt does not go to CSE but instead can add weight to reasonable suspicion. In light of the discussion above about secretive security agencies operating within democratic norms, this mode of argumentation should be sufficient to place the burden of proof squarely on CSE, which should provide clear public evidence that either contradicts the claims here or else acknowledges their validity and justifies secretly developing such an interception capability.

The chapter begins by closely examining several classified CSE documents that the Canadian Broadcasting Corporation (CBC) published based on those that Snowden released to journalists. Together these documents strongly suggest that CSE has sought and at times deployed the capability to conduct mass surveillance of Canadians, and that it is hiding this fact from the public. To strengthen these findings and render them more concretely relatable to everyday Internet practices, a growing body of Canadian Internet routing data is examined to identify the cities and telecom carriers through which CSE would most likely conduct its interception operations. Given the highly concentrated nature of both Internet switching facilities and service providers, it is unsurprising that the routing data show that it would be feasible for CSE to capture a large proportion of Canadian communications with relatively few interception points, accessed through partnerships with just a handful of Internet service providers (ISPs).

The chapter concludes by challenging CSE's current practice of total secrecy about its domestic interception capabilities. As an alternative, it proposes a basic "capability transparency" approach. To become more accountable and earn the trust of Canadians, CSE should adopt an openness policy that appropriately and demonstrably balances legitimate secrecy needs with disclosure of basic surveillance capabilities.

Does CSE Intercept Canadians' Internet Communications in Bulk?

While the Snowden documents offer significant public insight into the domestic mass surveillance operations of the NSA and of the Government Communications Headquarters (GCHQ) in the United Kingdom, comparatively little is known about similar activities of CSE. Fewer than forty of the hundreds of Snowden documents published to date relate directly to CSE. However, a careful reading of these documents, in combination with the more abundant materials about its Five Eyes partners and a basic understanding of Internet routing technique, offers sufficient basis for the reasonable suspicion that CSE is routinely intercepting Canadians' domestic Internet communications in bulk.

The "Airport Wi-Fi" Story – No Tracking Canadians at Airports, Just "Normal Global Collection"

Among the media exposés of CSE surveillance, the CBC's 2014 report "CSEC Used Airport Wi-Fi to Track Canadian Travellers: Edward Snowden Documents" sparked the greatest controversy.[6] The classified documents behind this story are also the most revealing of the reach and intensity of the domestic Internet interception capabilities that CSE had achieved by 2012. The CBC's central claim, that the CSE could track individual Canadians, backward and forward in time, who accessed the Internet via Wi-Fi hotpots as they passed through airports, hotels, libraries, and other popular locations, was based on a CSE presentation describing a trial program in which CSE took up the challenge "to develop [a] new needle-in-a-haystack analytic."[7] This involved linking travellers' user IDs with the IP addresses locally assigned to their devices. However, this was done not by intercepting Wi-Fi signals, as the article ambiguously suggests, but through the untargeted (i.e., bulk) interception of all Internet traffic passing through the switching centres of major ISPs. Only a small fraction of this traffic would include communications originating at public Wi-Fi spots, such as at an airport. To extract the communications of individuals using the airport Wi-Fi, analysts looked for originating IP addresses that showed specific characteristic usage patterns. From this, they developed a signature profile for various kinds of public Wi-Fi hotspots and inspected all the user IDs of individuals who moved between them.

To understand what data CSE had access to from its interception operations and how it could track individuals requires a closer look at the technical characteristics of Internet communications. An IP address, such as for the router at a Wi-Fi gateway, is included in the header of every packet originating from or destined for that router. These IP addresses used for routing fit the conventional definition of communication metadata, that is, of the "shallow" kind – "information used by computer systems to identify, describe, manage or route communications across networks."[8] However, the user IDs that CSE needed for tracking individuals from one site to another are not found in packet headers used for routing but only within the packet "payload."

The CSE presentation does not mention what was used as the basis for user IDs, but almost certainly it included some combination of individualized online account names (e.g., for accessing Facebook, Yahoo, or Gmail) and "cookies." To reliably extract these IDs from Internet communication collected in bulk, as would have been needed for the experiment described in the presentation, CSE would have had to use deep packet inspection (DPI) facilities to reassemble packets into the original full messages for analysis. This is because an account name or cookie may be broken across more than one packet. In other words, to achieve this fine degree of granularity, CSE must have access to message *content,* not just the metadata needed for routing.

Once user IDs have been extracted from intercepted communications, tracking them across the various sites from which they access the Internet, and especially back in time before becoming an ID of interest, involves a further impressive but ominous computational feat. Foremost, it requires the ability to intercept *all* the Internet communications in a target region, referred to as "full-take" capture. While much traffic, such as Netflix streaming video content, needs to be filtered out immediately to avoid overloading storage facilities, it still generates vast quantities of (meta)data to be sifted through. Furthermore, this form of tracking cannot simply be conducted in real time, just by inspecting data as they flow past, but requires storage of some duration and retrospective analysis of extraordinarily large volumes of intercepted communications. And this comprehensive Internet interception was not confined to the Canadian city with the international airport. For its proof of concept test, the CSE team also "swept a modest size city ... over 2 weeks."[9]

CSE helped confirm this interpretation of its capabilities. Within days of the CBC story, the Senate Standing Committee on National Security and Defence invited then CSE head John Forster, along with other government officials, to appear before it. Especially revealing is this statement in Forster's testimony: "This [CSE surveillance] exercise involved a snapshot of historic metadata collected from the global internet. There was no data collected through any monitoring of the operations of any airport. *Just a part of our normal global collection*" (emphasis added).[10] No doubt intended to reassure Canadians that they were not tracked individually at airports, this statement should heighten concerns about the extent of domestic Internet surveillance capabilities. Here Forster confirmed that CSE's analytic experiment did not require any new data collection. It wasn't just data from specific airports, Wi-Fi hotspots, or one "modest size city" covering a period of a few weeks, but "normal," "historic" data collection, presumably captured in pursuit of some combination of CSE's three mandates prior to 2019 mentioned earlier. The repeated use of the term "global" gives the impression that the collection was conducted outside Canada, but this of course doesn't exclude portions of the Internet on Canadian soil. Indeed, as subsequent releases of Snowden documents reveal, given the need for signals intelligence on threatening foreign agents that may be within Canada (Mandate A),[11] for IT security (Mandate B), or to provide assistance to internally focused federal law enforcement (e.g., RCMP) and security agencies (e.g., CSIS) (Mandate C), CSE's interception capabilities are very likely to be well represented inside Canada and cover several cities.

The "Cyberwarfare" Story – Integrating Domestic Interception Capabilities

Just over a year after the airport Wi-Fi story, the CBC published a series of further stories based on leaked CSE documents that provided a deeper insight into its domestic interception capabilities. Two top-secret PowerPoint presentations in particular revealed that by 2011 CSE operated or planned to operate several Internet interception programs or "sensors," including within Canada – Photonic Prism and CASCADE, the cover name for the EONBLUE, INDUCTION, THIRD-EYE, and CRUCIBLE programs.[12] EONBLUE is the most prominent and relevant of these. Both it and INDUCTION, its multi-line version, are capable of "full-take" collection of Internet communications in service of CSE's three broad mandates. Typically located on the premises of telecommunications companies, EONBLUE's and INDUCTION's deep packet inspection devices process data streams at 10 gigabits per second for each tapped line. Sensors in Canada accumulate in their repositories up to 300 terabytes (3 million gigabits) of full-take then filtered interception, "equivalent to 'months' of traffic." In addition, EONBLUE sensors forward both metadata and content to CSE central facilities for further analysis and storage, such as that required in the airport Wi-Fi example.[13]

These CSE presentations also point out limitations in the agency's surveillance capabilities. The slide deck "CASCADE: Joint Cyber Sensor Architecture" notes that CSE's IT Security deployments for protecting Government of Canada systems were "currently performing full take and storage of all monitored Traffic," but experiencing "System performance issues."[14] "While both ITS/SIGINT currently leverage EONBLUE Software ... The architectures are not aligned," making it "difficult to manage [the] current sensor environment" and "costly to grow." While maintaining the full-take strategy, the solution proposed is to standardize the various sensors and through interoperability synchronize them into a "Single Interconnected Sensor Grid" that could serve all three mandates (see Figure 7.1).

Looking beyond this sensor unification to 2015, the presentation identifies several strategic priorities. Prominent among them is "Expand Our Access Footprint ... We will increase SPECIAL SOURCE [i.e., telecommunications companies] access to include all international gateways accessible from Canada." Asserting that protecting gateways, devices, and end nodes is essential but not sufficient, the presentation calls for embedding sensors throughout the domestic Internet with the following goals:

- Detect threats as they enter our national networks, not at the Gateway
- Identify Exfiltration, Command and Control, anywhere in our national networks
- The network is your defence for all infrastructure

For the CSE presenters, this means that "EONBLUE will be integrated into the Network ... [to enable] Monitoring Core Infrastructure (Special Source) extending the reach to view national infrastructure." Under the catch phrase "The Network is the Sensor," the presentation anticipates that for domestic

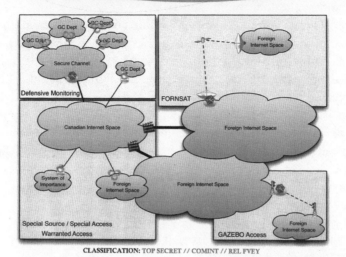

Figure 7.1 Canadian cyber sensor grid. This is a slide from a top-secret CSE presentation that shows the location of CSE's sensors in various parts of the global information infrastructure, including within the Canadian Internet Space and at entry points into Government of Canada networks. | *Source*: "CASCADE: Joint Cyber Sensor Architecture," https://snowdenarchive.cjfe. org/greenstone/collect/snowden1/index/assoc/HASH9a6d.dir/doc.pdf.

defence, "the same capabilities [as deployed for foreign signals intelligence (SIGINT) interception] will be integrated into the CORE of the [Canadian] Internet."

Some caveats are in order here about interpreting these CSE documents. These slide decks are not simply factual reports but are intended in part to impress colleagues with accomplishments and argue for more resources. And of course they are intended to accompany a verbal presentation within a wider security agency milieu to which the public has no access; they assume knowledge of obscure technical, tradecraft, and codeword terms; and they are several years old. Capabilities that may have existed at the time may have been discontinued, and new ones added. Many of the statements in the 2011 and earlier documents refer to interception capabilities in the planning stage, some of which may not have come to fruition. However, sensor performance reported in the

2012 document on which the airport Wi-Fi story was based is consistent with the operational and projected capabilities mentioned previously, and strongly suggests that CSE may have accomplished many of its goals around intercepting Internet communications within Canada.

Given CSE's clear ambitions, growing funding, and expanded collection during this recent period, it is reasonable to suspect that by 2020 CSE had successfully developed extensive domestic interception capabilities – that is, it is likely routinely intercepting within Canada, filtering, storing and analyzing Internet communications in bulk. To accomplish this, CSE would have needed the cooperation, whether willing or coerced, of major Canadian telecommunication providers in installing interception equipment. Furthermore, the data captured would go well beyond metadata, in the conventional meaning of CSE's definition above, and draw on message content. This kind of activity constitutes mass, population-wide, content-based, suspicion-less surveillance that would intrude upon the communications of millions of Canadians.

Where Might CSE Intercept Canadians' Internet Communications, and with Whose Assistance?

Building on this conclusion, that there are reasonable grounds to suspect that CSE is intercepting Internet communications in bulk throughout the Canadian Internet, the analysis turns to estimating the geographic locations of this interception. It further assesses which telecom service providers CSE would be most likely to make arrangements with for accessing the Internet infrastructure to accomplish this bulk interception.

The principal motivation for making these assessments within the broad aims of this chapter is to provide further support for the central claim – that CSE indeed has the capability to conduct such interception – by demonstrating that CSE can feasibly intercept a large fraction of Canadian Internet communications with relatively few interception points and partners. More provocatively, opening up the technical and institutional aspects of Internet surveillance to public scrutiny is an attempt to illustrate a form of capability transparency that CSE should consider adopting when reforming its total secrecy regime in the interests of becoming more accountable and trusted.

Interception at Canada's Border Cities

This investigation begins by asking where CSE would most likely place sensors to fulfill its missions to provide foreign intelligence (Mandate A) and protect national IT systems (Mandate B).[15] Most obviously, this means intercepting Internet traffic entering Canada from foreign countries and analyzing it for potential threats. Based on what the Snowden documents have revealed about

NSA and GCHQ surveillance operations, this interception is likely not done right at the border but at the first Internet exchange where the cross-border traffic is next routed to its various destinations.

An obvious way to identify the cross-border switching centres in Canada is to examine the route maps that various major telecom companies provide publicly for promoting their Internet businesses. These maps paint a consistent picture of the main fibre routes that cross the border and where they connect with the Canadian Internet backbone. Collating the information from the route maps of major Canadian carriers as well as large foreign carriers providing transit services in the Canadian market indicates that nine cities host nearly all the cross-border Internet connections: Victoria, Vancouver, Calgary, Winnipeg, Windsor, Hamilton, Toronto, Montreal, and Halifax/Dartmouth.

It would be reasonable to expect that CSE would seek to install interception devices at the main Internet switching centres in each of these cities, and thereby capture close to 100 percent of inbound Internet traffic. However, especially if resources are limited, some cities will be prioritized over others, depending on their relative volumes of traffic and which telecom providers will need to be enrolled. For this it is helpful to analyze the actual routes that data follow in practice. In the absence of public reporting of such detailed Internet traffic statistics, the IXmaps Internet mapping and analysis tool can provide useful insights.

IXmaps – An Internet Transparency Tool

As part of broader Internet transparency initiatives, the IXmaps project seeks to promote greater public understanding of Internet operations and related governance issues.[16] In particular, the IXmaps Internet mapping platform provides lay users with a means of probing hitherto obscure technical and institutional aspects of Internet routing, notably potential sites of mass surveillance.

In order to produce Internet data that reflect individual users' online activity and preferences, IXmaps takes a crowd-sourced approach to generating the traceroute data that it requires for mapping Internet routes. Traceroutes measure the paths data take across the Internet as a series of hops from one router to the next. IXmaps enables Internet users to contribute to a shared database the routes their data take when they visit websites of their choice. Based on estimates of the geographic location of the routers involved, users can then selectively map their own or others' traceroutes and check which ones pass through suspected security agency interception sites, as well as which Internet service providers carry their data en route.[17] (See Figure 7.2 for an example.)

The IXmaps database also provides a valuable research resource for estimating the most likely sites of CSE domestic Internet interception. In particular, it can

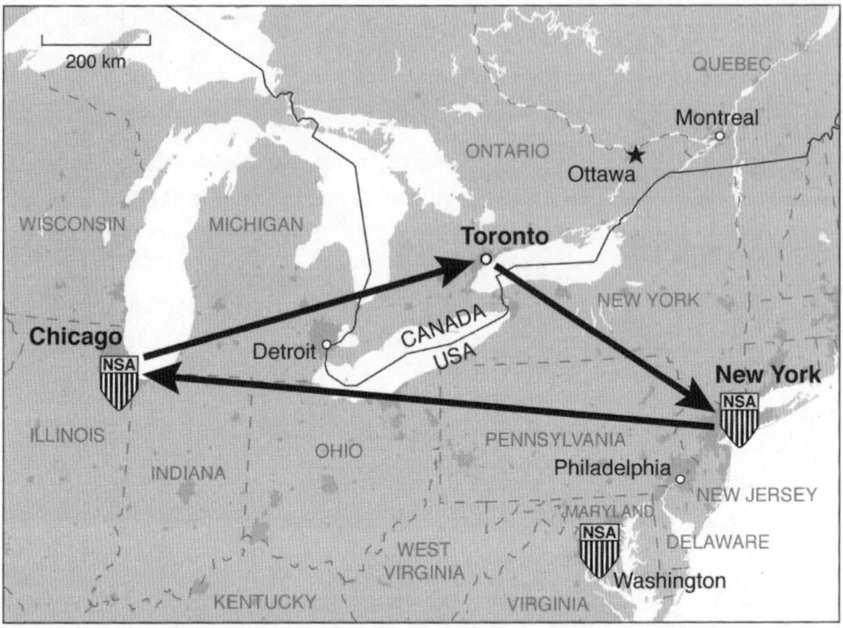

Figure 7.2 Boomerang route originating and terminating in Toronto. In this map showing southern Ontario and the northeastern United States, a line, representing a data path, is drawn from the origin in Toronto to New York City, then to Chicago, and finally to Toronto, the final destination. Both New York City and Chicago are marked with an icon indicating that they are sites of NSA surveillance. | *Source:* Adapted from Andrew Clement and Jonathan Obar, "Canadian Internet 'Boomerang' Traffic and Mass NSA Surveillance: Responding to Privacy and Network Sovereignty Challenges," in *Law, Privacy and Surveillance in Canada in the Post-Snowden Era*, edited by Michael Geist (Ottawa: University of Ottawa Press, 2015), 21. Cartography by Eric Leinberger.

show the main Internet routes entering and traversing Canada, and reveal the main network operators and their switching centres. The following analysis considers the more than 250,000 traceroutes users contributed to the database in the twelve-month period from 1 December 2016 to 30 November 2017. Of these, over 75,000 routes entered Canada. Table 7.1 shows in ranked order the top five metropolitan areas where the first router in Canada along the route is located. The percentages refer to the proportion of routes in relation to the number of routes for which a city can be identified. In other words, over 90 percent of incoming Internet routes make their first Canadian hop in just these five metropolitan areas before being routed to their ultimate destinations within Canada. It is these cities that CSE would be most likely

Table 7.1

Top border cities for Internet traffic entering Canada

City	% Inbound routes	Cumulative %
Toronto	34	34
Montreal	19	53
Vancouver	16	70
Ottawa	16	85
Calgary	7	92

Table 7.2

Top carriers bringing Internet data into Canada

Carrier	Country	% Inbound routes	Cumulative %
Hurricane Electric	USA	24	24
Bell	Canada	18	42
Cogent	USA	12	54
Peer 1	Canada	7	61
Zayo/Allstream	USA	5	66
TATA	India	5	70
Shaw	Canada	4	74
GTT	USA	2	76
Telus	Canada	2	79
Level 3	USA	2	81

to prioritize when developing interception capabilities for monitoring foreign threats.

As revealed in the documents released by Snowden and Mark Klein,[18] an earlier NSA whistle-blower, the preferred approach of signals intelligence agencies for intercepting Internet data is through arranging directly with telecom service providers to gain access to the switching equipment for installing their sensors. A similar analysis of traceroute data to that above indicates which carriers will be the most promising targets for CSE to approach. IXmaps reports the officially registered carrier for each router's IP address. Table 7.2 shows in ranked order the top ten carriers whose routers are the first encountered upon entry to Canada and that collectively account for over 80 percent of inbound traffic.

Boomerang Routing

It is important to note that within the stream of Internet data entering Canada from the United States, a significant portion (~10 percent) originated in Canada. These are known as "boomerang" routes because of their characteristic pattern of leaving Canada before returning to reach their destination. Figure 7.2 offers an example of a boomerang route that both originates and terminates in Toronto but transits via New York City and Chicago. While estimates vary, such routes constitute approximately one-quarter or more of domestic routes (Canada to Canada). Furthermore, nearly all Internet users in Canada that visit prominent Canadian websites, including those of federal and provincial governments, are likely to have their personal data transmitted in this way.[19] This is significant because CSE may have a legal basis to treat the data it intercepts in these inbound channels as foreign-based by default, which provides a lower level of protection. Only packet analysis *after* interception can indicate whether or not the data originate with someone in Canada.

Interception within the Core of the Canadian Internet

As noted above, CSE planned to integrate the same capabilities deployed for foreign SIGINT interception into "the CORE of the [Canadian] Internet" and, based on the airport Wi-Fi case, succeeded to a considerable extent. IXmaps data for routes that both originate and terminate in Canada help identify the most likely sites for sensor installation to accomplish CSE's ambition of "extending the reach [of EONBLUE] to view national infrastructure." Examining domestic Canadian Internet communications during the same period produces a similar picture. The following ten cities (metro areas), in decreasing order of approximate traffic volumes, account for over 90 percent of the hops routed through Canada's Internet core: Toronto, Vancouver, Montreal, Ottawa, Calgary, Edmonton, Winnipeg, Saskatoon, Saint John, and Thunder Bay.

Focusing on the hops by Canadian facilities-based carriers operating routers in the Internet core, over 90 percent are handled by just five carriers and their subsidiaries: Bell, Cogeco, Rogers, Shaw, and Telus. The leading foreign carriers providing transit but no retail services within Canada account for about 20 percent of the Canadian domestic hops where a carrier is known. These are Cogent, Hurricane Electric, TATA Communications, and Zayo (formerly Allstream).

Table 7.3 indicates the cities where each of the major carriers, both Canadian and foreign, predominantly operate their core Internet routers. While this analysis is partial and approximate, the pattern is clear. If CSE is routinely surveilling Canadians' Internet communications within Canada, it would be able to capture a large fraction (roughly estimated at 80 percent) of this

Table 7.3

Principal concentrations of Internet routers by metropolitan area and carrier

Carrier	Vancouver	Calgary	Edmonton	Winnipeg	Toronto	Ottawa	Montreal
Canadian							
Bell					x	x	x
Shaw	x	x	x		x		
Rogers	x				x		
Telus	x	x	x		x		
Cogeco/Peer 1	x				x		x
Foreign							
Hurricane	x	x		x	x		x
Cogent	x				x		x
Zayo	x			?	x	x	?
TATA	x				x		x

communication with relatively few, strategically positioned interception devices. The nine carriers listed in Table 7.3, as well as the cities where they handle the largest volumes of traffic, are likely to be those CSE would target first in this regard. An EONBLUE sensor installed in each of these 30 sites would represent just 15 percent of the 200 sensors that CSE had deployed globally by 2010.

Concentration of Canada's Physical Internet Infrastructure and Telecom Industry Facilitates Mass Interception

The finding that CSE could achieve effective and efficient Internet interception by arranging with a handful of carriers to access sensors in a small number of cities is not surprising given the highly concentrated character of Internet routing. The switching facilities located in relatively few centres connected by high-capacity fibre-optic trunk lines, which constitute the physical choke points of Internet routing, offer attractive sites for intercepting the greatest amount of traffic with the least effort. In this respect, the cloud metaphor for Internet operations is highly misleading. While Canada covers a vast terrain, its Internet infrastructure, like its population, is concentrated in large urban centres strung along the US border, each with its own well-established historical north-south and east-west transportation corridors along which fibre cable can be relatively easily strung.

Another factor enabling bulk interception is Canada's highly concentrated telecom industry. The top five groups – Bell, Quebecor (Videotron),

Rogers, Telus, and Shaw – account for approximately 83 percent of total industry revenues.[20] All of these are long-standing incumbents in the communications arena and depend on government licensing approval to stay in business. For years, they routinely provided individual subscriber information without a warrant when requested by law enforcement agencies, at least until the 2014 Supreme Court of Canada ruling in *R v Spencer*.[21] When lawful access legislation (Bill C-30) was introduced in 2012, Bell led a group of telecom companies that cooperated with the federal government around implementation issues while reportedly expressing no concerns about privacy, only about how they were to be compensated. These five therefore constitute "low-hanging fruit" from CSE's perspective when seeking interception "partners." Government of Canada relationships with foreign transit providers are less clear, but at least in the case of Cogent, Hurricane, and Zayo there is good reason to believe the NSA already conducts surveillance on their networks and facilitates CSE access.

The point of this analytic exercise is not to claim with certitude that CSE is intercepting Internet traffic in any particular Canadian city or that any particular carrier has agreed to become a Special Source Operation (SSO) by providing CSE with access to its network infrastructure. Rather it is to make a well-grounded case for suspecting the existence of bulk domestic Internet surveillance – one sufficiently strong to place the onus on CSE to be significantly more forthcoming with the Canadian public than it has been so far about what it is and is not doing in this respect.

Implications for CSE and Its Telecom Partners

The foregoing analysis of Snowden documents and Canadian Internet routing patterns provides reasonable grounds to suspect that:

- CSE is capable of intercepting the Internet communications of millions of Canadians within Canada.
- CSE conducts this interception at the Internet exchanges in the following cities: Calgary, Edmonton, Halifax, Hamilton, Montreal, Ottawa, Toronto, Vancouver, Victoria, Windsor, and Winnipeg.
- CSE accesses the Internet switching operations of leading facilities-based telecommunications providers such as Bell, Rogers, Shaw, Telus, and Videotron to conduct its bulk Internet interception.

These claims are not conclusive, nor are they allegations of illegal behaviour on the part of CSE or its telecommunications partners. They are, however, sufficiently well founded to call into serious question CSE's stock responses regarding possible domestic surveillance. CSE repeatedly asserts that it follows the law, but has yet to categorically deny that it intercepts Canadians' Internet communications in bulk. Since CSE is ultimately answerable to the Canadian public, the mounting evidence of domestic interception places a clear onus on CSE to be much more transparent and accountable about its Internet surveillance capabilities and activities.

In response to the airport Wi-Fi story, CSE mentioned only its foreign intelligence mandate for collecting communications, leaving open the possibility that it may have been collecting Canadian data used for the tracking experiment under another of its mandates. Such collection would be consistent with what we have seen earlier about the integration of sensors in the CASCADE program to serve multiple mandates. CSE further denied "targeting" Canadians' communication (i.e., focusing attention on already specified individuals), but what about data that is inevitably collected "incidentally" as part of full-take interception? It also denied "collection,"[22] but what does this actually mean? Is it equivalent to interception in the usual sense adopted here, or, following the NSA, does CSE regard collection as occurring only at the point that an analyst actually reads or listens to message content?[23]

An essential move for CSE to maintain the trust of Canadians would be to state plainly whether or not it has the capability to intercept Canadians' Internet communications in bulk, whether it is routinely doing so, and under what mandate(s). If CSE does intercept Canadians' communications, it would also need to be clearer about what personal communication data it captures and what measures are in place to ensure that personal and democratic rights are well protected. What content is intercepted? If "only" metadata is extracted and stored, what does this consist of? If not all message content is discarded immediately, is metadata extraction performed later?[24] While beyond the scope of this chapter, this opens a host of other questions concerning how CSE processes the data after the point of interception. Where are the data stored and for how long? What organizational entities have access to them and for what purposes? What can CSE and its partner agencies infer about individuals' lives from the metadata? What "minimization" and other protective procedures apply? While some of these questions may infringe on the sources and methods that security agencies legitimately keep secret, there should at least be some public understanding of how the boundary is drawn. Most fundamentally, Canadians need demonstrable assurance that any secrecy or other security measure is consistent with the *Canadian Charter of Rights and Freedoms* as well as established international human rights norms.[25] In particular, it should satisfy the four-part constitutional test based on *Oakes,* that any secrecy or other security measure be minimal, proportionate, necessary, and effective.[26]

Another aspect of the interception process calling for greater transparency is the role telecom carriers play in enabling CSE to access their facilities or the data flowing through them. Is it not reasonable to expect some degree of disclosure about whether ISPs are cooperating with CSE to facilitate surveillance? It would contribute to a better-informed public debate about national security to know whether Internet service providers are facilitating mass domestic surveillance. In particular, following the model of AT&T's likely cooperation with the NSA, does CSE have access to fibre-optic splitters and deep packet inspection devices installed on the premises of telecom carriers? If not, by what other means do CSE sensors access Canadians' data?

It is not surprising that CSE has been extremely reluctant to reveal anything publicly about its operational capabilities. It is typical of security-oriented organizations to treat any information they expose about themselves as potentially providing advantage to those who may pose a threat. Furthermore, CSE was founded in the wake of the Second World War and shaped by Cold War conditions for over half its life, so a deeply ingrained culture of secrecy and suspicion of outsiders is to be expected. As CSE pursues potential terrorist threats that are more difficult to distinguish within the civilian population than the foreign state agents that the agency was created to track (see Chapter 3), the tensions between secrecy and democratic rights, such as personal privacy, freedom of expression, and public accountability, are becoming more acute. This requires CSE to be more transparent in ways that imply significant organizational change.

There are undoubtedly areas of CSE activity that rightfully need to remain at the highest levels of secrecy for the agency to meet its legitimate mission. But the degree of secrecy and obscurity that it currently maintains appears to far exceed what is necessary or justified in this regard. The official response to the airport Wi-Fi story is typical of CSE's resistance to transparency about its activities: "The unauthorized disclosure of tradecraft puts our techniques at risk of being less effective when addressing threats to Canada and Canadians."[27] CSE has yet to make a substantive public case, however, that there is nothing that it can reveal about what it does without incurring risks. The Snowden revelations about NSA domestic surveillance provide abundant counter-evidence. Millions of AT&T and Verizon customers know that their ISP has enabled the NSA to intercept their personal communications, but there is no indication that this has compromised US national security. Much more obvious is that this new knowledge has fostered a vigorous and ongoing debate about the authority and legitimacy of this surveillance, even leading to modest legislative reform.

Also typical of CSE's position of secrecy is its response to a journalist reporting on its EONBLUE program: "CSE cannot comment further on operations, methods or capabilities, as that would constitute a breach of the Security of Information

Act."[28] However, the *Security of Information Act* prohibits only *unauthorized* disclosure of "special operational information," defined as that which the "Government of Canada is *taking measures to safeguard*" (emphasis added).[29] In other words, there appears to be nothing in this act to prohibit CSE from being more transparent if government policy were to change to provide the necessary authorizations and selectively declassify information for which current safeguards cannot be justified. Unfortunately, CSE's statements so far do not even acknowledge that there may be a public interest in disclosing some of its basic capabilities.

It is very difficult to see how clarifying this issue would so undermine CSE's effectiveness as to override the right and value of citizens knowing what their government is doing, and the risks that such surveillance may pose to constitutionally protected rights. Any serious adversary will already presume such surveillance, especially in light of the published Snowden documents, and adopt countermeasures. In the absence of a compelling rationale for why basic transparency about surveillance capabilities would harm the public interest, the main losers with CSE's ongoing refusal to be more forthcoming on this issue will be Canadian citizenry and democracy. This refusal fuels suspicion that CSE is hiding from public scrutiny not so much out of legitimate operational needs but to protect itself from exposing its own shortcomings, which, once revealed, will lead to embarrassment or worse. Postponing this through continued secrecy may be tempting as a short-term tactic but trust will continue to erode.

Between CSE's current total secrecy about all surveillance activities and secrecy that is demonstrably necessary for effectiveness, there is a broad middle ground of transparency and accountability worth exploring, especially related to domestic surveillance capabilities. Based on the preceding analysis, initial candidates for basic capabilities that belong in this middle ground, to be considered for public disclosure, include responses to such questions as:

- What proportion of Canadians' Internet communications can or does CSE routinely intercept?
- What types of information can CSE derive from these intercepted communications?
- What is the nature of the relationship between CSE and the telecommunications carriers it relies on for domestic interception?
- What safeguards does CSE adopt to ensure compliance with Canadian law and the Constitution?
- How operationally does CSE define the key terms that it uses in its official statements, such as metadata, content, target, collection, direct, intercept, monitor, use, surveil, personal information, private communication?
- How do these various capabilities and definitions relate specifically to CSE's former and current mandates?

This approach may be termed *capability transparency,* which intersects with and complements the approach outlined in Chapter 13, on horizontal accountability and signals intelligence.

CSE has significantly outgrown its Cold War signals intelligence agency role focusing its analogue transmission spying capabilities on a foreign state adversary (see Chapter 5). In the past two decades, it has greatly expanded its surveillance capabilities to include digital transmissions and it is now able to intercept and process enormous volumes of Internet communications, both domestically and internationally.[30] Along with the emergence of more diffuse threats under cybersecurity and anti-terrorism labels, CSE has also broadened the scope of its operations in ways that potentially implicate all Canadians and their everyday communications. However, there is little sign that it has acknowledged the new obligations that come with these transitions, especially regarding public accountability and reform of its legacy culture of adamant secrecy.[31] Good first steps in this direction would be for CSE to acknowledge its responsibilities for greater transparency and to clarify its capabilities for intercepting the Internet communications of millions of Canadians. The newly formed National Security and Intelligence Review Agency (NSIRA) and the Intelligence Commissioner offer some promise this might actually happen.

Acknowledgments

An earlier extended version of this chapter, with additional technical details and more extensive endnotes, is available at SSRN, https://ssrn.com/abstract=3206875.

I am grateful for the feedback on a preliminary presentation of this work from participants in the Security and Surveillance workshop held in Ottawa on 18–19 October 2017. In particular, my ongoing conversations with Chris Parsons as well as his "Canadian SIGINT Summaries" (https://christopher-parsons.com/writings/cse-summaries/) have provided invaluable insights into CSE activities. Bill Robinson, whose *Lux Ex Umbra* blog (https://luxexumbra.blogspot.com/) is an important resource for better public understanding of CSE, also contributed helpful feedback on an earlier draft of this chapter. The Snowden Surveillance Archive (https://snowdenarchive.cjfe.org/greenstone/cgi-bin/library.cgi), designed and built by archivists George Raine and Jillian Harkness, likewise assisted in finding and interpreting relevant Snowden documents. I also appreciate the contributions over many years of Colin McCann and other collaborators in the IXmaps (https://ixmaps.ca/) research project that provided the basis for the empirical analysis of Internet routing patterns. IXmaps research has received funding from Canada's Social Sciences and Humanities Research Council, the Office of the Privacy Commissioner of Canada, the Canadian Internet Registration Authority, and the Centre for Digital Rights. As is the norm for academic research, the views expressed here are those of the author alone and not of the funding organizations or others who have assisted in the research.

Notes

1   Communications Security Establishment (CSE), "Frequently Asked Questions" (13. Does CSE target Canadians?), 3 July 2015, https://www.cse-cst.gc.ca/en/about-apropos/faq#q13.

2 CSE, "CSE Statement re: January 30 CBC Story – January 30, 2014," 13 December 2016, https://www.cse-cst.gc.ca/en/media/media-2014-01-30.

3 Bill C-59, *An Act respecting national security matters*, 1st Sess, 42nd Parl, 2019 (assented to 21 June 2019), SC 2019, c 13.

4 Communication Security Establishment, "What We Do and Why We Do It," 1 August 2019, http://www.cse-cst.gc.ca/en/inside-interieur/what-nos.

5 See also Chapters 2, 5, 8, 13, and 14.

6 Greg Weston, "CSEC Used Airport Wi-Fi to Track Canadian Travellers: Edward Snowden Documents," *CBC News*, 31 January 2014, http://www.cbc.ca/news/politics/csec-used-airport-wi-fi-to-track-canadian-travellers-edward-snowden-documents-1.2517881. Unless otherwise indicated, quotes in this section are from this article. Since publication of the article, CSE no longer uses the acronym "CSEC."

7 CSE, "IP Profiling Analytics & Mission Impacts" (slide deck, 10 May 2012), http://www.cbc.ca/news2/pdf/airports_redacted.pdf.

8 CSE, "Metadata and Our Mandate," 1 August 2019, https://www.cse-cst.gc.ca/en/inside-interieur/metadata-metadonnees. See Chapter 14 in this book for the distinction between shallow and deep metadata.

9 The slide deck gives the impression that this was another Canadian city, but CSE denies this. See Amber Hildebrandt, "CSE Worried about How Its Use of Canadian Metadata Might Be Viewed," *CBC News*, 22 April 2015, http://www.cbc.ca/news/canada/cse-worried-about-how-its-use-of-canadian-metadata-might-be-viewed-1.3040816.

10 Laura Payton, "Spy Agencies, Prime Minister's Adviser Defend Wi-Fi Data Collection," *CBC News*, 3 February 2014, http://www.cbc.ca/news/politics/spy-agencies-prime-minister-s-adviser-defend-wi-fi-data-collection-1.2521166.

11 CSE, "What We Do and Why We Do It."

12 The principal CSE documents are "CSEC Cyber Threat Capabilities/SIGINT and ITS: An End-to-End Approach" (slide deck, October 2009), https://assets.documentcloud.org/documents/1690224/doc-6-cyber-threat-capabilities.pdf; and "CASCADE: Joint Cyber Sensor Architecture" (slide deck, 2011), https://s3.amazonaws.com/s3.documentcloud.org/documents/1690204/cascade-2011.pdf.

13 For more on CSE's sensor programs, see Chapter 13.

14 CSE, "CASCADE."

15 CSE, "What We Do and Why We Do It."

16 See http://IXmaps.ca.

17 Andrew Clement, "IXmaps – Tracking Your Personal Data through the NSA's Warrantless Wiretapping Sites," in *Proceedings of the 2013 IEEE International Symposium on Technology and Society (ISTAS)* (Toronto, 27–29 June 2013), 216–23, doi: 10.1109/ISTAS.2013.6613122.

18 Mark Klein, *Wiring Up the Big Brother Machine ... and Fighting It* (Charleston, SC: BookSurge, 2009).

19 Andrew Clement and Jonathan Obar, "Canadian Internet 'Boomerang' Traffic and Mass NSA Surveillance: Responding to Privacy and Network Sovereignty Challenges," in *Law, Privacy and Surveillance in Canada in the Post-Snowden Era*, edited by Michael Geist (Ottawa: University of Ottawa Press, 2015), 13–44. Available for free, open-access download at http://www.press.uottawa.ca/law-privacy-and-surveillance or http://hdl.handle.net/10393/32424.

20 Canadian Radio-television and Telecommunications Commission (CRTC), "Communications Monitoring Report 2017: The Communications Industry," https://crtc.gc.ca/eng/publications/reports/PolicyMonitoring/2017/cmr3.htm.

21 *R v Spencer,* 2014 SCC 43, https://scc-csc.lexum.com/scc-csc/scc-csc/en/item/14233/index.do; Alex Boutilier, "Government Agencies Seek Telecom User Data at 'Jaw-Dropping' Rates," *The Star,* 29 April 2014, http://www.thestar.com/news/canada/2014/04/29/telecoms_refuse_say_how_often_they_hand_over_customers_data.html.

22 CSE, "CSE Statement re: January 30 CBC Story": "No Canadian communications were (or are) targeted, collected or used."

23 For more discussion of the contested and ambiguous interpretations of key terms, see Chapters 2 and 8.

24 See Chapter 14 for a discussion of CSE's possible interpretation of metadata.

25 *Necessary and Proportionate: International Principles on the Application of Human Rights to Communications Surveillance,* May 2014, https://necessaryandproportionate.org/files/2016/03/04/en_principles_2014.pdf.

26 *R v Oakes,* [1986] 1 SCR 103, http://www.canlii.org/en/ca/scc/doc/1986/1986canlii46/1986canlii46.html.

27 CSE, "CSE Statement re: January 30 CBC Story."

28 Matthew Braga, "How Canadian Spies Infiltrated the Internet's Core to Watch What You Do Online," *Motherboard,* 11 February 2015, https://motherboard.vice.com/en_us/article/9ak8qa/how-canadian-spies-infiltrated-the-internets-core-to-watch-what-you-do-online.

29 *Security of Information Act,* RSC, 1985, c O-5, esp. ss. 8, 14, 16, and 17, http://laws-lois.justice.gc.ca/PDF/O-5.pdf.

30 In Chapter 6, Scott Thompson and David Lyon illuminate how CSE's expanded technical capabilities for bulk data collection have been accompanied by a significant transformation of the agency in terms of its conceptualization of data, policies, organizational structure, recruiting, and training. They conclude that the New Analytic Model's overreliance on technical skills at the expense of other disciplines may impair CSE's actual capabilities to appropriately interpret its newly available data and thereby create fresh problems.

31 Indeed, as Bill Robinson's *Lux Ex Umbra* blog post of 16 April 2018, "And Still Darker: CSE Stops Reporting Budget Breakdown," suggests, CSE appears to be heading for increased secrecy. https://luxexumbra.blogspot.ca/2018/04/and-still-darker-cse-stops-reporting.html#links.

Part 3
**Legal Challenges to Big Data Surveillance
in Canada**

Gleanings from the Security Intelligence Review Committee about the Canadian Security Intelligence Service's Bulk Data Holdings and the Bill C-59 "Solution"

Micheal Vonn

THE ISSUE OF mass surveillance by national security agencies in Canada has probably seen greater prominence in the last three years than ever before.

The national security landscape of Canada was radically altered in 2015. That year saw the enactment of an omnibus national security bill so notorious that it was generally known not by the name of the act but simply as "Bill C-51." It generated widespread public opposition. Greatly increased surveillance capacity and the potential for bulk data acquisition by national security agencies by means of new powers of "information sharing" between federal government bodies were among the most prominent of the concerns.[1]

The government that brought in Bill C-51 lost the next election. The new government (the Liberals) had supported Bill C-51, but with the promise that, if elected, they would make appropriate and needed amendments to the new law. In the run-up to the introduction of Bill C-59, which was the government's delivery of its promised changes, a series of reports and revelations brought critically important insight into the issue of Canada's national security surveillance more generally and bulk data acquisition and data analytics more specifically.

The revelations that were reported from the cache of documents disclosed in 2013 by Edward Snowden about the surveillance activities of the United States and allies brought the issue of bulk data acquisition prominently into public discourse in the Anglo-American press. More familiar terms like "mass surveillance" were generally used to discuss the practices that had been revealed, such as the secret interception of communications traffic through undersea fibre-optic cables. The question of how various countries conduct their national security intelligence, and particularly the scale, rationale, and legality of domestic spying activities, came into sharp focus in many countries, notably the United States and the United Kingdom.

By contrast, Canada's reaction to the Snowden revelations was muted. While the American and British governments had vigorous debates about domestic bulk surveillance powers after the Snowden revelations, the Canadian government was unresponsive to calls for an emergency debate on the surveillance activities of Canada's national electronic intelligence-gathering agency, the Communications Security Establishment Canada (now the Communications Security Establishment, or CSE).[2]

In 2013, the British Columbia Civil Liberties Association (BCCLA) filed a lawsuit against the CSE claiming unjustifiable infringement of rights under the *Canadian Charter of Rights and Freedoms* in respect of the statutory powers under the *National Defence Act* permitting the interception, retention, and use of private communications (including metadata) of persons in Canada as authorized by ministerial directives and authorizations.[3] As of 2020, the case has not been heard in court on its merits. In contrast, by 2019 the European Court of Human Rights had rendered a historic decision on bulk data surveillance by the British government and appeals had been filed.[4]

However, judicial and quasi-judicial initiatives, most notably those issuing from the Federal Court, have been a critical aspect of the limited transparency that has been brought to bear on Canada's intelligence agencies' bulk data acquisition. These decisions, alongside reports from oversight bodies, provide arguably the best insight available to the public on Canadian intelligence agencies' mass domestic surveillance.

The first part of this chapter discusses both what is reported and what can be gleaned from two recent annual reports by the Security Intelligence Review Committee (SIRC) about the Canadian Security Intelligence Service's (CSIS) bulk data holdings and use of big data surveillance and big data analytics. The second part outlines how Bill C-59, *An Act respecting national security matters,* proposes to address the problems identified with CSIS's bulk data program.[5]

In the fall of 2016, the Federal Court issued an explosive decision, *X (Re),* about information that had been gathered by CSIS.[6] It found that CSIS had breached its duty of candour to the court in failing, for over ten years, to alert the judges that had been issuing warrants under section 21 of the *Canadian Security Intelligence Service Act (CSIS Act)* that CSIS was indefinitely retaining information from these warrants about third parties unrelated to threats to the security of Canada.[7] The court found that CSIS was holding this information illegally. The information had been added to the data holdings of a program that appears to have since changed its name but was once known as the Operational Data Analysis Centre (ODAC). ODAC started in 2006, but CSIS had not disclosed its existence to the court. The court discovered its existence only inadvertently, through an annual report by SIRC.

SIRC is an external independent review body that conducts reviews of CSIS's activities and issues reports to Parliament. SIRC's 2015–16 annual report was particularly notable for including the findings of its first examination into the CSIS data acquisition program.[8] SIRC itself has broad authority to examine information in the control of CSIS, but its public reports on these examinations are terse, high-level, and tightly edited to protect national security. Consequently, these reports typically require some "unpacking" to extract the importance of the information provided by the review and to use it to sketch more of the picture (or of the likely picture) of CSIS activities.

SIRC's 2016 report of its first examination of the CSIS data acquisition program, in its characteristically measured, understated tone, managed to convey that CSIS's activities in this realm were essentially unmoored from law.

The Challenge of Bulk Data Acquisition for CSIS

Canadians have a much better idea about what kinds of mass surveillance activities are occurring among some of Canada's intelligence partners in the "Five Eyes" alliance than about the Canadian situation. Ongoing revelations about the activities of the US National Security Agency (NSA) and extensive information about mass surveillance in the United Kingdom disclosed through a historic legal challenge[9] have given Canadians fodder for speculation about what national security agencies in Canada might be doing, or trying to do, with respect to bulk data collection.

It is clear that the United Kingdom's security intelligence agency has been collecting vast troves of government, commercial, and telecommunications records on millions of people, but Canada's practices are still comparatively unknown. Regarding CSIS specifically, the question has been not only what bulk data it might be collecting but under what ostensible legal authority such collection could be occurring.

The *CSIS Act* sets a demanding test of "strict necessity" for data collection:

> s. 12(1) The Service shall collect, by investigation or otherwise, to the extent that it is strictly necessary, and analyse and retain information and intelligence respecting activities that may on reasonable grounds be suspected of constituting threats to the security of Canada and, in relation thereto, shall report to and advise the Government of Canada.[10]

As the 2016 SIRC annual report confirms that CSIS has a program of bulk datasets, this naturally invites the question of what kinds of bulk data collection – generally construed as "haystack hoovering" just in case any needles might be found – could meet the test for strict necessity.

Collection That Isn't Collection

One way in which CSIS justified its bulk data holdings was by claiming that the standard of strict necessity did not apply to certain classes of datasets that, on the CSIS interpretation, the agency had acquired without ever "collecting."

The 2016 SIRC report was the first public insight into the legal interpretation by CSIS that creates a category of acquired but "non-collected" datasets. As the report sets out, CSIS's bulk data holdings are used in many ways and are considered to be of two broad types. One type consists of information used mainly for verifying identification. CSIS calls these datasets "referential." The other type ("non-referential") consists of bulk data on a wide variety of individuals that are supposed to be retained only if they are determined to be relevant to an actual investigation. CSIS's position is that their referential datasets are not "collected" (and therefore not governed by section 12 of the *CSIS Act*) because they are all openly sourced and publicly available.

SIRC did not contest the principle that some "purely referential datasets would not constitute 'collection' per se" and cited the phonebook as an example of a dataset that would meet the criteria of being openly sourced and publicly available.[11] This statement by SIRC appears carefully worded. It is not a legal interpretation that is agreed to, but a "principle." Likewise, there appears to be a distinction introduced between referential and "purely referential" datasets. And SIRC does not precisely concede that some datasets held were not collected, but says rather that they were not collected "per se."

However, even assuming the validity of this "non-collected" categorization, which at least looks open to some dispute, SIRC finds that these bulk data holdings include data that are not publicly available and openly sourced, and so do not meet the criteria for inclusion in this category regardless of the category's validity.

A Threshold That Isn't a Threshold

Turning to the non-referential datasets, CSIS does not dispute that they are "collected" and thus subject to the collection threshold of "strict necessity." SIRC's findings in its audit of the non-referential datasets of CSIS are contained in a single, astonishing sentence:

> Despite this [CSIS's agreeing that section 12 of the act applied], SIRC found no evidence to indicate that CSIS had appropriately considered the threshold as required in the *CSIS Act*.[12]

Again, it is helpful to pay careful attention to the language. This was not a matter of a dispute about how the threshold was interpreted or even how an interpretation was applied in some cases. This was a case of there being no evidence to indicate that CSIS had even appropriately considered the threshold. It is arguable that this is a failure so vast and otherwise inexplicable as to suggest a contempt for the applicable legal requirements. While it is never expressly stated, the inescapable conclusion of SIRC's findings is that a very large amount (and, minus the phonebook, possibly all) of the CSIS bulk data holdings were not lawful.

SIRC issued recommendations (it has no order-making powers) that CSIS re-evaluate all its referential bulk datasets; undertake an assessment of its non-referential datasets to ensure they meet the "strictly necessary" threshold; and halt all acquisition of bulk datasets until a formal process of assessment exists to ensure that required standards are being met.[13]

Guidelines That Are (Probably) Not the Guidelines

SIRC then went beyond these recommendations and made public a proposal for guidelines to help interpret the strict necessity standard in the context of bulk data. In essence, SIRC weighed in to suggest that section 12, despite its high threshold, was not incompatible with bulk data collection and proposed criteria it implicitly advocated as principled and workable for making the necessary evaluation.

SIRC's proposal was a three-part test:

> *First,* for any bulk information, *a clear connection to a threat to the security of Canada* as defined in section 2 of the CSIS Act must be established. *Second,* it must be established that less intrusive means that would satisfy the intelligence requirements are not available as an alternative to bulk collection, consistent with the *principle of proportionality. Third,* if there is no reasonable alternative to bulk collection, CSIS needs to provide an *objective assessment of how closely connected the bulk information is to intelligence of value;* the broader the intended collection, the more strictly CSIS must establish the connection between the bulk information and the threat-related intelligence. [Emphasis added][14]

It is stated in the 2016 SIRC report's very brief "CSIS response" sidebar that CSIS agreed to review its bulk data holdings and to suspend further bulk data acquisition pending the implementation of its newly approved governance framework.[15] However, the "response" is silent as to whether that governance framework includes any of the criteria proposed by SIRC. The read-between-the-lines assessment would be that the SIRC guideline recommendations are not found in the new governance framework for bulk data acquisitions.

SIRC noted in this report that it had previously seen references in CSIS documents to "the need to validate the authority to collect and manage the risk of over-collection by confining collection to that which is 'strictly necessary.'"[16] SIRC reported that it was told that a (then) two-year-old draft of a governance framework existed but had never been finalized.[17] The CSIS "response" statement would suggest that it is this old governance document – drafted before the decision in *X (Re)* – that CSIS agreed to finalize and implement. It is difficult to understand why SIRC would be publishing its own proposal for criteria to evaluate bulk data collection in compliance with section 12 of the *CSIS Act* if no proposal was required because the CSIS governance framework already contained these criteria. The suggestion is that the governance framework does not contain guidance and interpretation of the kind proposed by SIRC.

The Program Previously Known as ODAC and Currently Known as [Redacted]

SIRC and the Federal Court have given us some inkling of what might be occurring in the data analytics program(s) of CSIS.

The 2016 SIRC report notes that

> CSIS uses bulk datasets in multiple ways. They can be used to conduct indices checks by taking information already connected to a potential threat – such as an address, phone number or citizen identification number – and using it to search for "hits" in the data. Datasets can also be used to enhance knowledge of a target by searching the data for previously undetected trends, links or patterns between and among data points. And data is used to support more focused inquiries, such as "data mining" to identify leads. Finally, SIRC was told that the data can be used to try to identify previously unknown individuals of interest by linking together types of information which have mirrored threat behaviour.

Overall, the addition of more datasets was expected to enrich CSIS's analytical capacity and enhance its ability to provide support for CSIS investigations.[18]

This indicates that CSIS uses bulk datasets in all of the following ways: to confirm identity, to learn more about targets, to detect networks and patterns, and to profile.

From *X (Re)* we learn:

> [37] In the early 2000's, the CSIS considered that the information it collected through investigations was underutilised as it was not processed through modern analytical techniques ... The ODAC was designed to be "a centre for excellence for the exploitation and analysis" of a number of databases.
>
> ...

[41] ... The present reasons should not give the impression that the Court is well informed of the [redacted] program; only very limited evidence was provided. Given that the program was still called the ODAC at the time of the application, I will use that term and not [redacted].

[42] The ODAC is a powerful program which processes metadata resulting in a product imbued with a degree of insight otherwise impossible to glean from simply looking at granular numbers. The ODAC processes and analyses [sic] data such as (but not limited) to: [redacted]. The end product is intelligence which reveals specific, intimate details on the life and environment of the persons CSIS investigates. The program is capable of drawing links between various sources and enormous amounts of data that no human being is capable of [redacted].[19]

Later, in its discussion of the arguments put forward by counsel about the privacy interests of the data at issue, specifically with respect to "information gleaned from granular metadata and from the products of its aggregation and analysis," the court noted that "the products of the CSIS's analytical methods are much more elaborate than methods or types of information at issue in prior Supreme Court of Canada cases."[20]

This signals that we are in a grey zone about what level of constitutional privacy protection the data – but, more specifically, the data processed *in this way* – requires. Whatever else this statement might be referring to, it almost certainly would be referring to national security profiling, which was cited in the 2016 SIRC report as one of the uses of the bulk data holdings.

Security of Canada Information Sharing Act in Action – Global Affairs Canada and Canada Revenue Agency

It is important to note that these revelations about CSIS's bulk data collection occurred against the backdrop of an increased ability of many government agencies to "share" their information, including entire databases, with national security agencies such as CSIS.

The *Anti-terrorism Act, 2015*[21] (also known as Bill C-51) is omnibus legislation that, among other things, created a free-standing statute called the *Security of Canada Information Sharing Act (SCISA)*.[22] SCISA allows seventeen federal government institutions to share information under a standard broader than any legal language in the Canadian national security context, namely, that the information relates to an "activity that undermines the security of Canada"[23] (versus the usual language of "threatens the security of Canada").

The Canadian government conducted a national consultation on security issues writ large in 2016 and the results of that consultation demonstrated "a great deal of concern" about *SCISA*.[24] As the consultation report noted:

> Many organizations recommended SCISA be repealed or fundamentally revised, with concerns – particularly among human rights, legal and community organizations – the current definitions of information that can and cannot be shared are too vague and that existing review mechanisms do not provide enough accountability.[25]

Despite the wide scope for expansion of information sharing under *SCISA*, SIRC reports that there has not been a large increase in the volume of sharing with CSIS. In its 2017 report, SIRC "noted that the volume of exchanges [between CSIS and other federal institutions] under SCISA has been modest."[26] There were two agencies – Global Affairs Canada (GAC) and the Canada Revenue Agency (CRA) – that did most of the *SCISA*-authorized exchanges with CSIS, and the 2017 SIRC report gives an overview of the information sharing with each.

These brief, high-level overviews provide only information subject to the limitations that all of SIRC's reporting is subject to. Even within these limits, SIRC manages to give a good indication of the formidable entanglement of legal and policy thresholds at play for information sharing and how these requirements from different bodies and in different pieces of legislation are supposed to mesh, but likely do not.

Walking through this with some of the information provided in the findings with respect to GAC, we note that CSIS and GAC share information relating to activities that undermine the security of Canada, as defined in *SCISA*. However, CSIS is allowed to "collect" information only "to the extent that it is strictly necessary,"[27] and it is not at all clear that the threshold for information to exit GAC (under *SCISA*) and the threshold for information to enter CSIS (under the *CSIS Act*) are the same thresholds, and if not, how such incompatibility is assessed and what happens as a result.

We learn from the 2017 SIRC report that CSIS and GAC signed an information-sharing agreement in 2016, but that discussions between the agencies are ongoing, in part due to disagreements on thresholds and triggers for disclosures of information (CSIS arguing for more, not less, disclosure).[28] The 2017 SIRC report also notes that a small number of disclosures of consular information were recorded as having been made under the *Privacy Act*,[29] which is perhaps unsurprising given that legal commentators have often noted that interplay between *SCISA* and the *Privacy Act* is extremely unclear.[30] Alternatively or additionally, it might signal that targeted information is being sought under one scheme and bulk data under the other.

From the 2017 report's findings about the CRA we learn that at least some of the information that is being shared by CRA with CSIS previously required a judicially authorized warrant for disclosure to CSIS, and that there is no memorandum of understanding in place with respect to information sharing of taxpayer information. In terms of aligning the thresholds for disclosing information with the thresholds for receiving information, the *Income Tax Act* was amended to allow for the disclosure of information to bodies like CSIS if "there are reasonable grounds to suspect that the information would be relevant to (i) an investigation of whether the activity of any person may constitute threats to the security of Canada as defined in section 2 of the *Canadian Security Intelligence Service Act*."[31] This is a low threshold requiring only suspicion (not belief) of information relevant (not necessarily evidence) to an investigation of whether the activity of any person may constitute threats to the security of Canada (not the activities of targeted persons, but whether any person's activities may possibly justify targeting). There does not appear to be any bar to bulk data sharing on this threshold.

Questions of Proportionality, Necessity, and Relevance

SIRC's discussion about the CRA data gives glimpses of ongoing disagreements about data access. The 2017 SIRC report notes that CSIS has had an internal directive since April 2016 that stipulates the specific internal authority that is required for CSIS to ask the CRA for taxpayer information.[32] In light of "the type of constitutional protections that have been found to apply to taxpayer information," SIRC makes a recommendation that CSIS "increase the required threshold for receiving taxpayer information from CRA" and "consider the appropriateness of seeking a Department of Justice case-by-case analysis of the proportionality of each request."[33]

These recommendations certainly signal that SIRC's view is that CSIS is over-collecting from the CRA and that this over-collection may be unconstitutional. CSIS "agreed to increase the required threshold for requesting taxpayer information from CRA," but did not agree to seek legal advice from the Department of Justice on a case-by-case basis, stating the view that its agreement to raise the threshold of the requests "better addresses the issue of proportionality from a CSIS perspective."[34]

This is an intriguing reference to "the issue of proportionality." Recall that SIRC's proposed guidelines for the "strict necessity" test incorporated a proportionality principle, specifically that "it must be established that less intrusive means that would satisfy the intelligence requirements are not available as an alternative to bulk collection."[35] It is not clear (and this chapter argues that it is unlikely) that CSIS has adopted SIRC's guidelines. Regardless of the guidelines

CSIS is operating from, however, there is an "issue of proportionality" on which CSIS has a perspective.

One aspect of the "perspective" may be on the meaning of the proportionality principle. It is possible, for example, that CSIS's perspective does not incorporate a "least intrusive means" test in its proportionality principle. CSIS may be interpreting "proportionality" along other lines, such as whether the nature of the intrusion is proportionate to the seriousness of the threat being investigated. Were that to be the case, it would effectively negate "proportionality" as a meaningful limit on data acquisition. If it is a given that national security threats are very serious, then any weighing of the data acquisition against the seriousness of the threat would tend to license very expansive acquisition.

Thus, it is important that "perspectives" on the meaning of the proportionality principle be drawn out and, where needed, challenged. At this juncture, it appears that "proportionality" is some component of the internal criteria being applied, but that the meaning of the term (that is, what is meant to be proportionate to what) may or may not align with ordinary understandings and expectations.

But proportionality is not the only principle that we can infer forms part of the criteria being used to assess the "strict necessity" test for collection. It also appears likely that there is a "relevance" criterion on the evidence that the 2017 SIRC report announces that two aspects of its ongoing work are reviewing CSIS's response to the Federal Court decision in *X (Re)* and "examining CSIS data set holdings to determine their relevance and necessity."[36]

The examinations with respect to relevance are likely of critical importance. The secret operational meaning of the standard of "relevance" in the national security context of our close ally the United States illustrates this point very graphically.

The Snowden revelations in 2013 made public a large trove of information about NSA surveillance programs. Among other outcomes, the revelations spurred a report by the US Privacy and Civil Liberties Oversight Board (PCLOB) into the NSA's telephone records program.[37]

The NSA program in question was an ongoing collection of the details of most Americans' telephone records. It did not collect the content of the calls, but did collect a rich repository of data about the calls. The ostensible authority for the program was section 215 of the *USA PATRIOT Act*, which authorizes the collection of certain business records where there are reasonable grounds to believe that the records are relevant to an authorized investigation. The US government's justification for its ongoing mass surveillance of the nation's telephone activity turned on the interpretation of "relevant."

To justify its position that the telephone records of the entire country are relevant to all its counterterrorism activities, the US government advanced two rationales. The first rationale was that the data are relevant on the basis that the NSA has analytical tools that are likely to generate investigative leads and that these tools require bulk data for analysis. Because bulk data is necessary to operate these analytical tools, the government argued that bulk data is relevant for the purposes of the statute. The second rationale was that "relevance" should have a very expansive interpretation drawing on analogous legal contexts, such as the discovery process. The PCLOB soundly rejected both rationales.

With respect to the argument that relevance is founded in analytical tools generating the necessity for bulk data, the PCLOB rejected the "elastic definition"[38] that "supplies a license for nearly unlimited governmental acquisition of other kinds of transactional information."[39]

> In the Board's view, this interpretation of the statute is circular and deprives the word "relevant" of any interpretative value. All records become relevant to an investigation under this reasoning, because the government has developed an investigative tool that functions by collecting all records to enable later searching. The implication of this reasoning is that if the government develops an effective means of search through *everything* in order to find *something*, then *everything* becomes relevant to its investigations. The word "relevant" becomes limited only by the government's technological capacity to ingest information and sift through it efficiently.[40]

The PCLOB also rejected the rationale that "relevance" has a particularized meaning in legal contexts that is more expansive than the ordinary dictionary definition of the term, arguing that while other legal processes demonstrate that "relevance" can have legitimately expansive interpretations, no definition can be so expansive as to effectively be no limit whatsoever.

> Simply put, analogous precedent does not support anything like the principle that necessity equals relevance, or that a body of records can be deemed relevant when virtually all of them are known to be unrelated to the purpose for which they are sought.
>
> ...
>
> Relevance limitations are a shield that protects against overreaching, not a sword that enables it.[41]

The disclosure of the NSA's mass surveillance of telephone records and the paradoxical interpretation of relevance that purported to authorize the program generated controversy on several fronts. The massive sweep of the program affected the privacy rights of nearly everyone in the United States. But further, it clearly demonstrated the dangers to the democratic process of secret legislative interpretations. Congressman Jim Sensenbrenner, a primary author of the *PATRIOT Act*, made public his views that the legislative intent of the impugned provision of the law had been fundamentally undermined by the administration's secret interpretations: "As I have said numerous times, I did not know the administration was using the Patriot Act for bulk collection, and neither did a majority of my colleagues."[42]

These are more than cautionary tales for Canada. The bulk data programs of CSIS are in service of data analytics of the kind that US counterparts have used to justify nearly unlimited data acquisition. Additionally, our democratic representatives may be just as in the dark as the general public as to the nature of the data acquisition that is occurring now or will occur under legislative proposals in the future. And the analytics in question can present their own problems. For example, CSIS appears to be conducting profiling of some kind, and yet there is a great deal of evidence to suggest that efficacious profiling for terrorism or serious criminality is not even possible.[43]

But the failures of democratic process run deeper still, in that Canada has never had a meaningful democratic debate about the shift from targeted surveillance to bulk data acquisition and analytics. We are currently forced to rely on the very thin disclosures provided through SIRC to piece together glimpses of the likely activities of CSIS in this respect and the promise that new legislative proposals will bring greater accountability.

Meanwhile, Bill C-59's "Solution" to the Bulk Data Controversy

The centrepiece of the response of the government to Canada's national security consultation is Bill C-59. It is a very complex, omnibus legislative scheme that, among other things, significantly revises the oversight and accountability of national security and intelligence agencies. In response to many calls for effective and integrated review, dating back many years, part one of Bill C-59 creates the National Security and Intelligence Review Agency (NSIRA). NSIRA is a kind of "super-SIRC" with a mandate that includes reviewing any activity carried out by CSIS, the Communications Security Establishment (CSE; Canada's signals intelligence agency), and other specified federal bodies whose activities relate to national security or intelligence.

The enactment of Bill C-59 means that NSIRA, rather than SIRC, has responsibility for examining CSIS's data holdings. NSIRA has the ability to make findings and recommendations that relate to legal compliance as well as the "reasonableness and necessity" of the exercise of the powers of CSIS and must report on these annually. Under Bill C-59, NSIRA is folded into a larger accountability architecture that includes, in part two of the bill, the creation of an

Intelligence Commissioner. The Intelligence Commissioner is a retired judge who, among other duties, must review several of the new powers that Bill C-59 gives to CSIS with respect to the collection of bulk data.

Part four of Bill C-59 sets out a raft of amendments to the *CSIS Act*. Particularly notable are the provisions about datasets. These changes expressly allow for datasets (defined as "a collection of information stored as an electronic record and characterized by a common subject matter")[44] to be acquired and used in a number of different ways. The two types of datasets probably most germane to Canadians and people in Canada are the "Canadian Datasets" and the "Publicly Available Datasets."

The minister of public safety can determine "classes" of Canadian Datasets that CSIS is authorized to collect. These are datasets that contain personal information that does not directly and immediately relate to activities that represent a threat to the security of Canada.[45] These datasets can be authorized for collection by CSIS if the minister concludes that the querying (conducting a specific search with respect to a person or entity for the purpose of obtaining intelligence) or exploitation (a computational analysis of one or more datasets for the purpose of obtaining intelligence that would not otherwise be apparent) of any dataset in the class could lead to results that are relevant to the performance of CSIS's duties and functions.[46] The Intelligence Commissioner reviews whether the minister's conclusions in determining what classes of datasets are authorized for collection are reasonable.

When CSIS acquires a Canadian Dataset, there is an evaluation period (ninety days) during which a designated employee must delete any information that relates to personal information that in CSIS's opinion is not relevant to the performance of its duties and functions and may be deleted without affecting the integrity of the dataset. CSIS must also delete any information in respect of which there is a reasonable expectation of privacy that relates to the physical or mental health of an individual, and delete any information subject to solicitor-client privilege.

At the end of the evaluation period, CSIS must make an application for judicial authorization to retain the Canadian Dataset. The judge may authorize the retention of the dataset if it is "likely to assist" CSIS in the performance of its duties or functions and the legislated obligations (authorized class, Intelligence Commissioner's review, etc.) have been fulfilled. A judicial authorization is valid for up to two years and the authorization can set out terms and conditions, including with regard to the querying or exploitation of the dataset or the destruction or retention of the dataset or a portion of the dataset. A judicially authorized Canadian Dataset can then be queried or exploited by CSIS "to the extent that it is strictly necessary" to assist in the performance of its functions and duties.[47] The results of these queries and exploitations may be retained if it is "strictly necessary" to assist CSIS in the performance of its duties and functions. NSIRA can review these activities.

Publicly Available Datasets are defined in the amendments to the *CSIS Act* as datasets "publicly available at the time of collection."[48] CSIS can collect a Publicly Available Dataset if it is satisfied that it is relevant to the performance of its duties and functions and is evaluated by a designated employee. CSIS can query and exploit Publicly Available Datasets and retain the results. NSIRA can review these activities.

Addressing or Excusing the Controversy of Bulk Data?

It is instructive to compare SIRC's proposals for standards and criteria applicable to bulk data collection with the scheme authorized by Bill C-59.

Recall that SIRC proposed a three-part test for the bulk data acquisition:

1 *Clear connection to a threat to the security of Canada.* A clear connection to a threat to the security of Canada as defined in section 2 of the CSIS Act must be established.

2 *No less intrusive means available.* It must be established that less intrusive means that would satisfy the intelligence requirements are not available as an alternative to bulk collection, consistent with the principle of proportionality.

3 *Objective assessment of intelligence value.* If there is no reasonable alternative to bulk collection, CSIS needs to provide an objective assessment of how closely connected the bulk information is to intelligence of value. The broader the intended collection, the more strictly CSIS must establish the connection between the bulk information and the threat-related intelligence.

Here is the "test" as set out in C-59.

For Publicly Available Datasets, the first item of concern is that what constitutes "publicly available" is not defined. In the referential databases that were reviewed by SIRC, SIRC disagreed with CSIS that it had collected datasets that were "publicly available and openly sourced." The proposed amendments to the *CSIS Act* leave the term "publicly available" undefined, leaving open a myriad of possible interpretations, some expansive enough to include hacked information that is posted to the Internet or personal information purchased from data brokers. It gives no comfort that elsewhere in C-59 we do see definitions, and when the new *Communications Security Establishment Act* uses the term "publicly available information," the definition is very expansive: "information that has been published or broadcast for public consumption, is accessible to the public on the global information infrastructure or otherwise or is available to the public on request, by subscription or by purchase."[49] C-59 allows CSIS to collect "publicly available" datasets (with no definition of that term) on the basis of a bare "relevance" standard.

As to Canadian Datasets, the personal information they contain is expressly acknowledged as *not* directly and immediately relating to activities that represent a threat to the security of Canada. The test is simply that the results of querying or exploiting this information could be relevant and that this assessment must be reasonable.

In theory, the privacy impact of this extremely wide-open funnel could be slightly moderated by the "evaluation" that requires that irrelevant personal information be deleted if this can be done without affecting the integrity of the dataset, but it is difficult to imagine how this would ever be effectively used. One of the main purposes of the dataset is for "searching the data for previously undetected trends, links of patterns between and among data points"[50] and providing "products" that "[draw] links between various sources and enormous amounts of data that no human being is capable of."[51] How could an evaluator assess whether a piece of personal information is irrelevant to a big data analytics process in which it is impossible to know the "relevance" of any particular type of data because the queries aren't set, predictable, or even decisions made by humans, in the case of analytics that use machine learning? In practice, it is likely that "the integrity of the dataset" will be cited in almost every case as the reason for keeping the dataset intact and not removing personal information.

The judicial authorization for the retention of the Canadian Datasets sounds like significant gatekeeping, but in fact it simply compounds the effect of all of the very low standards that lead up to it. Personal information that does not directly and immediately relate to activities that represent a threat to the security of Canada is allowed to be collected if it "could be relevant"; this assessment must be reasonable and the judge decides whether the dataset can be retained on the standard that it is "likely to assist."[52]

It is only at the point that the now fully approved dataset gets queried or exploited by CSIS that we see the introduction of the language that guided the entirety of SIRC's test, the language and interpretation of "strict necessity." NSIRA can review those decisions, and make findings as to reasonableness and necessity and report those findings, but NSIRA is not likely to be reporting non-compliance with the law. To be clear, it is obliged to report even possible non-compliance with the law to the attorney general, but the law as it applies to CSIS collection, use, and retention of bulk data is so broadly permissive that it is unlikely that CSIS will be exceeding such capacious boundaries with any frequency.

A "Solution" That Isn't a Solution

The matter of CSIS's unlawful bulk data collection, as revealed in *X (Re)*, relates to more than the rule of law. Certainly, it is critical to have confidence that CSIS is abiding by the law, and legislating express powers where they are needed is an obvious means of addressing some of the serious concerns that have arisen in the context of SIRC's reporting on bulk data acquisitions and the decision in *X (Re)*. However, it is arguable that what Bill C-59 contains does not even sufficiently address this component of the problem. The absence of definitions of such critically important and historically slippery and contested terms such as "publicly available" are serious invitations to the kind of "secret-law-by-secret-interpretation" problem that has historically plagued national security in many countries, Canada included.[53] Beyond the rule-of-law issue, however, there is of course the substantive issue of what kind and degree of bulk data surveillance is being authorized. Comparing the standards and criteria proposed by SIRC for bulk data collection with those contained in C-59, it is evident that the opportunity for a meaningful and measured approach to bulk data surveillance for national security purposes has been squandered. Under C-59, CSIS would have vast scope for bulk data surveillance and the national security accountability architecture, notwithstanding its importance, cannot provide an effective means of restraining excessive bulk data surveillance when the thresholds for surveillance it is empowered to enforce are shockingly low.

When the US Privacy and Civil Liberties Oversight Board undertook its assessment of the NSA's telephone records program and found that it was "not sustainable from a legal or a policy perspective,"[54] it warned against a response that would address only the legality and not the policy:

> The Board also recommends against the enactment of legislation that would merely codify the existing program or any other program that collected bulk data on such a massive scale regarding individuals with no suspected ties to terrorism or criminal activity. While new legislation could provide clear statutory authorization for a program that currently lacks a sound statutory footing, any new bulk collection program would still pose grave threats to privacy and civil liberties.[55]

In essence, this is what is occurring in Canada. While much remains opaque, the evidence suggests that the proposal for a new legal regime for bulk data acquisition will essentially codify former practices of surveillance on a massive scale regarding individuals who present no basis for any suspicion of wrongdoing. In short, Canada is addressing the process of bulk data acquisition but failing to meaningfully assess the substance of the rights violations at issue.

Notes

1 For further discussion of the security intelligence practices and agencies in Canada, see the section "Situating Security Intelligence" in the Introduction to this volume, pages 6–13.

2 Simon Davies, *A Crisis of Accountability: A Global Analysis of the Impact of the Snowden Revelations* (Privacy Surgeon, 2014), 24.

3 *Canadian Charter of Rights and Freedoms,* Part 1 of the *Constitution Act, 1982,* being Schedule B to the *Canada Act 1982* (UK), 1982, c 11, s 7; British Columbia Civil Liberties Association, Notice of Civil Claim, Supreme Court of British Columbia, 2013, http://bccla.org/wp-content/uploads/2013/10/2013-10-22-Notice-of-Civil-Claim.pdf.

4 *Big Brother Watch and others v United Kingdom (Applications nos 58170/13, 62322/14 and 24960/15)* (2018), ECHR 722; Rebecca Hill, "Bulk Surveillance Is Always Bad, Say Human Rights Orgs Appealing against Top Euro Court," *The Register,* 12 December 2018.

5 Canada, Bill C-59, *An Act respecting national security matters,* 1st Sess, 42nd Parl, 2017 (first reading 20 June 2017) [Bill C-59].

6 *X (Re),* 2016 FC 1105.

7 *Canadian Security Intelligence Service Act,* RSC 1985, c C-23 [*CSIS Act*].

8 Canada, Security Intelligence Review Committee, *Annual Report 2015–2016: Maintaining Momentum* (Ottawa: Public Works and Government Services Canada, 2016).

9 *Privacy International v Secretary of State for Foreign and Commonwealth Affairs & others,* [2017] UKIPTrib IPT_15_110_CH (UK).

10 *CSIS Act,* s 12(1).

11 Canada, Security Intelligence Review Committee, *Annual Report 2015–2016,* 24.

12 Ibid., 24.

13 Ibid., 24–25.

14 Ibid., 25.

15 Ibid.

16 Ibid., 24.

17 Ibid.

18 Ibid., 23–24.

19 *X (Re),* paras 37, 41–42.

20 Ibid., para 79.

21 *Anti-terrorism Act, 2015,* SC 2015, c 20.

22 *Security of Canada Information Sharing Act,* SC 2015, c 20, s 2 [*SCISA*]. SCISA was later amended and renamed *Security of Canada Information Disclosure Act* [*SCIDA*].

23 Ibid., s 2.

24 Public Safety Canada, *National Security Consultations: What We Learned Report* (Hill+Knowlton Strategies, 2017), 8.

25 Ibid., 4.

26 Canada, Security Intelligence Review Committee, *Annual Report 2016–2017: Accelerating Accountability* (Ottawa: Public Works and Government Services Canada, 2017), 22.

27 *CSIS Act,* s 12(1).

28 Canada, Security Intelligence Review Committee, *Annual Report 2016–2017,* 22–23.

29 *Privacy Act,* RSC 1985, c P-21.

30 Canada, Security Intelligence Review Committee, *Annual Report 2016–2017,* 23.

31 *Income Tax Act,* RSC 1985, c 1 (5th Supp), s 9(b)(i).

32 Canada, Security Intelligence Review Committee, *Annual Report 2016–2017,* 24.

33 Ibid., 24.

34 Ibid., 24–25.

35 Canada, Security Intelligence Review Committee, *Annual Report 2015–2016,* 25.

36   Canada, Security Intelligence Review Committee, *Annual Report 2016–2017*, 2.

37   Privacy and Civil Liberties Oversight Board, *Report on the Telephone Records Program Conducted under Section 215 of the USA PATRIOT Act and on the Operations of the Foreign Intelligence Surveillance Court* (2014).

38   Ibid., 62.

39   Ibid.

40   Ibid.

41   Ibid., 65.

42   Jim Sensenbrenner, "How Obama Has Abused the Patriot Act," *Los Angeles Times*, 19 August 2013.

43   See, for example, the comprehensive report on this subject from the Council of Europe: *Consultative Committee of the Convention for the Protection of Individuals with Regard to Automatic Processing of Personal Data* (Directorate General of Human Rights and Rule of Law, 27 June 2016).

44   Bill C-59, cl 92.

45   Ibid., cl 97.

46   Ibid.

47   Ibid.

48   Ibid.

49   Ibid., cl 76.

50   Canada, Security Intelligence Review Committee, *Annual Report, 2015–2016*, 23–24.

51   *X (Re)*, para 42.

52   Bill C-59, cl 97.

53   Elizabeth Goitein, *The New Era of Secret Law* (New York: Brennan Center for Justice at New York University School of Law, 2016).

54   Privacy and Civil Liberties Oversight Board, *Report on the Telephone Records Program*, 168.

55   Ibid., 169.

9

Bill C-59 and the Judicialization of Intelligence Collection

Craig Forcese

CANADA IS REMAKING its national security law through Bill C-59.[1] This law project constitutes the country's largest national security law reform since 1984 and the creation of the Canadian Security Intelligence Service (CSIS). And with its 150 pages of complicated legislative drafting, C-59 follows the pattern in other democracies of codifying once murky intelligence practices into statute.

On the cusp of being enacted in Parliament at the time of this writing, the bill responds to quandaries common to democracies in the early part of the twenty-first century. Among these questions: How broad a remit should intelligence services have to build pools of data in which to fish for threats? And how best can a liberal democracy structure its oversight and review institutions to guard against improper conduct by security and intelligence services in this new data-rich environment?

This chapter examines how Bill C-59 proposes to reshape the activities of both CSIS and the Communications Security Establishment (CSE) in fashions responding to these dilemmas. Specifically, it highlights C-59's proposed changes to CSIS's capacity to collect bulk data as part of its security intelligence mandate, and also the new oversight system proposed for CSE's foreign intelligence and cybersecurity regimes. The chapter examines the objectives motivating both sets of changes and suggests that in its architecture C-59 tries to mesh together the challenges of intelligence in a technologically sophisticated, information-rich environment with privacy protections derived from a simpler age but updated to meet new demands.

The Evolution of Intelligence Law

In 2008, then CSIS director Jim Judd raised concerns about "the judicialization of intelligence."[2] His focus was on anti-terrorism and the propensity after 9/11 for greater overlap between intelligence and police investigations. But his expression has a broader meaning, capturing a core disconnect between a covert intelligence function and the more overt culture of law and legal accountability. Intelligence needs are fluid. Law is rigid. Intelligence needs are immediate and exigent. Law can be laborious.

Nevertheless, law has inevitably encroached on intelligence. Wiretap powers constitute a case in point. In the 1950s, national security domestic intercept warrants were issued by the prime minister as an exercise of discretionary power under a Korean War–period instrument, the *Emergency Powers Act.*[3] This provided vague statutory standards for such surveillance[4] and certainly did not oblige independent judicial oversight.[5] In 1954, the deputy minister of justice issued the so-called Varcoe opinion, concluding that telephone communications could be intercepted for security purposes with a search warrant issued by a justice of the peace, under the then *Official Secrets Act.*[6] Twenty years later, in 1974, Parliament legislated the *Protection of Privacy Act of 1974,* now found as Part VI of the *Criminal Code.*[7] Part VI governs the intercept of "private communications" – in essence, any oral communication or telecommunication made or received in Canada in which the originator has a reasonable expectation of privacy.[8] Interception almost always requires advance authorization by a judge. And in 1984, Parliament followed this pattern in the *CSIS Act* and built CSIS search-and-seizure powers around a judicial warrant process, with the practical result that CSIS intercepts of private communications also require judicial preauthorization.[9]

The same year, the Supreme Court of Canada decided *Hunter v Southam,*[10] still the leading case on section 8 of the *Canadian Charter of Rights and Freedoms.* Section 8 provides, simply, that "everyone has the right to be secure against unreasonable search or seizure." Since *Hunter,* section 8 has protected against unreasonable invasions of reasonable expectations of privacy. The gold standard for a reasonable search in a criminal law context has been: "(1) prior authorization; (2) granted by a neutral and impartial arbiter capable of acting judicially; (3) based on reasonable and probable grounds to believe that an offence has been committed and there is evidence to be found at the place to be searched."[11]

Since then, in cases like the Federal Court of Appeal's decision in *Atwal,*[12] through to the Federal Court's recent decision in the *In the Matter of Islamist Terrorism* case,[13] intelligence search-and-seizure expectations (in these cases, conducted by CSIS) have been placed on a constitutional footing largely indistinguishable from that of criminal law. In the *Islamist Terrorism* case, for instance, the court pointed to the injuries that might befall an individual subject to an intelligence investigation and held that "the investigation of threats to the security of Canada ... and the collection of information or intelligence ... [is] closer in nature to the purposes of criminal legislation than to the purposes underlying the types of public welfare, regulatory or economic legislation in respect of which low expectations of privacy have been found to exist."[14]

Technological Conundrums in Information-Rich Environments

This "judicialization of intelligence" model has, to date, depended on judges serving as gatekeepers, obliging the state to show reasonable grounds to believe (or in some instances, suspect) that the information collected is tied to (in the case of the police) an offence or (in the case of CSIS) a threat to the security of Canada. Warrants also oblige a large measure of specificity, targeting individuals (or perhaps classes of individuals) who themselves are linked to these offences or threats.

Oversight has, therefore, been front-ended, in advance of the intercept or collection. And authorized information collection has then been relatively focused. To date, therefore, the judicialization model has not accommodated "bulk powers," an expression borrowed from the United Kingdom. A bulk power is one that allows intelligence agencies access to a large quantity of data, most of which is not associated with existing targets of investigation. In other words, it is the mass access to data from a population not itself suspected of threat-related activity. The commonplace example, since Edward Snowden's revelations, is Internet or telephony metadata for entire populations of communications users. But bulk powers can also involve content, and not just the metadata surrounding that content.

Bulk powers are controversial – they are the heart of the post-Snowden preoccupations. They inevitably raise new questions about privacy and, in the Canadian context, Charter rights, not least because bulk powers are irreconcilable with the requirements of classic warrants. There is no specificity. By definition, bulk powers are not targeted; they are indiscriminate.

However, whether bulk powers amount to "dragnet" or "mass" surveillance is a closely contested issue. Collection does not – and likely cannot, given resource constraints – mean real-time, persistent observation. It does mean, however, a sea of data that may then be queried and exploited. The distinction between querying of collected and archived data and a permanent, panoptic form of surveillance may be a distinction without a difference for members of the public and privacy advocates, but it is one that David Anderson, former UK Independent Reviewer of Terrorism Legislation, viewed as compelling in his 2016 report on bulk powers:

> It should be plain that the collection and retention of data in bulk does not equate to so-called "mass surveillance." Any legal system worth the name will incorporate limitations and safeguards designed precisely to ensure that access to stores of sensitive data (whether held by the Government or by communications service providers [CSPs]) is not given on an indiscriminate or unjustified basis.[15]

Put another way, surveillance means "watching," and not "potential watching." And "potential" is controlled by safeguards that mean collection does not morph seamlessly into watching. This is the philosophy that animated the United

Kingdom's 2016 *Investigatory Powers Act (IPA)*,[16] and now is reflected also in Bill C-59. Under the *IPA,* the world of bulk powers can be divided into bulk interception, bulk equipment interference, bulk acquisition, and bulk personal datasets. Canada's Bill C-59 addresses issues relating to bulk interception and bulk personal datasets. The bill does two things of note: for both CSE and CSIS, it superimposes new quasi-judicial controls on collection of certain sorts of information. For CSIS, it also creates judicial controls on retention, exploitation, and querying of at least some sorts of information.

Bulk Interception by CSE

Bulk interception is what it sounds like: the collection of transiting communications passing through communications providers or otherwise through the ether. Canadian law permits bulk collection by the Communications Security Establishment. Among other things, CSE is Canada's "signals intelligence" service, charged with acquiring foreign intelligence from the "global information infrastructure," that is, electronic emissions and now also information from other technology networks such as the Internet. It also has a cybersecurity mandate: "to provide advice, guidance and services to help ensure the protection of electronic information and of information infrastructures of importance to the Government of Canada."[17]

In conducting its foreign intelligence and cybersecurity function, CSE is to cast its eyes outward, beyond Canada: it cannot direct its activities at Canadians or any person in Canada. It also must take steps to protect the privacy of Canadians.[18] This privacy requirement responds to a technical problem: the inevitability of *incidental* acquisition of Canadian information. In acquiring information from the global information infrastructure or performing its cybersecurity role, CSE cannot know in advance whether Canadian or Canadian-origin data will be swept within its acquisition activities.

Under the current *National Defence Act,* therefore, CSE may (and does) obtain special "ministerial authorizations" under which it might inadvertently acquire Canadian "private communications" within the meaning of Part VI of the *Criminal Code* – essentially "telecommunications" with a nexus to Canada.[19] There are presently three authorizations for foreign intelligence and one for cybersecurity. The authorizations are broad – involving classes of activities and not individual activities.

The current rules suffer from two key problems, however. First, technology has evolved considerably since the original enactment of CSE's powers in 2001. Now, the focus is on metadata – the information that surrounds a communication, such as email addresses, routing information, duration and place of cellular calls, and the like. The government's view has been that these metadata are not a component of a private communication for which a ministerial authorization must be sought – a conclusion dependent on a narrow reading of the definition of "telecommunication" in the *Interpretation Act*.[20]

Second, whether or not CSE obtains a ministerial authorization, there are evident constitutional issues under section 8 of the Charter, ones anticipated many years ago but never resolved.[21] As noted, section 8 usually means that authorities may interfere with a reasonable expectation of privacy only under a warrant authorized in advance by an independent judicial officer, that is, someone able to act judicially.[22] As suggested, wiretaps of communications must be authorized by judicial warrant in almost all circumstances.

Whatever else he or she may be, the minister of defence is not an independent judicial officer, and yet under the current act it is his or her authorization that permits CSE's collection of private communication, a form of data in which the originator has, by definition, a reasonable expectation of privacy. For their part, metadata do not include the content of a communication. But pieced together (and even alone) they can be remarkably revealing of a person's habits, beliefs, and conduct. Metadata are often information in which there is a reasonable expectation of privacy, especially when compiled as a mosaic.[23] This conclusion is supported, if not quite decided, by the Supreme Court of Canada's decision in *R v Spencer*, holding that even the most innocuous of nameplate information tied to a digital trail – subscriber information associated with an IP address – attracts constitutional protection.[24]

The risk, therefore, is that CSE now acquires information that enjoys constitutional protection without going through the independent judicial officer process (or anything approximating the process) that the Constitution requires before the state acquires this information. That is, at core, the issue in a constitutional challenge brought by the British Columbia Civil Liberties Association (BCCLA) to CSE's law and metadata practices.[25]

The fact that CSE's acquisition of private communications and metadata is incidental to its outward-looking mandates should not matter, since the collection of at least some constitutionally protected information is *foreseeable* and *inevitable*. Canada's constitutional standards for search and seizure do not say, "You are protected against unreasonable search and seizures, except when the search and seizure is simply a predictable, foreseen accident stemming from other activities." Put another way, the fact that information in which Canadians have a reasonable expectation of privacy is incidentally but foreseeably (rather than intentionally) collected by the state should not abrogate the constitutional right (although I accept it may shape the precise protections that the Charter will then require; see below). As the government itself has now acknowledged, "because the authority to acquire private information through the GII [global information infrastructure] has the potential to interfere with privacy interests, it may engage section 8."[26]

Bill C-59 and a *Hunter* Approximation

Bill C-59 responds to these constitutional concerns primarily through a new system of quasi-judicial preauthorizations for CSE's recrafted foreign intelligence and cybersecurity mandates. Whereas under the current system, the defence minister alone issues an authorization, C-59 anticipates a quasi-judicial intelligence commissioner (IC) who will review the ministerial authorization before its execution. To be clear: this is not a warrant. It will lack specificity. It will be issued for classes of activities, not specific activities or operations. It is review of the reasonableness of a ministerial authorization, not the more hands-on warrant process. Moreover, the intelligence commissioner is not a sitting judge but rather a former judge occupying an administrative office at arm's length from executive government, and is not clothed with as robust independence as a court. Will this meet *Hunter's* section 8 standards? Some have argued it will not.[27] I am inclined to suggest it will pass constitutional muster, because the warrant cookie cutter cannot possibly apply to a form of bulk intercept in which intercept of section 8 rights-bearer communications is entirely incidental, and not targeted.

From past cases, we know that section 8 does not require an actual judge – but instead a person capable of acting judicially.[28] Nor does it oblige one-size-fits-all warrants for all forms of search and seizure. As the Federal Court of Appeal decided (in applying different criteria to a CSIS warrant than to a police wiretap): "To conclude ... a different standard should apply where national security is involved *is not necessarily to apply a lower standard but rather one which takes account of reality*" (emphasis added).[29] And so in that case, it made no sense to require CSIS to show that it was investigating a criminal offence – its mandate is to investigate threats to the security of Canada. This suggests that there is at least some flexibility in design, so long as we preserve the core essentials of the section 8 jurisprudence: advance authorization by an independent judicial officer.

CSIS Datasets and Bulk Personal Datasets

Turning to domestic-facing bulk powers, Bill C-59 creates new bulk powers for CSIS. Under the bill, CSIS would be empowered to collect bulk personal datasets. The British understanding of this expression also describes what is at issue in Canada:

> A bulk personal dataset includes personal data relating to a number of individuals, and the nature of that set is such that the majority of individuals contained

within it are not, and are unlikely to become, of interest to the intelligence services in the exercise of their statutory functions. Typically these datasets are very large, and of a size which means they cannot be processed manually.[30]

The C-59 approach to bulk personal datasets is a response, in part, to the Federal Court's 2016 decision on what was known as "ODAC."[31] But it also responds to a broader concern about the ambit of CSIS's threat investigation mandate.[32] That mandate is anchored in section 12 of the *CSIS Act*.

Under its section 12 mandate, CSIS collects, to the extent it is strictly necessary, and analyzes and retains information and intelligence on activities it has reasonable grounds to suspect constitute threats to the security of Canada. This passage has several "magic words": "to the extent that it is strictly necessary"; "reasonable grounds to suspect"; and "threats to the security of Canada." "Threats to the security of Canada" is the only passage defined in the *CSIS Act* (in section 2). "Reasonable grounds to suspect" has a generally well-understood meaning: "suspects on reasonable grounds" is a suspicion based on objectively articulable grounds that may be lower in quantity or content than the requirement of reasonable belief, but must be more than a subjective hunch.[33] It amounts to a *possibility* the threat exists, based on cogent evidence (and not simply a hunch).

Under section 12, CSIS commences an investigation on this standard. But where the means of that collection are sufficiently intrusive to trigger section 8 of the Charter or the Part VI *Criminal Code* prohibition against unauthorized intercept of private communications (for instance, a wiretap), it must get a Federal Court warrant. A judge will issue a warrant only if persuaded that CSIS has reasonable grounds to "believe" that it is required to investigate threats to the security of Canada.

"Reasonable grounds to believe" is a higher standard than the reasonable grounds to suspect standard that must be met for CSIS to begin an information collection investigation under section 12. Sometimes called "reasonable and probable grounds" in the constitutional case law, reasonable grounds to believe is less demanding than the criminal trial standard of "beyond a reasonable doubt." Instead, it is defined as a "credibly-based probability" or "reasonable probability."[34]

CSIS obtains warrants in a closed-court (i.e., secret) process in which only the government side is represented. The warrants can, and often do, impose conditions on CSIS investigations. There are templates for standard warrant applications. These templates are occasionally updated, a process that requires CSIS to apply to the Federal Court. The 2006 ODAC case came about through a belated updating process.

Operational Data Analysis Centre (ODAC)

CSIS collects much data in its section 12 investigations, including those aspects of the investigation conducted pursuant to a warrant. Not unreasonably, it wants to keep these data to pool them in a manner that it can then search to further investigations in the future. And so, it created ODAC in 2006. It did not tell the Federal Court about ODAC, at least not in any real concrete manner.

This is important because ODAC was pooling information collected via warrant. And that information included not only content and metadata produced by an investigative target's own communications (the collection of which was authorized by warrant), but also so-called associated data. As the court defined it, associated data are data "collected through the operation of the warrants from which the content was assessed as unrelated to threats and of no use to an investigation, prosecution, national defence, or international affairs." Presumably a lot of these would-be data from third parties – that is, communication-related information involving non-targets – are swept into the CSIS surveillance net. For telephony, this might include the speech of the person on the other end of a conversation, or the accompanying metadata (e.g., telephone number, geolocation of a cellphone, etc.). For email, this could be content and metadata totally unrelated to the target's communication. Email travels in packets across the Internet and packets bundle unrelated segments of individual emails. And so, intercepting a target's emails generally means intercepting all the packets, and the accompanying content and metadata of other people's communications bundled with them.

CSIS chose, in the ODAC, to retain some of this "associated data," specifically, the metadata, although not the actual content of the communication. The retention of these metadata raised a legal issue. For one thing, as noted above, it now seems certain that at least some metadata are protected by section 8 of the Charter. In addition, the *CSIS Act* determines what CSIS can do with the information it collects.

In the 2016 ODAC case, the court did not reach the section 8 issue, although it acknowledged that the matter had been argued before it. Instead it focused on the *CSIS Act* issue. And there, the key consideration was whether CSIS can retain the information it collects through its investigations. On this point, there are now two answers.

First, as per the Supreme Court of Canada's holdings in *Charkaoui II*,[35] CSIS has a constitutional duty to retain information related to its targets, or to threats to the security of Canada. As the Federal Court summarized this rule: "information that is indeed linked to threats to the security of Canada or to the target of a warrant must be retained in its original state by the CSIS to comply with the protected rights under section 7 of the Charter."[36] Or in lay terms: CSIS cannot destroy information collected on targets/threats, because people implicated in those threats may subsequently be subject to legal proceedings that oblige full government disclosure allowing for a fair trial. And if CSIS has destroyed the original collected information and (the argument would go) simply kept a cherry-picking summary, then no fair trial can be had.

Second, this *Charkaoui II* rule does not apply to information unrelated to the target or threats – that is, associated data. *Charkaoui II* was not about associated data, and so the Federal Court looked to the *CSIS Act* and concluded as follows: associated data, by definition, is non-threat-related. It is therefore not something that is "strictly necessary" to the investigation of threats to the security of Canada. Thus, collecting it is something CSIS should not be in the business of doing. Technology means it cannot help but collect it while undertaking its bona fide "strictly necessary" collection of threat-related information. And so, court warrants allow for this incidental collection. But authorizing incidental collection does not bless indefinite retention. And indeed, indefinite retention is not something any court could authorize without effectively usurping the "strictly necessary" standard found in section 12. And so CSIS retention of the associated metadata was illegal, because of the way the *CSIS Act* was drafted.

The Policy Issue

In this manner, the present *CSIS Act* ties information collection, retention, and analysis to a narrow band of threat investigations. The analogy is a fishing craft that must use a sonar with limited range and scope. Bill C-59 proposes relaxing these limitations and permitting the netting of more data, of a sort that would exceed the "strictly necessary" standard.

A spy service fishing in more ocean is, in some eyes, the stuff of Big Brother and nightmares. On the other hand, an intelligence service that cannot have access to the ocean when performing its functions is also not likely to perform its functions very well. And there is a lot of ocean out there in the digital era. As the government has urged:

> Today's threats to Canada's national security are fast, complex and dynamic, and threat actors are highly connected and mobile. The ease of movement across international borders and spread of social media networks and modern communications technology can be used by individuals and groups seeking to harm Canada. This creates some very real challenges for CSIS.[37]

The dilemma lies in reconciling oceans full of data generated by innocents with the intelligence function of clearing the fog of uncertainty and revealing not just the known threats but also the unknown threats.

Bill C-59 proposes its solution: judicializing a more sweeping fish-detecting sonar through a dataset system. Datasets are currently defined as collections of "information stored as an electronic record and characterized by a common subject matter." More importantly, this is information that CSIS would not be able to collect, retain, or analyze under its regular mandates because, for instance, it will not know they contain information significant to a threat investigation without searching them. Under C-59, new rules allow for the collection of publicly available, foreign, and Canadian datasets, subject to an array of checks and balances that vary in strictness. The most robust accountability regime concerns Canadian datasets. Here, the minister of public safety and the intelligence commissioner may approve collection of "classes" of Canadian datasets – datasets primarily comprising Canadian information. Once ingested, the bill then authorizes limited, firewalled vetting by CSIS to assess the usefulness of the dataset. And then any subsequent retention for actual use must be approved by the Federal Court, which is empowered to impose conditions on that subsequent use. Querying and exploitation of the retained dataset must thereafter generally be done with an eye to CSIS's mandates – for example, only where strictly necessary in performance of CSIS's section 12 mandate.

The system is enormously complex, sparking skepticism among those who look askance at the intrusion of law into intelligence. Privacy advocates, for their part, may question any expansion of the state's ability to collect personal information. The system does constitute a quid pro quo, however: CSIS's traditional section 12 constraints are loosened to the extent that it may consume a broader ocean of data, but retention (at least for Canadian datasets) requires judicial supervision.[38] This system recognizes that privacy interests extend beyond the point of collection and include retention and use. In so doing, it short-circuits inevitable frontier section 8 issues; namely, does section 8 attach to the big data analysis of information, the individual bits of which trigger no reasonable expectation of privacy (and thus, the initial collection of which attracts no constitutional protection)? C-59 anticipates (and pre-empts) this issue by superimposing independent judicial authorization guiding and conditioning the big data analysis.

By bundling the issue of collection, retention, and use of electronic information in the hands of CSIS into a specialized model, C-59 creates a system much more demanding than the now antiquated rules found in the federal *Privacy Act*. The latter includes no independent, direct oversight of personal type of information collected, retained, and used by the federal government, instead depending on periodic review audits by the privacy commissioner.

The C-59 system compares favourably, therefore, with other controls on government use of information. That said, I have one lingering doubt about this constitution proofing of CSIS dataset retention. The Federal Court retention authorization (and the IC approval of dataset classes) is limited to "Canadian datasets." Datasets primarily comprising information on foreign individuals outside Canada are processed under a separate regime, in which the IC decides the retention issue. Since Charter privacy rights are largely geographic in scope, this more relaxed system is probably justifiable. However, a third class of datasets comprises personal information "publicly available at the time of collection." Publicly available datasets are not subject to any independent oversight regime.

It matters, therefore, into which bucket information is placed. Some information may be publicly available (e.g., hacked private information dumped on the Internet) but still raises considerable privacy implications. CSIS has indicated before Parliament that it will not treat hacked information as publicly available. This is a policy decision, however, not one required by law. Should CSIS adopt an underinclusive policy that steers information about which a Canadian still has a reasonable expectation of privacy into the publicly available bucket, the constitutionality of this practice would be suspect. This would then become a high-risk practice, and raise the prospect of an ODAC controversy rerun.

The obvious solution would be to amend Bill C-59 to define "publicly available" as excluding "information in which a Canadian or person in Canada retains a reasonable expectation of privacy." This would have the effect of steering such information into the "Canadian dataset" bucket, with its more constitutionally robust oversight system. Since that amendment was not made in Parliament, the minister of public safety should, at minimum, issue a ministerial direction with the same effect – and ensure that this direction and any of its successors are public to create confidence in otherwise opaque internal procedures within CSIS.

Conclusion

Privacy is among the least absolute rights in international and Canadian human rights law. It has always been about equilibrium, from its inception as a common law concept in the eighteenth century. Balancing has depended, in the Canadian law tradition, on advance oversight by judicial officers. In relation to CSE, changes in technology have placed that agency out of alignment with this expectation. Bill C-59 tries to restore a more traditional pattern, albeit in circumstances where a classic judicial warrant model would prove unworkable.

Meanwhile, CSIS has laboured with an act designed for an analogue period. It has become an intelligence service largely incapable of fishing in an electronic sea. The challenge is to permit reasonable fishing but not dragnetting. Bill C-59 attempts to strike this balance by superimposing a judge, not to police CSIS's dataset fishing net but rather to determine what information captured within the net may be retained and analyzed. We are right to be wary of such a system, since it depends on close adherence to a complicated set of checks and balances. On the other hand, those checks and balances cannot become so burdensome that intelligence services are left to obtain, essentially, a warrant to obtain a warrant.

Put another way, C-59 seeks balance. Not everyone will agree, but in my view (and subject to my doubts about publicly available datasets), C-59 succeeds reasonably well in reconciling the "nightwatchman" role of the state's security services with the individual's right to be left alone.

Notes

1 Canada, Bill C-59, *An Act respecting national security matters*, 1st Sess, 42nd Parl, 2017, http://www.parl.ca/DocumentViewer/en/42-1/bill/C-59/first-reading. This chapter deals with C-59 as it existed at the time of writing: after first reading in the House of Commons.
2 Canadian Security Intelligence Service (CSIS), "Remarks by Jim Judd, Director of CSIS, at the Global Futures Forum Conference in Vancouver," 15 April 2008, Internet Archive, https://web.archive.org/web/20081012174022/http://www.csis-scrs.gc.ca:80/nwsrm/spchs/spch15042008-eng.asp.
3 RSC 1952, c 96.
4 Under the act, the minister of justice could require a communications agency to produce any communication "that may be prejudicial to or may be used for purposes that are prejudicial to the security or defence of Canada." David C. McDonald, "Electronic Surveillance – Security Service and C.I.B.," in *Reports of the Commission of Inquiry Concerning Certain Activities of the Royal Canadian Mounted Police* (Ottawa: Privy Council Office, 1981), vol 2-1, 158, http://publications.gc.ca/collections/collection_2014/bcp-pco/CP32-37-1981-2-1-2-eng.pdf.
5 The document is archived as Canada, "Privy Council Wiretap Order (St-Laurent Government)" (unpublished document, 1951), http://secretlaw.omeka.net/items/show/69, and was obtained by Dennis Molinaro under the *Access to Information Act*.
6 McDonald, *Reports of the Commission of Inquiry*, vol 2-1, 158.
7 RSC, 1985, c C-46.
8 Ibid., s 183.
9 RSC, 1985, c C-23, s 21.
10 [1984] 2 SCR 145.
11 Justice Canada, "Section 8 – Search and Seizure," https://www.justice.gc.ca/eng/csj-sjc/rfc-dlc/ccrf-ccdl/check/art8.html.
12 *Atwal v Canada*, [1988] 1 FC 107 (FCA).
13 2017 FC 1047.
14 Ibid., para 171.
15 David Anderson, *Report of the Bulk Powers Review* (London: Williams Lea Group, 2016), para 1.9, https://terrorismlegislationreviewer.independent.gov.uk/wp-content/uploads/2016/08/Bulk-Powers-Review-final-report.pdf.
16 2016, c 25.
17 *National Defence Act*, RSC, 1985, c N-5, ss 274.61 and 273.64(1) [*NDA*]. These mandates are preserved in Bill C-59, Part 3, *Communications Security Establishment Act* (*CSE Act*), ss 2, 16, 17, and 18 [*CSE Act*].
18 *NDA*, s 273.64(2); *CSE Act*, ss 17, 18, 23, and 25.

19 *NDA,* ss 273.65, 273.61; *Criminal Code,* RSC 1985, c C-46, s 183.
20 *Interpretation Act,* RSC, 1985 c I-21, s 35 (defining "telecommunications" as "the emission, transmission or reception of *signs, signals,* writing, images, sounds or *intelligence of any nature* by any wire, cable, radio, optical or other electromagnetic system, or by any similar technical system" [emphasis added]).
21 See, e.g., Stanley A. Cohen, *Privacy, Crime and Terror: Legal Rights and Security in a Time of Peril* (Markham, ON: LexisNexis Butterworths, 2005), 232.
22 *Hunter v Southam,* [1984] 2 SCR 145, 162.
23 For a fuller discussion of metadata and privacy rules, see Craig Forcese, "Law, Logarithms and Liberties: Legal Issues Arising from CSEC's Metadata Collection Initiatives," in *Law, Privacy and Surveillance in Canada in the Post-Snowden Era,* edited by Michael Geist (Ottawa: University of Ottawa Press, 2015), https://ssrn.com/abstract=2436615.
24 2014 SCC 43.
25 See BCCLA, "BCCLA v. CSEC: Stop Illegal Spying," 23 May 2014, https://bccla.org/our_work/stop-illegal-spying/. (In the interest of full disclosure: on behalf of BCCLA, I provided factual background information for use by the court in that proceeding.)
26 Justice Canada, "Charter Statement – Bill C-59: *An Act respecting national security matters,*" 20 June 2017, http://www.justice.gc.ca/eng/csj-sjc/pl/charter-charte/ns-sn.html.
27 See, e.g., Christopher Parsons, Lex Gill, Tamir Israel, Bill Robinson, and Ronald Deibert, "Analysis of the *Communications Security Establishment Act* and Related Provisions in Bill C-59 (*An Act respecting national security matters*), First Reading (December 18, 2017) (Citizen Lab/Canadian Internet Policy and Public Interest Clinic report, December 2017), 18, https://citizenlab.ca/wp-content/uploads/2018/01/C-59-Analysis-1.0.pdf.
28 *Hunter v Southam,* 162.
29 *Atwal v Canada,* para 35.
30 United Kingdom, Home Office, *Security and Intelligence Agencies' Retention and Use of Bulk Personal Datasets: Draft Code of Practice* (2016), para 2.2, https://www.gov.uk/government/uploads/system/uploads/attachment_data/file/557860/IP_Bill_-_Draft_BPD_code_of_practice.pdf.
31 *X (Re),* 2016 FC 1105.
32 See CSIS, "Amendments to the CSIS Act – Data Analytics," 20 June 2017, https://www.canada.ca/en/security-intelligence-service/news/2017/06/amendments_to_thecsisact-dataanalytics.html. ("When it was written, the *CSIS Act* could not have anticipated the technological changes of the last 30 years. The Federal Court acknowledged the age of the *CSIS Act* and that it may not be keeping pace with changing technology.")
33 *R v Kang-Brown,* 2008 SCC 18.
34 *R v Debot,* [1989] 2 SCR 1140. In the administrative law context, courts have described it as a bona fide belief of a serious possibility, based on credible evidence. *Chiau v Canada (Minister of Citizenship and Immigration),* [2001] 2 FC 297 (FCA).
35 *Charkaoui v Canada (Citizenship and Immigration),* 2008 SCC 38.
36 *X (Re),* para 195.
37 CSIS, "Amendments to the CSIS Act."
38 The Privacy Commissioner makes (essentially) this same point, and offered no recommendations for changes to the CSIS dataset regime in Bill C-59. See Canada, Office of the Privacy Commissioner of Canada, "Brief to the Standing Committee on Public Safety and National Security," 5 March 2018, 12.

10

The Challenges Facing Canadian Police in Making Use of Big Data Analytics

Carrie B. Sanders and Janet Chan

ADVANCED INFORMATION TECHNOLOGY is playing a progressively more important role in policing and security. This is in part driven by the growing complexity of the crime and security environment, and partly by the lure of new technology such as big data technology, which promises greater efficiency and innovation. The advent of big data technologies appears to be a continuation of a trend to combine statistical thinking and communication technology to present "risk data."[1] As Lucia Zedner points out, the impact of 9/11 and the changing and volatile nature of organized crime have put pressure on governments to "think and act pre-emptively," leading to an acceleration of the "trajectory towards anticipatory endeavor, risk assessment and intelligence gathering."[2] Big data technology has been increasingly deployed by policing and national security agencies to detect and/or prevent complex crime such as terrorism and organized crime.[3] For example, the apprehension and arrest of the 2013 attempted Via Rail bombers in Ontario not only illustrate the heightened role information, data, and analytics play in public safety decision making but also demonstrate the blurring boundaries between policing and national security intelligence practices.[4] Information and intelligence sharing among the RCMP, the Canadian Security Intelligence Service (CSIS), municipal and provincial police forces in Ontario and Quebec, the US Department of Homeland Security, and the FBI led to the early apprehension of the attempted Via Rail bombers. Indeed, Patrick Walsh's analysis of intelligence frameworks across the "Five Eyes" intelligence enterprises (United States, Britain, Australia, Canada, and New Zealand) demonstrates how intelligence frameworks are "evolving post 9/11" and concludes that "each framework ... demonstrates the blurring between what has been traditionally thought of as a 'policing and national security intelligence.'"[6]

The pursuit of security within policing is clearly evident in the adoption of new policing initiatives – such as intelligence-led and predictive policing – that rely upon "the collection and analysis of information to produce an intelligence end product designed to inform law enforcement decision making at both the tactical and strategic levels."[6] As Greg Ridgeway argues, "the demand for intelligence on offenders incentivized the creation of information technology that could feed the demand ... At the same time, with ready access to information, police have an opportunity to make links and connections that used to be more labor intensive."[7]

New technology such as big data analytics promises opportunities for police services to work more efficiently and effectively by identifying and predicting crime patterns in large datasets with the hope that such practices will enable "the opportunity to enter the decision cycle of [their] ... adversaries' [sic] in order to prevent and disrupt crime."[8] For example, the Vancouver Police Department has implemented a "city-wide 'Predictive Policing' system that uses machine learning to prevent break-ins by predicting where they will occur before they happen – the first of its kind in Canada."[9] The system is said to have 80 percent accuracy in directing officers to locations of break-ins.[10] While Vancouver is the first service in Canada to implement predictive policing software, other services are implementing technologies that enable them to collect and store large sets of data.[11] For example, Calgary Police Services, the Royal Canadian Military Police, the Ontario Provincial Police, and Winnipeg Police Services have all implemented Mobile Device Identifier technology (which mimics cellular towers) that enables them to intercept cellphone data.[12] Such examples demonstrate how big data and data analytics are being integrated in Canadian police services.

At present, the use of big data in policing has been largely limited to the collection and storage of DNA information, mass surveillance, and predictive policing.[13] While there is a lot of speculation about the possibilities (both good and bad) of these technologies, there is little empirical research available on how big data is used and experienced in policing.[14] Ridgeway identifies specific applications of big data in American policing, such as pushing real-time information to officers, tracking police locations, performance measurement, and predictive policing, but like others, notes that the "evidence so far is mixed on whether police can effectively use big data."[15] To date, much of the available literature on big data and policing is focused on predictive policing and originates in the United States, United Kingdom, and Australia – where police intelligence frameworks, policies, and practices differ.[16] For example, the United Kingdom has a National Intelligence Model (NIM) that provides police services with a standardized approach for gathering and analyzing intelligence for informing strategic and tactical decision making.[17] Canada, however, does not have a standardized model or approach to intelligence work, so significantly less is known about the use of technology and data science in the Canadian context.

This chapter presents empirical data on the challenges facing Canadian police in making effective use of technologies and data science, including big data technology, for intelligence practices. While Canadian police services are adopting data analytic practices, the extent of their integration and use varies signficantly across the country. Some large services in Canada, for example, are working actively to implement an organizational intelligence framework that facilitates the adoption of new technologies and standardized analytic practices throughout their services, while others, particularly smaller municipal services, are in the early phases of technological adoption and appropriation that facilitate data science practices. Drawing directly from interviews with thirteen Canadian police services, we identify technological, organizational, and cultural challenges for the integration and effective uptake of big data technologies. It is important to note that, similar to the variance in the integration and adoption of data science practices across Canadian services, the extent to which services experience these challenges will also vary.

Police Technology and Big Data: A Review of the Literature

Police technologies and data science – particularly big data technologies – are perceived to enhance work efficiency and effectiveness by improving the predictive capabilities of police services while simultaneously reducing subjectivity and bias.[18] Big data technology is generally defined using the three Vs: high volume (amount of data), high velocity (speed at which data are generated), and high variety (diversity of sources and formats).[19] More recently, other common features of big data technologies in policing have been identified, such as data being "exhaustive" (representing a census of all activity), "relational," and of "fine resolution" (which for police means greater precision in identifying the time and location), and data systems that are "flexible and scalable."[20] Yet, defining big data in these ways focuses analytical attention on the technological elements while ignoring the way broader contexts – such as culture and organizations – shape big data.[21] For example, research available on big data analytics has shown how "analytic platforms and techniques are deployed in pre-existing organizational contexts ... and embody the purposes of their creators."[22]

In order to analytically capture the "social shaping"[23] of big data technology, we use danah boyd and Kate Crawford's definition of big data as a "cultural, technological and scholarly phenomenon" that incorporates technology, analysis and mythology.[24] We extend this definition to include a fourth dimension concerning "actionability," which refers to the "action taken on the basis of the inferences drawn," because "the performing of algorithms and calculations, the drawing of inferences and the taking of action are all important stages in the use of big data analytics in ... decision-making."[25] The research available on police use of big data suggests that the capability of policing agencies to take advantage of big data technologies is uneven.[26] Conducting in-depth interviews with intelligence and security agencies in Australia, Janet Chan and Lyria

Bennett Moses found that most personnel did not have knowledge of, or first-hand experience with, big data. When asking their participants about the value and purpose of big data, they found that most law enforcement and security personnel focused on the value of these technologies for investigative or crime disruption purposes rather than for predictive purposes or for understanding broader crime trends.[27] Unlike Chan and Bennett Moses, Sarah Brayne's ethnographic study on the use of big data surveillance by the Los Angeles Police Department (LAPD) found that the LAPD increasingly used big data analytics for predictive rather than reactive or explanatory purposes.[28] Further, she found that big data analytics amplify prior surveillance practices, while also facilitating fundamental transformations in surveillance activities.[29] For example, she found that the integration of big data technologies, such as "alert-based technologies" instead of the old query-based technologies, made it possible for the LAPD to survey an unprecedentedly large number of people – people who would not normally be found in traditional police records systems.[30]

Whereas there are only a few empirical studies available on the in situ use of big data technologies, there are studies that discuss their potential uses. Alexander Babuta, for example, wrote a report exploring the potential uses of big data analytics in British policing. His report identified four ways in which big data analytics presently are, or could be, used: (1) predictive crime mapping; (2) predictive analytics for identifying individuals at risk of reoffending or being victimized; (3) advanced analytics "to harness the full potential of data collected through visual surveillance"; and (4) the use of "open-source data, such as that collected from social media, to gain a richer understanding of specific crime problems, which would ultimately inform the development of preventative policing strategies."[31] Yet, like other scholars in the field, he found that the empirical evidence on the use of big data analytics in these four ways is uneven.[32]

There have also been studies that identify a number of "fundamental limitations" to the implementation and effective use of big data technologies.[33] For example, Babuta notes that the "lack of coordinated development of technology across UK policing," fragmentation of databases and software, lack of organizational access to advanced analytic tools, and legal constraints governing data usage impede the successful use of big data.[34] In synthesizing the available research on the uptake and impact of police technology, Chan and Bennett Moses identify the importance of other factors – apart from technological capacity, such as police leadership, management of technology, organizational politics, and cultural resistance – for understanding technological adoption and use.[35] The research of Carrie Sanders, Crystal Weston, and Nicole Schott on the integration of intelligence-led policing practices in Canada demonstrates how cultural issues and management of innovation issues are intertwined. For example, in the six Canadian police services studied, they found that the use of analytic technologies to support intelligence-led policing was more rhetorical than real. In particular, the "occupational culture of information hoarding ... has shaped the use and functioning of police innovations."[36] In line with previous research on the "poorly understood and appreciated" role of crime and intelligence analysts,[37] the lack of knowledge and training about crime analysis on the part of police managers and officers has left analysts to engage in crime reporting instead of predictive analytics so that new technologies are used to support traditional policing practices.[38]

Methods

The empirical data driving our argument comes from sixty-four semi-structured interviews with personnel from thirteen Canadian police services. Our sample includes forty-one crime and intelligence analysts, three senior/lead analysts, six civilian managers of analytic units, three support personnel (including one junior support analyst and two policy developers), and eleven sworn officers who work with, or supervise, crime and intelligence analysts. Most of the interviews were conducted face to face, while a small portion (10 percent) were conducted over the telephone. Interviews were supplemented with participation at the Massachusetts Association of Crime Analysts training conference (2017); Canadian chapter of the International Association of Crime Analysts training conference (2017); International Association of Crime Analysts annual training conference (2017); South Western Ontario Crime Analysis Network (2015); and two meetings of the Canadian Association of Chiefs of Police (2016 and 2017).

Interviews and field observations were conducted by the lead author and a doctoral research assistant. All data were stored and analyzed in NVivo 10, a qualitative data analysis software program, using a constructivist grounded theory approach.[39] The data were thematically coded by the doctoral research assistant, with continual collaboration and consultation with the lead author. The lead author then used writing as an analytical device to make sense of, and theorize, the data. Through analytic memoing,[40] we saw many similarities between the state of police technology and data science in Canadian policing and that found in the United States, United Kingdom, and Australia. Of interest for this chapter are the ways in which technological, organizational, and cultural contexts create challenges for Canadian police in making effective use of big data technologies. Such challenges include fragmented technological platforms and information silos; resources and practical barriers; emphasis on tactical and operational intelligence (i.e., creating workups on offenders or cases) over strategic intelligence (identifying future offenders or emerging crime trends); and the uneven professionalization of analytics and user capacities.

Fragmented Technological Platforms and Information Silos

Police services work with a variety of information and communication companies (such as Sunguard, Niche, Versaterm, Palantir), technological platforms, and datasets (e.g., open-source media, Ministry of Transportation, internal records management systems, provincial police records systems, national police records systems, closed-circuit televisions, court databases, etc.). Presently, there are no uniform policies or guidelines for police services when it comes to technological adoption and appropriation for intelligence work, leaving each service to act independently.[41] As in the United Kingdom, the highly localized and devolved governance structure of Canadian policing has left services to work in relative isolation with autonomy over local policing strategies and technological adoption.[42] As a result, Canadian police services lack a standardized and systematic approach to the collection and analysis of intelligence, which has left data to be managed across multiple, separate systems that are not always compatible. Further, many traditional police data warehouses do not have the capacity to manage all of the structured and unstructured data available to them, and, for many, their warehouses "are not sufficient to meet the requirements of advanced analytics."[43]

While all Canadian analysts stress how they have access to a large history of data within their own service's records management system, they also identify how fragmented databases and technological platforms are a significant impediment to conducting crime and intelligence analysis:

> Back in 2007, the Solicitor General Office in [a Canadian province] went and talked to all of the police agencies and said we would like to get you on the same software with the same tools ... They selected [a private IT company] to deliver the computer aided dispatch and records management systems, business intelligence and [intelligence analysis] for doing analytics. We started working on that project with that vendor in 2010 – by 2012 it lost momentum. Policing is a world where people like their privacy and they like to do their own thing – like even within our own walls we have silos – so trying to get twelve agencies to work together and agree on something is impossible. (I27)[44]

Fragmented databases have left police services having to create "Band-Aid solutions" (I22) by purchasing off-the-shelf data management systems to facilitate interoperability – systems that often have proprietary regulations attached that create additional challenges for technological integration.[45] Without an integrated system, officers have to input the same data across different systems. Entering information in duplicate can lead to data entry errors – such as the misspelling of a person's name or an incorrect home address. When a name is spelt incorrectly or a person is linked to multiple addresses, separate entities are created in the data system. Further complicating the technological terrain is the lack of a standardized lexicon and system for querying databases. There are no strict guidelines or rules that officers must follow when writing reports, which means that officers can use different words to describe the same incidents. The lack of technological integration and standardization creates challenges for computerized searching and querying of databases, thereby requiring analysts to manually search, collate, and clean data from different systems.

Finally, the lack of a standardized process for gathering and analyzing intelligence has also led services to develop and implement different intelligence organizational structures. Of importance here is the way services have adopted crime and intelligence analysis. Some services have created clear and often hierarchical divisions between these roles and their responsibilities. For example, crime analysts are frequently employed (1) by administration and used largely for comp statistics (comp stat) policing activities (such as developing monthly crime reports and statistics), or (2) by front-line officers where they spend a great deal of their time "mapping crime," "making pretty pictures," and doing "workups" on people of interest.[46] On the other hand, intelligence analysts are assigned to specialized units (such as Gang Crime, Homicide, Sex Crime Unit, etc.) and tasked with doing tactical and operational intelligence analysis (such as "linkage charts," cellphone analysis). These organizational divisions have led analysts to work in isolation from each other and created informal "information silos" (fieldnotes).[47]

Resource and Practical Barriers

As described above, the multiplicity of informal information networks, data systems, repositories, and technological platforms, coupled with data quality issues, creates impediments for computational systems to effectively conduct advanced predictive analytics. The use of manual computation and analysis did not result solely from the fragmented technological platforms, although they do significantly contribute to them, but also stemmed from a series of organizational factors, such as a lack of organizational policies and legal frameworks, and user competencies. Many of the analysts interviewed did not have knowledge of technological platforms available to them that would enable them to analyze unstructured data, such as videos, images, and social media. Where analysts did have access to social media analysis, they identified a number of challenges to its integration. First, the costs associated with purchasing an open-source analytic software licence – that wouldn't leave a trace – were very high. Police services could afford to purchase only a small number of licences, which in turn left only a few computers in the service available for doing such work. This means that analysts and police personnel have to request access to the social media computer terminal – requiring them to physically move locations in the service – or request the assistance of a different analyst. Neither of these was perceived as an acceptable or ideal option.

Second, legislative barriers to accessing information and scraping data structure the types of open-source data and analytics that can be utilized for law enforcement purposes. In services where open-source data were available, there was often a lack of familiarity with, and awareness of, organizational policies or legal frameworks for analyzing them. As one analyst explained:

> We're very behind in our policy ... It's really due to a lack of understanding from upper management. They are slow to understand that most of our crime is moving online, or a lot of our evidence is moving to digital. And they don't understand the need for a policy ... We're not CSIS and we don't have those resources, but I'm sure that within there, there is what law enforcement can and cannot do (I6).

This analyst suggested that the lack of organizational policies concerning open-source analytics are the result of a broader problem around organizational knowledge and understanding of open-source data and the legalities of working with such data for intelligence purposes.

Lack of organizational training on open-source analytics was also identified as a challenge to the effective uptake of big data analytics. An analyst explained:

> We had this program [redacted] that was social media related ... Unfortunately, really, I didn't have the training to be able to fully know what I was doing with that program. So, as an example, we had a major incident that somebody said "[CITY] Shopping Centre had a bomb threat." There had been a number of tweets, as an example, coming from this area. Can you pinpoint exactly where these tweets are coming from? I didn't have the training to do that – which really to work that – you should really have it (I1).

This analyst explains how her service did provide her with a technological platform that made possible open-source big data analytics, but the service did not provide the training required to effectively integrate and use the software. Our findings mirror those of Jyoti Belur and Shane Johnson, who identified knowledge and process gaps that inhibit the integration of analysis. Specifically, they found that "knowledge gaps existed not only on the part of analysts as individuals and collectively, but also in terms of what policy-makers and senior leaders knew about analysis and analytical capability of the organization."[48]

Emphasis on Tactical and Operational Analysis over Strategic Analysis

Research on police intelligence work identifies different types of intelligence, such as tactical, strategic, and operational, which serve different purposes. However, there appears to be a lack of consensus and agreement – among both practitioners and academics – on how to classify intelligence and what the labels mean.[49] Marilyn Peterson defines tactical intelligence as information used to target specific cases and people, strategic intelligence as information used to identify broader crime trends and to recommend how resources should be allocated, and operational intelligence as work with larger cases to target crime.[50] When we spoke with police personnel – in both information technology departments and analytic roles – it quickly became apparent that procurement needs were shaped by traditional police uses of information, specifically tactical and operational needs, which left analysts having to work with "flat files" (I30) that required them to "pull the unstructured data (intelligence narratives) out of [the] records management system, compile it into a relational database, and reorganize it" (I39).[51] Police records management systems are structured around the information requirements for inputting information about a single incident or individual. Yet, as Ridgeway notes, police services "need to expand to data designs with a Big Data strategy in mind, which means having the ability to filter and link on data features."[52] Often, when describing their analytic process, analysts described a very investigative and targeted approach. For example, analysts explained how social media sites, such as Facebook, were frequently used in a "targeted" way "to see if they're [known suspects] posting photos with other people – certain people" (I2). In this way, analysts who were on social media were often using it to find evidence or information about people they already suspected.

While traditional uses of police information have shaped technological design and appropriation, we further argue that the tactical and operational focus of front-line policing – on reaction and arrest – has led to an emphasis on, and value for, tactical and operational intelligence over strategic intelligence. The following excerpt from an interview with a strategic intelligence analyst illuminates the service's emphasis on targeted, investigative tactical and operational analysis:

> I don't feel that I have moved to the analysis of anything – because we start out and say there are targets and all I do is run history, like I check all of the databases to identify their address, associates, vehicles and so on and so forth, but there are times that at least it is not required of me to go further and try to see the bigger picture, of the group because of the mandate for my team ... we don't go up on wire, we do basic investigative files ... I think one area that we are

lacking is looking at the final aspects of it ... there is a bigger network and we don't seem to focus on that as much – we are more just reactive – and we do very low level investigations. (I20)

Using analytics for "targeted" and "investigative purposes," this analyst argued, led to "low level" investigations that do not enable police services to identify and interrupt larger crime trends.

When we inquired about the use of predictive analytics and broader strategic intelligence analysis, all analysts noted the organizational emphasis on tactical and operational intelligence over strategic intelligence:

Even [in] our bigger investigations there is less of an appetite [for strategic analysis] because of the resources that are involved. So, as an analyst, we could pool all of that information and start seeing the connections and identifying what works – pull financial[s] of these individuals and see where the money is coming and going ... We don't have the resources because we don't have forensic accountants that are capable. We are requesting regular members to look into these documents ... so there is no appetite for that ... but they [police service] don't consider the impact that it has on the economy ... you can show, go to the media and say "look at all these drugs and weapons that we have seized and all this cash"[;] these are tangible things that you can show, but bank documents and wire transfers, no one cares for the paper. (I20)

This analyst contended that the organizational emphasis on tactical intelligence over strategic intelligence was shaped by the service's desire to demonstrate its ability to take guns and drugs off the street and make arrests in order to address visible street-level crime. The emphasis on tactical and operational intelligence, we argue, is also shaped by the fact that many analysts are tasked by uniform officers who do not possess analytic training and "are reactive and short-term goal driven."[53] Yet, for police services to effectively use big data technologies will require an organizational shift away from targeted investigative data gathering towards bulk data collection and analysis.

Uneven Professionalization of Analysts and User Capacity and Capability

A final challenge facing the integration of big data technologies in Canadian policing is connected to the uneven professionalization of crime and intelligence analysts. While the field has changed significantly over the past ten years, there are still very few post-secondary programs and recognized accreditation programs available on criminal intelligence analysis in Canada. Further, there are no recognized core competencies associated with this position.[54] The lack of formalized education and recognized core competencies has created challenges for the professionalization of the field, which has led to great variation in the educational background and disciplinary training of analysts.

The costs associated with analytic training means that many services are unable to send their analysts to advanced training courses. For many analysts, "experience and expertise were developed" (I06) through on-the-ground peer learning. The lack of high-quality training provided to analysts raises serious concerns about user capacity and capability. For example, a lead intelligence analyst from a large police service noted that they had hired an internationally recognized intelligence analyst to come and train their service on doing cellphone analysis, but the trainer was unable to run the training because the analysts did not have enough foundational training in Microsoft Excel to do advanced analytics (fieldnotes).

Training for, and knowledge of, big data analytics was also limited among the analysts and police personnel interviewed. When we asked analysts whether they use big data or conduct big data analytics, we received mixed responses:

I don't know. I guess – because I don't do a whole lot of – well at least to my knowledge of what big data refers to – because I do more of the intelligence stuff, so more research on individuals, as opposed to any large data – like, in terms of going over 10 years of information on volumes of shootings, stuff like that ... I don't personally use big data. (I1)

I haven't had to do anything that's been extensive, yet. But, in the sense of [internal records management system] being a large database, you have a lot of information in there. So, usually I am kind of going through that, yeah. (I3)

We are tactical analysts, and they are strategic analysts, and of course we feed off of each other ... But as for doing all the research, anything with big data, is done by [strategic analysts]. We don't have anything to do with it. (I12)

Thus, there are mixed understandings and definitions of what big data is. Over half of the analysts interviewed noted that their internal police records systems constituted big data, while the other half did not believe they worked with big data. Also, of interest in the quotes above, is the delineation between the value of big data for strategic versus tactical intelligence analysis. Both participant I1 and I12 believed that they did not access or conduct analysis with big data because they were focused on tactical intelligence. The mixed definitions of what big data is *combined* with mixed understandings of using it speaks to broader user capacity and capability issues. We believe the current situation is that a large number of analysts do not have the skills to match the functionality of the principal software packages supported by, or available to, police services.

Conclusion

The growing complexity of the post-9/11 security environment has blurred the boundaries of policing and national security intelligence. The changing security environment, combined with the digital revolution of the 1990s and a permissive legislative environment, has also shaped the ways in which police collect, store, analyze, and interpret intelligence for the purpose of detecting and disrupting crime.[55] There are growing claims in the United States and the United Kingdom, and more recently in Canada, about a movement towards predictive policing practices through the integration of big data technologies. The findings presented in this chapter problematize many of the claims surrounding big data and predictive policing by identifying how big data technologies are socially shaped by technological, organizational, and cultural contexts, which impede their effective integration and uptake by Canadian law enforcement.

The findings raise concerns about police services' knowledge and capacity to fully understand and utilize data analytics and big data technologies in police intelligence work. In fact, the empirical data informing this chapter demonstrate that few analysts have the technical skills and data literacy to use the technical tools to their full potential.[56] Yet, as Weston, Bennett Moses, and Sanders argue, "the increasing complexity of data science methods associated with pattern-recognition and prediction, particularly in the context of large volumes of diverse, evolving data, requires a relatively high level of technical sophistication."[57] Andrew Ferguson contends that while big data technology provides innovative potential for police services, choosing a big data system is a *political* decision rather than a *policing* decision. He argues that police administrators must be able to (1) identify the risks they are trying to address; (2) defend the inputs into the system (i.e., data accuracy, methodological soundness); (3) defend the outputs of the system (i.e., how they will impact policing practice and community relationships); (4) test the technology in order to offer accountability and some measure of transparency; and (5) answer whether their use of the technology is respectful of the autonomy of the people it will impact.[58] Our findings raise serious concerns about the risks associated with low-level data literacy skills and a police service's understanding of the capabilities and limitations of big data and predictive policing.

Lastly, throughout this chapter, we have demonstrated different ways in which police adoption and use of big data and data analytics can be plagued with "black data" – which results from "data bias, data error, and the incompleteness of data systems."[59] Further complicating the issues is that algorithmic predictive technologies can also have technical and subjective bias built in that can, if their users are not cautious, lead to discriminatory practices.[60] While the outputs of predictive technologies can be easily attained, due to proprietary algorithms the outputs lack transparency and accountability. Thus, while big data technologies hold great promise for police services to become more efficient, effective, and accountable, without strong data literacy and a sophisticated understanding of the political, effective implementation their success is questionable, and more importantly, the socio-political implications of their use are difficult to determine.

Notes

1 Richard Ericson and Kevin Haggerty, *Policing the Risk Society* (Toronto: University of Toronto Press, 1997).
2 Lucia Zedner, "Pre-Crime and Post Criminology?" *Theoretical Criminology* 11 (2007): 264.
3 Patrick F. Walsh, *Intelligence and Intelligence Analysis* (Oxford: Routledge, 2011).
4 Keeley Townsend, John Sullivan, Thomas Monahan, and John Donnelly, "Intelligence-Led Mitigation" *Journal of Homeland Security and Emergency Management* 7 (2010): 1–17.
5 Walsh, *Intelligence and Intelligence Analysis*, 130.
6 Jerry Ratcliffe, *Intelligence Led Policing* (Cullompton: Willan Publishing, 2008), 81.
7 Greg Ridgeway, "Policing in the Era of Big Data," *Annual Review of Criminology* 1 (2017): 409.
8 Charlie Beck and Colleen McCue, "Predictive Policing: What Can We Learn from Wal-Mart and Amazon about Fighting Crime in a Recession?" *Police Chief* 76 (2009): 19.
9 Matt Meuse, "Vancouver Police Now Using Machine Learning to Prevent Property Crime: 'Predictive Policing' Technology Uses Past Trends to Determine Where Break-ins Are Likely to Occur," *CBC News*, 22 July 2017.
10 Ibid.
11 Ibid.
12 Meghan Grant, "Calgary Police Cellphone Surveillance Device Must Remain Top Secret, Judge Rules: Alleged Gangsters Barakat Amer and Tarek El-Rafie Were Targets of the Cellphone Interception Tool," *CBC News*, 30 October 2017.
13 Alexander Babuta, "An Assessment of Law Enforcement Requirements, Expectations and Priorities" (RUSI Occasional Paper, ISSN 2397-0286, 2017).
14 Sarah Brayne, "Big Data Surveillance: The Case of Policing," *American Sociological Association* 82, 3 (2017), doi: 10.1177/0003122417725865 i.org/10.1177/0003122417725865.
15 Ridgeway, "Policing in the Era of Big Data," 408.
16 Babuta, "An Assessment of Law Enforcement"; Ridgeway, "Policing in the Era of Big Data"; Walt Perry, Brian McInnis, Carter Price, Susan Smith, and John Hollywood, *Predictive Policing: The Role of Crime Forecasting in Law Enforcement Operations* (Santa Monica, CA: RAND Corporation, 2013).
17 Jyoti Belur and Shane Johnson, "Is Crime Analysis at the Heart of Policing Practice? A Case Study," *Policing and Society* (2016): 2, doi: 10.1080/10439463.2016.1262364.
18 Brayne, "Big Data Surveillance."
19 Janet Chan and Lyria Bennett Moses, "Making Sense of Big Data for Security," *British Journal of Criminology* 57 (2017): 299–319; Adam Crawford, "Networked Governance

and the Post-Regulatory State? Steering, Rowing and Anchoring the Provision of Policing and Security," *Theoretical Criminology* 10, 6 (2006): 449–79.

20 Ridgeway, "Policing in the Era of Big Data," 408.

21 Lisa-Jo Van den Scott, Carrie Sanders, and Andrew Puddephatt, "Reconceptualizing Users through Rich Ethnographic Accounts," in *Handbook of Science and Technology Studies*, 4th ed., edited by Clark Miller, Urike Felt, Laurel Smith-Doerr, and Rayvon Fouche (Cambridge, MA: MIT Press, 2017).

22 Brayne, "Big Data Surveillance," 6.

23 Wiebe E. Bijker, "How Is Technology Made? – That Is the Question!" *Cambridge Journal of Economics* 34 (2010): 63–76.

24 danah boyd and Kate Crawford, "Critical Questions for Big Data: Provocations for a Cultural, Technological, and Scholarly Phenomenon," *Information, Communication and Society* 15 (2012): 663.

25 Lyria Bennett Moses and Janet Chan, "Using Big Data for Legal and Law Enforcement Decisions: Testing the New Tools," *University of New South Wales Law Journal* 37 (2014): 652.

26 Chan and Bennett Moses, "Making Sense of Big Data."

27 Ibid.

28 Brayne, "Big Data Surveillance."

29 Ibid.

30 Ibid.

31 Babuta, "An Assessment of Law Enforcement."

32 Ibid.

33 Ibid; Janet Chan and Lyria Bennett Moses, "Can 'Big Data' Analytics Predict Policing Practice?" in *Security and Risk Technologies in Criminal Justice*, edited by S. Hannem et al. (Toronto: Canadian Scholars' Press, 2019); Ridgeway, "Policing in the Era of Big Data."

34 Babuta, "An Assessment of Law Enforcement."

35 Chan and Bennett Moses, "Can 'Big Data' Analytics Predict Policing Practice?"

36 Carrie B. Sanders, Crystal Weston, and Nicole Schott, "Police Innovations, 'Secret Squirrels' and Accountability: Empirically Studying Intelligence-Led Policing in Canada," *British Journal of Criminology* 55 (2015): 718.

37 Colin Atkinson, "Patriarchy, Gender, Infantilisation: A Cultural Account of Police Intelligence Work in Scotland," *Australian and New Zealand Journal of Criminology* 50, 2 (2017): 234–51; Nina Cope, "Intelligence Led Policing or Policing Led Intelligence? Integrating Volume Crime Analysis into Policing," *British Journal of Criminology* 44, 2 (2004): 188–203; Belur and Johnson, "Is Crime Analysis at the Heart of Policing Practice?"

38 Walsh, *Intelligence and Intelligence Analysis;* Patrick F. Walsh, "Building Better Intelligence Frameworks through Effective Governance," *International Journal of Intelligence and Counter Intelligence* 28, 1 (2015): 123–42; Anthony A. Braga and David L. Weisburd, *Police Innovation and Crime Prevention: Lessons Learned from Police Research over the Past 20 Years* (Washington, DC: National Institute of Justice, 2006); Christopher S. Koper, Cynthia Lum, and James Willis, "Optimizing the Use of Technology in Policing: Results and Implications from a Multi-Site Study of the Social, Organizational, and Behavioural Aspects of Implementing Police Technologies," *Policing* 8, 2 (2014): 212–21; Carrie B. Sanders and Camie Condon, "Crime Analysis and Cognitive Effects: The Practice of Policing through Flows of Data," *Global Crime* 18, 3 (2017): 237–55.

39 Kathy Charmaz, *Constructing Grounded Theory: A Practical Guide through Qualitative Analysis* (London: Sage Publications, 2006).

40 Ibid.

41   Sanders, Weston, and Schott, "Police Innovations."
42   Babuta, "An Assessment of Law Enforcement."
43   Ibid., 5.
44   "I" denotes interviewee number.
45   James Sheptycki, "Organizational Pathologies in Police Intelligence Systems: Some Contributions to the Lexicon of Intelligence-Led Policing," *European Journal of Criminology* 1, 3 (2004): 307–32.
46   Sanders and Condon, "Crime Analysis and Cognitive Effects."
47   "Fieldnotes" refers to data acquired through direct field observations.
48   Belur and Johnson, "Is Crime Analysis at the Heart of Policing Practice?"
49   Walsh, *Intelligence and Intelligence Analysis.*
50   Marilyn Peterson, *Intelligence-Led Policing: The New Intelligence Architecture* (Washington, DC: US Department of Justice, 2005).
51   Sanders and Condon, "Crime Analysis and Cognitive Effects."
52   Ridgeway, "Policing in the Era of Big Data," 405.
53   Belur and Johnson, "Is Crime Analysis at the Heart of Policing Practice?" 8.
54   Crystal Weston, Lyria Bennett Moses, and Carrie Sanders, "The Changing Role of the Law Enforcement Analyst: Clarifying Core Competencies for Analysts and Supervisors through Empirical Research," *Policing and Society: An International Journal,* https://doi.org/10.1080/10439463.2018.1564751.
55   Walsh, *Intelligence and Intelligence Analysis.*
56   M. Burcher and Chad Whelan, "Intelligence-Led Policing in Practice: Reflections from Intelligence Analysts," *Police Quarterly* 22, 2 (2018): 139–60, doi: 10.1177/1098611118796890; Weston, Bennett Moses, and Sanders, "The Changing Role of the Law Enforcement Analyst."
57   Weston, Bennett Moses, and Sanders, "The Changing Role of the Law Enforcement Analyst," 8.
58   Andrew Ferguson, *The Rise of Big Data Policing: Surveillance, Race and the Future of Law Enforcement* (New York: New York University Press, 2017), 439.
59   Ibid., 446.
60   Janet Chan and Lyria Bennett Moses, "Is Big Data Challenging Criminology?" *Theoretical Criminology* 20, 1 (2016): 21–39.

Part 4
Resistance to Big Data Surveillance

11

Confronting Big Data

Popular Resistance to Government Surveillance in Canada since 2001

Tim McSorley and Anne Dagenais Guertin

STATE SURVEILLANCE HAS been a hallmark of government activities since before the official founding of Canada. As many have noted, the project of pacification – a more palatable term for colonization – of Indigenous populations was undertaken with thorough, widespread surveillance, ranging from tribal rolls to church records.[1]

Observers, notably Mark Neocleous, have pointed out that the first use of the word "pacification" traces back to the sixteenth century, and the concept was quickly incorporated into the approach of colonial countries in their quest for greater territory and resources.[2] King Philip II of Spain stated explicitly that in order to better achieve its colonial mission, his empire should adopt a policy of pacification, including to "gather information about the various tribes, languages and divisions of the Indians in the province."[3] This, of course, did not mean understanding the local populations in order to enter into a reciprocal relationship but rather to better quell unrest and integrate them into the colonial project. As Neocleous notes, "it implies the construction of a new social order as well as the crushing of opposition to that construction."[4]

As the colonial project has continued over centuries, with Indigenous communities continuing to face high levels of state surveillance, similar tools and tactics have been applied to other segments of the Canadian population. The greatest attention of the state surveillance apparatus continues to be directed towards communities who present – or are viewed as presenting – the greatest challenge to the status quo. This has alternately included trade unionists, communists, Quebec independence activists, LGBTQI+ people, anti-globalization activists, environmental activists, and Muslims and Arabs.[5]

Surveillance also goes beyond the targeting of identified populations, to the monitoring of society as a whole. Numerous scholars have detailed how overarching methods of surveillance, particularly through law enforcement and state bureaucracy, serve to keep a watchful – and acknowledged – eye on the population at large, serving to (once again) pacify while at the same time causing a chilling effect.[6] Canadians are sharing greater and greater amounts of their information with both private companies and the government. At the same time, new forms of surveillance technology have allowed government and private interests to collect information about people with or without their consent.[7]

This increase in surveillance has been motivated by several objectives, not the least of which has been "national security."[8] Indeed, the idea of national security – the protection of the Canadian state from external and internal threats – has been a prime motivator for surveillance since the earliest days of colonialism, through both domestic and international upheavals, until today.[9]

The idea of what constitutes a national security threat has changed greatly over the decades, and has been a topic of research in itself. This chapter will examine examples of government surveillance of Canadians but not the alleged threats that motivate them. More specifically, we will examine recent popular/ grassroots responses to government surveillance, analyzing their impact and the lessons they may hold for the future. To do so, we have selected three cases where we have interviewed a participant, carried out research on the campaign, and examined the results. The three cases are:

1 *Stop Illegal Spying* – The British Columbia Civil Liberties Association (BCCLA) launched an ongoing lawsuit against the Communications Security Establishment (CSE) in 2013, challenging CSE's work as infringing on Canadians' rights. Along with the court case, the BCCLA has engaged in a popular education campaign to raise awareness of problems with the CSE's work.

2 *Stop Online Spying* – A 2011 campaign initiated by OpenMedia against lawful access laws. At the time, the federal government framed the need for lawful access laws as necessary for the enforcement of criminal law.

3 *International Campaign Against Mass Surveillance (ICAMS)* – Begun in 2004, ICAMS was an international movement, modelled after the International Campaign to Ban Landmines, with the goal of bringing about internationally agreed-to limits on mass surveillance.

These three examples have been chosen because they address three different issues pertaining to mass surveillance: the actions of a specific surveillance agency, laws granting governments easier access to personal information, and global systems of mass surveillance. They were also chosen for their differing approaches: use of the legal arena, mass online mobilization, and an international coalition of civil society around a text-based campaign.

As we interviewed only one person per campaign, and as impact is sometimes difficult to determine and attribute accurately, our analysis has clear limitations. Thus, this chapter is not meant to be read as an authoritative guide to the most and least effective campaigning methods. As activists, we often do not have the time to reflect on past experiences, especially those of others. Thus, this chapter aims to present information about past campaigns that will hopefully be useful to today's anti-surveillance campaigners in determining their preferred approach and actions.

It has been nineteen years since Canada's first *Anti-terrorism Act* (Bill C-36),[10] and national security and surveillance legislation has only continued to multiply: by our count, no fewer than twelve bills have been passed to bring in new national security and surveillance powers over that time, culminating with Bill C-51, Canada's second *Anti-terrorism Act,* in 2015.[11] In June 2019, Parliament passed a new piece of national security legislation, Bill C-59 (the *National Security Act, 2017*), which has introduced sweeping changes, including to the powers and regulations surrounding mass surveillance in Canada.[12] Along with what we have learned through the revelations made by Edward Snowden and other whistle-blowers and journalists, it is an opportune time to look at popular responses to surveillance and their impact.

Case 1: Stop Illegal Spying

In 2013, the BC Civil Liberties Association filed suit in Federal Court against the Communications Security Establishment, Canada's cryptologic and signals intelligence agency. The suit alleges that CSE violates Canadians' Charter rights through its mass surveillance practices.[13] It followed long-standing and multiple concerns expressed by civil liberties organizations across the country. This case is based on an interview with Caily DiPuma, who at the time was the acting litigation director at the BCCLA and a member of the legal team for the association's lawsuit against CSE.

At the time, CSE's mandate was defined in a brief section of the *National Defence Act.* It allowed for the minister of defence to grant broad authorizations for, among other things, the interception of the private conversations of Canadians without any judicial oversight.[14] The adoption of the *National Security Act, 2017* has since created a new *CSE Act,* which establishes more explicit rules, as well as oversight, for the agency. Despite this, concerns remain about the scope of CSE surveillance, and an examination of the BCCLA's suit still holds lessons for today. The change in the law also does not eliminate the need for accountability for possible wrongdoing under the previous legal regime.

The Court Case

The case in Federal Court alleges that two aspects of CSE's activities violate the *Canadian Charter of Rights and Freedoms'* protections against unreasonable search and seizure and infringe on free expression: (1) the interception of the private communications of Canadians, and (2) the sweeping collection of metadata information produced by Canadians in their everyday activities online and through phone conversations.[15]

In 2014, the BCCLA followed up with a companion class action suit.[16] The goal of the class action is to provide a way for Canadians who have been impacted by CSE surveillance to seek remedy if the initial suit is successful in striking down the laws that allow CSE to collect Canadians' private communications and metadata. The action is being brought on behalf of all people who have used a wireless device – laptops, cellphones, etc. – in Canada since 2001.

The federal government and CSE have responded that CSE's mandate prohibits it from targeting Canadians' communications and that it would be unlawful for it to do so. They also argue that due to the nature of CSE's work, it is impossible for the agency to know whether or not Canadians' communications are being swept up in its surveillance activities, so "there may be circumstances in which incidental interception of private communications or information about Canadians will occur."[17]

Litigating against Mass Surveillance

Throughout its history, the BCCLA has used numerous tactics in its defence of civil liberties from the impact of national security and anti-terrorism laws, including lobbying, petitions, and public education.

In this instance, according to DiPuma, the BCCLA decided upon litigation because the CSE provisions in the *National Defence Act* were particularly weak and amenable to challenge in court. This is because the act did not establish any real statutory authority beyond the ministerial directives that delineated what CSE could do with Canadians' data.

The lack of details contained in the *National Defence Act* regarding what CSE could and could not do meant that, among other things, the authorizations granted to CSE for its surveillance activities were issued (1) without restrictions on the breadth of communications to be collected, (2) without a reasonable time limit, and (3) without adequate safeguards to ensure the accountability of CSE in the course of its collection of private communications.[18] The suit alleges that these issues violate section 8 of the Charter (freedom from unreasonable search and seizure). The BCCLA's statement of claim also argues that CSE violates section 2(b) of the Charter, which protects freedom of thought, belief, opinion, and expression.[19]

While the goal of the suit is to bring substantial change to the rules governing CSE's activities, the BCCLA has coupled it with a public outreach campaign, using infographics, social media sharing tools, backgrounders, and video.[20] The hope, said DiPuma, is that such court cases will also help bring more public attention to government surveillance and CSE, and that this will put political pressure on the government to act.

The timing of the case was also meant to capitalize on public awareness. The suit was filed shortly after the publication of information and documents leaked by former CIA contractor Edward Snowden, revealing global networks of mass surveillance, particularly on behalf of the United States and the United Kingdom, but also Canada.[21] According to DiPuma, the BCCLA hoped to take advantage of "an historical moment when people were paying attention to the issue of mass surveillance." Further revelations from the Snowden files would eventually implicate CSE in spying on Canadians as well as engaging in global mass surveillance operations.[22]

As the suit has yet to go to trial, there is no way to predict the outcome. The BCCLA is hoping for a favourable judgment, but DiPuma says that it is open to other outcomes too, including unilateral steps by the government to ensure that CSE's activities do not violate Canadians' rights. "Litigation can add to the overall policy discussion in a way that affects meaningful change in the law," says DiPuma, adding that if the government were to introduce laws that appropriately changed CSE's legal framework, the BCCLA would reconsider its suit.

Impact

It is difficult to attest to the impact of a lawsuit that is still before the courts. However, DiPuma points to what she sees as some impacts already:

- The suit has contributed to the public policy debate around CSE and government surveillance.
- The case has brought public awareness to a secretive regime.
- The BCCLA has learned new details about the operations of CSE, but which cannot be shared publicly yet.

These impacts are difficult to measure, but there are a few indications we can look to.

Public Awareness

Through its outreach and public discussions, the BCCLA has found that people were "shocked" and agreed that change was needed when the details of the case and the association's concerns with CSE's surveillance practices were explained to them.

In her experience, DiPuma said, there are mixed reactions among the public to the question of whether or not we need to be concerned about protecting privacy rights. In this case, however, the issues "resonated deeply." The secrecy around CSE makes it particularly important in this case to get people engaged, and to understand it, DiPuma said.

At the time the lawsuit was filed, the case garnered considerable media coverage across the country, including articles in the *Globe and Mail*, *CBC News*, and the *Vancouver Sun*.[23] Each time the case has come up in court, including the filing of the class action suit and the arguments over disclosure in the summer of 2016, there was a resurgence in media coverage of CSE and its surveillance practices.[24]

Although it is impossible to measure the exact impact of this lawsuit on public awareness, it is safe to say that such mainstream coverage at each stage of the lawsuit would have educated more than a few people. However, as CSE remains little known or understood by the Canadian public, it is also safe to say that much more public education and media coverage is necessary.

Disclosure

Another impact of such a lawsuit is disclosure of information. Information that to date has remained secret, unpublished, or inaccessible through other means may come to light through the disclosure process, once it is entered into evidence and become public. The disclosure of these documents helps to inform advocates and the public at large of new issues and concerns, and can lead to further action.

The BCCLA's suit has gone through the disclosure stage, including arguments over whether certain documents deemed sensitive to national security should be disclosed to the BCCLA and made available to be entered into evidence. While the bulk of disclosure is still being considered and will be made public only if and when it is entered into evidence, we have already been given a glimpse of the kind of information such cases can provide. In June 2016, the *Globe and Mail* published a comparison of two versions of a document detailing metadata collection by CSE.[25] The first version, received by the *Globe* through access to information requests, is heavily redacted and of modest value. The second version, received by the BCCLA through disclosure, is significantly less redacted and contains information on how metadata is defined and what analysts are able to do with the information. As the *Globe and Mail* notes:

> The BCCLA version of the document shows how CSE is under orders to indiscriminately collect and share metadata with allied agencies. But also revealed is the order to scrub out any "Canadian identifying information" after the fact.[26]

It is also important to note that it is difficult to challenge the operations of national security agencies when their regulations are kept secret. By simply obtaining more public disclosure of the rules that these agencies play by, civil liberties advocates are better able to identify potential flaws and weaknesses.

It is to be hoped that as the case heads to trial, more information that shines a light on CSE's mass surveillance activities will become public.

Policy

As with other impacts, it is difficult to show a direct relation between the pressure that a lawsuit puts on policy-makers and their decisions. This is especially true when it comes to national security, since so much of what drives government decision making is kept confidential. At the same time, one of the BCCLA's stated public goals with this suit is to change the practice and law around government surveillance. The association's suit also comes at a time of pressure from other organizations and sectors to reform CSE's activities to ensure that they do not violate Canadians' Charter rights (or engage in mass surveillance internationally, for that matter).

In June 2017, four years after the BCCLA filed its initial lawsuit, the federal government proposed a major revamp of CSE's legislation. Bill C-59, the *National Security Act, 2017*, includes the newly titled *CSE Act*. The act lays out in detail the policies and procedures that would govern the work of CSE, including parameters for surveillance and retention of data.[27] The bill was granted royal assent in June 2019.

The creation in the *National Security Act, 2017* of a new Intelligence Commissioner (IC), with quasi-judicial status (the IC must be a retired Federal Court judge), to approve surveillance authorizations before they are carried out may also be seen as a response to some of the issues addressed in the lawsuit (although without more information it is impossible to point to causality, and further research would be necessary to reach any conclusion). Such an approval process could, in theory, provide more certainty that authorizations are issued on reasonable and probable grounds, or at least under a clear and articulable legal standard (which, the lawsuit argues, does not currently occur).

While the BCCLA published a brief on the provisions of Bill C-59, including those related to CSE, it did not express an opinion on whether these changes address the concerns brought up in its court challenge.[28]

Analysis

Litigation can be an effective tactic to protect Charter rights: rather than rely solely on public pressure and advocacy, Charter challenges can result in concrete changes in law and put pressure on the government to act before the courts issue their decision. They can also draw media attention to an issue and provide an opportunity for public awareness campaigns. At the same time, they can be resource-intensive and drawn out, and there is little guarantee that a court ruling will support, in full or in part, the goal a campaign hopes to achieve. The decision then centres on whether to continue to pursue it through the courts or attempt to bring about change through other means.

The advantage of litigation is that a government with a parliamentary majority, as the Liberals are at the time of writing and the Conservatives were before them, is able to withstand public pressure to amend legislation unless it threatens its electability at the next polls. When dealing with surveillance and national security, which is often little known to the public and rarely determines how people vote, relying on pressure at the polls is difficult. The impact of a court ruling could force the government's hand to take action that other public advocacy campaigns could not achieve. Furthermore, court rulings, even if not completely favourable, can lead to momentum and openings for advocacy campaigns to push for important changes to the law, with the weight of a court decision behind them.

The possibility of a negative ruling can also push a government to act before it is issued, in the hope that the suit is dropped; even the possibility of disclosures during trial that could further damage the government's reputation or raise other legal concerns could motivate it to take action and reform the law.

Disclosure and access to information is another positive, if secondary, result of this kind of legal action. Often the most difficult part of understanding – let alone challenging – national security activities is accessing clear, comprehensive information about those activities, and the authorizations and analyses that underlie them. Disclosures in court can provide much more pertinent and complete information than the current access to information laws provide. While such disclosure would never be the primary reason for this kind of suit, it nonetheless helps complete the picture and lays the foundation for future work on these issues.

Finally, the fact that the government saw a need to finally detail the rules governing CSE's work in Bill C-59 could be seen as motivated by the BCCLA's suit – or at least a recognition that the lack of clear policy leaves the agency open to such challenge. It is of course impossible to attribute any kind of causality without further research. We would suggest that further investigation be carried out, including access to information requests and interviews with policy-makers, to ascertain what role this suit has played. The other question, of course, is whether the reforms contained in C-59 actually address the concerns raised in the lawsuit. This remains a matter of debate, but overall, civil society groups have judged the new *CSE Act* to be insufficient in addressing current concerns as well as granting troubling new powers to the agency.[29] The *CSE Act* in fact enshrines some of CSE's more controversial powers, including those related to the retention of Canadians' private information, in law. Instead of limiting CSE's activities, the adopted act may simply result in legitimizing them. In that case, continuation of the lawsuit with the possibility of a verdict favourable to the BCCLA's arguments could provide additional pressure to improve a problematic law.

Case 2: Stop Online Spying

In February 2012, the Conservative government introduced Bill C-30, the *Protecting Children from Internet Predators Act.*[30] Originally titled the *Lawful Access Act,* the bill would have given law enforcement authorities and national security agencies sweeping new powers to access private information without a warrant.[31] OpenMedia was central to organizing a coalition and online campaign, including a petition, that led to withdrawal of the bill.[32] In 2014, the government enacted a similar but significantly weakened bill, which, however, still expanded lawful access powers. This case is based on an interview with David Christopher, OpenMedia's interim communications and campaigns director.

The Campaign

Many will remember the fight against lawful access in Canada for Public Safety Minister Vic Toews's infamous words just before Bill C-30 was introduced – that Canadians "can either stand with us or with the child pornographers."[33] Within a year, the bill was dead.

The battle against lawful access had been ongoing for several years already, dating back to the 2005 Liberal government. Despite many attempts, no lawful access legislation was successfully adopted.[34] The Conservative party made it a key plank of its proposed omnibus crime bill, which it promised to enact within the first 100 days following its election with a parliamentary majority on 2 May 2011.[35] That June, however, a coalition of thirty public interest organizations, businesses, and concerned academics assembled by OpenMedia launched the Stop Online Spying campaign (www.stopspying.ca), calling for an end to lawful access legislation and for the Conservatives to exclude it from the proposed omnibus crime bill.

At the time, OpenMedia was known especially for its Stop the Meter campaign, which by mid-2011 had racked up more than 500,000 signatures on an e-petition calling on the government to put an end to usage-based billing (or metered Internet access). Such a large number of online petition signatures was unheard of in Canada at the time, and the campaign was a factor in having the government make the CRTC rule against the practice.[36] The campaign's success played a role in OpenMedia's taking on of lawful access issues.

OpenMedia believed that fighting lawful access in the same way could succeed. According to Christopher, the organization set out to bring together a wide coalition that bridged the political spectrum in order to put pressure on all political parties. Why would OpenMedia weigh in on online surveillance when, to that point, it was known for its focus on access to the Internet? As it stated in a press release:

"Every single provincial privacy commissioner has spoken against this bill," says OpenMedia.ca's Executive Director, Steve Anderson. "Law-abiding Canadians should be able to use the Internet and mobile devices without Big Telecom and government looking over their shoulders. These invasive surveillance bills will transform the Internet into a closed, rigid, and paranoid space."[37]

On 9 August 2011, coalition members followed up with an open letter to Prime Minister Stephen Harper outlining their concerns.[38]

The campaign appears to have met with some early success, with the Conservatives introducing their omnibus crime bill, C-10, without mention of lawful access.[39] Christopher attributes this outcome to cross-sector approach. The government, however, promised to provide what it described as necessary tools for law enforcement to fight child pornographers and organized crime. The campaign kept up the pressure by producing public service announcements and a short documentary explaining the dangers of lawful access legislation to Canadians' privacy; these garnered around 25,000 and 75,000 views, respectively. The Conservatives persevered, unsurprisingly since, with a majority government, they had just passed the omnibus crime bill that was also highly unpopular with civil liberties advocates. On 14 February 2012, they introduced Bill C-30 to a flurry of criticism.[40]

That same day, Toews made his infamous statement. His speech in the House of Commons led to the #TellVicEverything hashtag as Canadians bombarded him on Twitter with the minutest details of their lives, trending in Canada and worldwide on 16 February.[41] As Steve Anderson wrote on the OpenMedia website, OpenMedia and its coalition members had prepared for the tabling of the bill, pushing the online petition launched with the start of the campaign.[42] Besides the online petition and the August 2011 open letter, OpenMedia also divulged documents demonstrating that police forces had difficulty finding examples of cases that were hindered due to the lack of lawful access legislation.[43]

The controversy caused by Toews's statement helped propel the campaign forward, but, according to Christopher, the coalition also benefited from having prepared tools in advance and from the confidence gained from its success in the Stop the Meter campaign. At the time, said Christopher, OpenMedia, which now operates internationally, had a much smaller team with fewer resources, and was attempting to punch above its weight. The online petition, key to the Stop the Meter campaign and viewed as key to the new campaign, took off after Toews's statement and the momentum generated by the hashtag. By April, the petition had more than 130,000 signatures.[44]

Christopher points out that it is important to see this number in context. At the time, online petitions receiving mass support were something new, especially in Canada. Thus, as the petition passed each milestone – say, 25,000 signatures – the media reported on it, resulting in ever-growing momentum. On 30 April, the petition hits its peak, with 135,000 signatures – fewer than for Stop the Meter but still significant for a campaign on issues like online surveillance and lawful access, topics that were not often seen as causing strong public outcry.

Bill C-30 had passed only first reading and while opposition parties brought it up in debate, the government never returned it to the House of Commons. A year after its introduction, the government withdrew the bill. Justice Minister Rob Nicholson stated:

> We will not be proceeding with Bill C-30 and any attempts we will have to modernize the Criminal Code will not contain the measures in C-30 – including the warrantless mandatory disclosure of basic subscriber information, or the requirement for telecommunications service providers to build intercept capabilities within their systems ... Any modernization of the Criminal Code ... will not contain those.[45]

OpenMedia and other anti-surveillance activists greeted this as a major victory against lawful access at the time, having forced a majority government to roll back a key law – which rarely happens.

Analysis

While the Stop Online Spying campaign is remembered for the #TellVicEverything hashtag and the online petition, it was a multi-faceted campaign that also included coalition building, lobbying, and popular education through online videos and community screenings. These other tactics arguably helped build momentum towards the 135,000-signature petition.

Along with the multiple tactics, it is also important to acknowledge what Christopher called the "moment in time." This includes the resounding success of the Stop the Meter campaign (the largest online petition campaign in Canada to date), the novelty and newsworthiness of a viral online petition, and the government's miscalculations, particularly Vic Toews's "with us or with the child pornographers" proclamation.

It would appear that OpenMedia and its partners were able to take advantage of this moment to pressure the government and make it politically unpalatable for the Conservatives to proceed with Bill C-30. The online petition with 135,000 signatures served as visual evidence of the widespread disapproval of the bill that was necessary to cause the government to retreat.

Unfortunately, just as there had already been multiple attempts to bring in lawful access, the Conservative government did not give up. Several months later, Justice Minister Peter MacKay reintroduced lawful access legislation with Bill C-13. This time, the government framed the issue as an anti-bullying law to address cases like those of Amanda Todd and Rehtaeh Parsons – teenage girls bullied online to the point of suicide. Many, including Amanda Todd's mother, criticized the bill for combining two unrelated issues and decried it as a political manoeuvre.[46] The new amendments were scaled back, and did not, to the word, break Nicholson's earlier promise: the new legislation did not allow for warrantless access or force Internet service providers (ISPs) to build in technology that would allow back-door entrance for law enforcement. It did, however, lower the threshold for approval of certain kinds of access warrants, thereby making it easier than ever for law enforcement and national security agencies to access online personal data.

So while the laws have been loosened and the debate continues, it is fair to say that the Stop Online Spying campaign significantly slowed lawful access rules in Canada. It is telling that even in recent debates on lawful access, there continue to be references to the failure of Bill C-30 and the massive opposition Canadians have shown to warrantless surveillance.

Case 3: International Campaign Against Mass Surveillance

This case is based on an interview with the former International Civil Liberties Monitoring Group (ICLMG) national coordinator and initiator of ICAMS Roch Tassé. At the time, in 2004, ICLMG was a coalition of about thirty Canadian civil society groups. It now has forty-six member organizations and its mandate is the protection and promotion of human rights and civil liberties in the context of the so-called War on Terror.

What Is ICAMS?

In 2004, the ICLMG joined other well-known human rights groups from around the world – the American Civil Liberties Union (United States), Statewatch (United Kingdom), and Focus on the Global South (Philippines) – in launching the International Campaign Against Mass Surveillance, which calls on governments to end mass surveillance and global registration of entire populations.

Patterned in some respects after the international campaign to ban land-mines, ICAMS aims to build a movement of resistance to these measures around the world by circulating a core document, a summary of the docu-ment, and a declaration for endorsement.[47] In order to create such an international network, twenty ICLMG member organizations, Ben Hayes from Statewatch, Jameel Jaffer from the ACLU, and Walden Bello from Focus on the Global South organized a three-day conference in 2004 to discuss the impacts of mass surveillance. The first day of the conference was a private round-table meeting with about thirty guests. The second day was a public panel attended by about 150 people where Tassé, Hayes, Jaffer, and Bello made presentations and several guests spoke specifically of the impacts on Muslim communities. The final day was also a closed-door meeting to find a way to keep the momentum going, to find an action that could be accomplished by this new international partnership. What seemed the most pressing to the attendees was the consequences of national security legislation and surveillance on people's privacy. It was then decided that a campaign on that issue should be created in the next year, and a small coordination committee composed of the main organizers and Maureen Webb was put together and tasked with writing the core document. The document was eventually expanded into a book, *Illusions of Security,* writ-ten by Maureen Webb.[48] The conference and the campaign were carried out on the organizers' own time and dime.

After one year, the core document was ready. The campaign got its name, a website was created, and the document was distributed internationally. In just a few months, 300 individuals and organizations endorsed the ICAMS Declaration. At the end of the campaign, the number had grown significantly, although the exact number is unknown as the website is no longer active.

International Conference of Data Protection and Privacy Commissioners

In 2007, Montreal hosted the International Conference of Data Protection and Privacy Commissioners, with guests from Canada, Europe, and Africa, but not the United States.[49] A civil society conference was organized in parallel and the two sides met at the end of both conferences. The Office of the Privacy Commissioner of Canada (OPC) awarded ICAMS a grant of $150,000 to organ-ize the parallel conference. A staff person was hired for that purpose. After a few modifications, the ICAMS core document became the report of the civil society conference. The report was adopted as a resolution at the subsequent Conference of Data Protection and Privacy Commissioners.[50]

Impacts of ICAMS

The campaign had many positive results and impacts, including:

- the declaration signed by hundreds of organizations and individuals
- the book *Illusions of Security*
- global partnerships, the creation of a collaborative structure and culture, and regional networks that have lasted to this day
- the emergence of many individuals and groups working on privacy
- getting privacy groups to start doing policy work
- getting organizations from all sectors to start working on privacy as well
- the creation of a relationship between civil society and the OPC
- the civil society parallel conference
- adoption of the core document as a resolution by the Conference of Data Protection and Privacy Commissioners
- development of international awareness of mass surveillance
- influence on university researchers and federal opposition parties – for example, the Bloc Québecois and the New Democratic Party published a minority report calling for the abrogation of the *Anti-terrorism Act* of 2001 because of ICAMS's work,[51] and the ICLMG was frequently cited by them in the House of Commons.

Reflections and Lessons

Although the campaign did important work, created important networks, and had many positive impacts and outcomes, it has obviously not met its general goal of eliminating mass surveillance or, at the very least, augmenting privacy protections and reducing mass surveillance, in contrast to the success of the campaign against landmines. If anything, privacy protections have deteriorated and mass surveillance has crept into our lives and appears to be here to stay. We are not suggesting that ICAMS was a failure or that it had the responsibility to rid us of mass surveillance; that would be completely unfair. However, it is important to examine the campaign in order to identify the lessons for future courses of action against mass surveillance.

First, the size of the phenomenon makes it very difficult to tackle. Mass surveillance is an omnipresent but often invisible issue that is highly intertwined with technologies that have been integrated into our daily lives in numerous helpful and positive ways. This makes it difficult for most people to fully grasp the problem or to not feel powerless to protect themselves or others, and thus to mobilize against it. Second, the political climate was a huge problem: the Conservatives were in power at the time and they were highly unreceptive, although the campaign document was sent to all of them and privacy commissioners from around the world had adopted it. Thus, the campaign did not lead to any new government policies. Third, no country adopted the document or brought it before the United Nations, so no UN treaty was drafted, let alone signed. Roch Tassé wonders whether they should have given themselves more solid international structures or created a more formal international entity. However, it is difficult to say whether that would have worked or been more effective, he added.

Finally, the lack of time and resources had a big influence. Often, we feel that it is imperative to act against a terrible affliction such as mass surveillance, but resources and time limit what can be done. And although there were many influential individuals and researchers involved, they could not carry the entire burden. After a while, they moved on to other things or retired, with no one to succeed them.

Discussion of the Three Cases

Surveillance, especially for national security purposes, is difficult to address as so much is carried out in secret. In cases where the rules are explicitly stated, such as lawful access, it is difficult to know exactly what data are being intercepted, collected, and retained, as well as how they are being used. It is even more difficult when it comes to surveillance conducted by organizations like CSE, which has operated for over seventy years in relative obscurity and with very few written rules.

Each of the campaigns above was faced with the dual task of challenging unjust laws as well as uncovering and explaining to the public exactly what the laws, regulations, and surveillance activities were and why they presented a challenge to Canadians' Charter rights. Although it seems safe to say that mainstream media coverage of the BCCLA Charter challenge has educated some of the public regarding CSE and mass surveillance, it is difficult to measure the extent of its impact on policy changes.

It is clear, however, that Charter challenges in general can result in concrete changes in law. When dealing with surveillance and national security, relying on pressure from the public or at the polls can be difficult, and obtaining a ruling that forces a government (especially a majority government) to make legislative changes can therefore be a useful strategy. Furthermore, a lawsuit can put pressure on the government to act before the courts issue their decision, to save face or to avoid disclosure or further legal concerns. At the same time, lawsuits can be resource-intensive and drawn out, and there is little guarantee that a court ruling will support, in full or in part, the goal a campaign hopes to achieve. If the goal is to access and make public some information never before disclosed, or to change the law in situations where public pressure seems improbable or insufficient, and if one has the resources and the patience for such endeavours, then lawsuits and Charter challenges might be the better approach.

It would seem that the Stop Online Spying campaign contributed to the defeat of Bill C-30 thanks to not only its hashtag #TellVicEverything and its online petition but also its multi-faceted approach, including coalition building, lobbying, and popular education through online videos and community screenings. It would also appear that the campaign took advantage of a moment in time that, unfortunately, cannot be planned and thus cannot be replicated. As we have seen, no such moment enabled us to avoid the adoption of Bill C-13, a subsequent piece of lawful access legislation. Being able to recognize such a moment and being prepared to seize it are lessons we can take from the Stop Online Spying campaign. Although multi-faceted campaigns and viral online petitions also require resources, they are more accessible than lawsuits for many individual campaigners and non-profit organizations.

Mass surveillance being an international issue, an international campaign might be what is needed. The International Campaign Against Mass Surveillance offers a few lessons for such a project. One is that novel ways of framing and publicizing the issue of mass surveillance as a serious problem that can be solved appear to be essential in order to mobilize people. The political climate also needs to be taken into account in order not to waste precious resources and energy on governments that refuse to act on the issue. The creation of more solid international structures or a more formal international entity is a potential avenue to explore. Finally, a deeper collective reflection on the struggle against mass surveillance, as well as securing more resources and ensuring the succession within the movement, appears to be necessary in order to sustain this type of long-term campaign.

Unfortunately, it remains difficult to quantify the results or qualify any of these campaigns as complete successes (although campaigns often achieve partial or incremental reform). Or, perhaps more precisely, while each has in large part fulfilled its immediate goals, the broader goal of reversing (and eventually eliminating) intrusive, rights-undermining mass surveillance has yet to be achieved. There is a strong argument to be made that civil society campaigns have effectively slowed the growth of mass surveillance for national security purposes, but if we were to measure whether mass surveillance is more prevalent now than in 2001, it is clear that despite the revelations of Edward Snowden and other whistle-blowers, as well as the work of progressive legislators and of civil society groups, mass surveillance has continued to grow.

The lessons that we can draw from these cases are reflective of campaign strategies adopted in other sectors as well:

- Have clear, direct targets. Attacking the entire national security apparatus, while necessary, appears to be aiming at too broad a target. This makes it difficult to enunciate clear goals and engage the public in a clear campaign. Targeting of CSE or of lawful access made those campaigns more straightforward, with clear measures of success.
- Build coalitions across sectors. ICAMS went beyond civil society to build bridges and allies in the government bureaucracy through privacy commissioners' offices. OpenMedia reached out to conservative libertarians and business organizations that shared similar concerns over privacy as well as the cost to industry and users of forcing ISPs to integrate interfaces for government surveillance technology into their own infrastructure.
- Use a diversity of tactics. Although the more facets a campaign has, the more intense the use of resources (which are often limited for civil society organizations), by multiplying the kinds of tactics and tools used – targeted to the campaign's specific goal – each of these campaigns was able to achieve greater impact.

Another important aspect of these kinds of campaigns is how to address the underlying motivation for government mass surveillance. As mentioned at the outset of this chapter, government surveillance has often developed as a form of control or pacification. Others have also argued that what we are witnessing is a kind of change in equilibrium, towards a government that is wrapped in privacy and a population expected to live in public, whereas the democratic model is the opposite.

Surveillance, with the companion concept of national security, is also often developed as a means to control minority and marginalized groups or any community that poses a perceived threat to the status go. Integrating arguments for equality and justice – including anti-racist, feminist, and anti-colonial frameworks – into anti-surveillance campaigns may help stop specific laws as well as undermine the rationale for such laws. It can also allow for new and broader partnerships to form across organizations, including those from directly impacted communities. The difficulty lies in how to communicate to the public the current issue as well as the underlying motivations, which can be quite complex. Parallel campaigns, which address both the immediate legislative issues and more systemic concerns, can support each other. We see this in some of the work undertaken by the organizations addressed in this chapter, but would argue that more can be done (including at the ICLMG).

Conclusion

As mass surveillance becomes more and more normalized and ubiquitous, traditional and targeted campaigns and actions seem limited in their outcomes, especially if one's desired outcome is the abolition of mass surveillance. More research and reflection are necessary to identify the real impact of our campaigning and more radical methods to effect changes. The constant barrage of new legislation slowly allowing more and more surveillance makes it difficult to take the time to evaluate the efficiency of our advocacy, but it also makes it all the more urgent.

A broader research project that investigates both the actions and thought processes of campaigners as well as those of government officials through more interviews, access to information requests, and primary source documentation could help answer some of the outstanding questions raised in this chapter. Other interesting avenues to explore could be international comparisons of campaigns targeting similar surveillance concerns in different countries. For example, the Five Eyes countries often adopt similar laws, so an examination of successes and failures in different jurisdictions could be enlightening. Overall, however, we believe these three cases show how important it is for civil liberties and privacy groups to maintain long-term coordinated resistance to mass surveillance, and provide some indications that such resistance will continue to grow and hopefully achieve new victories in the coming years.

Notes

1 Tia Dafnos, Scott Thompson, and Martin French, "Surveillance and the Colonial Dream: Canada's Surveillance of Indigenous Self-Determination," in *National Security, Surveillance and Terror,* edited by Randy K. Lippert, Kevin Walby, Ian Warren, and Darren Palmer (Basingstoke, UK: Palgrave Macmillan, 2016), 324.
2 Mark Neocleous, *War Power, Police Power* (Edinburgh: Edinburgh University Press, 2014), 31–35.
3 Cited in ibid., 33–34.
4 Ibid., 34.
5 Gary Kinsman, Dieter K. Buse, and Mercedes Steedman, "Introduction," in *Whose National Security? Canadian State Surveillance and the Creation of Enemies* (Toronto: Between the Lines, 2000), 1–8; Luis A. Fernandez, *Policing Dissent: Social Control and the Anti-Globalization Movement* (New Brunswick, NJ: Rutgers University Press, 2008), 94–107.
6 Paul Bernal, "Data Gathering, Surveillance and Human Rights: Recasting the Debate," *Journal of Cyber Policy* 1, 2 (2016): 243–64; Jon Penney, "Chilling Effects: Online Surveillance and Wikipedia Use," *Berkeley Technology Law Journal* 31, 1 (2016): 117, SSRN, https://ssrn.com/abstract=2769645; Dafnos, Thompson, and French, "Surveillance and the Colonial Dream," 324.
7 Colin J. Bennett, Kevin D. Haggerty, David Lyon, and Valerie Steeves, eds., *Transparent Lives: Surveillance in Canada* (Edmonton: Athabasca University Press, 2014), 19–37.
8 Ibid., 12.

9 Gregory S. Kealey, *Spying on Canadians: The Royal Canadian Mounted Police Security Service and the Origins of the Long Cold War* (Toronto: University of Toronto Press, 2017), 1–13.

10 Canada, Bill C-36, *Anti-terrorism Act*, 1st Sess, 37th Parl, 2001, http://www.parl.ca/DocumentViewer/en/37-1/bill/C-36/royal-assent.

11 Canada, Bill C-51, *Anti-terrorism Act, 2015*, 2nd Sess, 41st Parl, 2015, http://www.parl.ca/DocumentViewer/en/41-2/bill/C-51/royal-assent.

12 Canada, Bill C-59, *An Act respecting national security matters*, 1st Sess, 42nd Parl, 2017, http://www.parl.ca/DocumentViewer/en/42-1/bill/C-59/second-reading [*National Security Act, 2017*]; International Civil Liberties Monitoring Group (ICLMG), "Breaking Down Bill C-59, the New National Security Act," http://iclmg.ca/issues/bill-c-59-the-national-security-act-of-2017/.

13 BC Civil Liberties Association (BCCLA), "BCCLA Sues Canadian Government to Stop Illegal Spying," https://bccla.org/stop-illegal-spying/protect-our-privacy-case-details/.

14 BCCLA, "Backgrounder on Spying: Civil Liberties Watchdog Sues Surveillance Agency over Illegal Spying on Canadians," 1 June 2016, https://bccla.org/wp-content/uploads/2016/06/2016_06_02_Backgrounder-BCCLA-Sues-CSE-1.pdf.

15 Ibid.

16 BCCLA, "Illegal Spying: BCCLA Files Class Action Lawsuit against Canada's Electronic Spy Agency," 1 April 2014, https://bccla.org/news/2014/04/illegal-spying-bccla-files-class-action-lawsuit-against-canadas-electronic-spy-agency/.

17 James Keller, "Ottawa Says CSEC's Collection of Canadians' Data 'incidental,'" *CTV News*, 24 January 2014, https://www.ctvnews.ca/canada/ottawa-says-csec-s-collection-of-canadians-data-incidental-1.1655231.

18 BCCLA to the Attorney General of Canada, Statement of Claim to the Defendant, 27 October 2014, https://bccla.org/wp-content/uploads/2014/12/20141027-CSEC-Statement-of-Claim.pdf.

19 Ibid.

20 BCCLA, "Stop Illegal Spying," https://bccla.org/stop-illegal-spying/.

21 BCCLA, "Spying in Canada: Civil Liberties Watchdog Sues Surveillance Agency over Illegal Spying on Canadians," 23 October 2013, https://bccla.org/wp-content/uploads/2013/10/Final-Press-Release-Spying-10_21_131.pdf.

22 Greg Weston, "CSEC Used Airport Wi-Fi to Track Canadian Travellers: Edward Snowden Documents," *CBC News*, 31 January 2014, http://www.cbc.ca/news/politics/csec-used-airport-wi-fi-to-track-canadian-travellers-edward-snowden-documents-1.2517881; Dave Seglins, "CSE Tracks Millions of Downloads Daily: Snowden Documents," *CBC News*, 27 January 2015, http://www.cbc.ca/news/canada/cse-tracks-millions-of-downloads-daily-snowden-documents-1.2930120.

23 Colin Freeze and Wendy Stueck, "Civil Liberties Groups Launch Lawsuit against Canadian Eavesdropping Agency," *Globe and Mail*, 22 October 2013, https://www.theglobeandmail.com/news/national/canadian-eavesdropping-agency-facing-lawsuit-from-civil-liberties-group/article14984074/; "Canadian Spy Agency Sued for Allegedly Violating Charter," *CBC News*, 22 October 2013, http://www.cbc.ca/news/canada/british-columbia/canadian-spy-agency-sued-for-allegedly-violating-charter-1.2158884; Gillian Shaw, "BC Civil Liberties Association Launches Lawsuit against Canada's Electronic Surveillance Agency," *Vancouver Sun*, 22 October 2013, http://vancouversun.com/news/staff-blogs/bc-civil-liberties-association-launches-lawsuit-against-canadian-government-over-csec-spying.

24 Liam Britten, "BCCLA Says Warrantless Spying on Canadians Must End," *CBC News*, 23 June 2016, http://www.cbc.ca/news/canada/british-columbia/bccla-cse-surveillance-1.3650286.

25 "The 'Top Secret' Surveillance Directives," *Globe and Mail,* 2 June 2016, https://www.the globeandmail.com/news/national/top-secret-surveillance-directives/article30249860/.

26 Ibid.

27 Monique Scotti, "Here's What You Need to Know about Canada's 'Extraordinarily Permissive' New Spying Laws," *Global News,* 6 February 2018, https://globalnews.ca/news/3999947/cse-c59-new-spy-powers-canada/.

28 BCCLA, "Written Submissions of the British Columbia Civil Liberties Association ('BCCLA') to the Standing Committee on Public Safety and National Security regarding Bill C-59, An Act respecting national security matters," 30 January 2018, http://www.ourcommons.ca/Content/Committee/421/SECU/Brief/BR9669809/br-external/British ColumbiaCivilLibertiesAssociation-e.pdf.

29 Christopher A. Parsons, Lex Gill, Tamir Israel, Bill Robinson, and Ronald J. Deibert, "Analysis of the Communications Security Establishment Act and Related Provisions in Bill C-59 (an Act Respecting National Security Matters), First Reading," *Transparency and Accountability,* December 2017, SSRN, https://ssrn.com/abstract=3101557.

30 Canada, Bill C-30, *An Act to enact the Investigating and Preventing Criminal Electronic Communications Act and to amend the Criminal Code and other Acts,* 1st Sess, 41st Parl, 2012, http://www.parl.ca/LegisInfo/BillDetails.aspx?Language=E&billId=5375610.

31 Sarah Schmidt and Jason Fekete, "Vic Toews Will 'Entertain Amendments' to Online Surveillance Bill," *National Post,* 15 February 2012, http://nationalpost.com/news/canada/protecting-children-from-internet-predators-act-vic-toews.

32 Gillian Shaw, "Stop Online Spying," *Vancouver Sun,* 15 September 2011, https://vancouversun.com/news/staff-blogs/stop-online-spying-openmedia-ca-launches-campaign -against-web-surveillance-legislation/.

33 Schmidt and Fekete, "Vic Toews Will 'Entertain Amendments.'"

34 Philippa Lawson, *Moving toward a Surveillance Society: Proposals to Expand 'Lawful Access' in Canada* (Vancouver: BCCLA, January 2012), https://bccla.org/wp-content/uploads/2012/03/2012-BCCLA-REPORT-Moving-toward-a-surveillance-society.pdf.

35 Laura Payton, "Internet Privacy Experts Raise Concerns over Crime Bill," *CBC News,* 9 August 2011, http://www.cbc.ca/news/politics/internet-privacy-experts-raise-concerns -over-crime-bill-1.1090482; Michael Geist, "The Conservatives Commitment to Internet Surveillance," *Michael Geist* (blog), 9 April 2011, http://www.michaelgeist.ca/2011/04/conservative-lawful-access-commit/.

36 OpenMedia, "A Look Back at Our Stop the Meter Campaign," https://openmedia.org/en/ca/look-back-our-stop-meter-campaign.

37 OpenMedia, "Invasive Surveillance Bills Will Cost Canadians in Cash and Civil Liberties, Says New Coalition," 22 June 2011, https://openmedia.org/en/press/invasive-surveillance -bills-will-cost-canadians-cash-and-civil-liberties-says-new-coalition.

38 OpenMedia to Right Honorable Prime Minister Stephen Harper, "RE: Omnibus Crime Bill," 9 August 2001, https://assets.documentcloud.org/documents/230754/letter-to-harper -re-lawfulaccess.pdf.

39 Daniel Tencer, "'Lawful Access' Legislation Missing from Omnibus Crime Bill, but Online Spying Fight Isn't Over," *Huffington Post Canada,* 20 September 2011, https://www.huffingtonpost.ca/2011/09/20/lawful-access-legislation_n_971965.html.

40 Postmedia News, "Online Surveillance Bill Critics Are Siding with 'Child Pornographers': Vic Toews," *National Post,* 14 February 2012, http://nationalpost.com/news/canada/online-surveillance-bill-critics-are-siding-with-child-pornographers-vic-toews.

41 Melissa Martin, "TellVicEverything an Internet Sensation," *Winnipeg Free Press,* 17 February 2012, https://www.winnipegfreepress.com/local/tell-vic-everything-an-internet -sensation-139501528.html.

42 Steve Anderson, "Stop Online Spying Hits 100k: Canadians Are an Inspiration," Open-Media.ca, 17 February 2012, https://openmedia.org/en/stop-online-spying-hits-100k -canadians-are-inspiration.

43 Ibid.

44 OpenMedia, "A Look Back at Our Stop Spying Campaign against Canada's Bill C-30," https://openmedia.org/en/ca/look-back-our-stop-spying-campaign-against-canadas -bill-c-30.

45 Canadian Press, "Conservatives Kill Controversial 'Child Pornographers' Internet Surveillance Bill," *National Post*, 11 February 2013, http://nationalpost.com/news/politics/ conservatives-kill-controversial-internet-surveillance-bill.

46 Evan Dyer, "Cyberbullying Bill Draws Fire from Diverse Mix of Critics," *CBC News*, 20 October 2014, http://www.cbc.ca/news/politics/cyberbullying-bill-draws-fire-from -diverse-mix-of-critics-1.2803637.

47 International Campaign Against Mass Surveillance (ICAMS), *The Emergence of a Global Infrastructure for Mass Registration and Surveillance* (ICAMS, April 2005), https:// web.archive.org/web/20070109200500/http://www.i-cams.org/ICAMS1.pdf; ICAMS, "The Emergence of a Global Infrastructure for Mass Registration and Surveillance: 10 Signposts," https://web.archive.org/web/20061219231540/http://www.i-cams.org:80/ Surveillance_intro.html; ICAMS, "Campaign Declaration," https://web.archive.org/ web/20061219231451/http://www.i-cams.org:80/Declaration_Eng.html.

48 Maureen Webb, *Illusions of Security: Global Surveillance and Democracy in the Post-9/11 World* (San Francisco: City Lights Books, 2007).

49 The Global Privacy Assembly (GPA), 18 May 2020, https://globalprivacyassembly.org/ the-assembly-and-executive-committee/history-of-the-assembly/; International Conference of Data Protection and Privacy Commissioners (ICDPPC), "Resolution on the Urgent Need for Global Standards for Safeguarding Passenger Data to Be Used by Governments for Law Enforcement and Border Security Purposes," 29th International Conference, Montreal, 2007, http://globalprivacyassembly.org/wp-content/uploads/2015/02/ Resolution-on-Urgent-need-for-global-standards-for-safeguarding-passenger-data-to -be-used-by-governments-for-law-enforcement-and-border-security-purposes.pdf.

50 ICDPPC, "Resolution on the Urgent Need for Protecting Privacy in a Borderless World, and for Reaching a Joint Proposal for Setting International Standards on Privacy and Personal Data Protection," 30th International Conference, Strasbourg, France, 2008, http://globalprivacyassembly.org/wp-content/uploads/2015/02/Resoltuion-on-the -urgent-need-for-protecting-privacy-in-a-borderless-world.pdf.

51 Serge Ménard and Joe Comartin, "Anti-Terrorism Act Dissenting Opinion," in *Rights, Limits, Security: A Comprehensive Review of the Anti-Terrorism Act and Related Issues*, Report of the Standing Committee on Public Safety and National Security, March 2007, http://www.ourcommons.ca/DocumentViewer/en/39-1/SECU/report-7/page-69.

12

Protesting Bill C-51
Reflections on Connective Action against Big Data Surveillance

Jeffrey Monaghan and Valerie Steeves

> Get a couple of beers in them and [privacy advocates] will fantasize about
> what they call the "Privacy Chernobyl" – the one privacy outrage that will
> finally catalyze an effective social movement around the issue.
> – PHILIP AGRE, CITED IN THE PRIVACY ADVOCATES:
> RESISTING THE SPREAD OF SURVEILLANCE

IN OCTOBER 2014, a homeless man killed a soldier standing guard by the National War Memorial in downtown Ottawa using an antique single-shot rifle, and then entered the front entrance of Parliament's Centre Block. Within minutes, he was shot and killed by parliamentary security. Days later, taking advantage of this tragic yet exceptional act of violence, Prime Minister Stephen Harper's government proposed sweeping reform to the policing and security powers contained in the *Anti-terrorism Act*. The legislation, known as Bill C-51, included increased powers of surveillance and information sharing, as well as contentious powers of disruption that would enable judges to sanction, in advance, police actions that would explicitly violate the *Canadian Charter of Rights and Freedoms*.[1]

Bill C-51 was among a number of surveillance and intelligence-sharing proposals that had been floated to strengthen the ability of security agencies to engage in big data practices of mass collection for the purpose of future preemptive action through algorithmic induction; indeed, critics suggested that the proposals were ready-made, simply waiting for the appropriate tragedy to be officialized.[2] In spite of the social backdrop of fear and anxiety, public criticism of Bill C-51 quickly emerged. Cross-country mobilizations included a number of national days of action that attracted thousands of protest participants in fifty-five cities across the country.[3] Newspapers, television news, and social media exploded with debate, and thousands of Canadians signed petitions and open letters of protest, gradually building a critical mass in opposition grounded loosely on concerns about civil liberties, privacy politics, and policing powers in the "War on Terror."

Although an amended version of the bill was enacted into law, the public response to Bill C-51 stands in stark contrast to the lack of public engagement in privacy issues noted by Colin Bennett in his study of privacy advocacy. In spite of the ongoing efforts of a long-standing coalition of civil society groups and academics working to slow the spread of surveillance, Bennett rightly concluded that efforts to reform privacy laws were largely in the hands of a global cadre of "privacy experts" and anti-surveillance politics was "still generally an elitist issue within government, business and civil society."[4] Less than ten years after the publication of Bennett's study, grassroots opposition to government surveillance would ignite.

In this chapter, we explore this shift and suggest that campaigning against C-51 represented a unique moment in Canadian politics when surveillance issues entered the domain of social movement mobilization. While resistance to surveillance is often characterized as interventionist (e.g., artistic installations, tactical disruptions, litigation), the C-51 campaign transcended a single issue of privacy and instead mobilized broader publics and politics in resistance to the expansion of policing powers and the prospects of enhanced big data surveillance. Although the movement may not have been sustained over the long term and was not rekindled when the subsequent Liberal government further enhanced surveillance powers under Bill C-59 (discussed elsewhere in this volume), we suggest that the mobilizations against C-51 provide certain strategic and tactical insights for organizing against the incursions of big data surveillance.

This chapter revisits aspects of the campaign against C-51 to provide perspective on contemporary efforts to expand and intensify surveillance, particularly the data collection and information-sharing components of big data practices. We conducted twelve semi-structured interviews with organizers in the campaign. Interview participants were grouped according to three criteria: (1) traditional privacy or civil liberties activists (five participants); (2) Internet and/ or broadly hacktivist (e.g., Internet freedom) activists (four participants); and (3) non-traditional activists whose activism was not at all related to surveillance but who joined the campaign (three participants).[5]

Based on data collected through these interviews, we develop two arguments that can be taken from the C-51 mobilizations. First, the movement against C-51 is an excellent example of a heterogeneous movement of what Lance Bennett and Alexandra Segerberg call connective action.[6] The movement does not conform to the collective action described by the strict Social Movement Organization (SMO) typology of social movement studies, but instead accords more with emerging models of hybrid movements enabled by digitally mediated personal action frames. Second, C-51 campaigning was successful as a hybrid movement not only because it built on the repertoire, quasi-organizational strengths, and public education campaigns of the previous decade vis-à-vis warrantless access and digital privacy work but also because it took advantage of specific affordances available at the moment. In particular, we address the affordances created by the Snowden revelations and the opportunities to use the ineffectiveness of the political environment as a mechanism for public education. We close with a discussion of the barriers or demobilization challenges that pre-dated the C-51 campaign and impacted the ability of surveillance critics to challenge Bill C-59. Although these challenges will continue to be relevant to any action against intrusive big data surveillance practices associated with national security, we suggest that the connective actions used in the C-51 campaign may provide a roadmap for resisting big data surveillance in the future.

Opposition to Bill C-51 as Organizationally Enabled Connective Action

Social movement scholarship has underlined how digitally enabled movements have transformed the study of contemporary protests and/or efforts to bring about political change.[7] Much of the early literature on social movements focused on *collective action* and evaluated the role of SMOs with respect to their mobilization of resources or how they fit into political opportunity structures. Especially because the literature was rooted in psychology and economics, theorists posited SMOs as rational actors that sought to effect change within an institutionally defined public sphere.

The rise of more fluid forms of digitally enabled movements has coincided with the waning influence of traditional SMOs as a bedrock for mobilizing the public.[8] Emerging scholarship is accordingly directed towards the role of digital technology in the formation and mobilization of a wide variety of different groups and individuals – what Bennett and Segerberg call *connective action* – as well as the new dynamics of group identities that bind movements and give them a sense of "we-ness" despite their heterogeneity.[9] In this sense, public mobilization is addressed by looking less towards the role of institutional actors and more towards what Ian Angus calls the "emergent publics": an amorphous social sphere that can be mobilized based on digital infrastructures of resonance.[10] Zeynep Tufekci uses the term "digitally networked public sphere" in recognition of how the public and the digital have been reconfigured where neither domain is exclusive of the other,[11] but where digital environments have become central to what Paolo Gerbaudo describes as "information diffusion, public discussions, and calls for mobilization."[12] This suggests that within the digitally networked public sphere, SMOs have become less central in the circulation of a mobilization economy that involves far more plural, heterogeneous actors.

At the same time, as Bennett and Segerberg argue, SMOs continue to be an important unit of analysis despite their diminished role because of their ongoing visible participation in contemporary mobilizations that are enabled through digital connections. Bennett and Segerberg accordingly apply "hybrid" network theory as a middle space between the logics of collective versus connective actions, and posit that hybrid networks feature "conventional organizations [that] operate in the background of protest and issue advocacy networks to enable personalized engagement."[13] These forms of "organizationally enabled connective action" are characterized by the "stepping back [of formal SMOs] from projecting strong agendas, political brands, and collective identities in favor of using resources to deploy social technologies enabling loose public networks to form around personalized action themes."[14]

In these types of contemporary mobilizations, Bennett and Segerberg have found three general characteristics: (1) familiar NGOs and other civil society organizations engage in loose collaborations to provide something of a networking backbone for (2) digital media networks to engage a broader public around contested political issues, yet with (3) fewer efforts and abilities to brand the issues around specific organizations, own the messages, or control the understandings of individual participants.[15] We suggest that these characteristics of organizationally enabled connective action are useful for understanding the Bill C-51 protests as a hybrid social movement that balanced a degree of formally organized action frames, but where SMOs enabled a broader public engagement with issues of surveillance and privacy that resonated through digital spheres of information consumption and diffusion. Given the lack of a coherent privacy movement in Canada, the strength of the Bill C-51 protest was notable for its hybridity. To begin with, the SMOs involved with issues related to privacy, civil liberties, or surveillance in Canada are quite small. More appropriately characterized as small advocacy groups or NGOs, these groups have limited experience with mobilizing a public in line with a more traditional SMO model. "The normal politics of privacy," writes Bennett in the *Privacy Advocates*, "involves the quite relentless and painstaking attempt to understand the policies and proposals of government and business and to inject privacy argumentation and reasoning."[16] Often involving technical and privacy-oriented engagements that create what Jonathan Obar calls technocratic divides, privacy issues have typically lacked a politics of contention that form a basis for social movement action.[17]

Yet our data suggest that the loose network of technically oriented actors involved in privacy issues had formalized their connections over the past decade or more of privacy- and surveillance-related issues. Blayne Haggart, for example, suggests that the Fair Copyright campaign of the early 2010s was a moment when the loose network of copyright advocates – closely associated with Internet freedom activism – was galvanized into a social movement through digitally enabled connective action.[18] Similarly, a number of our participants underlined the importance of campaigns against lawful access laws as formalizing the hybrid action network.[19] The lawful access debates provide an excellent example of what Jennifer Earl and Katrina Kimport describe as e-tactics and e-mobilizations.[20] However, the movement against lawful access never translated from online activism to protest mobilizations.

Based on the networks established through earlier campaigning, organizers were able to quickly come together and establish a new campaign as soon as the government introduced Bill C-51, using a variety of digitally mediated efforts. As described by another participant:

> [When] Bill C-51 [was announced] that's when we really kicked into high gear with the Charter challenge and petition and letter writing campaigns, social media campaigns, basically all the tactics ... [that] organizations like ours can use and we've been fighting that battle now for four years.[21]

Almost immediately, the C-51 campaign was also far more heterogeneous, attracting the participation of activists who were engaged more broadly in political/economic (e.g., labour unions) and Internet/Internet freedom issues (e.g., net neutrality). As one participant put it, "a lot more groups – a bit bigger diversity groups came in."[22] This brought with it a concomitant diversity of views about government surveillance and policing, and opened up more space for members of the public to engage with the campaign for their own purposes and from their own personal action frames. It enabled participants to act in concert, if not collectively, to push back against surveillance and move the opposition from online campaigning into protest organizing.

We turn now to the factors that supported this shift.

Affordances in the Post-Snowden Environment

Affordance theories have been used to explain how more fluid, or hybrid, social movement assemblages leverage specific opportunities to foster protest and dissent.[23] While affordance theories are often tied to technological repertoires, a key distinction when using affordance theory is its contrast to "opportunities" theories. Within SMO literature, opportunities are theorized statically: as precise conditions where movement organizations apply a calculus to guide actions towards social change. Affordances are far more fluid: they consider contentiousness as constantly in flux where contemporary political actions are mediated through social media and associative publics. Seeing connective actions as including heterogeneous groups who may (or may not) share collective political identities, affordance theory accords a broader scope of personal and organizational agency to political action.

In positing themselves against more traditional social movement theories that weigh rational activity with organizational resources or political opportunities within a more rigid "public" sphere, scholars who discuss practices of affordances stress the heterogeneous and mixed constellation of forces that are provoked or harnessed within our increasingly "networked public."[24] Describing how digitally enabled movements interact and make use of networked publics, Earl and Kimport suggest that "leveraged affordances" have opened a range of opportunities to mobilize publics both offline and online, while dramatically lowering costs associated with creating, organizing, and participating in protests.[25] While affordance theories have been critiqued for remaining overly techno-socio,[26] we stress that affordances are best conceptualized as opportunities for connective action within hybrid social movements.

In the context of the anti-surveillance movement, our participants reported that both collective and connective action had been limited pre-C-51 because of the high level of secrecy surrounding policing and national security information practices. The resulting lack of transparency made it difficult to hold agencies to account through the traditional political process, or to provide digitally enabled opportunities for people to protest. As one participant put it:

> Here's a statement of CSIS [the Canadian Security Intelligence Service]: "we will neither confirm nor deny and we will not tell you whether in our opinion we should get a warrant if we were ever to use one." I'm sorry, we will not tell you parliamentarians whether CSIS would get a warrant for the use of IMSI-catchers? What is that? That is a shocking level of disdain for democratic process.[27]

The lack of solid information about how and when surveillance was being mobilized made it particularly difficult to engage a public that was under-informed and fearful about security:

> I mean it's such a pervasive issue, and the PR machine of the governments and the spy agencies are so much bigger and they have so much ammunition to throw out there, especially with, you know, the fear mongering going on in the United States and around the world, it's a hard, hard battle to fight.[28]

Interestingly, our participants indicated that these two factors also combined to immobilize politicians and shut down dissenting voices among parliamentarians: "There is such fear and so that fear is even affecting our policy makers. So even if we can see sometimes and we can feel that yes they want to make these changes, it's like the political environment is really always pushing that in the other direction."[29] The creation of "an imbalance towards security" makes it even more difficult to obtain any transparency from government agencies engaged in surveillance. As one participant concluded, "again, we're not asking you for secret facts here. We're not asking you for operational secrets. We're talking about the rule of law and CSIS flips the bird."[30] When asked why the C-51 campaign was able to overcome the barrier of publicly debating security policies, many of our participants cited the Snowden revelations of 2013. Although much of the material released by Edward Snowden regarding the surveillance net created by the Five Eyes partners (Australia, Canada, New Zealand, the United Kingdom, and the United States) had been previously discussed in traditional media by whistle-blowers, the Snowden documents were seen as a central element of the success of the C-51 campaign. In what Bennett might call a "privacy Chernobyl,"[31] the Snowden documents – including information detailing the role of Canadian agencies – were quickly leveraged into wide-ranging debates regarding mass surveillance and privacy. One participant recounted:

> I mean it's a weird trade-off where I think that everyone knew that it was happening, but on the other side of the same coin you have the fact that if you bring that up, you're basically a tinfoil hat person. And I think that Edward Snowden made this more of a socially acceptable thing to talk about versus something that people didn't know. People already knew it was happening, but it was something that they didn't really want to talk about because they didn't want to seem like the crazy person. But now it's more acceptable to talk about.[32]

Another participant described the difficulties in addressing allegations of mass surveillance without having hard evidence, while also emphasizing the richness of the revelations that came from Snowden's leaks: "I make a joke about that that for a month after the Snowden revelations my outgoing message on my answering machine said, 'I told you so.' There were surprises even within the privacy community."[33]

As David Lyon has noted, the Snowden revelations have "done good service in showing how far state-based surveillance extends but also how much it depends on Big Data practices that implicate corporate bodies and connect directly with everyday practices of ordinary internet and cellphone users."[34] Participants echoed these claims by highlighting how the detailed evidence Snowden provided fed the critiques of mass surveillance and how the consequences of these big data surveillance practices were used in their public advocacy work. One participant noted: "But what Snowden did I think had a huge impact, not only raising the level of general understanding about what was going on, but actually putting tools in the hands of people who had been trying to crack this nut for a long time."[35] The transparency created by the Snowden revelations provided an important affordance for work on surveillance and privacy, and was also highlighted specifically as an important factor in the debates that emerged over Bill C-51: "I think Snowden helped [because it] really raised the ... salience of those issues [surveillance] to a broader set of people, which by the time C-51 rolled along ... I think helped [by] going outside the privacy bucket."[36]

That enlarged "privacy bucket" also provided a repertoire to the public at large. This was particularly true in the use of social media to tweet or share information regarding the impacts of C-51 in expanding information-sharing and surveillance practices. Using social media affordances that appeared as a result of the massive circulation of Snowden-related content, the hybridity of the C-51 movement created opportunities to leverage the *ineffectiveness* of the political environment. Often engagement with capital-P politics is conceived as an effort to reform or direct the legislative process, or the platforms of political parties.[37] Yet, from the perspective of C-51 movement participants, the political engagement around the proposed bill created opportunities to engage in public education and movement building. This was particularly true regarding work associated with attending parliamentary committee hearings. As with traditional SMOs, participating in institutional moments of lawmaking allowed C-51 critics to reach a much broader audience than merely the politicians themselves because of the media attention the bill attracted. But it also provided opportunities to leverage this focused attention to educate journalists and members of the public about the issues.

As one participant said:

It's not just a resonance ... [it's that] you get to the education component of it. Like you do build on it every time. So with C-51 – starting with the initial lawful access stuff, we had a lot of education to do – like journalists first. Like not – education's maybe the wrong word, but like we would have to – like it would take a while for journalists to get why this is a problem, how it works, etc., right? ... but we went through that process and then they get it ... then eventually they get it.[38]

A prominent example of this dynamic involved the issue of metadata, where the technology would have to be explained in the most basic form, but then journalists gradually understood and presented more comprehensive criticisms of the "just a postcard" argument. In order to get the criticisms to the public, some messaging work and explanations were developed first with the journalists that involved "explaining it over and over."[39]

Describing parliamentary committees as "a form of theatre," another participant remarked that "it is valuable [just] being able to get your position on the record and frankly, in Hansard," but the broader objective is to move "the public debate."[40] "I want to expand the public's sphere and expand the sphere of public space, and so those types of things are useful moments for that."[41] Again, the hybridity of the movement amplified the reach of debate beyond the more structured format of mainstream journalism by first engaging with journalists to expand their understanding of the issue, and then tweeting, blogging, and forwarding the information to feed into a broader public discussion.

In this way, our participants were able to work around the intransigence of the Conservative government of the day and work with a heterogeneous group of advocates and members of the public to mobilize against the bill. This was unexpected, particularly given the "tough on crime" stance of the Harper government and the nature of the attack in October 2014. In addition, the content of the bill itself raised few expectations that committee members were going to be open to significant debate or amendments. As one participant put it, "I'm not a lawyer but I, I asked our, our law-legal guy 'does that mean what I think it means?' And he was like 'yeah, this is pretty bad.' So pretty much right away, right on day one we knew we were in for a hell of a fight."[42]

In the early period after Bill C-51 was tabled, a loose network of privacy and civil liberties groups formed alliances with non-traditional privacy groups to educate and mobilize against the bill. One participant describes the early period: "We worked with a bunch of other organizations on a petition that ended up, getting over 300,000 signatures, which in a country the population of Canada is remarkable."[43] The connection with online activists was particularly fruitful, as it enabled the movement towards social media affordances to support a number of connective actions. These included petitions, social media campaigns, and several days of action. Consistent with the hybrid model, the SMOs took a backseat role; although the network tried to "craft a unified message," each member of the movement could "then take [it] to our individual constituencies and take it to the press and blast out across Canada."[44]

This set the stage that enabled social media calls for a national day of action to transform the campaign into a unique moment of large protest around privacy and surveillance issues. "It went viral and so it got like thousands of people signing up for this National Day of Action," described a participant from a non-traditional organization that joined the loose network because of potential chilling effects on its activist work. "And so from our perspective the Day of Action was a huge success ... And the rally here for example, in [city] was quite successful. We had over 5,000 people show up and [a] myriad of speakers."[45]

Describing the success in bringing a diverse group of participants to C-51 protests, a participant from a non-privacy background of activism noted:

> I went to the one protest here in [place] and seeing like, you know, people out on the streets of like [place] and [place] and like small towns right across the country on Bill C-51 was I think remarkable. So I think there's a huge public appetite out there for change.[46]

And that appetite for change was embraced by a wide variety of people who were mobilized by their own personal action frames. A participant from a traditional privacy group noted: "I participated in marches, in protests, in rallies and they were great, really great, great opportunities and great moments I would say to see people, not the usual suspects."[47] A participant from a non-privacy organization agreed:

> I mean a number of people from the C-51 campaign who were saying things like "oh this is my first time getting active in anything political." The number of people ... I've been to a bunch of different protests in [area] but was the – what was interesting about the C-51 one was – it definitely didn't seem to be like the usual kind of left wing kind of crowd that you would get.[48]

As a hybrid movement, the Bill C-51 days of action were created through a network that had been partially solidified from years of privacy activism related to surveillance, yet it was infused with organizations that had little history in protesting surveillance or privacy-related issues. Moreover, the affordances provided by the Snowden revelations, the negative political environment, and social media allowed for broad resonance and connective action with participants – not the "usual suspects" but those who had found what Bennett and Segerberg describe as "personalized" appeals to the protests. Although SMOs played an enabling role, the protests themselves became heterogeneous and far more diverse than previous moments of anti-surveillance activism.

As an example of organizationally enabled connective action, the C-51 movement was highly effective at changing public opinion on the bill. A combination of the political affordances and the mass mobilizations dramatically altered the framing that had been initially fostered by the Harper government. On participant recalled:

> You know, when C-51 was first brought on the books, something like 80 per cent of Canadians supported it and then that shifted almost immediately ... it was

almost a complete flip ... the fact that we were able to get so many Canadians so quickly to change their minds on it is incredible. Like, you don't see polls slip like that, ever ... I think the fact that we've gotten the media so on board with it is a huge success.[49]

This participant, who deals primarily with non-privacy–associated activism, summarized the success of the campaign as follows:

So I think we took a rather obscure topic and made it a point of national discussion ... I think we're able to sort of shift the frame, not for everyone but for a lot of people away from pure like security terrorism, to democratic debate, freedom, which I think is also helpful for a whole series of other debates that need to happen around, you know, net neutrality and a bunch of other things, where something that seems kind of obscure or almost benign actually is challenging, sort of like undercutting a lot of the underpinnings of [the] other types of freedoms we have.[50]

Framing connective action movements as heterogeneous amalgamations of actors is useful for understanding two successes that arose from the C-51 mobilizations. First, the concept of connective action helps explain how the campaign was able to move beyond the traditional frame of privacy advocacy – largely an elite exercise in legislative intervention – and merge SMO activities with mobilizations undertaken by a wide range of non-traditional actors approaching the problem from a variety of frames. This amplified the efforts of both SMOs and non-traditional actors because the deep reservoir of privacy-specific expertise was made available to support the interventions of others who could mobilize the information in their own ways and for their own purposes. Key to this was the willingness of the SMOs to let go of the need to define either the issues or the solutions. As Bennett and Segerberg note, tensions can arise when particular SMOs (especially political parties) vie to brand movements, yet the SMOs involved in the C-51 campaign demonstrated a tendency to remain more or less in the background. Second, the movement was successful in using affordances, as the participant above noted, to shift the frame of debate away from the "security" threats presented by the government. In part, this was accomplished by the use of personalized action frames that dramatically expanded the parameters of the debate, allowing an identification with a host of issues that connect to surveillance, privacy, democratic rights, policing powers, and so on. In expanding beyond the domains of privacy and anti-surveillance, the arena of political action was opened to more broad-based contentious political associations.

Discussion/Conclusions: Challenges in the Era of Big Data

In a rare example of public protests over surveillance, the organizationally enabled connective action against Bill C-51 parlayed opposition against mass surveillance into a flashpoint for anti-surveillance protests. Transparencies stemming from the Snowden revelations could be characterized as a "privacy Chernobyl" – an affordance that provided different contexts for people to interpret the negative consequences of Bill C-51 from their own personal action frames. SMOs could provide alternative perspectives on issues to support debate but they by no means had a leadership role during the protests. Instead, a broad and diverse array of concerned members of the public joined in protests against the bill. However, despite successes arising from the hybrid movement against Bill C-51, barriers continue to present obstacles to movements seeking to challenge big data surveillance. These challenges have been notable in recent efforts to contest the dramatic expansion of surveillance powers in Bill C-59 and, although they pre-date the C-51 protests, they remain just as (or even more) present in working against intrusive big data surveillance practices associated with national security.

Our participants were particularly cognizant of the enduring nature of these barriers. First was the secrecy associated with security governance practices, especially practices associated with big data. One participant recalled:

> We know SIRC [the Security Intelligence Review Committee] in its astonishing last annual report that does the first ever audit of CSIS' bulk data collections, bulk data holdings. And it's simply [a] gobsmacking finding that there is no evidence of any attempt to employ the correct legal standard in relation to those databases. We know the ongoing concerns with CSE [Communications Security Establishment], etc., etc. So check all those boxes. What are they all related to? They relate to bulk data. What are they about? They're about data analytics. We know that national security has been twisting themselves into pretzels to be able to for a minimum of the last 10 years – we think obviously much longer – to collect huge amounts of scraping of bulk data, C-51 of course giving them almost carte blanche to go dipping into it. They actually refer to "ingesting entire databases."[51]

While bulk data collection has been taking place for over a decade, security and policing agencies such as the RCMP, CSE, and CSIS have deliberately misled the public regarding the scope and objectives of its practices. The same agencies have also withheld vital information regarding bulk data collection from the courts. This development was spectacularly revealed in 2016 when the Federal Court lampooned CSIS for not meeting its duty of candour and deliberately withholding information on bulk data collection for ten years, including the existence of the Operational Data Analysis Centre (ODAC). Huysmans has characterized these securitarian practices as forms of political and security thickness.[52] In the current configurations, we see both forms of thickness deployed to make mass surveillance simultaneously diffuse and secretive. While political thickness is most associated with speech acts and the politics of fear that are used to rationalize more security and disallow – or delegitimize – critiques of security, security thickness refers to practices of security that are embedded in the proliferating fields of security and policing. In many aspects, security thickness is more acute – and more anti-democratic – in the sense that these fields of practices evade public knowledge due to their sensitive and specialized character. As one participant put it, "even for us who sit there and stare at those documents for months on end trying to figure out how it's gonna be used and talk to experts and whatever, it takes a while to get a fairly still murky picture [chuckles]."[53]

While the visibilities of social life are made more pronounced, including algorithmically, the visibility of security practices will continue to become more mercurial. Challenges to security thickness will likely accelerate and require sustained work from researchers, academics, and the legal community – the traditional domain of privacy advocates – although many participants raised the broader obstacle of having to mobilize the public in an increasingly fragmented environment. As a challenge that impacts social movements in the digitally mediated world, these dynamics are not unique to anti-surveillance movements, though some particular characteristics are worth reflecting upon.

One dynamic raised in the context of a discussion of post Snowden political implications was the overwhelming character of surveillance-related information. In making a point about potential ironies of the post-Snowden affordance, one participant noted that the public is overwhelmed with information about privacy and surveillance. A constant barrage of newspaper stories and discussions about surveillance often becomes "episodic discussions" about various technologies – but with little sustained debate or education. The outcome, suggested the participant, is that "they're just going to get overwhelmed. They're like, 'okay, well I'm screwed.' And they probably are to be honest. They probably are just screwed [chuckles]."[54]

The dangers of a post-privacy society are perhaps overstated, yet they correspond with a number of challenges facing SMOs working against mass surveillance. Oversaturated members of the public may increasingly tune out surveillance-related concerns, potentially closing the post-Snowden affordance. Post-privacy discourse is also mobilized by security and policing entities as a technique of security thickness, granting more space and opaqueness to their work. This is particularly evident with what one participant called the "allure of big data."[55]

Indeed, one of the most challenging dynamics in contesting big data is the supposed benefits – or "big data solutionism"[56] – espoused by its advocates. Appeals to big data solutionism are certainly not exclusive to security governance issues, but the dynamics of secrecy and potential for injustice that are rendered opaque by appeals to big data are particularly acute with security issues.

Despite the potential of post-privacy attitudes or the discourse of big data solutionism to obscure the ethical implications of the practices of mass data collection and algorithmic governance, the connective action that propelled Bill C-51 mobilizations may provide insight into practices that can challenge efforts to expand and intensify surveillance in the future. As Bennett and Segerberg have noted, the success of connective action results from the ability to "cast a broader public engagement net using interactive digital media and easy-to-personalize action themes, often deploying batteries of social technologies to help [people] spread the word over their personal networks."[57] Shifts in contemporary society towards personalized politics present challenges to the more traditional models and requirements of collective action, and a number of movements have made use of "personalized varieties of collective action" to spark public mobilizations.[58]

The movement from collective to connective action is represented as a move away from central organizations and a strong collective identity, as well as an opening of a broader field of political engagement. "Clicktivism," for example, has been associated with what Max Halupka characterizes as small, impulsive, non-ideological, political actions, such as clicking "likes" on Twitter or Facebook in an effort to raise awareness or contribute to social change through one's personal social media networks.[59] A far cry from the foundations of resource mobilization theories that require strong group identity and a recognition of political opportunities almost exclusively tied to capital-P politics, the personalized character of connective action offers more grounds for fluid, spontaneous political engagement. Yet, while connective action might be highly effective for contemporary mobilizations, from flash mobs to protest camps, are these new dynamics of public contestations effective at social change?

The broad spectrum of engagement around C-51 shows both an advantage and a disadvantage of connective action. While personalization can draw people into spontaneous resistance, the lack of organizational cohesion can result in quick dissipation and disaggregation unless SMOs adapt to shifting needs and continue to support new digital debates as they arise. Moreover, a growing area of concern – and attention – considers how digitally enabled actions have themselves become networked sites of mass surveillance, something we need to be very skeptical about.[60] Although the C-51 mobilizations demonstrate how connective action can translate into contentious politics, it is difficult to establish whether the contentiousness of such anti-surveillance politics have translated into action frames for broader resistance against both Bill C-59 and future surveillance-enhancing initiatives.

For connective action against creeping mass surveillance to continue, the hybrid organizational dynamics of the movement will have to create new personalizations that likely require new flashpoints or affordances to draw connectivity among members of the public along a spectrum of social justice issues, including, but not limited to, surveillance. Barriers of secrecy and media oversaturation are not new challenges, and strategies to mobilize can evolve from new repertoires of social movement action.

Notes

1 Craig Forcese and Kent Roach, *False Security: The Radicalization of Canadian Anti-Terrorism* (Montreal: Irwin Law, 2015).
2 Ibid.; Tamir Israel and Christopher Parsons, "Canada's National Security Consultation I: Digital Anonymity & Subscriber Identification Revisited ... Yet Again" (Canadian Internet Policy and Public Interest Clinic report, 2016), https://cippic.ca/uploads/20161005-CNSCI-RevisitingAnonymityYetAgain.pdf.
3 Michael Shulman, "Demonstrators Across Canada Protest Bill C-51," *CTV News*, 14 March 2015, http://www.ctvnews.ca/politics/demonstrators-across-canada-protest-bill-c-51-1.2279745.
4 Colin Bennett, *The Privacy Advocates: Resisting the Spread of Surveillance* (Cambridge, MA: MIT Press, 2008), 207. See also Colin Bennett and Charles Raab, *The Governances of Privacy* (Cambridge, MA: MIT Press, 2006).
5 Participant groups are denoted in the text as Traditional, Internet, and Other. Each interviewee has been given a number, e.g., Traditional 1.
6 W. Lance Bennett and Alexandra Segerberg, "The Logic of Connective Action: Digital Media and the Personalization of Contentious Politics," *Information, Communication and Society* 15, 5 (2012): 739–68.
7 Ibid.; Jennifer Earl and Katrina Kimport, *Digitally Enabled Social Change: Activism in the Internet Age* (Cambridge, MA: MIT Press, 2011); Paolo Gerbaudo, *Tweets and the Streets: Social Media and Contemporary Activism* (London: Pluto Press, 2012).
8 Jennifer Earl, "The Future of Social Movement Organizations: The Waning Dominance of SMOs Online," *American Behavioral Scientist* 59, 1 (2015): 35–52.
9 See debates on collective identity: Paolo Gerbaudo, *The Mask and the Flag: Populism, Citizenism, and Global Protest* (Oxford: Oxford University Press, 2017); Emiliano Treré, "Reclaiming, Proclaiming, and Maintaining Collective Identity in the #YoSoy132 Movement in Mexico: An Examination of Digital Frontstage and Backstage Activism through Social Media and Instant Messaging Platforms," *Information, Communication and Society* 18, 8 (2015): 901–15.
10 Ian Angus, *Emergent Publics: An Essay on Social Movements and Democracy* (Winnipeg: Arbiter Ring, 2001). See also Nancy K. Baym and danah boyd, "Socially Mediated Publicness: An Introduction," *Journal of Broadcasting and Electronic Media* 56, 3 (2012): 320–29.
11 Zeynep Tufekci, *Twitter and Tear Gas: The Power and Fragility of Networked Protest* (New Haven, CT: Yale University Press, 2017).

12 Gerbaudo, *The Mask and the Flag,* 135.
13 Bennett and Segerberg, "The Logic of Connective Action," 754. See also Andrew Chadwick, "Digital Network Repertoires and Organizational Hybridity," *Political Communication* 24, 3 (2007): 283–301; Sarah Anne Rennick, "Personal Grievance Sharing, Frame Alignment, and Hybrid Organisational Structures: The Role of Social Media in North Africa's 2011 Uprisings," *Journal of Contemporary African Studies* 31, 2 (2013): 156–74; Scott Wright, "Populism and Downing Street E-Petitions: Connective Action, Hybridity, and the Changing Nature of Organizing," *Political Communication* 32, 3 (2015): 414–33.
14 Bennett and Segerberg, "The Logic of Connective Action," 754, 757.
15 Ibid., 758.
16 Bennett, *Privacy Advocates,* 113.
17 Jonathan Obar, "Closing the Technocratic Divide? Activist Intermediaries, Digital Form Letters, and Public Involvement in FCC Policy Making," *International Journal of Communication* 10 (2016): 5865–88.
18 Blayne Haggart, "Fair Copyright for Canada: Lessons for Online Social Movements from the First Canadian Facebook Uprising," *Canadian Journal of Political Science/Revue canadienne de science politique* 46, 4 (2013): 841–61. See also Dan Mercea and Andreas Funk, "The Social Media Overture of the Pan-European Stop-ACTA Protest: An Empirical Examination of Participatory Coordination in Connective Action," *Convergence* 22, 3 (2016): 287–312; Jonathan Obar and Leslie Shade, "Activating the Fifth Estate: Bill C-30 and the Digitally-Mediated Public Watchdog," 23 July 2014, SSRN, https://ssrn.com/abstract=2470671 or http://dx.doi.org/10.2139/ssrn.2470671.
19 For an overview of the lawful access debates, see Christopher Parsons, "Stuck on the Agenda: Drawing Lessons from the Stagnation of 'Lawful Access' Legislation in Canada," in *Law, Privacy and Surveillance in Canada in the Post-Snowden Era,* edited by Michael Geist (Ottawa: University of Ottawa Press, 2015), 257–84.
20 Earl and Kimport, *Digitally Enabled Social Change,* 3–20.
21 Interview, Other 2.
22 Interview, Internet 4.
23 Ryan Calo, "Can Americans Resist Surveillance?" *University of Chicago Law Review* 83, 1 (2016): 23–43; Earl and Kimport, *Digitally Enabled Social Change;* Jeffrey Juris, "Reflections on #Occupy Everywhere: Social Media, Public Space, and Emerging Logics of Aggregation," *American Ethnologist* 39, 2 (2014): 259–79; Jonathan Obar, "Canadian Advocacy 2.0: An Analysis of Social Media Adoption and Perceived Affordances by Advocacy Groups Looking to Advance Activism in Canada," *Canadian Journal of Communication* 39, 2 (2014): 211–33.
24 danah boyd, "Social Network Sites as Networked Publics: Affordances, Dynamics, and Implications," in *Networked Self: Identity, Community, and Culture on Social Network Sites,* edited by Zizi Papacharissi (New York: Routledge, 2010), 39–58.
25 Earl and Kimport, *Digitally Enabled Social Change,* 10–12.
26 Gerbaudo, *The Mask and the Flag;* Juris, "Reflections on #Occupy."
27 Interview, Traditional 1.
28 Interview, Other 2.
29 Interview, Traditional 2.
30 Interview, Traditional 1.
31 Bennett, *Privacy Advocates,* 200, 209–10.
32 Interview, Internet 2.
33 Interview, Traditional 1.
34 David Lyon, "Surveillance, Snowden, and Big Data: Capacities, Consequences, Critique," *Big Data and Society* 1, 2 (2014): 11.

35 Interview, Traditional 1.
36 Interview, Internet 4.
37 See Calo, "Can Americans Resist Surveillance?"
38 Interview, Internet 4.
39 Ibid.
40 Interview, Internet 3.
41 Ibid.
42 Ibid.
43 Interview, Other 3.
44 Interview, Other 2.
45 Interview, Other 1.
46 Interview, Other 3.
47 Interview, Traditional 2.
48 Interview, Other 3.
49 Interview, Other 2.
50 Ibid.
51 Interview, Traditional 1.
52 Jef Huysmans, *Security Unbound: Enacting Democratic Limits* (New York: Routledge, 2014).
53 Interview, Internet 4.
54 Interview, Traditional 3.
55 Interview, Traditional 5.
56 See Ganaele Langlois, Joanna Redden, and Greg Elmer, "Introduction," in *Compromised Data – From Social Media to Big Data,* edited by Ganaele Langlois, Joanna Redden, and Greg Elmer (New York: Bloomsbury, 2014), 1–14.
57 Bennett and Segerberg, "The Logic of Connective Action," 742.
58 Ibid., 743. See also W. Lance Bennett, "The Personalization of Politics: Political Identity, Social Media, and Changing Patterns of Participation," *Annals of the American Academy of Political and Social Science* 644, 1 (2012): 20–39.
59 See Max Halupka, "Clicktivism: A Systematic Heuristic," *Policy and Internet* 6, 2 (2014): 115–32.
60 See Lucas Melgaço and Jeffrey Monaghan, "Introduction: Taking to the Streets in the Information Age," in *Protests in the Information Age: Social Movements, Digital Practices and Surveillance,* edited by Lucas Melgaço and Jeffrey Monaghan (New York: Routledge, 2018), 1–17.

Part 5
Policy and Technical Challenges of
Big Data Surveillance

13

Horizontal Accountability and Signals Intelligence
Lessons Drawing from Annual Electronic Surveillance Reports

Christopher Parsons and Adam Molnar

> *One of my biggest takeaways from the past 16 months is that we need to be more transparent. And, if we're going to profess transparency, we need to produce transparency, wherever we can.*
> – JAMES CLAPPER REMARKS AT THE 2014 AFCEA/
> INSA NATIONAL SECURITY AND INTELLIGENCE SUMMIT

THE COMMUNICATIONS SECURITY ESTABLISHMENT (CSE) is Canada's foremost signals intelligence (SIGINT) agency. Historically it has collected foreign signals intelligence, provided security and defensive information technology services to the government of Canada and systems critical to the government of Canada, and assisted domestic federal law enforcement and security agencies (LESAs).[1] CSE's activities are guided by parliamentary legislation and by the Minister of National Defence through ministerial authorizations and directives. The former can authorize CSE to engage in practices that would otherwise violate Canadian law without criminal liability, and the latter principally establishes conditions or limitations on the kinds of lawful activities CSE may conduct.[2] All of CSE's activities are subject to review by the Office of the Communications Security Establishment Commissioner (OCSEC).[3]

CSE's activities are routinely concealed from the public eye, with legislators and the public mainly reliant on the principles of ministerial responsibility, OCSEC reviews, rare unauthorized disclosures for classified activities, and (marginal) judicial oversight to ensure that CSE's activities comport with law. This present system of accountability that governs CSE activities has often been criticized as insufficient in the media and among some analysts.[4] And while legislation that was tabled in Parliament in 2017 may significantly restructure this historical relationship between CSE, its minister, and the OCSEC, and thus how CSE is rendered accountable to its minister and the public alike, we argue that both the current and proposed review and over-sight of CSE are insufficient to provide public accountability. We address these shortcomings by offering principle-based suggestions for facilitating such accountability.

We begin by unpacking the concepts of accountability, transparency, and democratic legitimacy as linked to lawful government surveillance activities. Next, we describe some of CSE's more controversial activities to reveal deficiencies in how its activities have historically been framed through legislation and publicly reviewed by its commissioner. The combined effect of such legislative framing and reviews has been to undermine assurances that CSE's activities could be democratically legitimated. We argue that the tabled legislative reforms that would affect CSE's accountability structures would be insufficient to rectify CSE's public accountability deficits. We conclude by sketching a principle-based framework that could ensure that CSE's activities are both made accountable to its minister and select parliamentarians, and as transparent as possible to Canadians, and, as a result, democratically legitimated.

Conceptual Terminology

Organizations that act transparently collate and present data to those outside the organization.[5] This disclosure of information can sometimes present data that are useful for the public.[6] Often, organizations act transparently when they are compelled to present information in a delimited format[7] or through their own methodologies to collate and disclose information.[8] In either case, organizations that "behave transparently" may be attempting to engender greater trust in their practices.[9] On this basis, scholars are advised to pay "careful attention to the human and material operations that go into the production of transparency"[10] because the revelatory character of transparency practices may be overemphasized absent critique.

One way that governments, in particular, demonstrate transparency is through the release of statutorily required reports. Electronic surveillance reports are an attempt to address social inequity in the social contract between governments and their citizens. By disclosing the regularity at which government surveillance practices occur, the disproportionate degree of intrusion of the state into the private lives of citizens is thought to be safeguarded. In contrast, the absence of any requirement to disclose these activities, or a failure to release such reports, can hinder legislatures and the citizenry from holding the government to account.[11] Without information about secretive government practices, the public, parliamentarians, and other stakeholders cannot evaluate whether government agencies are using their exceptional powers appropriately and in ways that cohere with public interpretations and expectations of how the law ought to legitimate such activities.[12]

Transparency in government activities is needed to ensure that civic agencies are held accountable to their minister, to Parliament, and to the public more broadly. A system of accountability exists "when there is a relationship where an individual or institution, and the performance of tasks of functions by that individual or institution, are subject to another's oversight, direction or request that the individual or institution provide information of justification for its actions."[13] In effect, an institution must be obligated to answer questions and there must also be a means of enforcing consequences should the institution refuse or fail to provide satisfactory responses.[14] In the context of a parliamentary democracy such as Canada, accountability can be manifested through ministerial responsibility or other formalized methods that empower the legislature to scrutinize an agency's practices.[15] However, accountability also exists through more informal measures, such as when non-governmental stakeholders hold government to account based on information tabled by government ministers or the government's independent officers.[16]

There are several ways to understand accountability.[17] In this chapter, we focus exclusively on informal, or horizontal, modes of accountability between government and non-governmental stakeholders. This mode can be contrasted with vertical accountability, which often involves ministers being formally compelled to account for their departments' activities to their respective legislatures.[18] Whereas ministers are obligated to explain their departments' activities and policies to the legislature, and the legislature is empowered to receive explanations and justifications and subsequently issue sanctions as appropriate,[19] the same is not true with regard to the government's relationship with external stakeholders. Horizontal accountability institutes accountability through civil engagement as a way to complement and enhance government accountability processes.[20] External stakeholders, however, cannot necessarily impose sanctions, and governments are not always required to provide an account to these stakeholders.[21] In place of formal legal tools, moral suasion is routinely used to sanction government behaviours. And while the disclosure of ethical impropriety and accompanying use of moral suasion may be amplified by the media, it is rarely premised on stakeholders having formal powers to compel the government to provide an account or modify its behaviours.[22]

The practice of holding governments to account is intended to control government conduct. Citizens can exert control through the ballot box as well as outside electoral periods.[23] Stakeholders engaged in horizontal accountability can work to identify problems so that legislators, or the government itself, can take up and attempt to solve challenging issues.[24] Moreover, through a proactive civil culture that proposes solutions to problems, government and legislators may realize previously unconsidered ways to correct them. External stakeholders can also testify or present information to government committees or members of the legislature. But for any of these means of exercising horizontal accountability to work, external stakeholders must have access to government information, possess a capacity to take on the work of ingesting and processing the information in question, and recognize that the state is capable, willing, and competent to receive external actors' concerns and has the potential ability to act on them.[25] Absent information provided by government, citizens may be inhibited from participating in political processes; such secrecy "compels the public to defer to the judgement of a narrow elite."[26]

By remaining open to external stakeholder analysis, critique, and problem solving, a government combats cynicism or doubts that it is not "of the people, for the people." An inability on the part of government to respond to civil society interests fosters cynicism and doubts about whether legislators can, or desire to, represent the citizenry. While most citizens may not be involved in holding their government to account, broader perceptions of accountability may be shaped by the government's receptiveness to civil society interventions.[27] If the electorate fails to see its representatives respond on policy issues raised by stakeholders, they may lose faith in legislators, and by extension in the representative democratic process of lawmaking itself.[28] Even if a government and its departments act based on laws passed within a legislative assembly, without adequate horizontal accountability laws may be seen as severed from the legitimating power of the citizenry itself. Such disconnection threatens to transform a democratic process bound through rule of law into a narrow and disconnected process that might be better understood as rule-with-law.[29] Severing "lawful activities" from democratic legitimation processes has been recognized as a core challenge that the second generation of intelligence oversight must overcome. Whereas in the past such oversight and review were concerned with detecting and preventing abuse and mischief, the second generation must reconcile economic, diplomatic, and strategic goals as well as secure the "consent of the governed" where public concerns are linked with the need for secrecy.[30]

Making the Past Clear?

CSE was formally established as part of the *National Defense Act* (*NDA*), though its origin dates back to the end the Second World War, when it secretly existed in different government departments.[31] The *NDA* imposed three mandates on CSE: (A) to "acquire and use information from the global information infrastructure for the purpose of providing foreign intelligence"; (B) to "provide advice, guidance and services to help ensure the protection of electronic information and of information infrastructures of importance to the Government of Canada"; and (C) to "provide technical and operational assistance to federal law enforcement and security agencies in the performance of their lawful duties."[32] The breadth of these mandates became truly apparent only following Edward Snowden's disclosure of classified national security documents to journalists, who subsequently selectively published from what they were given.

One of the most prominent Canadian-focused Snowden disclosures was a program covernamed CASCADE. CASCADE was operated on non–government of Canada networks and was designed to analyze network traffic. The analysis involved discovering and tracking targets, as well as isolating content or metadata from traffic exposed to the network probes.[33] Within the CASCADE program was a series of differently classified and covernamed network sensors. Some could capture metadata and content alike (EONBLUE and INDUCTION), whereas others could solely collect and analyze metadata (THIRD-EYE and CRUCIBLE).[34] All of these sensors relied on deep packet inspection technology, which enables operators to analyze the metadata and content of unencrypted communications and take actions on it, such as blocking certain traffic or modifying other traffic.[35]

INDUCTION operated at "Special Source Operations (SSO) sites," or within the premises of private Canadian organizations that had consented to CSE's activities. CRUCIBLE sensors, similar to INDUCTION sensors, were located in the pathways of networks that were designated "systems of importance" to Canada.[36] Such systems might belong to defence contractors, extractive resource companies, banks, or equivalent organizations whose compromise could detrimentally affect the governance of Canada. These sensors could also collect the metadata of communications that Canadians, and persons communicating with Canadians, were engaged in, as well as the metadata of devices that transmitted information into or out of Canada. Other aspects of CASCADE involved monitoring satellite communications as well as microwave towers that transmitted data.[37]

The purpose of CASCADE, when combined with an equivalent sensor network designed to protect the Canadian government's own networks (covernamed PHOTONIC PRISM, which was expected to be replaced by EON-BLUE),[38] was to use the entirety of the global information infrastructure as a means of defence. By tracking threat actors and their activities, CSE intended to "affect changes at the CORE of the Internet on detection" in collaboration with its Five Eyes partners. Such changes included modifying traffic routes, silently discarding malicious traffic, or inserting payloads into communications traffic to disrupt adversaries.[39] To achieve these ends, CASCADE would, in essence, be situated to grant fulsome awareness of domestic and foreign Internet activity throughout the world. The most controversial aspects of this program in Canada were principally linked to the extensive surveillance of Canadian-source, Canadian-bound, and Canadian domestic traffic, as well as CSE's efforts to work alongside private partners to conduct this global surveillance activity.

Fuzzy Mandates, Clarified?

The different mandates that CSE operates under authorize a broad spectrum of activities, including network discovery, exploitation, and attack; defensive cyber operations; the creation of information profiles useful for other agencies that engage in physical operations; and other activities intended to further or advance the missions of other government agencies.[40] The program discussed above reveals how seemingly restrictive mandates can be interpreted as authorizing mass surveillance practices in excess of imagined restrictions.

The CASCADE program goes beyond the concept of erecting a network perimeter and defending it in depth by envisioning monitoring of the entirety of the domestic and international Internet so that CSE can track all data emissions that might be harmful to Canadian interests. If Mandate B was principally considered to be instructing CSE to shield certain systems, the Snowden documents revealed that CSE took shielding domestic institutions to mean engaging in global mass surveillance as a prerequisite for such defensive policies. While monitoring data traffic internationally arguably falls under Mandate A, the identification of domestic networks of interest and subsequent generation of domestic content and metadata from these networks runs counter to Canadians' perceptions that CSE was not authorized to routinely monitor Canadians' activities.[41] Indeed, in internal slides, CSE recognizes that providing "defence" using CASCADE engages all three of its mandates: A, B, and C.[42]

Though the CSE is formally prohibited from deliberately collecting the personal communications content of Canadians or persons residing in Canada, the agency operates with a ministerial authorization that permits it to collect such data incidentally in the course of its operations – that is, CSE cannot direct its surveillance apparatus in a deliberate way towards specific or named Canadians or Canadian targets unless it is providing assistance to a foreign agency under warrant.[43] But these restrictions are not interpreted by the Canadian government or the OCSEC to preclude CSE from monitoring all metadata emanations from persons within Canada,[44] even though CSE, its minister, and its review body know that CSE has the capability to reidentify the persons with whom the emanations are associated. The OCSEC's conclusion that CSE behaved lawfully in the collection of metadata pertaining to Canadians' communications and devices was unsurprising: independent analysts have found that it is almost impossible for any activity conducted by CSE to be found unlawful given the nature of the OCSEC's role and interpretations of national security law.[45]

In 2017, the Canadian government introduced Bill C-59, which, among other things, was designed to clarify CSE's mandate while simultaneously updating the control and review structure for Canada's intelligence agencies. Based on the Snowden revelations, it was apparent that CSE was involved in a broader range of activities than many thought was already likely given its scope and perceived capabilities. While Bill C-59 may retroactively authorize these existing activities, it has made more explicit the expansive range of CSE's activities, which include collecting foreign intelligence through the global information infrastructure; engaging in cybersecurity and information assurance; conducting defensive operations to broadly protect federal institutions' systems and those deemed of importance to Canada; performing active cyber operations that may involve degrading, disrupting, influencing, responding to, or interfering with "the capabilities, intentions or activities" of non-Canadian parties; and providing technical and operational assistance to LESAs, the Canadian Forces, and the Department of National Defence.[46] There are provisions within the *CSE Act* that also permits CSE to collect information from any public source,[47] including perhaps grey market information brokers, as well as interfere with non-democratic foreign elections,[48] among other controversial measures.

The program that we have examined in this chapter can be situated within this expanded mandate. CASCADE could operate simultaneously under the collection of foreign intelligence, cybersecurity and information assurance, and (potentially) assistance mandates. When viewed through each of these mandate areas, CSE is permitted to acquire information as required, provide services to different government and non-governmental organizations that are meant to guarantee the respective organizations' digital security, and use collected information as appropriate to assist domestic LESAs or foreign-operating Canadian Forces to act on parties threatening Canadian organizations' digital systems. If it obtains authorization, activities in Canada could extend to active defensive operations. Furthermore, Bill C-59 explicitly authorizes CSE to infiltrate any part of the global information infrastructure for the purposes of collecting information that would provide foreign intelligence. This includes the types of attacks being launched towards Canadian networks or systems of interest, and also permits private companies to cooperate with CSE and, as such, operate as SSOs. Whereas CSE's current legislation does not explicitly state the conditions under which it can engage with private organizations (as envisioned under the CASCADE program), the cybersecurity authorizations for non-federal infrastructures under Bill C-59 establish the legislative framework for such cooperation. Notably, C-59 also includes emergency provisions for access to private organizations' infrastructure. These provisions might let CSE gain permission from either the operator of infrastructure, such as a party that is running software on, say, computer servers in a shared computing facility or, alternatively, from the party that owns the servers and leases them to the software-running party.[49] This can occur without having to get the activity approved by anyone besides

CSE's minister. Such access might be needed in some cases to establish, expand, or re-establish the defensive perimeter envisioned as part of the CASCADE program.

Beyond providing a broader range of activities that CSE might engage in, Bill C-59 also re-envisions how CSE's activities are authorized, controlled, and reviewed. Ministers will continue to issue authorizations and directives that guide and delimit the types of activities that CSE can engage in, with the minister of foreign affairs generally being consulted prior to CSE's engaging in defensive cyber operations or active offensive cyber operations. The Intelligence Commissioner, a new control-type body that was created as part of C-59, is typically responsible for (among other things) approving foreign intelligence authorizations and cyber security authorizations, and must also be notified of, and approve, significant amendments or repeals of such authorizations.[50] The Intelligence Commissioner provides annual reports to the minister. CSE's activities are subject to review by the National Security and Intelligence Review Agency (NSIRA), and thus assume responsibilities for CSE's reporting paralleling those held by the OCSEC. Neither the NSIRA nor any other body, including a committee of parliamentarians that reports principally to the prime minister, is required to evaluate whether or not CSE's activities are normatively appropriate or to focus extensively on whether they might, even if they are "lawful," still unnecessarily infringe upon Canadians' civil liberties. In the United States, the Privacy and Civil Liberties Oversight Board (PCLOB) provides this kind of external oversight of activities undertaken by the National Security Agency (NSA) and produces classified reports for the government as well as reports that are accessible to the public.

Bill C-59 requires both CSE and the NSIRA to produce annual reports. NSIRA's reports must include information about CSE's compliance with law and ministerial authorizations, and about the reasonableness and necessity of CSE's use of its powers. It does not, however, require *or* authorize the NSIRA to produce annual reports similar to those about the US National Security Agency. Those reports include statistics on the numbers of Americans targeted by the NSA under *Foreign Intelligence Surveillance Act (FISA)* Title I and Title III warrants and the proportion of persons targeted who are non-US versus US persons; estimates of the number of non-US targets affected by section 702 surveillance orders; the number of search terms used to query the section 702 database that concern a known US person and aim to retrieve the unminimized contents of their communications; and the number of section 702–based reports that contain US persons' identity information, among other statistics.[51]

The Performance of Legislative Legitimacy and Accountability

Bill C-59 is designed in part to reform how CSE is controlled and reviewed, and Bill C-22 established a committee of parliamentarians to evaluate some of CSE's activities and report on them to the Prime Minister's Office. Though judicial and other ways of evaluating the lawfulness of CSE's activities are important, they are limited in notable ways. As Kent Roach discusses, "even at its heroic best, judicial oversight will focus on issues of legality and propriety, not efficacy and effectiveness. Intelligence agencies will also have incentives – and often the ability – to take measures that avoid or limit any inconvenient judicial oversight."[52] Similarly, while the NSIRA is designed to prevent CSE and its partner agencies from avoiding or limiting review, members of the Canadian intelligence community have historically been willing to mislead judges and downplay questionable rationales of action to their reviewers.[53] Furthermore, the very *structure* of accountability raises some critical problems when it comes to roles played by legislators. For instance, "[g]iving legislators access to secret information but no mechanism for revealing their concerns may only allow the government to claim legitimacy for illegal and improper conduct ... Rather than relying on its members, much of the legitimacy of a legislative committee might come from constructive engagement with civil society."[54] Under Bill C-22, parliamentarians will be restricted in what they can examine, what they can report publicly, and who they can appoint as their chair and members.[55] So, while it is possible that the new control and review structures will improve accountability internal to formal government practices, nothing in Bill C-59 or the previously enacted Bill C-22 necessarily establishes enhanced *public* reporting of CSE's activities and thus do not promote horizontal accountability of CSE's activities.

Promoting horizontal accountability is vitally important to restore public trust in CSE. According to Zachary Goldman and Samuel Rascoff, trust "is, perhaps, the single most important determinant of how intelligence agencies will fare in liberal democracies."[56] Goldman argues separately that "[t]he [Snowden] leaks really, then, revealed" a lack of social agreement about the proper contours of the rules, "including about whether current interpretations of key constitutional provisions are consistent with society's expectations, rather than about significant illegal behaviour. Debates also revolved around policy choices by the [intelligence community] in areas where there is no direct legal authorization, such as whether the [National Security Agency] should stockpile zero-day exploits, or whether it should monitor communications of lawful foreign intelligence targets such as a foreign leader."[57] To promote horizontal accountability and restore the trust deficit between the population and CSE's lawful activities, the government might amend Bill C-59 or table new legislation that specifies certain statistical and narrative accounts of CSE's activities, as well as establish an independent review body responsible for evaluating the proportionality of the activities.

Any efforts to ensure that CSE is subject to horizontal accountability could include the following modes of transparency:

- *Legal transparency.* Decisions issued by the Federal Court should be made public and minimally redacted to assist external legal experts and scholars in understanding the development and shaping of law. As discussed by Daphna Renan, "[m]aking the overarching legal framework of surveillance programs more visible and participatory may make these programs more resilient ... the fundamental legal framework of intelligence programs belongs in the light."[58]

- *Statistical transparency.* The Office of the Director of National Intelligence in the United States voluntarily produces statistical reports concerning the National Security Agency's annual operations. While statistics may leave much to be desired, they show that information concerning the annual activities of the NSA can be disclosed without undue harm to national security. Reported information could also disclose the regularity with which CSE provides assistance to domestic LESAs to assuage concerns that CSE is routinely directing its activities towards Canadians or persons in Canada. A form of this reporting has been undertaken in Canada since the 1970s, and involves the federal and provincial governments issuing annual electronic surveillance reports that detail the regularity and efficacy of federal and provincial agencies' surveillance activities. To date, there is no evidence that such statistical transparency has negatively affected ongoing or concluded domestic LESA investigations.

- *Narrative transparency.* Legal or statistical transparency should be accompanied by narratives that help clarify the rationales for the actions undertaken by CSE. Such narratives should provide some information about the specific, annual activities of CSE and not merely refer to authorizing legislation under which the Establishment operates; though recent annual electronic surveillance reports in Canada generally fail to provide a useful narrative example to follow, federal reports pre-dating the mid-1990s that explain the situations associated with such surveillance may be a useful starting point for what such narrative explanations might include. Similarly, the narratives associated with the Office of the Director of National Intelligence's annual statistical reports indicate possible ways to explain how laws are interpreted and acted upon.

- *Proportionality transparency.* Though the review structures under Bill C-59 are expected to evaluate whether CSE's activities are reasonable or necessary for the agency to exercise its powers,[59] review and control bodies are not expected to focus on whether CSE's activities are proportionate to the impacts on civil liberties that result from those activities. The minister is required to take the proportionality of a measure into consideration before issuing a ministerial authorization, but this process is internal to government.[60] An external civil liberties board, similar to the PCLOB in the United States, could report on whether the specific activities undertaken by CSE are reasonable and proportionate when viewed against their intrusion into citizens' and foreigners' private lives alike.

Three of these measures of transparency are born from accountability reporting that the federal and provincial governments already include in their annual electronic surveillance reports. Such reports clarify the laws that authorize the surveillance, the regularity with which such surveillance is conducted, and the broad impacts of the surveillance, and they are supposed to provide some narrative explanation of the surveillance. The fourth measure we propose, focused on proportionality transparency, draws from measures established by Canada's close allies. Admittedly, the proposals we make extend beyond what the current annual electronic surveillance reports include – these current reports do not, for example, include discussions or decisions linked to secret case law associated with wiretapping or other live forms of surveillance – but, importantly, our proposals are not a radical adoption of entirely novel forms of government transparency and accountability.

Promoting transparency of government intelligence operations would result in important gains for horizontal accountability. Stakeholders could play a role in providing critical insights and analyses to parliamentary committees, legislatures, and regulatory bodies that routinely experience resource shortages or lack appropriate technical expertise. These stakeholders, who are often area experts, could play an important role by representing their communities' interests in debating the often thorny issues of secretive government surveillance activities that historically have "touched" the information of far more Canadian citizens and residents as well as visitors to Canada than previously suspected.

In general, emboldening horizontal accountability through meaningful public disclosure can inform the broader democratic process in an area of governance that is well known for its capacity to engender distrust and skepticism among the citizenry. Elsewhere, we have noted how even when legislation might exist to authorize a particular secret activity, information asymmetries between government lawyers and the public mean that the lawfulness of an activity may lack legitimation given the disconnect between legislation, law, and practice. In effect, by becoming more transparent in secret operations and thereby better enabling horizontal accountability processes, the lawful activities that are undertaken may be subject not *just* to critique but also to approval of how a measure is authorized and the policies to safeguard against misconduct, overbreadth, or infringements on civil liberties.

Conclusion

Patrick Walsh and Seumas Miller have argued that "[t]he Snowden leaks now provide the opportunity for 'Five Eyes' governments to do a root and branch review of current organizational, ministerial, parliamentary and other standing oversight bodies to ensure they remain fit for purpose."[61] Goldman has separately insisted that "although the institutions designed to ensure compliance work well, these same institutions have difficulty with a broader role."[62] We agree with these points and argue that a review of the intelligence community and its transparency and accountability structures must also consider how to empower stakeholders external to government to better engage in horizontal accountability. Indeed, in an environment characterized by rapid technological innovation, extensive legal ambiguities, and associated tensions with traditional liberal democratic principles, horizontal accountability is an essential component of meaningful regulation.

In this chapter, we have argued that horizontal accountability can help legitimate secretive government activities that are authorized by legislation. We proposed four separate measures, focused on legal, statistical, narrative, and proportionality, to enhance the information available to external-to-government stakeholders. This information could then be taken up and used to understand and critique some activities, while also ensuring that parties external to government could identify and propose solutions to thorny legal issues, could better explain the protections and safeguards established to protect civil liberties and human rights, and ensure that the stakeholders they represent are better informed about the actual, versus hypothetical or hyperbolic, issues linked to government surveillance activities.

A continuation of the status quo, where citizens are kept in the dark concerning the activities and laws that authorize secret intelligence activities, "undermines the capacity of citizens to determine whether a new balance of security concerns and basic rights has been struck."[63] The status quo also threatens to magnify the already disturbing gap between legislation as it is written, as it is interpreted by Department of Justice and other government national security lawyers, and as it is acted upon by Communications Security Establishment staff. This gap fundamentally threatens the legitimacy, if not the lawfulness, of CSE's activities. No government party benefits from the perpetuation of this gap: while it may be tactically helpful in advancing specific operations or activities, it ultimately threatens to poison the legitimacy of organizations themselves and, by extension, turn tactical outputs into components of a broader strategic blunder.

Ultimately, it is only once citizens, often facilitated by academic and civil society actors, know what is being done in their name, and why and how those measures are linked to the activities authorized by their legislators, can the accountability gap be bridged. As Canada undertakes national security consultations today and into the future, and engages in legislative action and reforms, the time to start bridging the gap is now.

Acknowledgments

Financial support for the research, authorship, and publication of this chapter was provided by the John D. and Catherine T. MacArthur Foundation.

The authors would like to thank the participants of a national security round table held at the 2017 Annual Citizen Lab Summer Institute for their insights concerning the *CSE Act* and other relevant aspects of Bill C-59. They would also like to thank members of the Communications Security Establishment for providing numerous briefings about different aspects of the Establishment's mandate, challenges it seeks to overcome, and how Bill C-59 might affect its practices.

The authors declare no potential conflicts of interest with respect to the research, authorship, and/or publication of this chapter.

Notes

1 *National Defence Act,* RSC 1985, c N-5, ss 273.64(1)(a)–(c).
2 Office of the Communications Security Establishment Commissioner (OCSEC), "Frequently Asked Questions," 24 February 2017, https://www.ocsec-bccst.gc.ca/s56/eng/frequently-asked-questions.
3 Ibid.
4 Bill Robinson, "Does CSE Comply with the Law?" *Lux Ex Umbra* (blog), 14 March 2015, https://luxexumbra.blogspot.ca/2015/03/does-cse-comply-with-law.html; Ronald Deibert, "Who Knows What Evils Lurk in the Shadows?" OpenCanada.org, 27 March 2015, https://www.opencanada.org/features/c-51-who-knows-what-evils-lurk-in-the-shadows/; Greg Weston, Glenn Greenwald, and Ryan Gallagher, "CSEC Used Airport Wi-Fi to Track Canadian Travellers: Edward Snowden Documents," *CBC News,* 30 January 2014, https://web.archive.org/web/20140131064055/https://www.cbc.ca/news/politics/csec-used-airport-wi-fi-to-track-canadian-travellers-edward-snowden-documents-1.2517881.
5 Robert Bushman, Joseph Piotroski, and Abbie Smith, "What Determines Corporate Social Transparency?" *Journal of Accounting Research* 42, 2 (2004): 207; Sylvester Eigffinger and Petra Geraats, *Government Transparency: Impacts and Unintended Consequences* (New York: Palgrave Macmillan, 2006).
6 Roger Cotterrell, "Transparency, Mass Media, Ideology and Community," *Journal for Cultural Research* 3, 4 (1999): 414–26.
7 Archon Fung, Mary Graham, and David Weil, *Full Disclosure: The Perils and Promise of Transparency* (New York: Cambridge University Press, 2007).
8 Ibid., 7; Christopher Parsons, "The (In)effectiveness of Voluntarily Produced Transparency Reports," *Business & Society* 58, 1 (2019): 103–31, https://journals.sagepub.com/doi/full/10.1177/0007650317717957.
9 Kent Wayland, Roberto Armengol, and Deborah Johnson, "When Transparency Isn't Transparent: Campaign Finance Disclosure and Internet Surveillance," in *Internet and Surveillance: The Challenges of Web 2.0 and Social Media,* edited by Christian Fuchs, Kees Boersma, Anders Albrechtslund, and Marisol Sandoval (New York: Routledge, 2012), 239–54.
10 Hans Krause Hansen, Lars Thoger Christensen, and Mikkel Flyverbom, "Introduction: Logics of Transparency in Late Modernity: Paradoxes, Mediation and Governance," *European Journal of Social Theory* 18, 2 (2015): 117–31.

11　Douwe Korff, Ben Wagner, Julia Powles, Renata Avila, and Ulf Buermeyer, "Boundaries of Law: Exploring Transparency, Accountability, and Oversight of Government Surveillance Regimes" (University of Cambridge Faculty of Law Research Paper No. 16/2017, 3 March 2017), SSRN, https://papers.ssrn.com/sol3/papers.cfm?abstract_id=2894490.

12　Christopher Parsons and Tamir Israel, "Gone Opaque? An Analysis of Hypothetical IMSI Catcher Overuse in Canada" (Citizen Lab/Canadian Internet Policy and Public Interest Clinic report, August 2016), https://citizenlab.org/wp-content/uploads/2016/09/20160818-Report-Gone_Opaque.pdf; Adam Molnar, Christopher Parsons, and Erik Zouave, "Computer Network Operations and 'Rule-with-Law' in Australia," *Internet Policy Review* 6, 1 (2017): 1–14.

13　Riccardo Pelizzo and Frederick Stapenhurst, *Government Accountability and Legislative Oversight* (New York: Routledge, 2013), 2.

14　Andreas Schedler, "Conceptualizing Accountability," in *The Self-Restraining State: Power and Accountability in New Democracies*, edited by Andrew Schelder, Larry Diamond, and Marc Plattner (Boulder, CO: Lynne Rienner, 1999), 13–28; Andrew Blick and Edward Hedger, "Literature Review of Factors Contributing to Commonwealth Public Accounts Committees Effectively Holding Government to Account for the Use of Public Resources" (National Audit Office, Overseas Development Institute, 2008); Richard Mulgan, "The Process of Public Accountability," *Australian Journal of Public Accountability* 56, 1 (1997): 26–36; Jonathan Anderson, "Illusions of Accountability," *Administrative Theory & Praxis* 31, 3 (2009): 322–39.

15　Dale Smith, *The Unbroken Machine: Canada's Democracy in Action* (Toronto: Dundurn, 2017); Bruce Stone, "Administrative Accountability in the 'Westminster' Democracies: Towards a New Conceptual Framework," *Governance* 8, 4 (1995): 502–25.

16　Carmen Malena, Reigner Forster, and Janmejay Singh, "Social Accountability: An Introduction to the Concept and Emerging Practice" (Social Development Paper 76, World Bank, 2004).

17　See, for example, Richard Mulgan, "'Accountability': An Ever-Expanding Concept?" *Public Administration* 78, 3 (2000): 555–73; Linda Deleon, "Accountability in a 'Reinvented' Government," *Public Administration* 76, 3 (1998): 539–58; Amanda Sinclair, "The Chameleon of Accountability: Forms and Discourses," *Accounting, Organizations and Society* 20, 2–3 (1995): 219–37; David Corbett, *Australian Public Sector Management*, 2nd ed. (Sydney: Allen and Unwin, 1996); James March and Johan Olsen, *Democratic Governance* (New York: Free Press, 1995).

18　Smith, *The Unbroken Machine*; Stone, "Administrative Accountability."

19　J. Ll. J. Edwards, "Ministerial Responsibility for National Security as It Relates to the Offices of the Prime Minister, Attorney General and Solicitor General of Canada," in *The Commission of Inquiry Concerning Certain Activities of the Royal Canadian Mounted Police* (Ottawa: Supply and Services Canada, 1980); Donald Savoie, *Breaking the Bargain: Public Servants, Ministers, and Parliament* (Toronto: University of Toronto Press, 2003).

20　Malena, Forster, and Singh, "Social Accountability."

21　Mark Bovens, "Analyzing and Assessing Accountability: A Conceptual Framework," *European Law Journal* 13, 4 (2007): 447–68.

22　Malena, Forster, and Singh, "Social Accountability"; Maxwell McCombs, *Setting the Agenda: Mass Media and Public Opinion* (Hoboken, NJ: John Wiley and Sons, 2014).

23　Bovens, "Analyzing and Assessing Accountability."

24　Alisdair Roberts, "Transparency in the Security Sector," in *The Right to Know: Transparency for an Open World*, edited by Ann Florini (New York: Columbia University Press, 2007), 309–36.

25　Malena, Forster, and Singh, "Social Accountability."

26　Roberts, "Transparency in the Security Sector."

27 Jan Aart Scholte, "Civil Society and Democracy in Global Governance," *Global Governance* 8, 3 (2002): 281–304; Julie Fisher, *Non Governments: NGOs and the Political Development of the Third World* (West Hartford, CT: Kumarian Press, 1998).

28 Jürgen Habermas, "On the Internal Relation between the Rule of Law and Democracy," in *The Inclusion of the Other: Studies in Political Theory*, edited by Ciaran Cronin and Pablo De Greiff (Cambridge, MA: MIT Press, 1998), 253–64; Jürgen Habermas, "Three Normative Models of Democracy," in Cronin and De Greiff, 239–52; Christopher Parsons, "Beyond Privacy: Articulating the Broader Harms of Pervasive Mass Surveillance," *Media and Communication* 3, 3 (2015): 1–11.

29 Ben Bowling and James Sheptycki, "Global Policing and Transnational Rule with law," *Transnational Legal Theory* 6, 1 (2015): 141–73; Molnar, Parsons, and Zouave, "Computer Network Operations."

30 Zachary K. Goldman and Samuel J. Rascoff, "The New Intelligence Oversight," in *Global Intelligence Oversight: Governing Security in the Twenty-First Century*, edited by Zachary K. Goldman and Samuel J. Rascoff (New York: Oxford University Press, 2016); see also "Intelligence Reform in a Post-Snowden World," YouTube video, 1:28:12, from a panel hosted by the Center for Strategic and International Studies, 9 October 2015, https://www.csis.org/events/intelligence-reform-post-snowden-world-0.

31 *National Defence Act*; Bill Robinson, "An Unofficial Look inside the Communications Security Establishment, Canada's Signals Intelligence Agency," *Lux Ex Umbra* (blog), 5 November 2000, http://circ.jmellon.com/docs/html/communications_security_establishment_unofficial_webpage_020623.html.

32 *National Defence Act*, ss 273.64(1)(a)–(c).

33 Communications Security Establishment (CSE), "CSEC Cyber Threat Capabilities: SIGINT and ITS: An End-to-End Approach" (slide deck, October 2009), https://christopher-parsons.com/Main/wp-content/uploads/2015/03/doc-6-cyber-threat-capabilities-2.pdf.

34 CSE, "CASCADE: Joint Cyber Sensor Architecture," 2011, Technology, Thoughts and Trinkets, https://christopher-parsons.com/writings/cse-summaries/#cse-cascade-joint.

35 CSE, "CSEC Cyber Threat Capabilities"; Christopher Parsons, "Deep Packet Inspection in Perspective: Tracing Its Lineage and Surveillance Potentials" (working paper, New Transparency Project, 2008), http://www.sscqueens.org/files/WP_Deep_Packet_Inspection_Parsons_Jan_2008.pdf.

36 CSE, "CASCADE: Joint Cyber Sensor Architecture."

37 Ibid.

38 CSE, "Cyber Network Defence R&D Activities," 2010, Technology, Thoughts and Trinkets, https://christopher-parsons.com/writings/cse-summaries/#cse-cyber-threat-capabilities; CSE, "CASCADE: Joint Cyber Sensor Architecture."

39 CSE, "CSEC Cyber Threat Capabilities."

40 Deibert, "Who Knows What Evils Lurk in the Shadows?"

41 Weston, "CSEC Used Airport Wi-Fi to Track."

42 CSE, "CSEC Cyber Threat Capabilities."

43 Based on discussions between the authors and senior CSE staff, we understand that in such warranted cases, information is cordoned off from CSE's more general repositories and thus inaccessible to many, if not all, CSE staff and operations.

44 "Defence Minister Insists Spy Agency Did Not Track Canadian Travellers," *CTV News*, 31 January 2014, http://www.ctvnews.ca/canada/defence-minister-insists-spy-agency-did-not-track-canadian-travellers-1.1664333; OCSEC, "Frequently Asked Questions." See also Craig Forcese, "Faith-Based Accountability: Metadata and CSEC Review," *National Security Law: Canadian Practice in Comparative Perspective* (blog), 13 February 2014,

https://www.craigforcese.com/blog/2014/2/13/faith-based-accountability-metadata
-and-csec-review.html?rq=faith-based%20accountability%3A%20metadata%20
and%20csec%20review.

45 Robinson, "Does CSE Comply with the Law?"

46 Canada, Bill C-59, *An Act respecting national security matters,* 1st Sess, 42nd Parl, 2017,
pt 3, ss 17–21 [Bill C-59].

47 Ibid., pt 3, s 24(1)(a).

48 Ibid., s 33(1)(b).

49 Ibid., s 41(4).

50 The tabled bill initially included a caveat: the Intelligence Commission is not required to
first approve emergency authorizations (pt 3, s 42(2)).

51 See, for example, US Office of the Director of National Intelligence (ODNI), "Statistical Transparency Report Regarding Use of National Security Authorities for
Calendar Year 2016," April 2016, https://www.dni.gov/files/icotr/ic_transparecy_report_
cy2016_5_2_17.pdf.

52 Kent Roach, "Review and Oversight of Intelligence in Canada: Expanding Accountability Gaps," in Goldman and Rascoff, *Global Intelligence Oversight,* 181.

53 *X (Re),* 2014 FCA 249 (CanLII), http://canlii.ca/t/gf63j; *X (Re),* [2017] 2 FCR 396, 2016
FC 1105 (CanLII), http://canlii.ca/t/gwo1x.

54 Roach, "Review and Oversight of Intelligence in Canada," 187–88.

55 Anne Dagenais Guertin, "Our Analysis of C-22: An Inadequate and Worrisome Bill,"
International Civil Liberties Monitoring Group, 30 June 2016, http://iclmg.ca/our-analysis
-of-c-22-an-inadequate-and-worrisome-bill/; Scott Newark, "Ensuring Independence
for the Parliamentary National Security Committee: A Review of Bill C-22" (Macdon-
ald-Laurier Institute publication, November 2016), http://www.macdonaldlaurier.ca/
files/pdf/MLICommentaryNewark11-16-webV2.pdf.

56 Goldman and Rascoff, "The New Intelligence Oversight," xxix.

57 Zachary K. Goldman, "The Emergence of Intelligence Governance," in Goldman and
Rascoff, *Global Intelligence Oversight,* 219.

58 Daphna Renan, "The FISC's Stealth Administrative Laws," in Goldman and Rascoff,
Global Intelligence Oversight, 135. Though beyond the scope of this argument, such proceedings could also include special advocates as much as possible to avoid *ex parte* hearings
that might lead to legal interpretations that unduly impact the civil liberties of those
affected by CSE's surveillance operations.

59 Bill C-59, pt 1, s 3(a), as well as pt 3, ss 13–21.

60 Ibid., pt 3, s 35(1).

61 Patrick F. Walsh and Seumas Miller, "Rethinking the 'Five Eyes' Security Intelligence
Collection Policies and Practice Post-Snowden," *Intelligence and National Security* 31, 3
(2016): 345–68, 365–66.

62 Goldman, "The Emergence of Intelligence Governance," 220.

63 Roberts, "Transparency in the Security Sector," 320.

14

Metadata – Both Shallow and Deep
The Fraught Key to Big Data Mass State Surveillance

Andrew Clement, Jillian Harkness, and George Raine

> *We kill people based on metadata.*
>
> – GENERAL MICHAEL HAYDEN, FORMER HEAD OF
> THE NATIONAL SECURITY AGENCY

UNTIL RECENTLY, METADATA – literally "data about data" – was unfamiliar outside the information fields, where it is a term of art used in describing a wide variety of information objects to enable cataloguing and retrieval. However, since Edward Snowden's 2013 whistle-blowing exposures of the extraordinary scope of secret mass state surveillance and the key role that metadata plays in such surveillance, the term has now entered public discourse. As national security agencies have adopted new techniques for intercepting electronic communications, notably "upstream" programs that tap into Internet data flows at key routing centres and major fibre-optic cables, they are turning to metadata analysis techniques to process the extraordinarily expanding volumes of intercept data (see Chapter 7 for a more in-depth discussion). We are also learning that with the application of big data collection and analysis techniques, metadata can be much more revealing of an individual's behaviour, movements, beliefs, affiliations, and social connections than previously understood.

In the hands of state actors, metadata can provide the basis for highly intrusive intervention into people's lives. While the coming into prominence of metadata draws attention to a relatively new and potent mode of mass surveillance, distinct from the popular image of individually targeted eavesdropping or surreptitious reading of communications, it remains an ambiguous and contested term. In particular, officials who lead state security agencies often deploy the term publicly in ways evidently designed to reassure audiences skeptical of their behind-the-scenes surveillance activities but that, given its ambiguity, also raise serious questions about their actual practices and trustworthiness. This is significant because metadata enjoys lower legal and constitutional protection than communication content. Furthermore, recurring discrepancies between what security and law enforcement agencies say about metadata and what they actually do with it call into question the adequacy of democratic governance of these powerful and often necessarily secretive arms of the state.

This chapter seeks to clarify the multiple meanings of metadata as defined and operationalized in various settings. More specifically, it seeks to determine whether the practices of the Five Eyes signals intelligence agencies – notably the US National Security Agency (NSA), the British Government Communications Headquarters (GCHQ), and Canada's Communications Security Establishment (CSE) – in relation to metadata conform to their public statements as well as the conventional and legal understandings of the term. To set the stage, we summarize the various definitions of metadata (and its equivalents) as they have appeared in academic, professional, legal, and popular discourses as well as in the emerging field of big data analytics.

The core of the chapter draws on our study of the more than 500 secret documents of the Five Eyes alliance published by the media based on Edward Snowden's leak, as found in the Snowden Digital Surveillance Archive.[1] Using the archive's various search and index features, we selected and analyzed documents for what they reveal about how the security agencies actually generate metadata from their global communication interception apparatus and subsequently organize, access, and use it in their intelligence operations.

Conventional Meanings of Metadata

Ever since the Snowden revelations prompted journalists to explain the technical aspects behind mass surveillance, an understanding of the term "metadata" has, for the average citizen, been largely shaped by the news media. These definitions are varied; often they are simplified accounts echoing those put forth by government offices, such as a commonly used definition from the Canadian Broadcasting Corporation (CBC), where metadata is defined as "information associated with communication that is used to identify, describe or route information," and more specifically as possibly including "personal information, including phone numbers or email addresses, but not the content of emails or recordings of phone calls."[2] More elaborate and insightful definitions have also sometimes been offered by the media; in 2013, *The Guardian* explained that "metadata provides a record of almost anything a user does online, from browsing history – such as map searches and websites visited – to account details, email activity, and even some account passwords. This can be used to build a detailed picture of an individual's life."[3] The *Guardian* example helps the public to understand the ramifications of metadata collection, whereas in the more common definition, as shown in the example from the CBC, these details remain vague.

Within legal frameworks, at least in the United Kingdom, the United States, and Canada, the term "metadata" is rarely if ever used. The concept of metadata within the law developed historically out of the ways in which the law has approached communications technology, insofar as this technology facilitates the production of personal information that may or may not be subject to privacy laws. How metadata is interpreted in Canadian law is still being worked out by regulators and the judiciary.[4] Referring to private communications, Part VI of the *Criminal Code* states that

> private communication means any oral communication, or any telecommuni-
> cation, that is made by an originator who is in Canada or is intended by the
> originator to be received by a person who is in Canada and that is made under
> circumstances in which it is reasonable for the originator to expect that it will
> not be intercepted by any person other than the person intended by the origina-
> tor to receive it.[5]

Whether or not metadata can be defined as private communications has been discussed in Canadian courts. Authoritative voices such as Craig Forcese and the Office of the Privacy Commissioner cite court cases as well as the Supreme Court interpretation of the *Criminal Code,* which protects "any derivative of that communication that would convey its substance or meaning."[6] As a deriva-tive of a communication, metadata has been shown to provide significant details about the meaning of a communication[7] and "may permit the drawing of infer-ences about an individual's conduct or activities."[8] This definition focuses, as in the media definitions, on the surface or contextual information about a com-munication but acknowledges the potential sensitivity of this information when analyzed and linked with other available data. The Office of the Privacy Com-missioner further asserts that "metadata can reveal medical conditions, religious beliefs, sexual orientation and many other elements of personal information."[9] Commenting on how the debate has played out in Canadian courts, Forcese reads the 2014 Supreme Court of Canada decision in *R v Spencer* as the "clear authority" that some forms of metadata, in this case "the name, address, and telephone number of a customer associated with an IP address," can be used to reveal details about private lives and should be protected as personal information.[10]

Like those in Canada, laws in the United Kingdom and the United States do not use the term "metadata," but focus more specifically on the technical aspects of the type of communications information. In the United Kingdom, the *Regu-lation of Investigatory Powers Act (RIPA)* defines "communications data" in part as including "(a) any traffic data comprised in or attached to a communication (whether by the sender or otherwise) for the purposes of any postal service or telecommunication system by means of which it is being or may be transmitted ... (b) any information which includes none of the contents of a communication (apart from any information falling within paragraph (a))."[11] In the United States, one example of metadata, "Call Detail Records," is legally defined as "session-identifying information (including an originating or terminating telephone number, an International Mobile Subscriber Identity number, or an International Mobile Station Equipment Identity number), a telephone calling card number, or the time or duration of a call" and "*does not include* – (1) the contents ... of any communication; (2) the name, address, or financial information of a subscriber or customer; or (3) cell site location or global positioning system information" (emphasis added).[12]

The differences in these varying approaches reveal how metadata can imply very different things across varying communities of practice. In her *Introduction to Metadata 3.0*, leading archival scholar Anne J. Gilliland explicates the "widely used but frequently underspecified term" within the framework of the archival discipline.[13] She notes that the term originated with data management and today in practice metadata is generally "the sum total of what one can say about any information object at any level of aggregation." An information object can vary from a film or book to email or phone call; therefore "metadata" in this definition suggests anything one could say about these items, from a title to any salient feature of the contents. For archivists and information managers, metadata reflects an information object's content, context, and structure, and enables preservation as well as "intellectual and physical access."[14]

Despite at times recognizing that communications metadata may reveal a significant amount of personal information, media and legal definitions of metadata tend to limit their focus to the specific types of information that can be read from the "surface" of the information object without delving into the object's content. By contrast, the archival definition of metadata, as put forth by Gilliland, acknowledges that varying levels of aggregation and detail, as well as relationships between information objects and systems, may impact how one defines metadata as opposed to data, or context as opposed to content.[15] Gilliland notes that these "distinctions ... can often be very fluid and may depend on how one wishes to use a certain information object."[16]

Role of Metadata in Big Data Analytics

Questions of how metadata is used, and by whom, are often missing from the simplified accounts of metadata collection. Critics of these popular and governmental definitions note the dismissal of metadata's importance to big data analysis,[17] which takes advantage of the ease with which this kind of structured data can be processed automatically to link very large collections of data elements and find patterns in order to create meaning and draw conclusions.[18] Proponents of big data analysis claim that metadata enables efficient "distill[ing of] terabytes of low-value data ... to ... a single bit of high-value data."[19] Through the development of mobile communications technology, an environment has emerged in which ordinary users, often without realizing it, produce large amounts of metadata on a daily basis.[20] Access to this mass of personal data, when analyzed through big data analytical techniques and software, allows for broad and deep access to personal information. Arguably, this access has been downplayed through the conventional meanings of metadata summarized above, to the benefit of both corporate business practices and surveillance agencies.[21]

Metadata from a Five Eyes Perspective

The Five Eyes, frequently abbreviated "FVEY" or "5VEY" in their internal documents, is an intelligence alliance among the United States, United Kingdom, Canada, Australia, and New Zealand dating back to the Second World War. Each of these countries maintains several intelligence agencies that participate in the alliance, but it is those focused on signals intelligence (SIGINT) that concern us here; they are, respectively, the National Security Agency, the Government Communications Headquarters, the Communications Security Establishment,[22] the Australian Signals Directorate (ASD), and the Government Communications Security Bureau (GCSB). During the Cold War, FVEY developed a globe-spanning signal interception capability known as ECHELON.[23] Initially targeted at the Soviet Union, whistle-blowers[24] and journalists[25] have recently revealed that this alliance, led by the NSA, has greatly expanded this network into a comprehensive surveillance apparatus of extraordinary scope and domestic penetration, albeit of highly questionable efficacy in its principal stated mission to aid in the "War on Terror."[26]

The classified internal documents that Edward Snowden leaked to journalists in June 2013 and subsequently published in major news media[27] have offered an unprecedented glimpse into these highly secretive surveillance agencies. The Snowden trove reveals for the first time in fascinating detail their inner workings, identifying hundreds of individual surveillance programs.[28] But the view offered is at best a sliver of the full picture. So far, well under 1,000 of the more than 50,000 documents that Snowden leaked have been made public.[29] Some vast surveillance programs are mentioned only in extremely abbreviated summaries. Many of the documents have been released to the public only in fragmented form, with heavy redactions by both government officials and newspaper editors. They are full of obscure, cryptic acronyms, code words, and arcane technical details that call for security expertise and organizational experience to properly decipher.

Nevertheless, while keeping these limitations in mind, there is already such an abundance of material in the Snowden trove dealing with metadata that we have a good basis for painting a reliable, if preliminary, picture of how these agencies discuss and operationalize our topic at hand.

For our study of metadata within the FVEY, we relied extensively on the Snowden Digital Surveillance Archive, a publicly accessible finding aid to the full corpus of published Snowden documents and related media articles that we designed and built, and that is now hosted by the Canadian Journalists for Free Expression.[30] From working with the documents in building the archive, we developed strong suspicions that internally the FVEY agencies take a much more expansive view of metadata than suggested by their public statements and reinforced in the popular media definitions discussed above. In switching to a research role, we sought to test our suspicions while being open to possible disconfirming evidence. We initially made use of the archive's full-text search, indexing, and document description features to locate documents and stories relatively dense in details about metadata, and then pursued thematic linkages between documents, such as by surveillance program, to amplify the contexts in aid of interpretation.

Metadata is evidently an important topic within the FVEY. A search in the archive on "metadata" produced 1,644 word hits. Fourteen documents contained "metadata" in their title, which we examined first. The surveillance programs, legal justifications, and internal policies mentioned therein informed further archival searches. The domain knowledge we had gained from arranging and describing the Snowden documents also greatly aided our initial searches in identifying fertile points for research as well as in understanding the documents we selected.

While we expected that exploring such a conceptually vague and varied phenomenon as metadata would yield a mix of results, we were struck by the breadth and heterogeneity of metadata produced by FVEY agencies. For example, disparate GCHQ surveillance programs harvest hotel room bookings (ROYAL CONCIERGE), social media activity (STELLARWIND), and text message geolocation data (in partnership with the NSA under DISHFIRE). Each different program generates different types of metadata, making classification of the surveillance agency's handling of metadata difficult. To facilitate comparison of the various agency interpretations of metadata with each other, with their public statements, and with the various legal definitions in their respective jurisdictions, we looked at the three most relevant agencies in turn – NSA, GCHQ, and CSE.[31] We also focused on those surveillance programs in which metadata plays a particularly prominent role, notably XKEYSCORE, which provides a front-end interface to many signals intelligence databases around the globe and is accessed by all members of the alliance as well as by selected third-party agencies.

Metadata in the NSA

Several documents in the Snowden trove across a span of several years use identical language that the NSA has apparently adopted as its standardized definition of metadata:

> Communications metadata refers to structured "data about data": it *includes all information associated with,* but not including *content,* and includes any data used by a network, service or application to facilitate routing or handling of a communication or to render content in the intended format; it includes, *but is not limited to,* dialing, routing, addressing, or signaling information and data in support of various network management activities (e.g. billing, authentication or tracking of communicants). [Emphasis added][32]

The key phrase here is "includes all information associated with, but not including content." But what does this actually mean? A colloquial interpretation, based on the caveat "but not including content," would confine communications metadata to the surface features, such as the oft-referenced "outside of the envelope" data. In which case, this could be reworded as "includes all information associated with the message, but *excluding anything based on message content.*" However, another plausible but very different interpretation would be that metadata "includes all information that can be derived from a message and its content, but excluding the content itself." This version would be consistent with metadata in archival theory and practice as described above. It would also be consistent with the NSA's often expansive, and secret, interpretation of its legal mandate, thereby opening the door for the agency to justify unfettered algorithmic analysis of communications content as metadata extraction. We find strong support for this latter interpretation when we examine the NSA's most prominent analysis engine, XKEYSCORE. Compared with many other tools and surveillance programs mentioned in the Snowden documents, important aspects of XKEYSCORE are extensively described, enabling a relatively comprehensive understanding of its capabilities, scope, and use.

XKEYSCORE is one of the NSA's most powerful tools and is often in demand among its trusted "second party" (i.e., other members of the Five Eyes) and "third party" partners.[33] Access to the tool has been shared with the GCHQ, ASD, CSE, GCSB, *Bundesnachrichtendienst* (Germany), and National Defence Radio Establishment (FRA) (Sweden). Described in the *Intercept* as "the NSA's Google,"[34] this tool gives analysts unprecedented access to communications metadata largely harvested by the NSA from fibre-optic cables and cached in over 700 servers at 150 storage sites scattered throughout the world. An unofficial user's guide to XKEYSCORE developed by Booz Allen Hamilton gives a technical description of the operation of the tool aimed at surveillance analysts. It includes detailed illustrations of its user interface, as well as specifications of how different metadata fields can be used to query the NSA's vast archives of intercepted communications. These fields are very valuable in identifying the NSA's operational interpretation of metadata.

Conventional metadata fields are well represented – unsurprisingly, analysts have the ability to query communications by IP address, phone number, email account, and so on. However, metadata query capabilities extend far beyond the obvious to include accessing anything contained in email messages, web searches, text chats, and file attachments – in short, the full range of communications content.

The user's guide describes various algorithmic metadata "extractors," including for phone number and email address. These tools appear to scan digital communications traffic for any mention of email addresses and phone numbers, not just in the routing data but within the message bodies, and retrieve these as distinct metadata fields: "The phone number extractor query looks through the *content* of an email for phone numbers ... XKEYSCORE may be your only hope at finding an email address for a target where you only have their phone number as lead information" (emphasis added).[35] Another document similarly describes the email address extractor query: "The query searches within bodies of emails, webpages and documents for ... (you guessed it) ... Email Addresses."[36]

The NSA and its intelligence partners, chief among them the GCHQ, use these content-derived metadata extraction capabilities not only for counterterrorism but also in other pursuits, including diplomatic advantage. Targeting the offices of at least thirty-five world leaders, FVEY agencies intercepted both phone and email communications from officials and staffers,[37] extracting phone numbers and email addresses to be used in identifying further targets.[38] Beyond phone numbers and email addresses, other XKEYSCORE documents make clear its ability to query the content of email messages and their attachments for arbitrary text strings: "Allow queries like ... show me all documents that reference Osama Bin Laden."[39]

Interestingly, the XKEYSCORE documents refer to this kind of database querying via metadata as "contextual" search. Arguably "context" is an even more ambiguous term than "metadata," providing for wide interpretative flexibility. The conflation of metadata with context is illustrated in excerpts from another XKEYSCORE training document, *Guide to Using Contexts in XKS Fingerprints* (see Figure 14.1).

These examples provide clear evidence that, in practice, the NSA subscribes to a view that anything it can derive algorithmically from communications

SECRET//COMINT//REL TO USA, AUS, CAN, GBR, NZL

Guide to using Contexts in XKS Fingerprints
Version 1.0

Example 1
```
$a = cc('pk') and (web_search('jihad') or document_body('planning
for jihad'))
```

Definition
(S//REL) Contextual expressions are those that restrict the search space for a particular expression. In example 1 above, we are looking for the string 'jihad' only in the normalized text of a web search, and 'planning for jihad' only in the context of the UTF-8 normalized text of an office document.

(S//REL) For example, web_search is a *scan* so web_search('jihad') will hit on web searches like:

"I want to participate in jihad"
"How do I avoid jihad"
"jihadi"
"bigjihad"

Communications Content

...

communication_body
  Description:
  (U//FOUO) The UTF-8 normalized text of all office document, email, and chat bodies.

  Aliases:
  doc_email_body

  Context Type:
  Scan
  Aliased to email_body, chat_body and document_body.

  Eample:
  communication_body('how to' and 'build' and ('bomb' or 'weapon'))

Figure 14.1 "Context" as metadata category in XKEYSCORE. A one-page excerpt from the classified secret Five Eyes document titled "Guide to Using Contexts in XKS Fingerprints." It shows that Communications Content is considered a form of Context of Type "Scan." | *Source*: Snowden Digital Surveillance Archive, https://is.gd/n7brJJ.

traffic can be regarded as metadata, including information extracted from the communications content itself. Short of a human analyst actually reading a message or listening in on a phone call, any distinction between content and metadata has been erased. As XKEYSCORE is shared among all Five Eyes

SIGINT partners, notwithstanding any jurisdictional differences between them, they all have in effect adopted this expansive view of metadata.

Metadata in the GCHQ

One particularly useful document in the Snowden archive, "Content or Metadata? Categorisation of Aspects of Intercepted Communications – GCHQ Policy Guidance,"[40] delineates the GCHQ's official understanding of metadata. This document clearly specifies whether certain elements of an Internet communication (such as an email) are to be classified as content or metadata, and which particular "class" under the *Regulation of Investigatory Powers Act* the communication falls under.

What is notable about this schema is how different it is from the NSA's. The contents of attachments to emails are labelled "content," in marked contrast to the NSA, which, as we saw above in XKEYSCORE, operationalizes this element as a class of communications metadata.[41] Interestingly, the GCHQ also identifies a class of "content derived data," including analysis of the language of the communication itself, presumably derived from analysis of the content of the message.[42] The document seems to imply that this class of data is considered conceptually distinct from both metadata and content.

However, the GCHQ, along with the other surveillance agencies in the Five Eyes, has access to XKEYSCORE. It is unclear how it utilizes this tool in accordance with its specific legal and policy requirements, as XKEYSCORE has been described as lacking any meaningful oversight and accountability features.[43]

Metadata in CSE

In Canada, CSE collects or, more precisely, generates metadata as part of its mandate, through the *National Defence Act,* "to acquire and use information from the global information infrastructure for the purpose of providing foreign intelligence."[44] The act broadly defines "global information structure" as "electromagnetic emissions, communications systems, information technology systems and networks, and any data or technical information carried on, contained in or relating to those emissions, systems or networks." This mandate is limited by "measures to protect the privacy of Canadians in the use and retention of intercepted information," as outlined in the *Criminal Code.*[45]

Unlike other intelligence agencies, the Canadian CSE displays its public definition of metadata on its website:

Metadata is the context, but not the content of a communication. It is information used by computer systems to identify, describe, manage or route communications across networks. For example, metadata can refer to an internet protocol address or a phone number or the time of a transmission or the location of a device ... While metadata reveals a certain amount of information about devices, users and transmissions, it is contextual and does not expose the content of emails, phone calls or text messages.[46]

In 2016, the director of CSE reiterated this distinction between content and metadata-as-context in responding to a *Toronto Star* editorial calling for more oversight of the agency – "Context, not content."[47] As we saw above, however, context in the eyes of these agencies is much different from how we conventionally understand the term and is deeply tied to communication content. As in the case of the GCHQ, it is difficult to square this definition with the agency's continued use of XKEYSCORE.

One CSE surveillance experiment in particular aptly reveals the power of metadata in surveillance activities. The leaked document titled "IP Profiling Analytics & Mission Impacts" describes a trial program where CSE profiled the users of Wi-Fi networks at an international airport located on Canadian soil.[48] The CBC incorrectly reported this as involving the interception of Wi-Fi signals in the airport, but as analyzed in greater depth in Chapter 7, the actual practices are far more disturbing. Especially revealing is the statement by John Forster, then chief of CSE, who told the Senate committee investigating the apparent violation of Canadian law that the experiment involved no actual monitoring at an airport, but simply "a snapshot of historic metadata collected from the global internet ... [as] part of our normal global collection."[49]

Through comprehensive capture, analysis, and storage of Internet communication, CSE spotted visitors to the airport based on the IP address of the airport's public Wi-Fi service. Analysts were then able to track individuals to other locations with identifiable IP addresses, both forward and backward in time, based on the user IDs extracted from message content. This case illustrates not only CSE's expansive interpretation of metadata but also the remarkably broad scope and fine detail of its domestic surveillance capabilities.

"Deep" versus "Shallow" Metadata

This review of the meanings of metadata in varied settings shows that notwithstanding a general recognition that metadata is ambiguous and difficult to distinguish from content, we can discern two distinct sets of meanings to the term. In the popular and legal discourses as well as in the official public statements by security agencies, we observe what can be termed narrow, conventional, "shallow" metadata,[50] characterized by the various forms of data about a communication act or information object that can be read externally, without examining the actual content. In contrast, "deep" metadata goes significantly beyond conventional metadata to include data that can be derived algorithmically from the content.

It is this "deep" metadata that we find defined in the archives field and operationalized in the big data surveillance activities of Five Eyes security agencies. An immediate disturbing conclusion from this finding is that under the rubric of "metadata," the mass surveillance operations of these agencies are potentially even more revealing of people's lives than previously understood. A more hopeful, mitigating conclusion is that attempts to maintain a sharp distinction between communication content and metadata, used as the basis for the weaker protection of the latter, are now more clearly untenable. In the context of Internet communication, current metadata practices that combine both shallow and deep forms are at odds with the *Criminal Code*, which in the interpretation of the Supreme Court of Canada protects "any derivative of that communication that would convey its substance or meaning."[51] While the judiciary is showing strong signs of updating its understanding of metadata in light of contemporary practices, journalism, privacy regulation, and the law need to catch up.

Implications

These conclusions hold implications for the various actors interested in mass surveillance.

For Surveillance Researchers

For researchers seeking to understand the nature and implications of contemporary big data surveillance practices across the private and public sectors, our findings highlight the need to avoid restricting their conceptualization of metadata to the conventional, "shallow" definition of metadata and to broaden it to include the "deep" form. Their protestations to the contrary, state security agencies widely practise metadata analysis in this deeper sense based on algorithmic processing of communication message bodies. Very likely commercial enterprises with access to large volumes of personal information do likewise. It is clear that this form of data mining involves large-scale, systematic algorithmic analysis of communication content intended to draw out potentially anything that may be of interest to the surveillance analyst. In short, metadata is a principal means for analyzing and accessing "content," and hence is effectively inseparable from it.

For Security Intelligence Agencies

State security intelligence agencies such as CSE, NSA, and GCHQ are legitimately in the business of maintaining secrecy and deceiving perceived opponents, but in healthy democracies they are also ultimately accountable to the citizens they are mandated to protect. While it may run against institutional culture, maintaining the necessary public confidence and trust requires significant transparency, honesty, and demonstrable compliance with legal and constitutional norms. Especially at a time when there is growing and well-founded skepticism that these agencies are neither in compliance with the law nor being effective in their missions, for their official statements to consistently rely on a narrow interpretation of metadata at odds with their actual practices is hardly reassuring. Misleading the public about such an important term as "metadata" only heightens concerns. Security agencies coming clean about what they really do with our data may initially provoke adverse reaction, but in the long run is far better than fuelling the vicious cycle of deception and public skepticism.

For Those Calling for State Surveillance Accountability and Reform

For civil liberties and democratic governance advocates, parliamentarians, privacy regulators, journalists, and citizens working to bring greater accountability and reform to state surveillance agencies, our findings point to several recommendations. They should:

- continue to revise their working definitions and metaphors of metadata to include "deep" metadata[52]
- treat statements about metadata, especially by government officials who repeat the conventional definition of metadata, with skepticism and avoid reiterating them
- instead adopt and publicize the more comprehensive meaning of metadata, its practical indistinguishability from message content, and the greater risks that deep metadata can pose to personal privacy
- call to account state security and law enforcement agencies that make misleading public statements and go beyond their legal authorizations
- press for metadata to receive privacy protection equivalent to content (e.g., in the *Criminal Code*).

These suggestions contribute to the wider effort to achieve stronger transparency and accountability of organizations with access to large volumes of personal information, especially state security and law enforcement agencies. In particular, they can help ensure that state security and law enforcement agencies are more transparent and accountable, and operate within the norms of democratic governance.

A Methodological Note on Researching with the Snowden Archive

Although we began constructing the Snowden Digital Surveillance Archive in 2014, this report reflects our first attempt to make use of the archive ourselves for research purposes. We are pleased that it provided us with an opportunity to examine in a comprehensive and seamless way all the documents Snowden released and subsequently published. We did not face a priori divisions based on agency, national jurisdiction, or publishing source. This enabled us to draw a more holistic picture of the role of metadata in mass surveillance at the international level. We found document descriptions and links to media reports developed during the archival process particularly helpful in contextualizing documents that are often heavily redacted and excerpted. We also became acutely aware of some of the limitations of the current implementation, notably the lack of a controlled vocabulary and technical limitations of the Greenstone digital library software the archive is built on. These were more of a nuisance than a major obstacle to our research, however. Our experience studying metadata using the Snowden Digital Surveillance Archive suggests that other researchers interested in big data surveillance, particularly by the Five Eyes agencies, may find the archive a valuable research tool.

Notes

1   Canadian Journalists for Free Expression, Snowden Digital Surveillance Archive (SDSA), https://snowdenarchive.cjfe.org.
2   Ashley Burke, "'Difficult to Determine' Scope of Privacy Breach in Five Eyes Data Sharing," *CBC News,* 23 February 2016, http://www.cbc.ca/news/politics/cse-metadata-five-eyes-sharing-1.3459717. A nearly identical definition was used again in the following article: Alison Crawford, "Canada's Electronic Spy Agency to Get New Rules for Sharing Data with Allies," *CBC News,* 29 August 2017, http://www.cbc.ca/news/politics/sajjan-cse-data-sharing-five-eyes-1.4265583.
3   James Ball, "NSA Stores Metadata of Millions of Web Users for Up to a Year, Secret Files Show," *Guardian,* 30 September 2013, http://www.theguardian.com/world/2013/sep/30/nsa-americans-metadata-year-documents.
4   Office of the Privacy Commissioner of Canada (OPCC), *Metadata and Privacy: A Technical and Legal Overview* (Gatineau, QC: Office of the Privacy Commissioner of Canada, 2014), 9.
5   *Criminal Code,* RSC 1985, c C-46, pt 6, s 183, https://laws-lois.justice.gc.ca/eng/acts/C-46/page-41.html#h-118715.
6   As quoted in Craig Forcese, "Laws, Logarithms, Liberties: Legal Issues Arising from CSE's Metadata Collection Initiatives," in *Law, Privacy, and Surveillance in the Post-Snowden Era,* edited by Michael Geist (Ottawa: University of Ottawa Press, 2015), 137.
7   Ibid., 137, 148.
8   OPCC, *Metadata and Privacy,* 10.
9   OPCC, "Backgrounder: Privacy and Canada's National Security Framework," 6 December 2016, https://www.priv.gc.ca/en/opc-news/news-and-announcements/2016/bg_161206/.
10 OPCC, *Metadata and Privacy,* 148.
11 *Regulation of Investigatory Powers Act 2000,* 2000 c 23, s 21.4.

12 *USA Freedom Act,* Pub L No 114-23, s 107 ("Definitions"), 129 Stat 268 (2015).

13 Anne J. Gilliland, "Setting the Stage," in *Introduction to Metadata,* edited by Murtha Baca (Los Angeles: Getty Research Institute, 2008), 1.

14 Ibid., 2.

15 Ibid.,14.

16 Ibid., 14–15.

17 David Lyon, "Surveillance, Snowden, and Big Data: Capacities, Consequences, Critique," *Big Data and Society* 1, 2 (2014): 3, 10.

18 Seref Sagiroglu and Duygu Sinanc, "Big Data: A Review," in *2013 International Conference on Collaboration Technologies and Systems (CTS)* (San Diego: Institute of Electrical and Electronics Engineers, 2013), 43; Danyel Fisher, Rob DeLine, Mary Czerwinski, and Steven Drucker, "Interactions with Big Data Analytics," *Interactions* 19, 3 (2012): 53.

19 Fisher et al., "Interactions with Big Data Analytics," 50.

20 Lyon, "Surveillance, Snowden," 3; Gilliland, "Setting the Stage," 8.

21 John Laprise, "Exploring PRISMS Spectrum: Privacy in the Information Age," in *The Turn to Infrastructure in Internet Governance,* edited by Francesca Musiani, Derrick L. Cogburn, Laura DeNardis, and Nanette S. Levinson (New York: Palgrave Macmillan, 2016), 208, 214; Lyon, "Surveillance, Snowden," 10.

22 Also formerly referred to as the Communications Security Establishment Canada (CSEC). It is this now unofficial name and acronym that appears most frequently in the Snowden documents.

23 In the mid-1970s, "the very existence of GCHQ and the [worldwide US/UK] Sigint network were then closely guarded secrets." Duncan Campbell, "GCHQ and Me: My Life Unmasking British Eavesdroppers," *Intercept,* 3 August 2015, https://theintercept.com/2015/08/03/life-unmasking-british-eavesdroppers/.

24 Notably Mark Klein, William Binney, Thomas Drake, and Edward Snowden.

25 Notably James Bamford, James Risen, Eric Lichtblau, Glenn Greenwald, Laura Poitras, Barton Gellman, and Ryan Gallagher,

26 Zach Whittaker, "NSA Is So Overwhelmed with Data, It's No Longer Effective, Says Whistleblower," *ZDNet,* 27 April 2016, http://www.zdnet.com/article/nsa-whistleblower-overwhelmed-with-data-ineffective/.

27 Notably the *Guardian, Washington Post, Der Speigel, Intercept, New York Times.* See SDSA, https://is.gd/ze5urh.

28 See SDSA, http://bit.ly/SnowdenArchive-Surveillance_Programs.

29 As of mid-2018, Snowden Doc Search reported a total of 2,176 documents in its searchable database, of which 1,571 were individual articles that appeared in *SIDToday,* the internal newsletter for the NSA's Signals Intelligence Directorate, https://search.edwardsnowden.com/.

30 SDSA, https://snowdenarchive.cjfe.org.

31 We exclude Australia's DSO and New Zealand's GCSB from our treatment here as there are relatively few Snowden documents that relate to these partners, nor does metadata appear prominently among them.

32 This definition appears in several different documents found in the Snowden Digital Surveillance Archive, e.g., National Security Agency (NSA), "Sharing Communications Metadata across the U.S. Intelligence Community – ICREACH" (slide deck, 15 March 2007), SDSA, https://is.gd/9j9vRA; and "Memorandum for the Director of National Intelligence: Sharing Communications Metadata across the Intelligence Community – Decision Memorandum," SDSA, https://is.gd/N1zoqR.

33 "XKEYSCORE" (slide deck, 25 February 2008), SDSA, https://is.gd/RLB6U6.

34 Morgan Marquis-Boire, Glenn Greenwald, and Micah Lee, "XKEYSCORE: NSA's Google for the World's Private Communications," *Intercept,* 1 July 2015, https://theintercept.com/2015/07/01/nsas-google-worlds-private-communications/.

35   Booz Allen Hamilton, "The Unofficial XKEYSCORE User Guide," 10, SDSA, https://is.gd/QX8VrU.
36   "Email Address vs User Activity" (slide deck, 24 June 2009), slide 2, SDSA, https://snowdenarchive.cjfe.org/greenstone/collect/snowden1/index/assoc/HASH0164/d967fedd.dir/doc.pdf.
37   James Ball, "NSA Monitored Calls of 35 World Leaders after US Official Handed Over Contacts," *Guardian*, 24 October 2013, http://www.theguardian.com/world/2013/oct/24/nsa-surveillance-world-leaders-calls.
38   "Intelligently Filtering Your Data: Brazil and Mexico Case Studies," SDSA, https://is.gd/ljFRcC; "3G Impact and Update" (slide deck, November 2009), SDSA, https://is.gd/gfOjhZ.
39   "XKEYSCORE" (slide deck, 25 February 2008), slide 26, SDSA, https://is.gd/RLB6U6.
40   "Content or Metadata?" SDSA, https://snowdenarchive.cjfe.org/greenstone/collect/snowden1/index/assoc/HASHd8b5.dir/doc.pdf. We could not find similar technical documents for the other two major surveillance agencies.
41   Ibid.
42   Ibid.
43   Kari Rea, "Glenn Greenwald: Low-Level NSA Analysts Have 'Powerful and Invasive' Search Tool," *ABC News*, 28 July 2013, http://abcnews.go.com/blogs/politics/2013/07/glenn-greenwald-low-level-nsa-analysts-have-powerful-and-invasive-search-tool/.
44   *National Defence Act*, s 273.64.1.
45   Ibid., s 273.64.2.
46   Communications Security Establishment (CSE), "Metadata and Our Mandate," June 2017, https://www.cse-cst.gc.ca/en/inside-interieur/metadata-metadonnees.
47   Greta Bossenmaier, letter to the editor, *The Star*, 3 March 2016, https://www.thestar.com/opinion/letters_to_the_editors/2016/03/03/metadata-is-crucial-cse-insists.html.
48   Greg Weston, "CSEC Used Airport Wi-Fi to Track Canadian Travellers: Edward Snowden Documents," *CBC News*, 31 January 2014, http://www.cbc.ca/news/politics/csec-used-airport-wi-fi-to-track-canadian-travellers-edward-snowden-documents-1.2517881.
49   Laura Payton, "Spy Agencies, Prime Minister's Adviser Defend Wi-Fi Data Collection," *CBC News*, 3 February 2014, http://www.cbc.ca/news/politics/spy-agencies-prime-minister-s-adviser-defend-wi-fi-data-collection-1.2521166.
50   This terminology of "shallow" versus "deep" metadata is inspired in part by the similar distinction used in the XKEYSCORE document of 25 February 2008. It also echoes the "deep packet inspection" techniques employed by FVEY agencies in generating metadata from intercepted communication traffic. See "XKEYSCORE" (slide deck, 25 February 2008), slides 9 and 10, SDSA, https://snowdenarchive.cjfe.org/greenstone/collect/snowden1/index/assoc/HASH56fe.dir/doc.pdf.
51   As quoted in Forcese, "Laws, Logarithms, Liberties," 137.
52   For example, the OPCC's 2014 *Metadata and Privacy* statement could be expanded to make explicit the forms of deep metadata we highlight above.

Afterword

Holly Porteous

THIS BOOK RAISES serious questions about preserving civil liberties *and* national security in a big data era. In reflecting on these questions, it became apparent to me that lingering gaps in our knowledge are forcing us to rely on assumptions that may prove incorrect should our access to government information and research output increase over the next few years. What I am proposing here, building on the excellent contributions of this book's authors, is to identify areas requiring further research, knowledge gaps, and where we need to strengthen our collective analysis.

First, delimiting our subject matter more precisely and with the necessary nuances appears urgent. Reading this book, I was struck by its enormous breadth. Among other things, it discusses the evolution of Canadian SIGINT collection, the complexity of Canada's current national security legal framework, the use of (or failure to use) big data analytics by Canadian intelligence and law enforcement agencies, mobilization of the public against proposed national security legislation, and challenges in achieving informed consent to access personal information.

Going forward, I believe there will be value in selecting elements of this broad discourse for closer scrutiny. For example, do we wish to examine in greater detail how and for what purposes the Canadian security and intelligence community and law enforcement exploit big data? If so, will our goal be to stop these activities entirely or to identify and recommend measures to mitigate the potentially negative consequences to individuals? Given the enthusiasm for algorithmic approaches by some government agencies, perhaps our interest is in ensuring that the state exploits big data more effectively to fulfill its duty to protect its citizenry? Do we wish instead to examine and address the roles and responsibilities of the private sector and academia in supporting and developing Canada's big data policy and capabilities? What about the role of big data and cybersecurity; specifically, are we interested in examining and commenting on the growing involvement of SIGINT agencies in defending critical infrastructures operated by the private sector? What are our views on "outsourcing" aspects of critical infrastructure protection to private sector actors, such as telecommunications providers? Finally, given artificial intelligence's evolving capabilities, what are our views on ensuring the interrogability and reliability of currently deployed technologies and the safety of future technologies being developed in well-funded labs around the world? Choosing among these questions will help us better marshal our multidisciplinary effort and resources.

Even a research agenda focused on the first question alone – how the Canadian security and intelligence community and law enforcement exploit big data – suggests to me that knowledge gaps persist and our assumptions need to be revisited. Let me present some examples to support this claim. The first example highlights the possibility that, for a SIGINT agency such as the Communications Security Establishment (CSE), the utility of big data techniques varies according to the intelligence collection context. The purpose of intelligence collection is generally understood to be the provision of assessed information on the capabilities and intentions of individuals, groups, or foreign countries to help state and law enforcement officials make decisions. Capabilities are relatively easy to assess; intentions, not so much. Humans can say one thing and do another. Their minds are essentially black boxes. Big data's pattern matching can offer some insight into hidden intentions but, absent a reliable template for what bad intentions look like ("indicators and warnings," in the parlance), the results may not be a reliable predictor of future actions.

The mismatch between what big data analytics can deliver and the intelligence task at hand is a recurring theme in this book. Big data analytics, it has been found, are largely ineffective in detecting and preventing terrorist threats. Likewise, algorithms may be creating more nightmares for the financial institutions forced to use them to meet their FINTRAC (Financial Transactions and Reports Analysis Centre of Canada) reporting requirements than for terrorist financiers. Finally, the enthusiasm of Canadian police services for big data is not necessarily matched by an informed understanding about how to integrate associated tools and techniques.

The story may be different, however, for cyber threats. Readers will recall that each of the Five Eyes SIGINT agencies, including CSE, also has a cybersecurity mandate. That means they are in the business of producing intelligence on cyber threats. Other Canadian agencies also have a mandated interest. For its part, the Canadian Security Intelligence Service (CSIS) has a requirement to investigate and assess *all* threats to the security of Canada, including cyber threats such as cyber espionage. The RCMP investigates criminal activities, including cyber crime.

In contrast to terrorists working in the physical world alone (increasingly, a near-impossible enterprise), cyber threats are bounded by the technical protocols and characteristics of the global information infrastructure through which they operate. In the cyber domain, it is possible – though data-intensive – to determine what normal activities look like. Therefore, it is also possible to identify anomalous and potentially malicious traffic. Cyber threats are thus conducive to big data analysis.

Indeed, for intelligence agencies, police, and systems security administrators more generally, network and host defence has always been about parsing massive logs of transmissions traffic, hunting for patterns that indicate malicious activities. Until recently, much of the work in this area has focused on recreating events after an attack, so-called digital forensics. Now, thanks to advances in artificial intelligence, it is increasingly realistic to speak of intrusion prevention through near-real-time, automated responses to suspected malicious traffic.

SIGINT agencies, whose intelligence collection activities have been conducted through the global information infrastructure for decades, are interested in marrying their leading-edge capabilities with commercially available big data tools to achieve intrusion prevention.

So, for cybersecurity, the big data tools are finally catching up to a long-standing demand. With the explosive growth of the poorly secured Internet of Things and increasingly aggressive Russian and Chinese cyber attacks, intelligence officials say building automated defence capabilities into our networks has become a "red lights blinking" undertaking. There is no choice but to fight their algorithms with our algorithms.

Those who track public statements of Five Eyes SIGINT agency officials know that cybersecurity now stands equal to, if not greater than, counterterrorism among national security priorities. Yes, terrorism remains a significant concern and big data does have some utility in this domain, but SIGINT agencies have for some time been re-engineering their foreign intelligence collection capabilities to tip and queue automated cyber defence capabilities.

Chapter 8 provides a sense of this policy trajectory. The programs it discusses indicate that, along with hacking into adversary networks, bulk data collection and machine learning are viewed as fundamental to national cyber defence.

If collecting bulk datasets for cybersecurity is an inescapable part of the national security picture, then we must understand the implications. For example, is the price of better securing our digital lifestyle a reduced expectation of privacy and an expanded peacetime role for intelligence agencies and the military? What role will private sector entities such as communications service providers play in defending Canada's cyberspace? How can we ensure that data collected for cybersecurity purposes is stored, used, and disposed of properly? Can our cyber defence systems be turned against us, either from within or from without? In a related vein and drawing on observations made in Chapter 5, how will smaller businesses who can't afford tailored algorithms protect themselves against cyber threats? Regarding SIGINT agencies' use of zero-days, through what mechanisms are vulnerabilities equities issues being addressed and who speaks for proportionality concerns?[1] What consideration is being given to other forms of civil defence against cyber attacks, such as enhancing societal resilience through preservation of analogue mechanisms for critical services? To what extent are we handing over potential life-and-death decisions to machines?

A second example inspired by this book also reveals a rich vein of follow-on research questions. It entails an exploration of what transparency and accountability mean in an age of algorithms. Some believe there are limits to what can be achieved in this context. For example, Mike Ananny and Kate Crawford highlight the inutility of transparency measures that "privilege seeing over understanding."[2] Useful transparency, they say, not only provides the visibility of a system but also affords observers sufficient understanding of the system's internal and external dynamics to debate and change it. In this connection, I would draw your attention to recent revelations that the CSE Commissioner learned about a technical glitch that had caused CSE to share unminimized Canadian metadata with foreign allies for years only because CSE volunteered the information itself. SIGINT watchdogs in the United Kingdom and United States have also reported similar glitches and "technical irregularities."

With current approaches to machine learning, where even a system's creator may not be able to explain how it works, useful transparency may not be achievable. Still, proponents of causality modelling in machine learning – Judea Pearl being foremost among this group[3] – may help lead the way to enhanced *and* transparent artificial intelligence. Simply put, to be able to ask learning machines useful questions, including questions about their internal reasoning, we need to put more work into framing how these machines approach cause and effect when we design them.

A word about achieving big data transparency through horizontal accountability mechanisms. Parliament, the judiciary, media, and civil rights groups each contribute to the public's awareness and thereby to informed debate. For example, even if the judiciary's accountability function is limited to the application of existing laws, its public disclosures of redacted versions of key national security decisions provide valuable information to Canadians about current and proposed national security activities, including bulk data collection. Journalists, the dedicated ones anyway, do their bit by continuously requesting the release of government records under the *Access to Information Act*. Finally, and as this book attests, Canada is in the remarkable position of being home to a pioneering group of scholars and civil rights activists who are all focused on the big data issue.

But the question remains: Is this accountability matrix up to the task of engaging government in meaningful and productive ways on big data used *within* a national security context? Does each element have access to sufficient information and expertise to recognize poor practice and challenge it? Alternatively, is each element capable of recognizing and supporting sound practices in this area? If not, what measures would enhance capacity while respecting secrecy requirements?

Regarding secrecy requirements, I would draw attention to the exceedingly small pool of individuals in this country who can claim genuine expertise in the operational aspects of intelligence collection. Most of these individuals are bound to secrecy for life under the *Security of Information Act* and they steer well clear of providing any public commentary that would shed light on intelligence collection sources and methods. This situation presents a challenge for those who would like to expand their knowledge.

Given the far-reaching policy decisions that Canada is poised to take regarding a national data strategy, perhaps there may be value in examining what is being said on this matter in our own Parliament and in the legislatures of other allied jurisdictions. Out of this examination should come a sense of where civil rights fit into this discussion. Now is also the time to consider what constitutes an appropriate balance between personal data sovereignty and the public goods that can accrue from machine learning.

Long before the Snowden leaks, legal scholars were voicing concern about intelligence agencies' outsourcing of data collection to the private sector. Indeed, the two editors of this book have for many years been instrumental in educating the public about how surveillance assemblages are being created out of these types of linkages.

With the recent controversy over Facebook's sharing of personal data from millions of its users' accounts with a political consulting firm possessing Canadian connections, the time is ripe for additional research on how data brokers operate in this country. Certainly, there is a gap in our knowledge regarding the specifics of how CSE and CSIS plan to use proposed new authorities to collect and use datasets containing "publicly available" information. A key public policy question would be whether these new authorities could incentivize increased private sector data collection.

Of course, it appears that we are all doing our bit to help private sector service providers collect our personal data. As this book has shown, the death of privacy often takes place in the fine print. Our "ignoring culture" leads most of us to hurry past consent form documentation, clicking quickly on the consent button at the end to gain access to desired services. If being informed about the privacy implications of gaining access to a "free" service means reading through pages of impenetrable legalese, nobody wants to be informed. While efforts are being made to use plain(er) language on consent forms, the documentation sweet spot may never be found.

Perhaps part of the solution lies in the broader public discourse about the deleterious effects of surveillance capitalism that giant social media platforms like Facebook, Twitter, and Google have come to personify. Related to this discussion is the question of user choice. Increasingly, citizens are being herded towards a digital monoculture that makes no room for analogue service delivery. Can people truly consent to sharing their personal data when, to access critical services such as public transit, they are forced to use a smart card?

In many ways, this book is the result of a breakdown in trust. It would not exist were it not for elements of the US national security community who did not like what they were seeing and decided to publicly disclose what they knew. Though they excoriated Edward Snowden as a traitor, even some senior US national security officials have come to admit that the ensuing public debate about previously classified matters has been necessary and useful. Here in Canada, recent polling indicates that most Canadians trust government to protect their privacy but still think they should be given more information about how it collects and uses their personal information. The same polling also shows that most Canadians don't know that their own intelligence agencies exist, let alone what they do.

Here, too, I see an opportunity for research, and thereby education.

Notes

Holly Porteous is an analyst with the Justice and National Security section of the Library of Parliament's Parliamentary Information and Research Service. The views she expresses here are hers alone and do not reflect those of the Library of Parliament.

1 The term "vulnerabilities equities" refers to the choice between enhancing overall cyber-security through public disclosure of previously unknown exploitable cyber vulnerability information and protecting an operational capability by maintaining secrecy.
2 Mike Ananny and Kate Crawford, "Seeing without Knowing: Limitations of the Transparency Ideal and Its Application to Algorithmic Accountability," *New Media and Society* 20, 3 (2016): 973–89.
3 See Judea Pearl and Dana Mackenzie, *The Book of Why: The New Science of Cause and Effect* (New York: Basic Books, 2018). See also Judea Pearl, "Theoretical Impediments to Machine Learning with Seven Sparks from the Causal Revolution," 11 January 2018, arXiv:1801.04016.

Contributors

Anthony Amicelle is an associate professor of criminology at the University of Montreal. In light of repeated corporate, corruption, and tax evasion scandals as well as the pervasiveness of terrorism financing issues, his research examines the policing of economic activities and money flows, with a specific focus on financial surveillance technologies in the digital age. His recent publications include the edited volume *The Policing of Flows: Challenging Contemporary Criminology* (2019) and "Research Ethics at Work: Accountabilities in Fieldwork on Security," in *Secrecy and Methods in Security Research*, edited by Marieke de Goede et al. (2019).

Janet Chan is a professor in the Faculty of Law, University of New South Wales, Sydney, and co-leader of the Data Justice Network at the Allens Hub for Technology, Law and Innovation. Her research analyzes the conceptualization of police culture – e.g., *Changing Police Culture* (1997), *Fair Cop: Learning the Art of Policing* (2003) – and its relationship with the use of technology such as information systems, big data, and artificial intelligence in policing.

Andrew Clement is a professor emeritus of information at the University of Toronto. With a PhD in Computer Science, he has had long-standing research and teaching interests in the social implications of information/communication technologies and privacy/surveillance issues. Among his recent/ongoing research projects are IXmaps.ca, an Internet mapping tool that helps make more visible National Security Agency mass Internet surveillance activities and the Snowden Surveillance Digital Archives, an online searchable collection of all documents leaked by former NSA contractor Edward Snowden and subsequently published by news media. He is currently a collaborator in the Big Data Surveillance project and a member of Waterfront Toronto's Digital Strategy Advisory Panel.

Anne Dagenais Guertin is the communications and research coordinator of the International Civil Liberties Monitoring Group. Anne has a master's degree in Law and Social Justice from the University of Ottawa, a certificate in Women's Studies from Concordia University, and a Bachelor in International Studies from the University of Montreal. Prior to working at ICLMG, Anne was a teaching and research assistant at the Human Rights Research and Education Centre of the University of Ottawa. Anne also organizes with Indigenous Solidarity Ottawa, is an advocate for consent, anti-oppression, and safer spaces, and writes political screenplays.

Craig Forcese is a full professor at the Faculty of Law (Common Law Section), University of Ottawa. He is also an adjunct research professor and senior fellow at the Norman Paterson School of International Affairs, Carleton University (from 2017 to 2022), and a National Security Crisis Law Fellow, Center on National Security and the Law at Georgetown Law (Washington, DC) (from 2017 to 2020). Craig sits on the executive at the Canadian Network for Research on Terrorism, Security and Society (TSAS), and is a past president of the Canadian Council on International Law and the Canadian Association of Law Teachers.

David Grondin is a professor of communication at the University of Montreal. His work examines how issues of security and mobility are adjudicated as part of a nexus, notably as it relates to infrastructures, borders, and citizenship in the digital age. His current project focuses on the technological control of mobilities, taking into account the surveillance, algorithmics, and infrastructures (such as digital platforms, big data, and artificial intelligence) ensuring the secured mobility of people, data, and objects. His recent publications include *Biometrics: Mediating Bodies* (*PUBLIC: Art/Culture/Ideas* special issue, co-edited with Aleksandra Kaminska, 2020), and *Movies, Myth and the National Security State* (with Dan O'Meara, Alex Macleod, and Frédérick Gagnon, 2016).

Jillian Harkness has a master's degree from the University of Toronto Faculty of Information, where she worked as an archival assistant helping to build the Snowden Digital Surveillance Archive. She continues to explore privacy, technology, and education in her current role as the Head of Library and Learning Resources at the United World College of the Adriatic in Duino, Italy.

Stéphane Leman-Langlois teaches criminology at Laval University, Quebec. He has written extensively on policing, national security intelligence, and terrorism. He is currently working on two books, one on the radicalization of the extreme right in Canada (with Aurélie Campana and Samuel Tanner), and the other on the state of policing in Quebec (with Gregory Gomez del Prado).

David Lyon is a professor of sociology and director of the Surveillance Studies Centre at Queen's University, Ontario. Author or editor of many books on surveillance, from *The Electronic Eye* (1994) through *Surveillance Studies* (2007) to *The Culture of Surveillance* (2018), Lyon's work offers a commentary on surveillance in the modern world. His responses to surveillance events such as the expansion of video surveillance, 9/11, and the Snowden revelations sit alongside treatments of the wider meanings of surveillance seen in *Surveillance as Social Sorting* (2003) or in *Liquid Surveillance* (with Zygmunt Bauman, 2013).

Tim McSorley is the national coordinator of the International Civil Liberties Monitoring Group. He combines his passion for civil liberties and social justice with his background in journalism, research, and analysis in his work with colleagues and partners to fight for social change. Previously, he was an editor with the Media Co-op and *The Dominion* magazine, and served as coordinator for the Voices-Voix Coalition. He is a graduate of Concordia University in Montreal, with a degree in journalism and political science.

Adam Molnar is an assistant professor in the Department of Sociology and Legal Studies at the University of Waterloo, Ontario, where he is also a member of the Waterloo Cybersecurity and Privacy Institute. Prior to joining the department in 2019, he was a lecturer in criminology at Deakin University in Australia. He completed his PhD at the University of Victoria, British Columbia, and a postdoctoral fellowship at the Queen's University Surveillance Studies Centre. Much of his work focuses on socio-legal practices of technology-led policing and security intelligence, which also considers the implications for civil liberties, social justice, and the politics of associated regulatory responses.

Jeffrey Monaghan is an associate professor of criminology and sociology at Carleton University in Ottawa. His research examines the policing of social movements as well as broader policing and surveillance practices influenced by the "War on Terror." Along with Andrew Crosby, he co-authored *Policing Indigenous Movements* (2018), which details how policing and other security agencies have developed a prolific surveillance regime that targets Indigenous movements as national security threats. He is also the co-editor, with Lucas Melgaço, of *Protests in the Information Age: Social Movements, Digital Practices and Surveillance* (2018).

David Murakami Wood is former Canada Research Chair (Tier II) in Surveillance Studies and associate professor of sociology at Queen's University. He has a BA in modern history from Oxford and an MSc and PhD from Newcastle, on the subject of secret Signals Intelligence bases in North Yorkshire, UK. He is a widely published specialist in the sociology and geography of surveillance, security, and global cities, particularly in Japan, where he was a Japan Society for the Promotion of Science Fellow in 2013–14, and most recently a 2019 Japan Foundation Fellow examining the security preparations for the Tokyo Olympics. He was co-founder and is co-editor-in-chief of the journal *Surveillance & Society,* and co-editor, with Torin Monahan, of *Surveillance Studies: A Handbook* (2018).

Midori Ogasawara is a Banting Postdoctoral Fellow in the Department of Criminology at the University of Ottawa. She completed her PhD in sociology at Queen's University in 2018, where her dissertation explored the Japanese colonial biometric systems in occupied Northeast China in the 1920s to 1945, to unpack a historical origin of today's digital surveillance. She had a personal interview with NSA whistle-blower Edward Snowden via video channel in 2016, as Snowden's first Japanese interviewer, and has published two books and numerous articles on the NSA's activities in Japan. She was an investigative reporter for Japan's national newspaper, *Asahi Shimbun,* and was awarded a Fulbright Scholarship and John S. Knight Professional Journalism Fellowship at Stanford University in 2004–05. She was appointed an assistant professor in the Department of Sociology at the University of Victoria, where she will start teaching in January 2021.

Christopher Parsons received his bachelor's and master's degrees from the University of Guelph, Ontario, and his PhD from the University of Victoria. He is a senior research associate at Citizen Lab, in the Munk School of Global Affairs and Public Policy at the University of Toronto. His research focuses on third-party access to telecommunications data, data privacy, data security, and national security. Besides publishing in academic journals and presses on topics such as national security, Internet privacy, and government surveillance practices, he routinely presents findings to members of government and the media. His work has been recognized by information and privacy commissioners, Canadian political parties, and national and international non-profits as advancing the state of privacy discourse.

Holly Porteous is an analyst with the Library of Parliament's Justice and National Security section. Since joining the Library in 2009, she has provided parliamentarians with non-partisan analysis on a broad range of national security issues. Her previous employment spans over two decades of work on defence and national security matters in Canada, the United Kingdom, and the United States, within various Government of Canada departments and agencies, the private sector, and academia. A prolific author, her work has appeared in print in various media, including academic journals, specialized trade journals, and government-sponsored reports.

Christopher Prince has been a strategic policy analyst with the Office of the Privacy Commissioner of Canada since 2007, where his focus has been privacy implications of national security programs, surveillance practices, oversight, and domestic laws governing interception of private communications. Before that, he was a researcher with the federal Treasury Board Secretariat and the National Archives of Canada. He has also worked on information management issues in the commercial aerospace, death care, and financial services sectors. He holds a master's degree from McGill University's School of Information Studies and a bachelor's degree from the University of King's College, Nova Scotia.

George Raine is a researcher based in Toronto. He is a graduate of the University of Toronto's Faculty of Information, where he completed a Master of Information Degree specializing in Archives and Records Management. He is the winner of the Toronto Area Archivists Group Award. His research focuses on the dynamics that operate between access and privacy in governmental archives, and how these dynamics are impacted by modern communications technologies.

Bill Robinson owns the blog *Lux Ex Umbra* (luxexumbra.blogspot.com), which focuses on Canadian signals intelligence activities past and present. He is frequently consulted by journalists about Canadian SIGINT activities, helped the CBC analyze the Snowden revelations, and provided research assistance to the British Columbia Civil Liberties Association for its legal challenge to CSE monitoring of Canadians. Since 2017, he has been a research fellow at the Citizen Lab at the Munk School of Global Affairs and Public Policy, University of Toronto. From 1986 to 2001, he was on the staff of the Canadian peace organization Project Ploughshares.

Carrie B. Sanders is an associate professor of criminology at Wilfrid Laurier University, Ontario, and Director of the Centre for Research on Security Practices (CRSP). Her research focuses on police technologies, intelligence analysis, and technologically mediated interactions in criminal justice. Her research has been published in high-impact international journals such as *Gender and Society, British Journal of Criminology,* and *Policing and Society,* and has received national funding by the Social Sciences and Humanities Research Council of Canada. Her new book (with Stacey Hannem, Christopher Schneider, Aaron Doyle, and Antony Christensen) is *Security and Risk Technologies in Criminal Justice: Critical Perspectives* (2019).

Valerie Steeves is a full professor in the Department of Criminology at the University of Ottawa. She is the principal investigator of The eQuality Project, a seven-year partnership funded by the Social Sciences and Humanities Research Council of Canada examining young people's experiences of privacy and equality in networked spaces. She co-edited (with Jane Bailey) the award-winning volume *eGirls, eCitizens,* which examines the ways in which young people negotiate with governance structures in networked spaces. As the lead researcher for Young Canadians in a Wired World, she has collected quantitative and qualitative data on digital citizenship since 2004.

Scott Thompson is an assistant professor in the Department of Sociology at the University of Saskatchewan, a research fellow in the Surveillance Studies Centre at Queen's University, and associate editor of the journal *Surveillance & Society*. Often focusing on historical case studies, his work on government surveillance also adopts Access to Information research methods in order to explain and address current and pressing issues in the areas of criminology, sociology, and surveillance studies.

Micheal Vonn is a lawyer and was policy director of the British Columbia Civil Liberties Association from 2004 to 2019. She has been an adjunct professor at the University of British Columbia in the Faculty of Law and in the School of Library, Archival and Information Studies, where she has taught civil liberties and information ethics. Her publication credits include the *Birkbeck Law Review, Surveillance & Society, Journal of Parliamentary and Political Law,* and *Case Western Reserve Journal of International Law*. Ms. Vonn has been a frequent speaker on a variety of civil liberties topics, including national security, policing, surveillance, and free expression. She is a collaborator on the Big Data Surveillance project, an Advisory Board member of Ryerson University's Centre for Free Expression, and an Advisory Board member of Privacy International. In September 2019, she became the chief executive officer of PHS Community Services Society in Vancouver.

Index